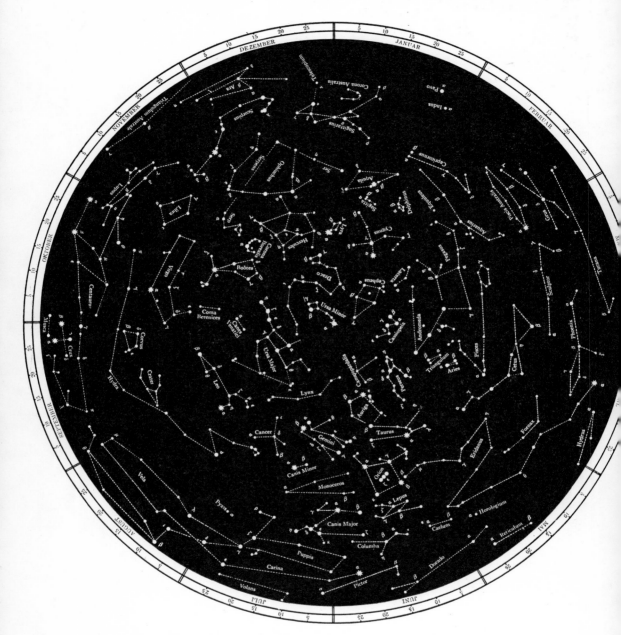

Modern Star Map. Publisher: Astronomy Charted Worcester (Mass.).

SCIENCE AWAKENING II

SCIENCE AWAKENING
II
THE BIRTH OF ASTRONOMY

by

Bartel L. van der Waerden

with contributions by

Peter Huber

NOORDHOFF INTERNATIONAL PUBLISHING
LEYDEN

OXFORD UNIVERSITY PRESS
NEW YORK

© 1974 Noordhoff International Publishing

A division of A. W. Sijthoff International Publishing Company B.V.,
Leyden, The Netherlands

NIP   ISBN 90 01 93103 0
OUP ISBN 0 19 519753 4

Library of Congress Catalog Card Number A54-7774

Sole publishers for North America
Oxford University Press
New York

Printed in the Netherlands by
Van der Loeff/Drukkers - Enschede

TABLE OF CONTENTS

CHAPTER 8. The spread of Babylonian astronomy 284-324

PREFACE

Whoever wants to understand the genesis of modern Science has to follow three lines of development, all starting in antiquity, which were brought together in the work of ISAAC NEWTON, namely

1. Ancient Mathematics $\Rightarrow$ DESCARTES $\Rightarrow$ PASCAL
2. Ancient Astronomy $\Rightarrow$ COPERNICUS $\Rightarrow$ KEPLER $\Rightarrow$ NEWTON
3. Ancient Mechanics $\Rightarrow$ GALILEO $\Rightarrow$ HUYGENS

In Science Awakening I (Dutch edition 1950, first English edition 1954, second 1961, first German edition 1956, second 1965) I have followed the first line, giving an outline of the development of Mathematics in Egypt, Babylonia, and Greece.

Volume II, dealing with Egyptian and Babylonian Astronomy first appeared in German under the title 'Die Anfänge der Astronomie' (Noordhoff, Groningen 1965 and Birkhäuser, Basel 1968). The volume was written in collaboration with PETER HUBER (Swiss Federal School of Technology, Zürich). HUBER has written considerable parts of Chapters 3 and 4, in particular all transcriptions of cuneiform texts in these chapters. I also had much help from ERNST WEIDNER (Graz), MARTIN VERMASEREN (Amsterdam), JOSEF JANSEN (Leiden) and MANU LEUMANN (Zürich).

The present English edition of Volume II is not just a translation: it is a completely revised text. Its history is roughly as follows. First, the German text was translated by MICHAEL HELL; next, the English version was revised and brought up to date by the author. Tedious calculations were suppressed, new parts were added, recent publications were used to simplify and to modernize the presentation. The more difficult chapters were put at the end of the book in order to make it easier for the reader. KLAUS BAER (Oriental Institute, Chicago) helped me to improve Chapter 1, which deals with Egyptian astronomy. Finally, the wording of the text was thoroughly revised by WILLYS BANDLER (University of Essex, Colchester). ERWIN NEUENSCHWANDER and PETER WIRTH helped me to correct the proofs and to compose the Index. To all these my hearty thanks!

The most important changes were made in Chapter 5, which deals with Astrology and Cosmic Religion. The last part of this chapter, on the identification of planets with gods in ancient Persia, and on the attitude of CYRUS and DARIUS towards Astrology and Zervanism are completely new.

The publisher generously fulfilled all my wishes concerning printing and illustrations. Many thanks to Mr. MOLENKAMP and Mrs. STEPHANIE VENEMA-NOORDHOFF!

Zürich, December 1972

B. L. VAN DER WAERDEN

THE ROLE OF ASTRONOMY IN THE HISTORY OF CIVILIZATION

Astronomy is the oldest physical science. It was highly developed by the Babylonians and Greeks, far more than physics, chemistry and technology. This, and indeed the fact that man studies astronomy at all, calls for some explanation.

The purpose of astronomy

Today, astronomy is studied because it is an essential part of natural science. It is scientific curiosity that drives us to explore what goes on in the universe. Celestial mechanics was the prototype of mechanics in general, and astrophysics is an indispensable part of physics. It is true that the results of astronomical research are used by astrologers, but this application is not the principal purpose of astronomy.

In antiquity and the Middle Ages it was different. According to a study by E. S. KENNEDY (*Trans. Am. Phil. Soc. 46*, Part 2, 1956), well over 100 sets of astronomical tables existed in the Islamic world. It was not purely scientific curiosity that prompted the calculation, copying, correction and recopying of these tables, but principally the fact that they were indispensable for astrology. The princes who contributed great sums for the construction of observatories and precision instruments expected something for their money, and not merely fame as promoters of science, but also astrological forecasts. This was also the position in Europe around 1600, at the time of the great astronomers TYCHO BRAHE and KEPLER.

It is true that the Islamic countries had excellent observers and outstanding theoretical astronomers. It is true that these theoreticians were interested in the structure of the universe. But there are only a few books that testify to this purely theoretical interest. Most table sets contain neither observations nor theory, but only numerical tables and rules for their application.

What we have just said about the Islamic countries is even more markedly true for India. In Indian astronomical handbooks of the period from 500 to 1900 A.D. I have not found a single observational report or mathematical derivation, but only numerical data, rules for calculations and dogmatic assertions about the universe, for which no justification is given. All that is needed for astrology is there, but the question 'Why is this so?' finds no answer, apart from incidental references to older traditions or divine revelation.

We enter a completely different world when we read the masterpiece of the great

Greek astronomer PTOLEMY, written about 140 A.D., the so-called 'Almagest'. Here purely theoretical interest predominates. The observations used are cited, the theoretical assumptions justified and the calculational rules firmly established. But this same PTOLEMY also wrote an astrological handbook, the 'Tetrabiblos', and published 'handy tables' containing no theory, but only rules for calculations: these were frequently used by later Byzantine astrologers[1]).

Going further back in time, we come next to Egyptian tables for the dates of entry of planets into zodiacal signs, belonging to the period from AUGUSTUS to HADRIANUS. As these tables originate from the very heyday of horoscopical astrology and are eminently suitable for the casting of horoscopes, it is to be assumed that they were composed for just this purpose.

The oldest cuneiform texts giving the position of the planets in the zodiac date from the second half of the fifth century B.C. To just this period, and to Babylon too, belongs the oldest horoscope that has been preserved[2]). It seems reasonable to assume that the positional data served just this end, namely to enable astrologers to cast horoscopes.

But this is only one part of the truth. We must consider yet another aspect[3]).

The divinity of the stars

Greek astronomy was already highly developed at the time around 300 B.C. when BEROSSOS, a priest of the Babylonian god Bel, founded the first Greek school of astrology on the island of Kos. Seventy years earlier EUDOXOS had made significant contributions to astronomy, but he did not believe in the prophecies of the astrologers (CICERO, De Divinatione, II, 87). It follows from this that the principal motive of the Greeks in developing their scientific astronomy was not the astrological application, but rather a specific interest in astronomy itself.

PTOLEMY motivates his personal interest as follows:

> 'Only Mathematics . . . offers her children sure and unassailable knowledge
> . . . This is also the reason that induced us to dedicate ourselves with all our
> strength to this preeminent science, . . . especially to that branch which deals with
> knowledge of the divine celestial bodies, for this science alone is devoted to the
> study of an eternally unchanging world'.
>
> (Almagest, Prooemium)

There are two motives put forward here: first, the attraction of the mathematical

---

[1]) VAN DER WAERDEN: Die handlichen Tafeln des Ptolemaios. *Osiris, 13*, p. 54 (1958).
[2]) A. SACHS: Babylonian horoscopes. *J. Cuneiform Studies, 6*.
[3]) This harmless little sentence contains two words of astrological origin: *consider* and *aspect*. This shows how important astrology once was!

method, which alone imparts certain knowledge; and second, the sublime subject-matter of astronomy — the eternally unchanging, divine celestial bodies.

Only few people are susceptible to the attractions of the mathematical method, but awe of the beauty of the starry sky is a universal human attribute. Even to-day there are many astronomers, both amateur and professional, who have become involved in the study of the stars principally because the beauty and sublimity of the starry firmament has so deeply impressed them. This motive was even stronger for the people of antiquity, who worshipped the Sun, the Moon, the Planets and the Sky as Gods.

Stellar religion, however, leads not only to astronomy, but also to astrology. Because the stars were considered to be mighty gods, it was supposed that they had a decisive influence on our fate.

Thus there are two kinds of impulse that derive from cosmic religion, both of which have been very influential in promoting astronomy. First, admiration of the stars and belief in their divinity had the direct effect of interesting mankind in the movements of the celestial bodies. Second, this same belief led to astrology, which in turn required astronomy as an auxiliary science, and therefore promoted it.

In this book, we shall study the history of Egyptian and Babylonian astronomy in connection with stellar religion and astrology. In this way we shall avoid taking astronomy out of the historical and cultural context to which it belongs. In Chapter 5 we shall see that this method is even necessary for the history of astronomy. The history of Babylonian astronomy in the Chaldaean and Persian reign, hitherto rather obscure, can actually be divided into periods by putting astronomy into the correct perspective relation to astrology and religion.

ASTRONOMICAL INTRODUCTION

This book is intended not only for astronomers and mathematicians, but for all those who are interested in the history of science and the cultural history of antiquity. I have therefore made it my concern to give clear explanations of all astronomical concepts in the text of the book. The elementary knowledge required for the understanding of these explanations is assembled in the next few pages.

The stellar sphere, poles and equator

To understand ancient astronomy, we must adopt the *geocentric standpoint*, that is, consider all phenomena from the Earth and determine the concepts of 'rest' and 'motion' relative to the Earth. In this sense, it is the sun and fixed stars that move, while the Earth is at rest. We must forget all we know about planets circling round the sun. For an observer standing on the ground and looking at the sky, the Earth is at rest, while the sun, moon and stars move through the sky — facts which are embedded in our language, as when we speak of stars 'rising and setting'.

The fixed stars are considered, as they were by the Greeks, to be located on a spherical surface called the *stellar sphere*. The sun, moon and planets are projected, from our eye, onto this sphere.

For an observer looking southwards, the sphere of the fixed stars rotates with a uniform motion to the right, i.e. from East to West, as does the sun in its daily motion. In this rotation two points of the sphere remain at rest: the *South Pole* and the *North Pole*. For an observer on the Northern hemisphere only the North Pole is visible.

The great circle whose points are equidistant from the North and South Poles is called the *Equator*. The angular distance of a star from the equator is called the *declination* of the star. Southerly declinations are marked by a minus sign.

On the modern stellar map opposite the title page the stars are depicted with their angular distances from the North Pole correctly reproduced. The more southerly constellations are consequently sharply distorted, namely stretched in the East-West direction. We should further observe that in antiquity, the North Pole did not occupy the same position among the stars as it does to-day: it was 11 to 12 degrees away from its present position in the centre of the map.

The zodiac

Besides the daily rotation of the sphere of the fixed stars, in which they all participate, the sun, moon and the five classical planets also have a slower *individual motion* in relation to the fixed stars. They always remain within the *zodiacal belt* or *zodiac*, which contains the *zodiacal constellations*. These are:

Aries, Taurus, Gemini,
Cancer, Leo, Virgo,
Libra, Scorpio, Sagittarius,
Capricornus, Aquarius, Pisces.

In the middle of this belt runs the *ecliptic*, the apparent path of the sun. The sun traverses this path annually towards the left, i.e. in opposite direction to its daily motion. The name 'ecliptic' is due to the fact that eclipses of the sun and moon occur only when the moon is directly in front of or directly opposite the sun, that is, in the ecliptic or very close to it.

The ecliptic is inclined with respect to the equator. It is divided into 12 equal segments, the *zodiacal signs*. They derive their names from the constellations just mentioned:

(1) Aries, the Ram
(2) Taurus, the Bull
(3) Gemini, the Twins
(4) Cancer, the Crab
(5) Leo, the Lion
(6) Virgo, the Virgin

(7) Libra, the Scales
(8) Scorpio, the Scorpion
(9) Sagittarius, the Archer
(10) Capricornus, the Ibex or the
    Goat-Fish
(11) Aquarius, the Water-bearer
(12) Pisces, the Fishes.

The starting point of the division is arbitrary. Contemporary astrologers follow the majority of the Greek astronomers in placing the origin of Aries at the *vernal point*, where the ecliptic climbing northwards intersects the equator. When the sun stands at this point, we have the *vernal equinox*. Equinox means equal day and night. When the sun is at the opposite intersection, we have the *autumnal equinox*.

The Babylonian astronomers and some of their Greek and Indian colleagues as well as many astrologers did not place the origin of Aries at the vernal point, but defined the starting points of the zodiacal signs by their positions relative to the fixed stars. For example, the star Spica (α Virginis) was taken to be at 28° or 29° of Virgo. We shall return later to this *sidereal division of the zodiac*. Here I should remark only that the vernal point is not fixed relative to the fixed stars, but moves slowly back along the ecliptic, i.e. to the right. This is the *precession of the equinoxes*, which was discovered by the Greek astronomer Hipparchos (about 130 B.C.).

Each sign of the zodiac is divided into 30 *degrees*, so that there are 360 degrees in the complete circle. Each degree is subdivided into 60 *minutes of arc* ($1° = 60'$), each minute into 60 *seconds* ($1' = 60''$) and so on. This division was known to both the Babylonians and the Greeks. Whenever necessary, the process of sexagesimal division was carried further on ($1'' = 60'''$, etc.).

The position of a star relative to the ecliptic is denoted by the *longitude* λ and the *latitude* β of the star. The *longitude* is reckoned from the origin of the ecliptic leftwards (that is, following the sequence of the signs of the zodiac) to the base of the perpendicular from the star on to the ecliptic. The *latitude* is the angular distance of the star from the ecliptic (with negative sign if the star is south of it).

The moon

The moon and sun move leftwards in the zodiacal belt, following the sequence of the signs — Aries, Taurus, etc. This is called *direct motion*. The path of the moon is slightly inclined to the ecliptic. The intersections of the path of the moon and the ecliptic are called the lunar nodes. It is only in the neighbourhood of the lunar nodes that eclipses can occur.

Shortly after new moon, the moon sickle becomes visible for the first time in the evening sky: this is the *crescent*. A fortnight later, the *full moon* stands in opposition to the sun and shines the whole night.

The *synodic month* is the period from one new moon to the next. The time in which the moon returns to the same node is called the *draconitic* or *dragon month*, because the nodes are obviously the habitation of the dragon which swallows the sun or moon at an eclipse.

The motion of the moon in its path is not quite uniform: it has an *anomaly*. The time required for the moon to pass from one maximum of its speed through the minimum to the next maximum is the *anomalistic month*.

The phases of the fixed stars and planets

A star like Sirius, which is not visible the whole year, appears for the first time in the morning sky on a certain day. This appearance is called the *morning rising*. Thereafter the star appears somewhat earlier every night until it rises just after dusk at the beginning of the night. This is the *evening rising*.

When the star sets at the end of the night, it is the *morning setting*. Thereafter it sets somewhat earlier every night until finally it is only just visible in the evening sky for the last time. This is the *evening setting*.

For stars in the zodiacal belt and south of it the sequence of annually returning phenomena is

Morning Rising or *Morningfirst* (MF)
Morning Setting
Evening Rising
Evening Setting or *Eveninglast* (EL).

The planets

The motion of the planets in the zodiacal belt is generally direct, but it is sometimes *retrograde*, i.e. to the right. The points where the retrograde motion begins and ends are called *stationary points*. They play an important part in Babylonian astronomy.

The time taken by a planet to pass once through the whole zodiac is called its *sidereal period*. The sidereal period of Saturn is $29\frac{1}{2}$ years, of Jupiter nearly 12 years, and of Mars nearly 2 years. The two *inferior planets* Venus and Mercury are never far from the sun, so their sidereal period (from the geocentric point of view) is exactly 1 year.

The three *superior planets* Saturn, Jupiter and Mars move more slowly than the sun. Near the sun they are, of course, invisible. They become visible for the first time in the morning sky at the *Morning Rising* or *Morningfirst* (MF). At the Morning Stationary Point or *Morning Station* (MSt) they change to retrograde motion, come into *Opposition*

(Op) to the sun and change back to direct motion again at the *Evening Station* (ESt). Then comes the *Evening Setting* or *Eveninglast* (EL), the time of last visibility in the evening sky, and shortly thereafter the *conjunction*, defined by the fact that the planet has the same longitude as the sun. The time from one conjunction to the next is called the *synodic period* of the planet. During this period we therefore have the following phenomena:

MF, MSt, Op, ESt, EL.

The planet Venus overtakes the sun at the *superior conjunction*, appears for the first time as an evening star at the *Eveningfirst* (EF), turns retrograde at the *evening stationary point* (ESt) and is visible for the last time as an evening star at the *Eveninglast* (EL). Then follow in rapid succession the *inferior conjunction*, the *Morningfirst* (MF) and the *morning stationary point* (MSt), where the planet returns to direct motion. At the Morninglast (ML) Venus is visible for the last time as a morning star.

The *synodic period* of Venus, from one superior conjunction to the next, is on the average 584 days. During this period, six phenomena take place:

EF, ESt, EL   MF, MSt, ML
evening star   morning star

The phenomena for Mercury are similar to those for Venus, except that it can happen that Mercury is not visible at all as an evening star or a morning star during a synodic period.

Historical and astronomical reckoning of years

In the usual historical counting of years, there is no 'year zero'. The first year A.D. is immediately preceeded by the first year B.C. In astronomical calculations, this is inconvenient. Therefore the year 1 B.C. is counted as 'year 0' by the astronomers, and generally the year $n + 1$ B.C. is counted as year $- n$:

$$\text{Year} - n \text{ (astron.)} = \text{Year } (n + 1) \text{ B.C.}$$

In the case of approximate dates such as 'circa $- 100$' it naturally makes no difference whether the astronomical or historical counting is used. However, if an exact date such as $- 524$ is quoted, the year 525 B.C. is meant.

CHAPTER I

ASTRONOMY IN ANCIENT EGYPT

HISTORICAL PERIODS

Egyptologists use to distinguish three periods of high civilization:
1. The *Old Kingdom* (2664-2155 B.C.)
2. The *Middle Kingdom* (2052-1786 B.C.)
3. The *New Kingdom* (1554-1072 B.C.)

For the dates and the methods, by which they were obtained, see R. A. PARKER: Calendars and Chronology, in: The Legacy of Egypt (Oxford Univ. Press).

Each of the three great periods was followed by a time of decline. In 670 B.C. Egypt was conquered by Assyria.

Of great importance for our investigation is the *Late Egyptian Period* (670-332 B.C.). Under the Dynasty of Sais (664-525) there were many contacts with Phoenicia, Syria, Lydia and Greece. From 525 to 404 and again from 341 to 332 B.C. Egypt was a part of the Persian Empire.

With ALEXANDER's conquest in 332 B.C., a period of high civilization under Greek rulers begins: the *Ptolemaeic Period*. Alexandria became the main centre of Greek civilization. Astronomy was highly developed. However, in this book we shall not deal with Greek astronomy. We shall first discuss the little we know about the astronomy of the Old Kingdom. Next we turn to the astronomy of the Middle and New Kingdom. Finally we shall show that during the Late Egyptian Period (670-332) a new development started, in which influences from Babylonia and Persia dominated.

THE RISING OF SIRIUS AND THE EGYPTIAN CALENDAR

Sirius as herald of the new year

The ancient Egyptians worshipped Sothis, that is Sirius, as 'herald of the new year and of the flood'. These words[1] are inscribed on an ivory tablet found in a First Dynasty

---

[1] KLAUS BAER (Chicago) informs me that the reading 'Sothis, herald of the new year and the flood' is not certain.

tomb in Abydos. The tablet was published by W. M. FLINDERS PETRIE: The Royal Tombs of the First Dynasty, London and Boston, 1901, Vol. II, Pl. V 1 and VIa 2; see also R. A. PARKER: Calendars of Ancient Egypt, p. 34, § 172.

To determine their precise significance, let us first consider the flood. The flooding of the Nile over its banks is the most important event in the Egyptian agricultural year. It gives new life to the parched land.

This event is heralded some weeks beforehand by a striking event in the firmament, namely the first visibility of Sirius in the morning sky. This is called the *heliacal rising* of Sirius. A more convenient expression, which we shall adopt, is *morning rising* or morningfirst (MF). In ancient Egypt this occurred on or around the 20th of July (Julian Calendar).

Thus we learn from our text, if the reading given above is correct, first that the morning rising of Sirius heralds the flooding of the Nile, and second, that the New Year also begins about this time.

The Egyptian year

To understand what is meant here by the beginning of the New Year, we must first look at the Egyptian calendar. The most commonly used Egyptian year was a 'wandering year' of exactly 365 days. It was divided into 12 'months' of 30 days each, with 5 supplementary days at the end of the year. The names usually given to the months were, from the New Kingdom to the Roman reign and even later:

1. Thoth	5. Tybi	9. Pachon
2. Phaophi	6. Mechir	10. Payni
3. Athyr	7. Phamenoth	11. Epiphi
4. Choiak	8. Pharmuti	12. Mesori.

Similar individual names were in use as early as the Middle Kingdom. However, in written texts, the first four months were named
'floods months',
the next four
'months of growth' or 'of seed'
and the last four
'hot months' or 'months of harvest'[1]).
Hence the months are named in the written texts as though they belonged to definite times of the year. The solar year, however, has approximately $365\frac{1}{4}$ days, so that every four years the Egyptian New Year falls a day behind in the solar year. In the course of the

---

[1]) I am indebted to KLAUS BAER for this information.

centuries, therefore, the beginning of the Egyptian year wanders through all the seasons of the year; hence the expression 'wandering year'.

This division of the year into periods of flood, growth and heat indicates that, at the time of the introduction of the 365-day year, the Egyptians thought in terms of a farmer's year, beginning with the Nile flood and consisting of three seasons. The Nile flood was heralded by the morning rising of Sirius, which took place a few weeks earlier.

There are texts from the Middle and New Kingdoms, in which the morning rising of Sirius is designated as the 'beginning of the year'. Scholars differ in their opinions about the kind of year this is meant to be. Some assume it to be a 'Sothis year', lasting precisely from one Morning Rising of Sirius to the next. On the other hand, R.A. PARKER in his most instructive book 'The calendars of ancient Egypt' (Univ. of Chicago Press, 1950) put forward the hypothesis that the year began with the day of the disappearance of the moon next after the Morning Rising of Sirius. According to this hypothesis there would be 12 or 13 lunar months in each of these years.

No astronomy is required for setting up such a Sirius calendar. The simple observation of the first appearance of Sirius and the subsequent last visibility of the old moon in the morning sky suffices.

Was there a scientific astronomy in the Egyptian Old Kingdom?

We do not know. The above-mentioned ivory tablet from Abydos is, as far as I know, the only text from the time of the Old Kingdom that makes reference to astronomical matters.

It has often been asserted that there is mathematical or astronomical wisdom concealed in the measures of the pyramids, but the only fact ever adduced as proof is that certain numbers calculated from these measures correspond to certain other numbers derived from modern science. It seems to me that such correspondences prove nothing. There are so many possible ways of making the measures of the pyramids fit into some apparently natural system of units and there are so many numbers and number relations in modern science, that a correspondence can always be found, provided that the seeker is diligent in his search and is convinced from the start of the comprehensive wisdom of the ancient Egyptians.

The Sothis period

The Egyptian calendar with its months and years of strictly constant length was very convenient for the civil administration of Egypt, but for fixing the right time for sowing, for harvest etc., the wandering year created a difficulty. In spite of this, the Egyptians retained the wandering year for many centuries. It was only in the time of the emperor

AUGUSTUS that a change was made by inserting a sixth supplementary day every fourth year and so making the average length of the year $365\frac{1}{4}$ days. This is the *Alexandrian calendar*. The astronomer PTOLEMY, who otherwise always employed the more convenient Egyptian calendar for his astronomical calculations, used the Alexandrian calender in his book *Phaseis* in order to fix the dates of the annually recurring phenomena of the fixed stars (such as Morning Rising and Evening Setting). He described the Alexandrian calendar as 'the calendar in common use among us to-day'.

In the Alexandrian calendar the date of the morning rising remains approximately the same from year to year, or, to put it a different way, the Alexandrian year is nearly the same as the Sirius year. The following exact equation holds:

(1)   1460 Alexandrian years = 1461 Egyptian years.

Thus it follows that after 1461 Egyptian years Sirius' morning rising again occurs on about the same date in the Egyptian calendar. The period (1) is called the *Sothis Period*, Sothis being the Egyptian name for Sirius.

Starting from any observation, the Sothis period can be counted backwards at will. Thus, the astronomer THEON of Alexandria, starting from the morning rising of Sirius in the Julian year 139, which took place on the 1st of Thoth in the Egyptian calendar, calculated that in the years

$$- 4241, \ - 2781, \ - 1321$$

the morning rising also occured on the 1st of Thoth. This whole calculation has little or no connection with ancient Egyptian chronology. THEON knew as little as we do, whether in fact the Egyptian calendar was already in use in the year $- 4241$, or whether Sirius was observed on 1st Thoth of that year. So far as I know, no mention is made of the Sothis period anywhere in ancient Egyptian texts.

The phases of stars in HESIODOS' poem

Other stars besides Sirius were observed by the peoples of antiquity. Weather predictions and farming rules were attached to their annual risings and settings. The oldest known Greek text containing such 'peasant rules' is the poem 'Works and Days' of HESIODOS. We may quote from lines 383-387:

When the Pleiades, daughters of Atlas, are rising, begin your harvest, and your ploughing when they are going to set. Forty nights and days they are hidden and appear again as the year moves round, when first you sharpen your sickle.

(Translated by H. G. EVELYN-WHITE, Loeb Classical Library)

According to HESIODOS there are thus 40 days and nights between the evening setting and morning rising of the Pleiades. This cannot be intended as more than an approximation. Actually, the period of invisibility varies from year to year, because the visibility of such faint stars depends very much on the weather.

HESIODOS then describes the autumn, when the power of the scorching sun abates, when Zeus sends the rains and Sirius shines longer in the night. Year by year the voice of the crane gives the signal for sowing and heralds the winter rains. Sixty days after the winter solstice the evening rising of Arcturus marks the end of winter:

> When Zeus has finished sixty wintry days after the solstice, then the star Arcturus leaves the holy stream of Ocean and first rises brilliantly at dusk.

Here, too, the number of days is naturally rounded off to 60. In fact, the evening rising of Arcturus in Boeotia in Hesiod's time took place about two months after the winter solstice.
Lines 609-611 read:

> But when Orion and Sirius come into mid-heaven, and rosy-fingered Dawn sees Arcturus, then cut off all the grapeclusters, Perses, and bring them home.

In lines 614-616 we read:

> ... But when the Pleiades and Hyades and strong Orion begin to set, then remember to plough ...

In lines 619-622 and 663-665, the favourable and unfavourable times for sea-faring are discussed:

> When the Pleiades plunge into the misty sea to escape Orion's powerful strength, then truly gales of all kinds rage. Then keep ships no longer on the sparkling sea, ...
> Fifty days after the solstice, when the season of wearisome heat is come to an end, is the right time for men to go sailing ...

These examples are sufficient to give an idea of HESIODOS' division of the year. The summer and winter solstices, the morning rising and evening setting of the Pleiades, the evening rising of Arcturus, these are the five fixed points of the year. On the basis of these fixed points, the year is divided into seasons and the right times are given for sowing and harvest, for vintage and sea-faring.

What we have here is no astronomical year, but a farmer's year, divided by celestial phenomena which anybody can observe for himself. True, this farmer's calendar can be made into a precise astronomical calendar, but for this sytematic observations are required. METON and EUKTEMON, DEMOKRITOS and EUDOXOS made such observations in the decades around −400 and produced astronomical calendars which were widely used for a long time. Thus, the farmer's calendar of HESIODOS was a first step towards Greek astronomy.

The significance of the phases of the stars for agriculture

For farmers in a land such as ancient Greece or Mesopotamia, agricultural rules of the kind handed down by HESIODOS were a vital necessity. Modern farmers do not need anything of the kind, because scientists have placed at their disposal a perfect calendar based on the solar year.

Ancient Babylonian calculation of time was based, like that of the Greeks, on the Moon. In the evening, when the new moon first became visible, a new Babylonian month began. Even to-day the Jewish Sabbath begins at sunset. Twelve or thirteen Babylonian months were combined into a *lunisolar year*. In Babylonia, the year began about the time of the spring equinox, but the sequence of years with 12 and 13 months was very irregular in ancient times, so that the year began sometimes earlier and sometimes later. The farmer could not, therefore, rely upon the official beginning of the year, but was dependent on direct observation of the fixed stars and the sun. Just as in Egypt the agricultural year began with the morning rising of Sirius, and just as HESIODOS divided his farmer's year by stellar phases and solar solstices, so, too, in Babylonia the farmer paid attention to certain annually recurring celestial phenomena, which, for example, gave him advance notice of the beginning of the rainy season.

Old Babylonian farming rules have not come down to us, but we find from a very early date Babylonian and Assyrian lists of stars and constellations, arranged according to the twelve months of the year. Most of these stars, as we shall see later, have their morning rising in just those months to which they belong in the texts (see Chapter 4). The lists also contain references to the seasons, the weather and agriculture.

In summarizing, we can say that in Egypt as well as in Greece, the connections between celestial phenomena and the seasons of the year were known before the beginning of scientific astronomy. Stellar phases, such as the morning rising of Sirius or the morning setting of the Pleiades, were taken as announcing the Nile flood or as a reminder to plough. These farming rules form a first step towards scientific astronomy.

THE EGYPTIAN DECANS

The Egyptians gave their aristocratic dead everything they might need on their long journey through space and time: food, riches, books and directions for telling the time by the stars. It is these latter that are of interest to us here, and we shall first consider the so-called diagonal calendars.

The diagonal calendars

Diagonal calendars are found on the inside of sarcophagus lids from the time of the Middle Kingdom (−2050 to −1700) and indeed, even earlier, from the 9th and 10th Dynasties (about −2100). The two halves of such a lid, from the grave of TEFABI (or TEFIBI or 'It'ib) at Asyut, are shown in plates 1 and 2.

A complete diagonal calendar should contain 36 transverse columns: 18 to the right of the central picture opposite the mummy's head, and 18 to the left. There are lids surviving with all these 36 columns, but TEFABI's contains only 32: there was no room left for the rest. It is possible that the preserved coffin lids were only bad copies of inscriptions on royal sarcophagi. Such inscriptions also survive, but the earliest ones date only from the New Kingdom.

From the extensive literature on astronomical tomb inscriptions[1]) I can recommend the following three treatises, as being not only especially informative but also conveniently brief:

A. POGO, Calendars of coffin lids from Asyut, *Isis 17* (1932) p. 6.

O. NEUGEBAUER, The Egyptian 'Decans', *Vistas in Astronomy 1* (1955).

R. BÖKER, Miszellen, *Z.f. ägypt. Sprache 82* (1957).

We shall use Plates 1 and 2 to illustrate the principal results of these researches. Place the plates with the right-hand long side horizontal, so that the legs in the picture of the Gods point to the left. Then the birds in the text all face to the right; the hieroglyphs are to be read from right to left, and the columns similarly are to be numbered from right to left. Plate 1 contains columns 1 to 18. Plate 2 columns 19 to 32 to the left of the picture of the gods.

Each column contains a heading and twelve names of stars (six above and six below the long middle line). The headings indicate thirds of months. Over col. 1, for example, we read: 1st third of the 1st month of the Flood season. The stellar names below denote either individual stars like Sirius, or constellations like Orion or frequently parts of constallations. Altogether, there are 36 names of stellar groups.

In the oldest texts these stars were apparently selected just for their suitability for telling the time. In the course of the centuries these Stars of Time became Gods of Time and Destiny. The Greek astrologers called these heavenly powers *Decans* and allocated to each an arc of 10° on the ecliptic. The Egyptians themselves called them 'rams' or simply 'stars'.

---

[1]) See the standard work by O. NEUGEBAUER and R. A. PARKER: Egyptian Astronomical Texts I & II (Lund Humphries, London, 1960 and 1964).

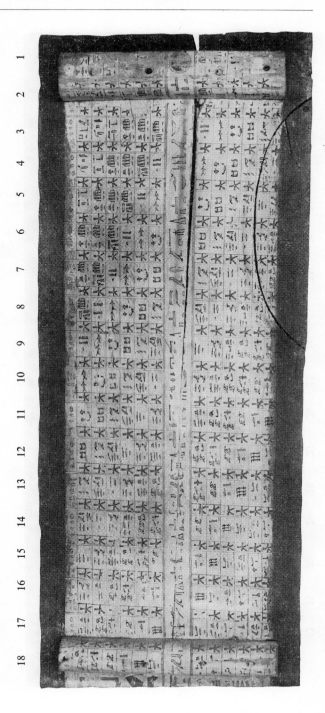

Plate 1. Lid of the coffin of TEFABI, from Asyut (about 2100 B.C.). On the left the lower part, reproduced on a small scale. On the right the upper half (columns 1 to 18) on a larger scale. In every column the names of the 12 decans rising during the night are written in hieroglyphs.

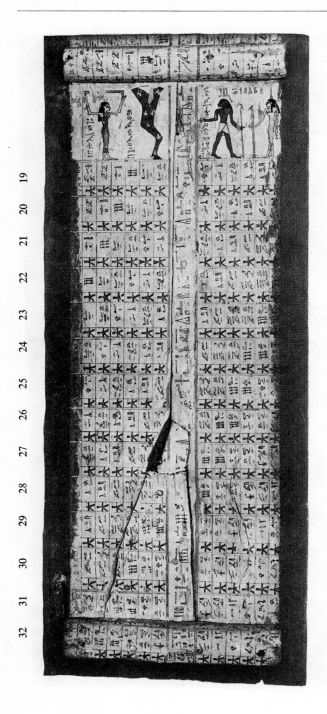

Plate 2. Coffin lid of TEFABI, lower half (col. 19 to 32). In every column 12 decans are named; in the next column the decans are shifted to the left one place. See explanation on page 17.

On closer examination of the hieroglyphs in Plates 1 and 2, it can be seen that the star name at the bottom of any column appears one place higher in the next column, one place higher still in the subsequent column, and so on.

To explain this diagonal arrangement, let us consider col. 18, where the bottom decan is Sopdet (= Sothis = Sirius). The Egyptians took it that, during the ten days to which col. 18 refers, Sirius rises right at the end of the night, immediately before dawn, and similarly for all the other columns. More precisely, we may say that on the first of these ten days Sirius is just visible for the first time in the morning. Each day hereafter Sirius rises 4 minutes earlier. On the first of the next ten days Sirius will become visible some 40 minutes before the end of the night. At the end of the night the next decan will be just visible, and so on. Every ten days all the decans move one place up, and a new decan appears in the bottom rank.

'One decan dies, one decan lives every tenth day', as Papyrus Carlsberg 1 says. 'Death' here is the evening setting, the disappearance of the star into the underworld, 'life' the morning rising, the first appearance of the star in the morning sky.

The position of the decans in the sky

Let a star P become visible in the morning sky for the first time. Its position is then a little above the horizon, stars on the horizon not being visible in these conditions; but to simplify the calculation of the morning rising, the calculation is made for the moment in which the star is exactly on the horizon, ten or twenty minutes before it becomes visble.

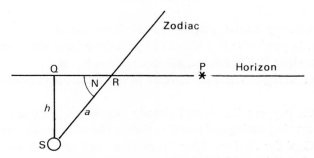

Fig. 1. Morning Rising of a Star at P, Sun at S.

For a star to become visible, the sun must, at the moment of the star's rising, be a certain distance below the horizon (see Fig. 1). The distance QS = h is an arc on the celestial sphere called the *arc of vision* (arcus visionis) of the star. For bright stars like Sirius this arc is only 9 or 10 degrees at the morning rising, given favourable weather conditions; for faint stars it is much larger[1]). Naturally, h also depends on the weather.

The position of the sun S on the celestial sphere lies always in a fixed circle, called the *ecliptic*. The Greeks called it the *circle through the middle of the zodia* (zodia = zodiacal signs). The intersection R of this circle with the eastern horizon is called the *ecliptic point rising with the star P*; it is also said of the star P that it *rises simultaneously with the point R*. These simultaneously rising stars (in Greek, *Paranatellonta*, from para = beside and anatellon = rising) play an important part in Greek descriptive astronomy and in astrology.

Given the distance h and the angle of inclination N of the ecliptic to the horizon, we can calculate the arc of the ecliptic a = SR. For Egypt the angle of inclination N is never very small, so that a is rather larger than h, but not very much larger. For Egypt a lies between $10°$ and $20°$ in most cases.

We shall now make an approximation, setting a equal to $15°$ in all cases. The same approximation is made by the Greek astronomer AUTOLYKOS in his book on the rotating sphere.

The time from the morning rising of one decan to the morning rising of the next decan is 10 days according to the Egyptian theory. In these 10 days the sun moves back along the ecliptic almost $10°$. In our schematic treatment we shall make this exactly $10°$.

If the position of the sun at the moment of Sirius' morning rising be marked on the ecliptic and from this point steps of $10°$ be taken in the direction of increasong solar longitude, 36 equidistant points on the ecliptic are obtained. Moving now $15°$ backwards from each of these points, to obtain the ecliptic points R which rise with the decans, we obtain a set of 36 equidistant points on the ecliptic:

$$R_1, R_2, \ldots, R_{36}.$$

If the Egyptian theory is taken literally, the 36 decan stars are paranatellonta to these 36 ecliptic points. In particular R_{36} is that point on the ecliptic that rises simultaneously with Sirius. As soon as R_{36} is known, all other points $R_1, R_2, \ldots$ can be constructed, and next one can find regions near the horizon in which the decan constellations must lie (see Fig. 2).

According to the papyrus Carlsberg 1 already mentioned, every decan is invisible for 70 days between evening setting and morning rising. The star remains 'in the underworld, in the house of Geb' for 70 days. There 'it purifies itself and rises on the horizon like Sothis'. It seems that Sirius, which indeed remains invisible for about 70 days, was taken as a model for all decans.

If a star remains invisible for 70 days, it must, like Sirius, be well south of the ecliptic. For stars on the ecliptic remain invisible for only 30 or 40 days, and stars to the north

---

[1]) For more accurate data, see B. L. VAN DER WAERDEN, Die Sichtbarkeit der Sterne am Horizont, *Vierteljahresschr. d. Naturf. Ges. Zürich 99* (1954).

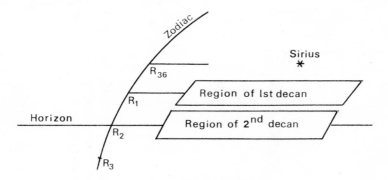

Fig. 2. The Situation of the Decans in the Sky.

of it for even shorter periods. This is why, in Fig. 2, the regions of the first and second decan are depicted as quadrilateral areas to the south of the ecliptic. The quadrilateral areas so obtained for the 36 decans all lie in a belt to the south of the ecliptic. Even if the assertions of the texts are only approximately correct, the decans must lie in this belt. This very remarkable result was obtained by O. NEUGEBAUER.

The rising of the decans in the night

Let us now consider why there are just 12 rows in the diagonal calendars.

As we have seen, each column relates to a period of ten days. The column contains 12 decans, of which the last rises at the end of the night. If now the first decan of the same column could be supposed to rise at the beginning of the night, the rising of the 12 decans could be used for telling the time at night.

In checking this, we can obviously substitute for the decans P the simultaneously rising ecliptic points R. The question then becomes, how many of these 36 points R rise in the course of a night.

At the end of the night, the sun rises in S. At the beginning of the night the sun sets, and the opposition point T rises. The points S and T lie on the ecliptic 180° apart, so that there are exactly 18 points R between them. These 18 points and the simultaneously rising decan stars therefore rise one after another in the course of the night. We should thus expect not 12, but 18 rows.

So far, however, we have not taken into consideration the periods of dawn and dusk. At these times only the very brightest stars in the neighbourhood of the horizon are visible. To make the Egyptian schema fit exactly, 3 decans both at the beginning and at the end of the night must be left out. This means, on the average, 2 hours at dusk and 2 hours at dawn — a pretty generous allowance! It appears that the Egyptians did in fact allow 2 hours each for dawn and dusk. In an inscription of the 13th century B.C.,

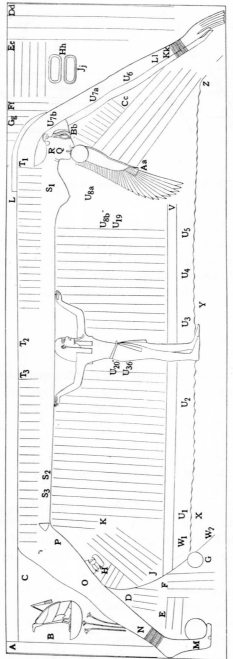

Plate 3a. Ceiling of Sarcophagus Chamber in the Cenotaph of SETI I (Osireion) at Abydos (circa 1300 B.C.). The Sky Goddess Nut, carried by Shu, the Air, spans the Cosmos between her outstretched arms. Drawing reproduced from NEUGEBAUER and PARKER: Egyptian Astronomical Texts I, p. 39 (Lund Humphreys, London 1960). The letters A to Z denote parts of the inscription in hieroglyphs, in which the rising and setting of the decans is explained (see p. 18).

Plate 3b. Photograph of right part of the inscription on the Cenotaph of SETI I drawn on Plate 3a. From NEUGEBAUER and PARKER: Egyptian Astronomical Texts I, Plate 30.

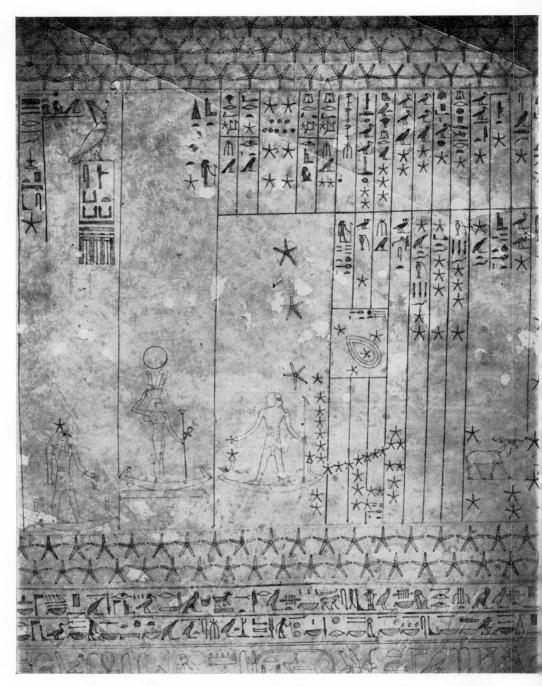

Plate 4. Part of the tomb ceiling of SENMUT (circa 1500 B.C.), the chancellor of HATSHEPSUT. The three large stars in the middle represent the girdle of the constellation Orion. Just below we see Oriris, followed by the great goddess Isis, both on boats. Isis was connected with Sirius, and Osiris with Orion. The text on the right gives the names of the decans and related gods. Photo Metropolitan Museum of Arts, Egyptian Expedition.

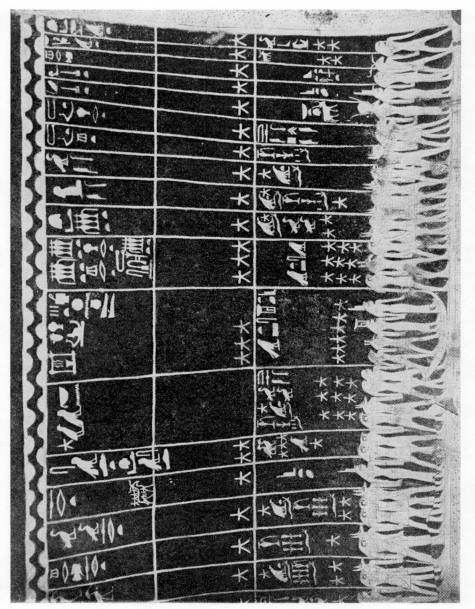

Plate 5. Cenotaph of SETI I (1300 B.C.). Below one sees the decans. In their middle Isis and Osiris on a boat Photo Metropolitan Museum of Arts, Egyptian Expedition.

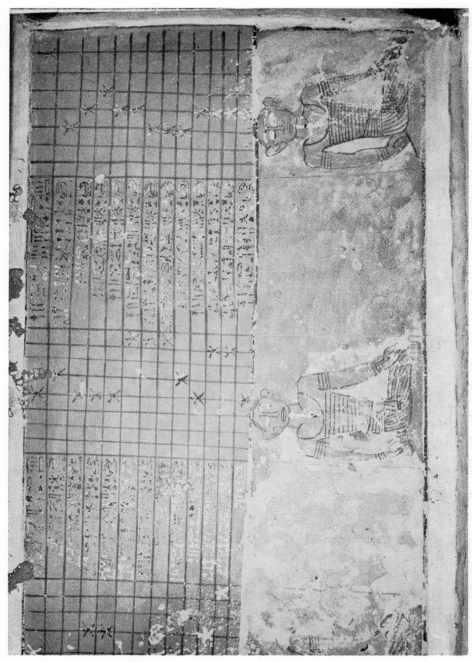

Plate 6. Tomb of Ramses VII in Luxor. Above each seated man one sees 13 horizontal lines representing the beginning of the night and the end of 12 consecutive hours of night. On each line a star is placed in one of 9 possible positions: just above the front of the man, or above his left or right eye or ear, or above his left or right shoulder, etc. The names of the stars are written in a table between the beside the symbols of the stars. Photo Oriental Institute, University of Chicago.

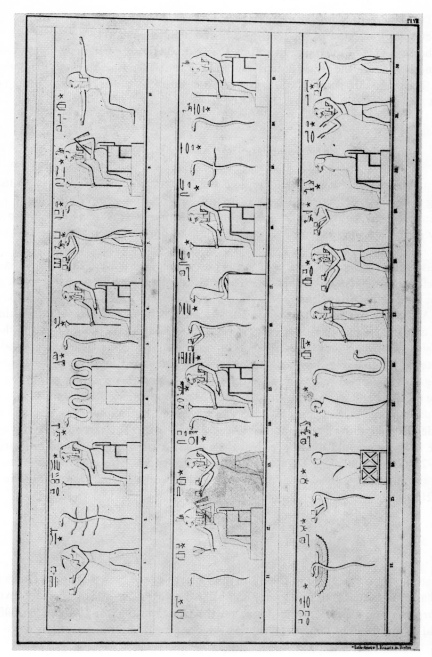

Plate 7. The first 32 decans in the Temple of Edfu (Ptolemaic, second century B.C.), ordered in groups of 3 decans. The middle decan of each group is pictured as a snake. Most probably, every group of 3 belongs to a zodiacal sign. Preproduced from H. BRUGSCH, Monumens d'Egypte, first series, Plate VII.

we read: 'Two hours pass in the morning before sunrise, and two hours also in the evening after sunset, because of the weariness of the night hours'.[1])

During the dark part of the night, therefore, the 12 decans mentioned in a column rise one after another. Thus, the rising decans can be used to tell the time through the night until dawn. The diagonal calendars are, as NEUGEBAUER correctly remarked, not calendars proper, but stellar clocks.

The headings of the columns

Each column in our text has a heading, indicating a definite period of 10 days. Thus, the heading of the 18th column, in which Sirius appears for the first time at the bottom of the column, reads: Last third of the sixth month (Mechir). The first day of this period, i.e. the day of the morning rising of Sirius according to our text, would be the 21st of Mechir.

As we have seen, the morning rising of Sirius was an important event in the Egyptian year. Therefore we may suppose that our diagonal calendars were arranged in such a way that the date of the Sirius rising would come out correctly or nearly so for the author's own time. According to the calculation of THEON, Sirius rose in the year −2781 on the 1st Thoth, and it rose one day later every 4 years. After 680 years, i.e. in −2101, the morning rising of Sirius should therefore occur on the 21st Mechir. The modern calculated date may differ by a few days from the date calculated according to THEON. This is unimportant, since we are interested only in an approximate dating of our text. Because the morning rising can easily occur some 4 or 5 days earlier or later than THEON's calculated date, a tolerance of some 20 years either way must be allowed. To remain on the safe side we shall allow a tolerance of 40 years either way. The sarcophagus lids of the Middle Kingdom would thus trace their origin to a pattern which should be dated between −2140 and −2060, just before the Middle Kingdom. This conclusion is confirmed by the fact that the oldest known diagonal calendar stems from the period around −2100.

Later development of the decan theory

The decan theory is explained in the tomb inscriptions of the New Kingdom (−1560 to −1080) and connected with cosmology and solar theology. The most important texts for our purposes are S and R, inscriptions on the cenotaph of SETI I (about −1300, Plate 3) and on the tomb of RAMSES IV (about −1155, Fig. 3). Both inscriptions consist

---

[1]) H. FRANKFORT, The Cenotaph of Seti 1 at Abydos, Memoir 36 of the Egyptian Exploration Society (1933), p. 78.

of a large picture of Nut, the goddess of Heaven, spanning the universe with her out-stretched arms and legs, and a text explaining this picture and describing the universe. There is a very informative commentary P on these texts which has been published by LANGE and NEUGEBAUER[1]). The central part of this commentary P is devoted to the decan theory. It tells us that at any time there are seven decans in the 'Duat' (underworld). These 7 decans are invisible all night long. The remaining 29 decans are divided as follows:

8 decans 'on the East side of the Heaven',
12 decans, that 'work in the middle of the Heaven',
9 decans 'in the West'.

The first 8 decans rise one after another in the East before the dark part of the night ends, but they do not reach the 'middle of the Heaven', i.e. the meridian. The 12 decans that 'work' in the middle of the Heaven are those that culminate during the night, the first at the beginning of the night, the last at the end. The last 9 decans have already passed the meridian at the beginning of the night: these follow one another down the western sky.

Ten days later one decan has emerged from the underworld and one has disappeared. All the decans have then moved one place on in the series.

The commentary P follows the course of a decan through the whole year, and mentions three important events:

A) *the evening culmination*. On its culmination a decan indicates the first hour of the night. In the next ten days it will culminate before the beginning of the night: at the end of the ten days it will therefore have its last visible culmination. The commentary describes this thus: 'This is the day when it ceases to work'.

B) *the evening setting*. The decan is visible for the last time in the evening sky. One day later it will be invisible. In the words of our commentary, 'the Evening Decan, that goes to the underworld without being in the underworld, namely in order to enter it, this is the decan that stands in the mouth of the underworld'. This decan is obviously the last of the 9 decans 'in the West'. Thus 90 days go by from the evening culmination to the evening setting. This agrees with the inscriptions S and R.

C) *the morning rising*. A decan becomes visible for the first time in the morning sky, or, as the commentary puts it, 'It ascends into the sky from the underworld on this day'. The previous day this decan was still invisible, being the last of the 7 decans in the under-world. Thus 70 days go by from evening setting to the day before the morning rising.

The inscriptions S and R and the commentary P pay special attention to the morning rising of Sirius. They all agree that this event takes place on the 26th of Pharmuti.

[1]) H. O. LANGE and O. NEUGEBAUER, Papyrus Carlsberg No. 1, *Kon. Danske Vid. Selskap Hist.-fil. Skrifter 1*, No. 2 (1940). New publication of all texts with valuable commentary by R. A. PARKER and O. NEUGEBAUER in Egyptian Astronomical Texts III (Lund Humphreys, London 1969).

Historical consequences

Assuming that this date was based upon an actual observation, we can find limits for the year in which the observation was made. Fairly wide limits, found by the method applied above, would be −1880 and −1800.

On the other hand, our texts S and R belong to the period after −1300. We thus reach the astonishing conclusion that the texts, given to the dead kings of the New Kingdom as manuals for telling the time, depended on observations from the period before −1800. The fact that the date of Sirius' morning rising had shifted some $4\frac{1}{2}$ months in the 7 centuries from −1840 to −1300 did not bother the author of the inscription S in the least. He simply copied an old text as if it had eternal validity, and the writer of Inscription R, some 150 years later, followed his example.

We conclude from this that the whole decan-astronomy is a product of the Middle Kingdom, that it stagnated completely after −1800 and was only copied and commented on thereafter. Obviously the scribes of the New Kingdom had nothing better than this long outdated theory; otherwise they would surely have placed a better theory at the disposal of the mighty SETI I.

The date Pharmuti 26 differs from the date Mechir 21 on the older sarcophagus lids. Hence it follows that the theory had not yet stagnated in the period of the Middle Kingdom. Observations were made until about −1840 and the theory was fitted to them.

The Middle Kingdom was apparently the golden age of ancient Egyptian astronomy, as it was indeed for ancient Egyptian mathematics (see my Science Awakening I).

Other astronomical tomb-inscriptions

SENMUT, the rich and mighty chancellor of Queen HATSHEPSUT (about −1500), likewise had an astronomical inscription placed on his tomb: a part is reproduced in Plate 4. The text in the narrow columns on the right enumerates the decans and their related gods. In the middle we see a god in a boat with three large stars over it, and above these, six stars in a narrow rectangle that are intended to portray the constellation Orion. According to POGO (*Isis, 14*, p. 319), the three large stars below portray the girdle of Orion as he rises above the horizon. Beneath is Osiris, the god of the constellation Orion, and behind him Isis, the goddess of Sirius, who follows Osiris.

Very similar representations are to be found in the Amon temple at Thebes, which was completed by RAMSES II about −1280[1]). Isis and Osiris are also to be seen in the middle of the decan series on the tomb of SETI I (Plate 5).

In the tombs of RAMSES VI, VII and IX (12th century B.C.) we find a new method of time determination, which represents an advance over the old decan method[2]). On Plate 6

---

[1]) H. BRUGSCH, Monumens de l'Egypte, Berlin 1857, Pl. V-VI.
[2]) O. NEUGEBAUER, The Exact Sciences in Antiquity, 2nd ed., Brown Univ. Press, Providence, 1957, p. 89.

we see a sitting man, one in a row of twenty-four — one for the 1st and 16th day of each month. The inscription above has 12 rows. In each row is mentioned one star, which is to be seen at a particular hour in a definite position. The text describes the positions as follows: 'over the left ear' or 'over the left shoudler', etc.

According to O. NEUGEBAUER, the text was mechanically copied again and again without the scribe noticing that after a time the dates could no longer be valid. In later times these methods fell into oblivion. The Babylonians and Greeks had much better methods for astronomical time determination and much more accurate star catalogues.

The decans in astrology

We find the decans once again in the 2nd Century B.C., under the Ptolemies, in the pronaos of the Great Temple at Edfu. Their names have survived practically unchanged, but their pictorial representation is markedly altered. They are mostly pictured as snakes or as gods with human or animal heads. Further, the decans are divided into groups of three, the middle decan of each trio always being shown as a snake (Plate 7).

Different again is the representation of the decans in the Temple of Dendera, which dates from Roman times (Fig. 3). We have here in the upper row a picture of the zodiac. From right to left we recognize Aquarius, Pisces, Aries and Taurus above, and Leo, Virgo with Spica, Libra and Scorpio below. These pictures are, as we shall show later, of Babylonian origin and Egyptianised in style only. Beneath, the decans are portrayed as Egyptian gods on boats. At the very bottom we see Nut, the Goddess of Heaven, who embraces the whole with her arms and legs.

On the circular ceiling-picture from Dendera we see in the middle again the signs of the zodiac and other celestial powers or constellations with the 36 decans encircling them on the outside. The names written beside them are almost the same as in the Egyptian decan lists. The forms resemble partly those from Edfu, partly those from the rectangular picture from Dendera, but new forms also appear.

Together with the form the concept of the decan has also changed. Whereas originally the decans were plain and simple constellations that lent themselves conveniently for telling the time at night, in the astrological literature of later times they appeared as gods determining men's fate. 'From their might derives everything that humanity encounters in the way of disasters', says the revelation of Hermes Trismegistos[1]). The texts show that the zodiac was divided into 36 segments of 10° each, and that to every such segment a decan was ascribed. As FIRMICUS MATERNUS says, the decans exercised 'their dominion and power over 10 degrees each'.

[1]) The evidence is assembled in W. GUNDEL, Dekane und Dekansternbilder (Studien Bibl. Warburg, 1936), pp. 342—355.

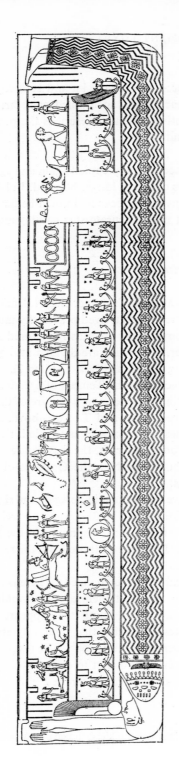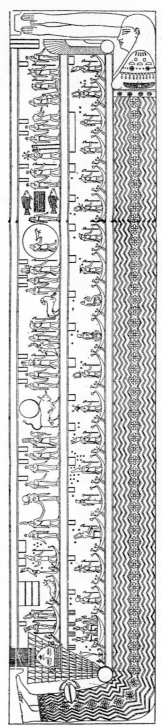

Fig. 3. 'Rectangular zodiac' in Dendera (Roman period). Above the zodiacal signs and other stellar Gods, below the decans on boats.

Plate 8. 'Round Zociac' on the ceiling of the Temple of Dendera (Roman period). Within the inner circle constellations. Below the center to the right Leo, the Lion. Just above the Lion one sees Cancer, the Crab. The other zodia are not so clear on the photgraph; on the drawing (Plate 13, opposite page 122) they are easier to recognize. Standing on the circumference the Decans are pictured as walking men, snakes and other animals. Photo Archives photographiques Paris HHLE 86, 23 189.

According to Hermes Trismegistos the decans can also be called 'horoskopoi' — hour indicators. The decan that rises in the hour of the birth of a child determines the nature of the child (W. GUNDEL, Dekane, p. 344 and 347).

Figure 4 shows Japanese drawings of twelve decans. Plates 9 en 10 show two particularly fine Italian pictures with decans.

THE LATE EGYPTIAN PERIOD

From 670 to 663 B.C. Egypt was part of the Assyrian Empire, and from 525 to 404 it belonged to the Persian Empire. The reigning dynasty between these two periods of foreign domination, i.e. from 663 to 525, was that of Sais, who used mercenaries from Greece and Asia Minor in their bid for power. This interlude was a period of prosperity and cultural development. Increasing sea trade and wars brought in their train manifold contacts with Phoenicians, Greeks, Jews and Syrians.

These contacts are an essential factor in the proper understanding of the civilization of the 'late Egyptian period', that is from about 670 to 332 B.C. If we come upon signs of cultural developments which are not readily intelligible in terms of the Egyptian tradition, we must always bear in mind the possibility of foreign influence.

In fact, there are several testimonies about the science and religion of this period which do not fit in at all with the picture of Egyptian culture obtained from earlier sources.

Most of these testimonies are known from Greek sources, but in the domain of astrology we have an original Egyptian document. So let us start with astrology.

Astrology

An astrological papyrus in demotic script from the Vienna National Library was published by R. A. PARKER[1]) in 1959. It was probably written in the first century A.D., but it certainly goes back to an original of the Persian period. 'With a rather high decree of confidence' writes PARKER, 'we can date the original of text A to the late sixth or early fifth century B.C.'.

The text discusses the significance of solar and lunar eclipses. At the beginning of the part that has been preserved there is a concordance of Babylonian and Egyptian months, of the following kind:

Nisan is the lunar month Choiak,
Iyyar is the lunar month Tybi, etc.

---

[1]) R. A. PARKER, A Vienna Demotic Papyrus on Eclipse- and Lunar-Omina. Brown Univ. Press, Providence, (1959).

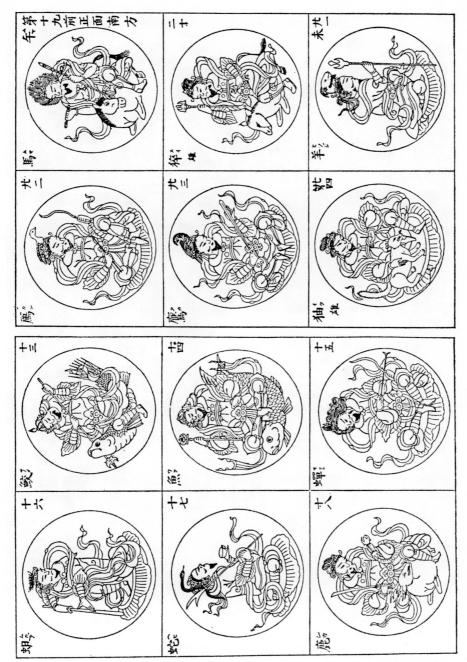

Fig. 4. Twelve decans, Japanese drawing. From GUNDEL: Dekane und Dekansternbilder (Studien Bibl. Warburg 1936).

Plate 9. Fresco in Palazzo Schifanoia in Ferrara, month March. In the middle a ram, because in March the sun stands in Aries. In the same rectangle the three decans of Aries. Below: Agriculture in March, and other scenes. Photo ALINARI.

Plate 10. Fresco in Palazzo Schifanoia, month April. The sun (visible in the middle) stands in Taurus, the Bull. In the same rectangle the three decans of Taurus. Above Triumph of Venus. To her right and left one sees the young people born under Venus, amorously playing and making music. On a rock the three graces. See F. BOLL and C. BEZOLD, Sternglaube und Sterndeutung, third ed. (1926). Photo ALINARI.

The fact that the Egyptian year wanders through all the seasons, whereas the Babylonian begins about the time of the spring equinox enables us to establish the date of the
text. The equations Nisan = Choiak (etc.) are approximately valid only if it is supposed
that the text was written between 630 and 480 B.C.

According to PARKER, the text was probably written during the reign of DARIUS
(521-486 B.C.). The king's name is mentioned in the text, but unfortunately only the last
letter of the name is preserved. Now it is known that it was just in Darius' reign (521-486
B.C.) that the Egyptian UDJEHARRESNET received the command to return from Persia to
Egypt and there to reorganize the 'houses of life', in which religious and medical books
were kept. The time of Darius therefore fits well.

The zodiac is not mentioned in the text. This also fits with the dating of the text to the
time before 480 B.C. Later Babylonian astrological texts are usually based on the division
of the zodiac into 12 signs.

The text allocates the 12 months of the year to four countries. If the months Choiak
etc. are numbered as the corresponding Babylonian months Nisan (I) etc., the allocation,
for solar eclipses (Col. II, line 29ff.) and lunar eclipses (IV, line 19ff.) alike, is:

I	Crete	V	Crete	IX	Crete
II	Amor	VI	Amor	X	Amor
III	Egypt	VII	Egypt	XI	Egypt
IV	Syria	VIII	Syria	XII	Syria

The allocation in old Babylonian eclipse texts is very similar:

I	Akkad	V	Akkad	IX	Akkad
II	Elam	VI	Elam	X	Elam
III	Amurru	VII	Amurru	XI	Amurru
IV	Subartu	VIII	Subartu	XII	Subartu

If an eclipse occurs in one of the twelve months, its meaning holds for the corresponding country, e.g.

If the Moon be eclipsed in the month Phamenoth, this month belonging to the country of the Syrian
it means: . . . in the country of the Syrian and great hunger likewise (IV, lines 23—24).

The Babylonian omen texts of the earlier period contain very similar expressions.
This seems to indicate that the method of prediction was taken over from Babylon and
adapted to the particular circumstances of Egypt.

The astrology of this text is rather primitive and requires little astronomical knowledge.
Later, in Ptolemæic times, Egypt became a center of astrology and astronomy. Many
astronomical and astrological texts were written in Greek, but some papyri in demotic

script are preserved. The walls and ceilings of Ptolemaeic temples were filled with astrological symbols and pictures of the Powers of Heaven: zodiacal signs, decans, constellations and planets (see plate 7). Some of these pictures show a definite Babylonian influence (see plates 12 and 13).

Astronomy

In his Meteorology 343 ARISTOTLE reports:

> The Egyptians say that the planets come into conjunction with one another as well as with the fixed stars,

and in De Caelo II 12 (292A):

> We have observed how the moon was once semi-circular and passed below the planet Mars, which disappeared into the dark half of the moon and reappeared from the light half. Similar reports are also given about other stars by the Egyptians and Babylonians, who have studied these matters thoroughly since time immemorial, and through whom we have many reliable reports about each of the stars.

Aristoteles lived in Athens in the middle of the fourth century B.C. As regards Babylonian observations, his statement is completely borne out by the cuneiform texts. It is from his report that we now learn that the Egyptians too carried out and recorded long-term observations of conjunctions of planets with one another and with the moon and fixed stars. This kind of observational astronomy is quite distinct from the older Egyptian decan astronomy and is quite unintelligible in terms of the Egyptian tradition. We are compelled to assume a Babylonian influence.

Calculation of periods

Babylonian astronomy was very much concerned with observations and periods. We have just seen that the Egyptians also made collections of systematic observations, and we therefore ask whether they concerned themselves with the periods of the heavenly bodies as well. Some late testimonies seem to point in this direction.

A hieroglyphic list of books from the Library of the temple of Horos at Edfu (built between 145 and 116 B.C.) mentions two books with the titles:

'Law of the Recurrence of the Stars',

'On the Science of the Recurrence of the Two Lights (Sun and Moon)'.

Similar titles are to be found in a list of four 'Hermetic Books' transmitted by CLEMENS
of Alexandria[1]). CLEMENS relates that in a procession of Egyptian priests one of them,
the 'hour watcher' (horoskopos), carried two astronomical instruments on display, and
that this priest must know by heart four books with the following titles:
  1) On the Disposition of the Fixed Stars and on Stellar Phenomena,
  2) On the Disposition of the Sun and the Moon and on the Five Planets,
  3) On the Syzygies and Phases of the Sun and the Moon,
  4) On Risings.

We have a papyrus 'Carlsberg 9' of the Roman period containing rules for calculating
the dates of new and full moon[2]). The rules are based upon the period relation

$$25 \text{ Egyptian years} = 309 \text{ synodic months} = 9\,125 \text{ days.}$$

We may conjecture that the book on the Syzygies and Phases of the Sun and the
Moon contained similar rules and period relations, for the expression 'Syzygy of sun
and moon' means their conjunction, i.e. the New Moon.

The first book mentioned by CLEMENS has a very similar title to that from Edfu:
'Law of the Recurrence of the Stars'. Presumably, this book mentioned at least the Sirius
year of $365\frac{1}{4}$ days. Certainly the Sirius year was assumed to be known in the famous
'Canopus Decree' of -237, in which the introduction of an extra intercalary day every
four years is prescribed[3]). The Sirius year in turn forms the basis of the Sothis period:

$$1460 \text{ Sirius years} = 1461 \text{ Egyptian years.}$$

The book 'On Risings' will presumably have contained dates for the annual risings of
fixed stars. Lists of dates of this kind are known from Babylonia as well as from Greece
and Hellenistic Egypt. A Babylonian list, called MUL APIN, will be discussed in Chapter
III; the oldest extant copy of this list is dated 687 B.C. Greek lists of dates of stellar phases
are called 'parapegmata'. The oldest parapegma was composed by EUKTEMON, who
observed the summer solstice in 432 B.C. in Athens. For the history of parapegms see
the article 'Parapegma' by Rehm in Pauly-Wissowa's 'Realenzyklopädie des klassischen
Altertums'.

One of the latest parapegmata was composed by PTOLEMY; it is contained in his Opera
under the title 'Phaseis'. In this book, PTOLEMY mentions the names of several astronomers who observed the phases of fixed stars and composed parapegms. One group of

---

[1]) See O. NEUGEBAUER, Egyptian Planetary Texts, *Trans. Amer. Phil. Soc. 22*, p. 209.
[2]) O. NEUGEBAUER and A. VOLTEN, Ein demotischer astronomischer Papyrus. (Pap. Carlsberg 9), Quellen
u. Stud. Gesch. Math., B 4, p. 383.
[3]) W. KUBITSCHEK, Grundriss der antiken Zeitrechnung, Handbuch d. Altertumswiss., I, 7, p. 89.

observers is called 'The Egyptians'. PTOLEMY tells us that the Egyptians made their observations in Egypt. Quotations from 'the Egyptians' are also found in other parapegmata.

It is possible that the book 'On Risings' mentioned by CLEMENS is identical with the parapegma of the Egyptians. In any case we may conclude that the Egyptians paid much attention to the annual phases of the fixed stars, to the duration of the year and to lunar periods.

Did this development take place in the Ptolemaeic and Roman period under the influence of Greek science, or already in the Late Egyptian period, i.e. before 332 B.C.? To answer this question we may quote a statement from the Geography of STRABON (Loeb's Classical Library) Chapter 17:

> The Egyptian priests taught Platon and Eudoxos the parts of the day and the night which must be added to the 365 days in order to complete the year, whose length was till then not known to the Hellenes.

I feel we can accept this statement, because it accords well with what we know from other sources.

EUDOXOS' *Egyptian journey*

DIOGENES LAERTIOS reports of EUDOXOS:

> With support from his friends and equipped with a letter of recommendation from Agesilaos to Nektanabis, he undertook a journey to Egypt in the company of the physician Chrysippos. Nektanabis is said to have introduced him to the priests. There he remained a year and four months; he shaved his pubic hair and eye-brows and, according to some, wrote the *Oktaeteris*.

DIOGENES LAERTIOS is a late and not very reliable author, but in this case his report seems to convey valuable information from much older and better sources. EUDOXOS did indeed compose an 'Oktaeteris': a calendar for 8 years containing data of stellar and lunar phases. Such details as the letter of introduction from AGESILAOS to the Pharaoh NEKTANABIS must come either from a source contemporary with EUDOXOS (about 370 B.C.) or from a historian very familiar with the chronology of this period. Compilers like DIOGENES LAERTIOS usually do not take the trouble to find out such details. The fact of EUDOXOS' Egyptian journey is therefore something we must accept, all the more so as it is attested by STRABON and other authors as well. STRABON writes:

> In Heliopolis . . . we were shown the living room of Platon and Eudoxos; for

> Eudoxos too came there with Platon and both lived there for 13 years with
> the priests, as some relate
>
> (Strabon, Geography XVII 806).

In the next section STRABON speaks of the city of Kerkesura, which lies on the left
bank of the Nile 'opposite Eudoxos' observatory'. 'For just outside the city of Heliopolis
one is shown . . . an observatory, where he (Eudoxos) determined some motions of the
heavenly bodies'.

Maybe STRABON just repeats the information given him by his guide in Heliopolis.
Part of this may be embellishment. One can imagine that the Greek visitors to Heliopolis
pestered their guides with such questions as 'Where did Platon and Eudoxos actually
live?' and that the guides built the rest of the story up on this basis. This explanation,
however, assumes that by the time of STRABON's travels in Egypt (around 25 B.C.) there
was a widespread tradition asserting that EUDOXOS had gone to Egypt to undertake
further studies of the motions of the celestial bodies.

What could EUDOXOS have learned in Egypt? First, according to STRABON, the year's
excess over 365 days. He did in fact need such information to compose his parapegma[1]).
The earlier parapegma of EUKTEMON was based on a 19-year cycle; similarly Eudoxos'
parapegma was probably based on an 8-year cycle, an Oktaeteris. We have seen above
that in later times the Egyptians had a star-calendar, in which the dates of annual risings
of fixed stars were noted. It is possible that such a calendar existed already at the time of
EUDOXOS, and that he used it in composing his own parapegma.

It appears that he also learned something about the movement of the planets. SENECA
writes: 'Eudoxos was the first to bring these movements to Greece'. We already know
from ARISTOTLE that the Egyptians collected observations of the conjunctions of the
planets, while CLEMENS states that the Egyptian priests had books about the five planets.
All our authors are unanimous in assuring us that the astronomers with whom EUDOXOS
dealt in Egypt were priests. In addition to this, we may quote another passage from
ARISTOTLE (Metaphysics A 1, 981B): 'Therefore the mathematical arts were first pursued
in Egypt, where the priests had time at their disposal'.

To sum up, the various reports that we have about Egyptian astronomy and about
EUDOXOS are in excellent agreement with one another. In EUDOXOS' time the Egyptians
had observations and a knowledge of astronomical periods and possibly lists of annual
risings of fixed stars, so that EUDOXOS could take over from them a variety of data he
needed for his parapegma and his planetary theory.

Other wise men are also reported to have travelled to Egypt. In De vita Pythagorica,
Ch. 4, IAMBLICHOS reports: 'Pythagoras spent 22 years in the temples of all Egypt, where
he studied astronomy and geometry and took part in all sacred ceremonies'. This report
probably stems from an old Pythagorean tradition; we do not know how reliable it is.

---

[1]) On EUDOXOS' parapegma, see P. TANNERY, Mémoires scientifiques II, p. 236.

Geometry

HERODOTOS (II 109), ARISTOTLE (*Metaphysics*, A 1) and all later writers are in agreement over the fact that geometry originated in Egypt. PROKLOS, whose source is probably the lost History of Mathematics of EUDEMOS, describes the circumstances more exactly:

> Just as trade and business resulted among the Phoenicians in the beginnings of the exact science of numbers, so too the reasons indicated gave rise to geometry among the Egyptians. This science was first transplanted to Greece by Thales after his Egyptian journey . . .

(PROKLOS, Commentary on the Elements of Euclid, p. 65 Friedlein).

A deductive geometry in the Greek sense is not to be found in the older Egyptian texts. The Egyptians of the Middle Kingdom had methods for calculating areas and volumes, but there is no textual evidence of a geometry with constructions and proofs. Furthermore, so far as we know, the mathematical texts of the Middle Kingdom were no longer copied after the Hyksos period. We are left, as I see it, with only two possibilities: either we abandon the statements of HERODOTOS, ARISTOTLE and EUDEMOS as completely worthless, or we assume with the Greek authors that there was a true geometry in Egypt at the time of THALES.

The picture the Greek authors had of this geometry is made more clear by a fragment of DEMOKRITOS, which has come down to us by way of CLEMENS of Alexandria:

> In the construction of lines with proofs I am not surpassed, not even by the so-called Harpendonaptai of the Egyptians.
>
> (Stromata I, p. 357, ed. Potter)

The Harpendonaptai or 'rope stretchers' were, according to GANDZ (Quellen u. Studien Gesch. Math. B 1, p. 255), surveyors, who also had a function to perform in the laying of foundation stones for temples. What DEMOKRITOS here ascribes to them is at the very least great competence in geometrical constructions. Whether he ascribes to them the relevant proofs as well, or limits this ascription to himself, is not clear. But there is nothing to indicate that he is speaking of surveyors from a legendary past. He is talking, it seems to me, of people from his own time or an immediate past, with whom he himself was in competition as a geometer.

To sum up, in the late Egyptian period, roughly between −600 and −330, we find several signs of renewed activity in geometry, astronomy and astrology. In the case of astrology, we can establish that this activity was taken over from Babylon. As astrology and astronomy are very closely inter-related, it is to be supposed that the astronomical activity in Egypt also received its impulse from Babylon. In fact, the Egyptian observations reported by ARISTOTLE are similar to the observations of planetary conjunctions which are known to us from such cuneiform texts.

The question remains, whether the same is true of geometry. We know nothing of any geometrical activity in Babylon during the Persian period. This could be due to the paucity of our source material. To judge, we must try to ascertain the significance of geometry for the astronomy of this time.

The significance of geometry for astronomy

From the first information that became available about Babylonian mathematics, it appeared that its character was algebraical and arithmetical rather than geometrical. This general characterization must, however, be somewhat modified. The Babylonians used the 'Theorem of Pythagoras' and also solved geometrical problems. In Science Awakening I (p. 72) there is a discussion of the text VAT 8512. This text had earlier been used (by NEUGEBAUER and VAN DER WAERDEN) as a proof of the basically algebraical nature of Babylonian thinking. However, quoted there is a solution proposed by P. HUBER (Isis 46, p. 104), which makes it likely that the problem was solved directly by the application of a rectangle to the desired triangle. The geometrical element in Babylonian thought seems to be stronger than was originally supposed.

The position is similar when we come to astronomy. Babylonian astronomical texts of the Seleucid period employ purely arithmetical methods; so much is certain. But in the text ^{mul}APIN the zodiac is presented as an inclined circle divided into four equal parts by two parallel circles. Trisection of the four parts of the zodiac produced the 12 signs of the zodiac. Star catalogues give the longitude of certain stars in relation to the 12 signs. To achieve these measurements, a circle on some measuring instrument must have been divided into 12 parts and these in turn divided into smaller parts. This could not have been done without geometrical constructions.

Similarly, ANAXIMANDROS must have used geometrical constructions in erecting his gnomon in Sparta around 550 (DIOGENES LAERTIOS II 1). For the gnomon 'showed' the equinoxes and solstices. At the equinoxes the sun stands in the plane of the equator. A plane through the top of the gnomon paralell to the plane of the equator cuts the base plate in a straight line g. When the end of the shadow falls on g, that is the exact moment of equal day and night. ANAXIMANDROS must have constructed this line g and incised it on the plate; otherwise, his gnomon could not possibly have shown the equinoxes.

According to HERODOTOS (II 109), the Greeks took over the gnomon from the Babylonians. There is therefore at the very least a historical relation between Babylonian astronomy and Greek geometrical instrument technology. It is possible that the Babylonians had constructed gnomons even before the time of ANAXIMANDROS.

Around 440 lived OINOPIDES of Chios, astronomer and mathematician. He discussed the problem of dropping a perpendicular from a point to a line in the plane, because he found this construction necessary for astronomy (PROKLOS, Commentary on Euclid I, 12). He determined the inclination of the ecliptic. Shortly afterwards a Pythagorean found the construction for the regular 15-sided polygon inscribed in a circle[1]). According to PROKLOS, this construction was included in the Elements because of its utility in astronomy, for the side of the regular 15-sided polygon is just the distance between the poles of the ecliptic and equator. This means that the inclination of the ecliptic was assumed to be just 24°.

If the application to astronomy was one of the purposes behind the Greek studies of geometrical constructions, it may be assumed that this application was one of the purposes of geometry for the Egyptians as well.

New trends in religion

We have already quoted IAMBLICHOS saying that PTYHAGORAS studied astronomy and geometry in Egyptian temples and took part in all sacred ceremonies. This combination of astronomy, geometry and religion may seem strange to us, but in antiquity it was quite common. The Pythagoreans were primarily a religious community, but they also developed a system of mathematical sciences. The extant books of 'Hermes Trismegistos' contain a mixture of religious, astronomical and astrological doctrines[2]). The 'Introduction to Arithmetic' of the Neo-Pythagorean NIKOMACHOS of Gerasa starts with a long introduction, in which religious and philosophical ideas about numbers and the creation of the world are developed.

Let us follow IAMBLICHOS' lead and ask: What religious ideas could PYTHAGORAS learn in Egypt?

PYTHAGORAS taught that the soul is immortal and that after the death of an individual the soul passes into other living beings. According to the Greek historian HERODOTOS, he had this idea from Egypt. HERODOTOS writes:

> The Egyptians were the first to teach that the human soul is immortal, and at the death of the body enters into some other living being then coming to birth; and after passing through all creatures of land, sea, and air it enters once more into a human body at birth. It completes this cycle in three thousand years. Some of the Greeks, early and late, have used this doctrine as if it were their own. I know their names, but do not here record them

(HERODOTOS, Histories II 123, transl. by A. D. GODLEY, Loeb Classical Library).

---

[1]) For details and references see PAULY-WISSOWA, Real-Encycl. der Altertumswiss., article on the Pythagoreans, col. 289 middle.
[2]) See A. J. FESTUGIÈRE: La révélation d'Hermès Trismégiste, 4 Vols, Paris, Gabalda 1949—54, and W. GUNDEL: Neue Texte des Hermes Trismegistos.

Egyptologists are of the unanimous opinion that HERODOTOS is wrong on this point. The doctrine of transmigration of souls as presented here is foreign to Egyptian religion. This may well be true of earlier Egyptian religion, as known to us from sarcophagus texts and books of the dead; but must it be that Egyptian religion in the time of HERODOTOS (about 450 B.C.) coincided in every respect with that of the middle and new kingdoms? There may well have been different religious currents in Egypt, as there were in Iran at the time of ZARATHUSTRA, in Greece at the time of PYTHAGORAS and in the Persian empire at the time of DARIUS and XERXES. The whole period from 700 to 400 B.C. was, after all, a time of violent religious fermentation throughout the ancient world. KAMBYSES seems to have meddled with Egyptian religion, for he is reported to have killed the bull of Apis (HERODOTOS III 29). The story may or may not be true, but in any case there must have been a religious conflict. Other religious influences of Persian or Babylonian origin may surely have made themselves felt as well. We do not know and therefore have no grounds for saying that HERODOTOS is wrong.

It has been supposed that PYTHAGORAS' doctrine of transmigration derives from India. It may be so, but we do not know by what route it finally reached Greece. HERODOTOS may well be right that Egypt was an intermediate station.

There is another very remarkable passage in HERODOTOS II 81:

> Nothing woollen is brought into the temples, or buried with them (the Egyptians); for it is not lawful. In this they agree with the ritual called Orphic and Bacchic, but which is in truth Egyptian and Pythagorean; for those that partake of these rites may also not be buried in woollen garments.

HERODOTOS here speaks of Greek mysteries which were commonly called 'Orphic' and 'Bacchic'. He says that the mysteries are 'in truth Egyptian and Pythagorean'. Let us examine more closely the significance of this remark.

'Orphic' mysteries are probably those in which 'Books of ORPHEUS' were recited or were the basis of the rites. A whole bundle of such 'Books of ORPHEUS' was available in the time of PLATON (Republic, 364e); but in the general opinion of philologists both ancient and modern, they do not originate from ORPHEUS himself. Amongst the authors of Orphic books Pythagoreans too were named[1]). We can therefore readily understand HERODOTOS' saying that the Orphic mysteries are actually Pythagorean.

HERODOTOS, however, says not only that the mysteries are Pythagorean, but also that they are 'Egyptian'. He obviously means that the Pythagorean and Orphic sects took over these mysteries from the Egyptians.

In considering the credibility of this report, we should note first that HERODOTOS is not given to fantasy. His basic principle is 'I record whatever is told me as I heard it' (II 123). He did himself visit Egypt. In the case of the earlier reports about transmigration

---

[1]) W. K. C. GUTHRIE, *Orpheus and Greek Religion*, London 1935, p. 217.

of souls it could be objected that he possibly misunderstood the statements of the Egyptian priests, or that the latter tried to lay claim to a Greek doctrine as ancient Egyptian wisdom. But his statement about the mysteries is a rather different case. A secret rite such as the Eleusinian mysteries is not merely a doctrine in words which could be misunderstood, but an institution, a cult action, conducted by priests with the participation of the initiated. So, when HERODOTOS speaks of a truly Egyptian rite, we cannot simply set this aside as a misunderstanding. In later times there were Isis mysteries in Egypt and in Rome whose participants ritually accomplished the rebirth of the soul to immortality[1]). It is not at all impossible that such mysteries did already exist in HERODOTOS' time.

My own inclination is to take HERODOTOS seriously, to assume that there was a religious movement in Egypt in the 6th and 5th centuries like the Pythagorean, a movement whose adherents believed in the transmigration and immortality of the soul, and that PYTHAGORAS was somehow connected with them.

---

[1]) APULEIOS: The Golden Ass, Book XI

CHAPTER II

OLD-BABYLONIAN ASTRONOMY

In Babylonia and Assyria astronomy made much more progress than in Egypt.

In this chapter we shall confine ourselves to the Old-Babylonian period, i.e. to the time of the HAMMURABI dynasty. The oldest known astronomical cuneiform texts belong to just this period.

HAMMURABI AND HIS DYNASTY

The dating of HAMMURABI's reign is a central problem of Babylonian-Assyrian chronology. Three chronologies have been proposed — a 'short', 'middle' and 'long' one. The short chronology places HAMMURABI's reign in the years 1728-1686 B.C. In this case his dynasty, the dynasty of Amurru, would have ruled from 1830 to 1531. All these dates must be put back 56 or 64 years according to the middle chronology and 120 years according to the long chronology. The reasons why just these figures are possible and no others will be explained in our discussion of the Venus tablets of AMMIZADUGA.

Old-Babylonian civilization stems from the more ancient civilization of the Sumerians. The Sumerians invented cuneiform writing; the Babylonians used it and adapted it to their Semitic language, while retaining many Sumerian word-signs in their original meaning as 'ideograms'. Such Sumerian signs were frequently used as technical terms in mathematics and astronomy. They had the advantage of brevity: most of them could be written with a single symbol. Accadian words, that is words of the Semitic spoken language, could also be written phonetically by dividing them into syllables and denoting each syllable by a Sumerian word symbol.

An example may make this clearer. The constellation Libra is called in Accadian *zibanitu(m)*, in Sumerian RIN. Both words have the same meaning: 'scales'. Consequently the constellation Libra can either be denoted by one cuneiform sign RIN (pronounced rin or *zibanitu*), or by four coneiform signs: *zi-ba-ni-tum*.

The Babylonian method of writing numbers was also taken over from the Sumerians. Integers under 60 were written simply by repetition of the symbols for 10 and 1. The sign for 10 was a wedge, for 1 a vertical stroke. Thus, two wedges and three strokes mean 23. For larger numbers and fractions a *positional notation* was used, similar to our decimal system, but with base 60. Thus, the notation 1, 1, 15 can be read as

$$60^2 + 60 + 15 = 3675.$$

It could, however, be that the 15 is to be read as 15×60^k: in that case the number 3675 will have to be multiplied by 60^k. Finally 15 can be intended to be read as $15/60^k$; in this case the number 3675 must be divided by 60^k.

For the convenience of the reader and to avoid ambiguties, we shall in our transcription of Babylonian numerals use a semicolon to separate units from sixtieths, and write 0 in empty places, as in our decimal system. Thus, 1, 0, 0 means 60^2 and 0; 0,15 means $15/60^2$.

The Sumerians had tables for multiplication, reciprocals, squares and square roots. The highly developed Sumerian calculational techniques were the foundation on which Old-Babylonian arithmetic and algebra were built. The Babylonians knew how to solve systems of linear and quadratic equations, and also certain cubic and biquadratic equations, and they could add up arithmetical and other series. They were also acquainted as early as the time of the HAMMURABI dynasty with the 'Theorem of PYTHAGORAS'. For a fuller description of Babylonian mathematics see Volume I of this series[1]).

HAMMURABI was a great lawgiver. Parts of his Legal Code derived, it is true, from older Sumerian laws and common law, but the Code as a whole represents something new and of great stature.

The priests and scribes of HAMMURABI unified the gods of the old city-states into one great Pantheon, subjecting them to the God of Babylon, Marduk. Marduk was declared to be the Creator of the Universe.

Besides law and religion, the calendar too was unified. The Babylonian names of the months were introduced throughout the whole kingdom. They were:

I	Nisannu	VII	Tashritu
II	Aiaru	VIII	Araḫsamna
III	Simanu	IX	Kislimu
IV	Duzu	X	Tebetu
V	Abu	XI	Shabatu
VI	Ululu	XII	Adaru

The month always began in the evening with the first sighting of the lunar crescent. Therefore the months had 29 or 30 days in irregular succession. The mean value of the month is 29·530 days.

The year always began with the beginning of a new month, in the spring. The years contained 12 or 13 months. In the years with 13 months either a 'second Ululu' VI_2 or a 'second Adaru' XII_2 was taken as the intercalary month. This intercalation occurred quite irregularly until the Persian period. We have a royal decree of the Neo-Babylonian King NABUNAID, stating that in the current year 15 (beginning 541 B.C.) there shall be a second Adaru. It was only after 528 B.C. that the intercalations became regular.

---

[1]) B. L. VAN DER WAERDEN, Science Awakening I (second edition). Noordhoff, Groningen, 1961.

They follow first (from 527 to 502) an 8-year cycle, and then (from 499 with an exception in 385) a 19-year cycle, such as is still used to-day for the Jewish and Christian calculation of Easter, with 7 intercalary months in 19 years. The 19-year intercalary cycle was maintained in astronomical cuneiform texts until the year 75 A.D.

As regards the division of the day, we must differentiate between the popular and the astronomical method of telling the time. For everyday purposes the night was divided into three 'watches' and the day likewise. In summer the night watches are therefore shorter and the day watches longer than in winter. In the 'astrolabe texts', which we shall discuss in detail in the next chapter, the day watches are further subdivided into half and quarter watches.

On the other hand, the astronomers divided the whole day (= day + night) first into 12 equal double-hours called *bēru* (miles) and then each *bēru* into 30 USH or *degrees of time*. One degree of time is therefore equal to exactly 4 modern minutes.

The beginning of astrology

Whether the Sumerians were interested in astrology and astronomy or not, we do not know. The oldest astronomical and astrological texts that we have, namely a single astrological and a single astronomical text, belong to the Old-Babylonian period.

The astrological text[1]) offers prognoses based on the course of the moon and the state of the sky on the day when the crescent becomes visible at the beginning of a new year. The text begins thus:

> 1. If the sky is dark, the year will be bad.
> 2. If the face of the sky is bright when the New Moon appears and (it is greeted) with joy, the year will be good.
> 3. If the North Wind blows across the face of the sky before the New Moon, the corn will grow abundantly.
> 4. If on the day of the crescent the Moon-God does not disappear quickly enough from the sky, 'quaking' (presumably some disease) will come upon the Land.

These prognoses are altogether primitive in nature. The moon and the sky are observed in the evening when the New Year begins, and the character of the year is deduced from this observation by analogy.

Old-Babylonian astrology was not interested, or at least not in the first place, in the fate of the individual. Its principal interest was the well-being of the country. Its

---

[1]) V. ŠILEIKO: Mondlaufprognosen aus der Zeit der ersten babyl. Dynastie. *Comptes Rendus Acad. Sci. U.R.S.S.*, (1927), p. 125. See also TH. BAUER, *Z.f. Assyriol.*, *43* (1936), p. 308.

predictions concern the weather and the harvest, drought and famine, war or peace and of course also the fate of the Kings.

It was clear to the Babylonians that the regular succession of days, months, seasons and years, and also the whole of agricultural life, depended on the course of the great gods Moon and Sun. Perhaps they also knew that ebb and flow are controlled by the moon; for the old land of Sumer, the southern part of Mesopotamia, lies directly on the Persian Gulf. At any rate the Moon and Sun were revered as very powerful Gods.

Ishtar, the Goddess of Love, Goddess also of the planet Venus, formed with the Moon and Sun a trinity of great Gods. That love plays a great part in our lives was as well known to the Babylonians as it is to us. It was therefore important to pay close attention to the appearance of her planet in the sky and its effect on earth.

In fact we find in the great collection of omens 'Enuma Anu Enlil', which was probably assembled in the Cassite period, a large number of Venus omens, i.e. phenomena of the planet Venus having astrological significance. For example:

> If Venus appears in the East in the month Airu and the Great and Small Twins surround her, all four of them, and she is dark, then will the King of Elam fall sick and not remain alive.[1])

According to Schaumberger, this omen is probably old; it could very well go back to the time of the Dynasty of Akkad (about 2300 B.C.). There are omens in which the names of the Kings SARGON of Akkad and IBI-SIN if Ur are mentioned (E. F. WEIDNER, Mitteil. d. altoriental. Ges., 4, p. 231 and 236). Omen-astrology thus appears to go back to the time before HAMMURABI.

The series 'Enuma Anu Enlil'

This extensive series of cuneiform texts is, so to speak, a compendium of the astrology of the second millenium B.C. It was continuously quoted, commented upon and used in the first millenium. If, for example, an Assyrian king wished to know whether the omens were favourable or unfavourable, the Royal Astrologer would reach for the old Omen Series, quote an omen therefrom and explain its application to the situation immediately confronting them. The archives of these Court Astrologers have been preserved to a large extent in the library of ASSURBANIPAL, so that we have numerous fragments and quotations from the series. There are also tables of contents, from which we can conclude that the series consisted of 70 or more tablets, altogether containing some 7000 omens. See E. F. WEIDNER, Die astrologische Serie Enuma Anu Enlil, *Archiv f. Orientforschung 14*, p. 173.

[1]) J. SCHAUMBERGER, 3. Ergänzungsheft zu F. X. KUGLER, Sternkunde u. Sterndienst in Babel (Münster, 1935), p. 344.

THE VENUS TABLETS OF AMMIZADUGA

Most important for the history of astronomy is a series of observations of the planet Ve-nus made during the reign of the king AMMIZADUGA. The records of these observations are contained in the 63rd tablet of the series 'Enuma Anu Enlil', of which various copies are partly preserved. Although the copies do not always agree and although they contain many obvious errors, it is still possible to reconstruct the greater part of the original text from them. The astronomical calculations carried out by KUGLER and others prove that the major part of the dates in the text is correct and that these dates must be based on actual observations. The standard edition of the tables is: LANGDON and FOTHERING-HAM, The Venus Tablets of Ammizaduga, Oxford 1928. KUGLER's first investigation of the tables was given in his book: F. X. KUGLER, Sternkunde und Sterndienst in Babel I (1907) and II (1910). See also J. D. WEIR, The Venus Tablets of Ammizaduga (Publ. Institut historique et archéologique Istambul 1972).

The most complete copy, namely text K 160 from the library of ASSURBANIPAL, consists of three parts labelled A_1, B and A_2 by KUGLER. Part B contains no observations, but rather schematic calculations of the appearance and disappearance of Venus, with related astrological predictions. Parts A_1 and A_2 contain observations of the same phenomena with astrological interpretations. The Italian astronomer SCHIAPARELLI was the first to recognize that there is no break between the observations of A_1 and A_2.

On uniting A_1 and A_2 and completing A_1 with the help of other texts such as K 2321, we obtain an almost complete list of observations of the heliacal risings and settings of Venus over a period of 21 years, with astrological interpretations of the following kind:

(Year 1) 'If on the 15th day of the month Shabatu Venus disappeared in the west, remaining absent in the sky 3 days, and on the 18th day of the month Shabatu Venus appeared in the east, catastrophes of kings; Adad will bring rains, Ea subterranean waters; king will send greetings to king.'

(Year 10) 'If on the 10th of Araḫsamna Venus disappeared in the east, remaining absent 2 months and 6 days in the sky, and was seen on the 16th of Tebetu in the west, the harvest of the land will be successful.'

The sequence of tenses: If (past tense) then (future) is very peculiar. It seems to indicate that the phenomenon was actually observed in the past and that from this observation a prediction was derived: Whenever the same phenomenon will be observed, the same consequences will follow.

Before we discuss the text, we must describe the principal phenomena of Venus during a synodic period, as seen from the earth. Here I follow KUGLER (Sternkunde u. Stern-dienst, I, p. 16).

The phases of Venus

For us, observers on the northern hemisphere facing southwards, the sun, moon and stars in their daily motion move to the right, that is from East to West by way of South. The sun and moon, however, in their annual and monthly motion in relation to the fixed stars, move to the left. It is in this sense that the words 'to the right' and 'to the left' are to be understood here and throughout the whole book. The daily motion which Venus shares with all the stars does not concern us for the moment; we restrict ourselves now to the slow motion of Venus in the girdle of the zodiac, using the fixed stars as landmarks.

Let Venus first be in its *superior conjunction* with the sun, i.e. in that conjunction where Venus is beyond the sun. The glaring sunlight makes the planet invisible. The sun and Venus move in the Zodiac towards the left, but the planet moves more quickly. After some 40^d its easterly elongation from the sun is $10°$. Then Venus becomes visible for the first time in the evening *(evening rising)*. In the following six months the elongation increases continuously, while the planet comes ever nearer the earth and becomes ever brighter. After some 222^d (calculated from the conjunction) it reaches its greatest easterly elongation (about 46 or 47 degrees). Its daily motion in relation to the fixed stars now decreases rapidly. After 272^d at an elongation of $28°$ the planet comes to rest *(evening stationary point)*. From here on its motion is *retrograde*, i.e. it moves to the right in the zodiac and with increasing velocity. After some 287^d it disappears at an elongation of $10°$ in the rays of the sun *(evening setting)*. After some 14 days of invisibility, during which it passes the sun *(inferior conjunction)*, it appears for the first time in the morning sky *(morning rising)*. The planet still moves retrogradely, but after some 314^d comes to a standstill *(morning stationary point)*. The retrograde motion which has taken it through some $15°$ in 42^d has ceased; from now on Venus again moves eastwards, but more slowly then the sun. After 364^d it reaches its greatest *westerly elongation*. Its brightness now declines and after 546^d it disappears at an elongation of some $10°$ in the rays of the sun *(morning setting)*. After the completion of a *synodic period*, which lasts on average 584 days, Venus is again in its superior conjunction with the sun.

The figures given are only approximate averages. The period of invisibility at the inferior conjunction can last 2 days or nearly 3 weeks, depending on the season of the year.

LANGDON, FOTHERINGHAM and SCHOCH have introduced the following very convenient notation:

$$
\begin{aligned}
\text{MF} &= \text{Morningfirst} = \text{Morning Rising} \\
\text{ML} &= \text{Morninglast} = \text{Morning Setting} \\
\text{EF} &= \text{Eveningfirst} = \text{Evening Rising} \\
\text{EL} &= \text{Eveninglast} = \text{Evening Setting.}
\end{aligned}
$$

After this preparation let us turn to the text proper.

The 'Year of the golden throne'

In our text, the eighth year is called 'Year of the golden throne'. Such titles for designating a particular year are found in many Old-Babylonian texts, but not in those from the subsequent Cassite period. There is only one single year that is found designated by this title 'The Year of the golden throne' in the Old-Babylonian texts, namely the 8th Year of King AMMIZADUGA. This king reigned for 21 years, and the observations of our text also cover just 21 years. Accordingly KUGLER (Sternkunde u. Sterndienst II, p. 280) concluded that the observations were made in the reign of AMMIZADUGA.

The time intervals

KUGLER next determined the time intervals between the observations. For this purpose, it was necessary to find out which years of AMMIZADUGA had an intercalary month VI_2 (second Ululu) or XII_2 (second Adaru). An example will make this clear.

The first two observations were an Eveninglast on the 15th and a Morningfirst on the 18th of the month XI (Shabatu). We shall denote these observations by

Year 1, EL XI 15
MF XI 18.

The third observation was a Morninglast:

Year 2, ML VIII 11.

KUGLER's investigations on intercalations showed that the year 1 was a normal year, i.e. a year with 12 months. Hence the time between the second and third observation was 9 months minus 7 days. This time of visibility of Venus as a Morning Star is quite reasonable.

Errors in the text

Some text dates are obvious errors: the time intervals are either too long or too short. Thus, in the year 9, the text has:

EL III 11, invisible 9 months and 4 days, MF XII 15.

The invisibility period of 9 months and 4 days is quite impossible: it ought to be a few days. If the first date III 11 is corrected into XII 11, the dates are all right.

Sometimes there are deviations between the extant copies of our text; in these cases we may choose the most probable dates. In other cases, impossible or highly improbable dates have to be left out of account. For details I refer to the German edition of this book.

At the end we are left with the following 35 corrected dates:

Corrected dates

Year	EL	MF	Year	ML	EF
1	XI 15	XI 18	2	VIII 11	X 19
3	VI 23	VII 13	4	IV 2	VI 3
5	II 2	II 18	5	IX 25	XI 29
6	VIII 28	IX 1	7	V 21	VIII 2
			8	XII 25	
9	XII 11	XII 15	10	VIII 10	X 16
11		VI$_2$ 8			
13		II 12	13	IX 21	XI 21
14		VIII 28	15	V 20	VIII 5
16	IV 5	IV 20	16	XII 25	
			20	III 25	
21	I 26		21	X 28	XII 28

From this table one sees that the Venus phenomena are nearly repeated after 8 years, or more precisely after 99 Babylonian months minus 4 days. Thus, the Eveninglast in year 1 takes place on XI 15. After exactly 99 months minus 4 days, in year 9 on XII 11, another EL was observed. The period of invisibility in year 1 was 3 days; after 8 years the duration of invisibility was 4 days. Just so the MF of the year 3 is repeated after 99 months minus 5 days in the year 11. Every period of 8 years contains just 5 synodic periods, i.e. 5 complete cycles of phenomena EL, MF, ML, EF.

The chronological problem

It is known that AMMIZADUGA came to the throne exactly 146 years after HAMMURABI. The dating of HAMMURABI is a fundamental problem of Babylonian chronology. From Assyrian lists of kings and other data we may deduce[1]) that HAMMURABI began his reign at some time between −1900 and −1680, and hence AMMIZADUGA between −1754

[1]) See M. B. ROWTON, The date of Hammurabi, *J. Near Eastern Studies 17*, p. 97.

and −1534. Our problem is: What dates between these limits are compatible with the Venus observations?

In the eleventh month of the first year of AMMIZADUGA the time of invisibility between EL and MF was, according to our text, only 3 days. So short a period of invisibility occurs only once or twice every eight years. According to our text the first period of 8 years contained just two short periods of invisibility, of 3 days each, in the years 1 and 6.

Now if we try to assign Julian year numbers to these years, we must take care to choose such a period of 8 Julian years, in which the first and sixth years have very few days of invisibility between EL and MF. An example is furnished by the 8 Julian years from −1701 to −1694. Of course, we must shift the years a little, because the Babylonian years begin in the spring. Thus, when talking of the year −1701, we shall mean a year beginning in the spring of −1701 and ending in the spring of −1700. In this year, Venus was invisible (according to modern calculation) for just 3 days at the end of March, −1700, and 5 years later the duration of invisibility was 4 days. Thus, it would be possible to identify the first year of Ammizaduga with the year −1701, but not with one of the seven following years. The next possibility, as far as the durations of invisibility are concerned, would be −1693, and then again −1685, and so on.

However, we must also take into account the Moon's phases. In the year 1 of AMMIZADUGA, the EL of Venus took place, according to our text, on the 15th of a month, i.e. 14 days after the first visibility of the crescent. According to modern calculation, this would be correct for the year −1701, but not for −1693 or −1685. Within the limits −1754 and −1534 which we have assigned to the first year of AMMIZADUGA, only the following four possible years would give a reasonable agreement between the ancient observations and modern calculation:

$$-1701, \; -1645, \; -1637, \; -1581.$$

Accordingly, the following proposals have been made by modern authors:
1. *Long chronology*, proposed by SIDERSKY and GOETZE: Accession year of AMMIZADUGA −1701.
2. *Middle chronology*, proposed by SIDNEY SMITH and UNGNAD: Accession year −1645 or −1637.
3. *Short chronology*, proposed by CORNELIUS and ALBRIGHT: Accession year −1581.

Now, if the four phenomena of Venus are calculated for the four possible periods of 21 years:

$$-1701 \text{ to } -1681$$
$$-1645 \text{ to } -1625$$
$$-1637 \text{ to } -1617$$
$$-1581 \text{ to } -1561$$

and compared with the text dates, one sees that the last possibility, i.e. the short chronology, gives by far the best agreement. The details of the calculation were given in the German edition of this book.

If the calculation is made for the accession year −1645, the differences between text dates and calculated dates are almost all negative, and for −1637 they are almost all positive. For the year −1701 the distribution of the positive and negative signs is all right, but the number of clear errors in the text is about twice as large as for −1581. Therefore the short chronology appears much more probable than the long and the middle one.

The short chronology is also confirmed by the historical investigation of ROWTON quoted before, and by Radiocarbon Dating. Hence we may confidently assert:

> The dynasty of HAMMURABI reigned from −1829 to −1530,
> HAMMURABI reigned from −1727 to −1685,
> AMMIZADUGA reigned from −1581 to −1561.

Schematic calculation of the phases of Venus

Schematic calculations are to be found in Part B of text K 190, which is inserted between Parts A_1 and A_2. The text begins thus:

> If in the month Nisannu on the 2nd day Venus rose in the East, there will be need in the land. Until the 6th Kislimu she will stay in the East, on the 7th Kislimu she will disappear. Three months she remains out of the sky. On the 7th Adaru will Venus appear again in the West, and one King will declare hostilities against the other.

In the next section it is assumed that Venus appears in the West in the month II on the 3rd day, in the following one that Venus appears in the East in the month III on the 4th day, and so on. The number of the month and of the day of the month is each time increased by 1, the period of visibility remains constant at 8 months and 5 days. The period of invisibility from ML to EF is always 3 months, from EL to MF 7 days. The numbers run as follows:

> 1) MF I 2, ML IX 6, invisible 3 months, EF XII 7;
> 2) EF II 3, EL X 7, invisible 7 days, MF X 15;
> 3) MF III 4, ML XI 8, invisible 3 months, EF II 9; and so on till
>
> 12) EF XII 13, EL VIII 17, invisible 7 days, MF VIII 25.

The dates follow one another, as we see, in arithmetic progression. What we have here is the first application of arithmetic progressions to astronomy. The application is certainly primitive and, to our way of thinking, of little significance. But later generations of Babylonian astronomers greatly refined the application of this mathematical divice to the calculation of celestial phenomena.

An important insight which finds clear expression in our text is that of the *periodicity of the celestial phenomena*. The time of visibility of Venus as a morning or evening star is always the same, according to the text, while the times of invisibility alternate between 7 days and 3 months. This is indeed a pronounced simplification of the true situation, but such simplifications are a necessary first step in ascertaining the regularities of celestial phenomena.

It is not known how the Babylonians arrived at these constant periods (8 months 5 days, 3 months and 7 days). KUGLER supposes that it was by averaging the intervals between the observations contained in A_1 and A_2. Such a procedure would provide an explanation not only of the correct value 7^d, but also of the much too large figure of 3 months, because the observations in the tables contain some erroneous, excessively large values for the time of invisibility between ML and EF.

The time from which these schematic calculations originate is not knwon. The limits within which it must fall — and very ample they are — are the end of the reign of AM- MIZADUGA (-1561) on the one hand and the destruction of ASSURBANIPAL's library by the Medes (-611) on the other. The name for Venus in text B, namely NIN.DAR.AN.NA, is not otherwise met in the Assyrian period; this perhaps favours an early dating.

The identity of the morning and evening star

This identity is expressed in the very wording of the observations: 'If NIN.DAR.AN.NA on the 15th disappeared in the West, remained 3 days invisible and on the 18th appeared again . . .'

The knowledge that the morning and evening star are identical was not the common property of all peoples in antiquity. This can be seen from the fact that the Greeks treated the discovery as something relatively new, ascribing it variously to PARMENIDES or PYTHAGORAS[1]). These ascriptions could not have been made if the matter had been one of general knowledge. It is all the more remarkable that the Babylonians recognized the identity as early as the time of AMMIZADUGA and called the planet Venus by the single name ^{d}NIN.DAR.AN.NA, that is, 'bright Queen of the Sky'.

---

[1]) DIOGENES LAERTIOS, Lives of the Philosophers, VIII 14 and IX 23.

Astral religion

What can have been the reason for so meticulously observing, recording and transmitting observations of the appearances and disappearances of Venus over a period of 21 years?

In some cases astronomical observations are needed to regulate the calendar. Examples of this (the rising of Sirius in Egypt, the summer solstice and the phases of the Pleiades in Hesiod) have already come our way. However, the observation of the planet Venus contributes nothing to the solution of calendaric problems. We must look in other directions for the motives behind these observations.

Three possibilities present themselves, namely interest in astronomy, in astrology and in astral religion.

1. It is possible that the Venus observations were undertaken out of purely scientific curiosity, out of the desire to investigate regularity in the appearances and disappearances of Venus. This is not a far-fetched possibility; it finds support in part B of the text, which was inserted in between the observations. Here the phases of Venus are calculated by a simple arithmetical law. To discover this law, it was necessary first to make observations, and then to eliminate the irregularities of the observed intervals by averaging over a number of periods. It might therefore be assumed that the observations were made just to serve this purpose.

But this immediately raises the question why the observations were copied again and again for centuries. Certainly not our of pure scientific interest, but because of the astrological interpretation. The Venus tablets formed part of the astrological series Anuma Anu Enlil, and were combined with astrological predictions.

2. Another possibility is that the observations were originally made solely to obtain empirical material for astrological predictions. The Venus phenomena were brought into connection with important events occurring at the same time or soon after. This explanation was suggested by O. NEUGEBAUER (Exact Sciences in Antiquity, 2nd ed., p. 100), and we may say in its favour that the appearance and disappearance of Venus are combined in the text itself with astrological predictions.

However, this explanation in its turn leaves one question open namely, how it came about that the Venus phenomena were regarded as being related to the events on earth, and treated as causes or at least portents of these events.

3. It seems to me that the reason for this is to be found in astral religion. The Venus phenomena were important to the Babylonians because the planet Venus was considered to be the visible manifestation of the great Goddess Ishtar. Just as the great Gods Sin (the moon) and Shamash (the sun) are obviously responsible for the regular procession of months, days and years, and thus influence our entire life, so it was thought that the Goddess Ishtar communicates important things to us by her appearances and disappearances. (That the planet is only the plaything of gravitational force could not be

suspected at that time.) Thus one was impelled to observe and record the phases of Venus carefully, and to connect them with events near at hand.

These three explanations are not mutually exclusive; rather, they complement one another. The first leaves a question open, which is satisfactorily answered by the second. This in turn leaves a question open, the answer to which requires a consideration of astral religion.

Not only the moon, the sun and Venus were revered as Gods; the other stars were also. This can be seen clearly in a well-known prayer, written in Old Babylonian times to accompany the still older practice of divining the future by examining the entrails of a sacrificed animal:

Prayer for a Haruspicy at night[1])

> They are lying down, the great ones.
> The bolts are fallen; the fastenings are placed.
> The crowds and people are quiet.
> The open gates are (now) closed.
> The gods of the land and the goddesses of the land,
> Shamash, Sin, Adad, and Ishtar,
> Have betaken themselves to sleep in heaven.
> They are not pronouncing judgement;
> They are not deciding things.
> Veiled is the night;
> The temple and the most holy places are quiet and dark.
> The traveller calls on (his) god;
> And the litigant is tarrying in sleep.
> The judge of the truth, the father of the fatherless,
> Shamash, has betaken himself to his chamber.
> O great ones, gods of the night,
> O bright one, Gibil, O warrior Irra,
> O bow (star) and yoke (star),
> O pleiades, Orion, and the dragon,
> O Ursa major, goat (star), and the bison,
> Stand by, and then,
> In the divination which I am making,
> In the lamb which I am offering,
> Put truth for me.

[1]) Translation by F. J. STEPHENS, in J. B. PRITCHARD: Ancient Near Eastern Texts relating to the Old Testament. (Princeton, 1950) p. 390.

Here it is apparent that the very ancient art of haruspicy is being placed by the poet under the tutelage of the celestial gods. No longer is knowledge of the future to come from the sacrificial lamb itself, nor even from the particular god to whom it is offered, but from the stars, called upon to witness and implant the truth. The whole prayer breathes with the religious awe of the poet in the presence of the starry firmament.

Modern man is still deeply moved, sometimes, beneath the stars. Many amateurs and professionals have been won to astronomy because the vision of the star-strewn sky evokes in them ever freshly a feeling of wonder and reverence. This feeling lies, it seems to me, at the deepest root of astral religion.

Astral religion and astrology

As far back as we know, the Babylonians always identified the planets with gods or at least allocated them to their gods. Jupiter was ^{mul} ^{d}Marduk, i.e. 'star god Marduk' or 'star of the god Marduk'. Venus was identified with Ishtar, the goddess of love, Mars with the war-god Nergal. Correspondingly, the astrological interpretations of the Mars phenomena relate mostly to war and destruction. The Venus omina deal frequently with love and fertility, but also with war, because Ishtar was also goddess of battle. Three examples from the series Enuma Anu Enlil may be cited in illustration:

'When Mars approaches the star SHU.GI, there will be uprising in Amurru and hostility; one will kill another . . .'

(GÖSSMANN, Planetarium Babyloniacum, p. 182).

'When Venus stands high, pleasure of copulation . . .'

(GÖSSMANN, p. 37).

'When Venus stands in her place, uprising of the hostile forces, 'fullness' of the women shall there be in the land . . .'

(GÖSSMANN, p. 39).

These examples show that Babylonian astrology depended essentially on astral religion. Mars as the star of Nergal proclaimed war and destruction, whereas the phenomena of Venus, the star of Ishtar, were connected with love, marriage and fertility. The guiding concept of astrology, that the gods of the sky rule our lives, was a religious concept. Very right were the Fathers of the Church to condemn astrology!

CHAPTER III

THE ASSYRIAN PERIOD

TIME TABLE (the years are B.C.)

I. Old-Babylonian Reign

Dynasty of Amurru, HAMMURABI Dynasty		1830-1530
HAMMURABI	1728-1686	
AMMIZADUGA	1582-1561	
(Observation of Venus)		
Hittite Invasion, End of Reign		1530

II. Cassite Reign

Approximate Duration of Cassite Reign	1530-1160
Astrological Series 'Enuma Anu Enlil',	Date unknown
Distances of Fixed Stars (HILPRECHT's Text)	between 1300 and 1100

III. Some Assyrian Kings

ASSUR-UBALLIT I	1356-1320
TUKULTI-NINURTA I	1235-1198
(Assyrian Copy of Astrolabe about 1100)	
ASSURNASIRPAL II	884-859
TIGLAT-PILESAR III	746-727
(Contemporary in Babylon: NABONASSAR 748-734)	
Sargonid Kings:	
SARGON II	722-705
SANHERIB	705-681
ASSARHADDON	681-669
ASSURBANIPAL	669-630
Nineveh and its Library Destroyed	612

IV. Chaldaean Kings

For the Chaldaean Kings see Chapter 4.

General survey[1])

During the reign of HAMMURABI's son and successor SAMSU-ILUNA the political power of Babylon began to decline. Its end came finally in 1530 when the Hittite king MURSILI I on a raiding expedition captured Babylon and sacked it. MURSILI could not keep the town permanently, but it never regained its old status. The Cassites, a people from the Eastern mountain country, took the opportunity to extend their empire over Babylon.

The Cassite reign ended about 1160 B.C. Meanwhile Assyria was strengthened under ASSUR-UBALLIT I (1356-1320), and reached the first peak of its power under TUKULTI-NINURTA I (1235-1198), known to the Greeks as Ninos. From this time on, except for occasional breaks, Assyria was politically dominant in Mesopotamia until 626 B.C.

Although in the second half of the second millenium Babylon played a rather subordinate role politically, the brilliance of its civilization shone more clearly than ever before. The Babylonian dialect of Akkadian became a leading language throughout the Near East, as is shown by the clay tablet archives from El-Amarna in Egypt and from Boghazköy in the heart of Asia Minor. It is also significant that, from the time of ASSUR-UBALLIT, the Assyrian kings composed their inscriptions not in their own Assyrian dialect, but in Babylonian.

There must have been a very lively intellectual life in Babylonia and Assyria from about 1350 to 1100 B.C. Older traditions were collected and systematized; for example, it was probably at this time that the gigantic astrological series Enuma Anu Enlil was composed. Many epics, prayers and other religious literary works were reshaped or created. Thus, probably in the 12th century, a highly gifted poet moulded the magnificent Gilgamesh Epic into its final form[2]). We shall see that this period also produced astronomical calculations.

In the first millenium B.C., Assyrian civilization remained to a large extent dependent on Babylon, though there is one achievement which we must mention as that of the Assyrians themselves — the unique bas-relief art of the time of ASSURNASIRPAL II (884-859).

There was a final flowering of Assyrian culture under the rulers of the Sargonid dynasty: SARGON II (722-705), SANHERIB (705-681), ASSARHADDON (681-669) and ASSURBANIPAL (669-630). ASSURBANIPAL is important for us because he built in his palace a great library that was to hold the entire cuneiform literature in the Sumerian and Akkadian language.

Only a few years later, however, the Assyrian kingdom fell. In 614 Assur, and then in 612 Nineveh, were taken by the Babylonians and Medes and completely destroyed.

---

[1]) This survey relies largely upon the excellent monograph by W. von Soden: 'Herrscher im alten Orient' (1954).

[2]) The most recent translation is in German: 'Das Gilgamesch-Epos', translated by A. SCHOTT, revised and supplemented by W. VON SODEN, Reclam 1958.

THE EARLIER TEXTS

Our source material from the early Assyrian period is rather sparse. We have only three astronomical texts that can be ascribed with some measure of certainty to the second half of the second millenium, namely:

(I) HILPRECHT's Text HS 229 from Nippur;

(II) the so-called 'Astrolabes': lists of 36 stars connected with the 12 months of the year.

Related to the astrolabes, but probably still older are:

(III) the star lists of Elam, Akkad and Amurru.

Some writers have believed that HILPRECHT's text demonstates the existence of a highly developed Old Babylonian scientific astronomy. We shall first clear away this legend and then pass on to a discussion of the more important Astrolabes. We shall see that HILPRECHT's text is merely a mathematical exercise belonging to the prescientific stage of Babylonian astronomy. On the other hand, the Astrolabes mark the beginning of scientific astronomy. They represent the first attempt to systematize the prescientific popular knowledge about stars that become visible in the sky at the different seasons of the year. Granted, the system was still very imperfect, but it was a good beginning.

Later texts, especially the two tablets of the ^{mul}APIN series, modified and completed the system of the astrolabes. By studying and comparing these texts, we shall gain insight into the development of astronomy in Mesopotamia.

For references and details see VAN DER WAERDEN, Babyl. Astron. II, *J. of Near Eastern Studies 8*, p. 6-26.

I. HILPRECHT's text HS 229

Some lines of this text were published by HOMMEL in 1908 in the 'Münchener Neuesten Nachrichten'. They read as follows:

44, 26, 40 times 9 is 6,40. (Therefore:)

13 *bēru* 10 USH is the distance of the star SHU.PA beyond the star BAN.

44, 26, 40 times 7 is 5, 11, 6, 40. (Therefore:)

10 *bēru* 11 USH 6$\frac{1}{2}$ GAR 2 *ammatu* is the distance of the star GIR.TAB over the star SHU.PA.

Explanation: The sexagesimal number 44,26,40 can be read as 44,26;40, i.e. as

$$44 \times 60 + 26 + 40/60.$$

This number, multiplied by 7, gives 5,11,6;40.

As in the majority of mathematical texts, the unit of length is 1 GAR = 12 *ammatu* (cubits). 60 GAR make 1 USH, and 30 USH 1 *bēru* (double hour), or in terms of travelling distance, nearly 11 km. Therefore it is correct that 5,11,6;40 GAR is just 10 *bēru* 11 USH 6½ GAR 2 *ammatu*, as the text says.

HOMMEL's publication caused a violent argument between KUGLER and WEIDNER over the accuracy of the measurement of stellar distances or right ascension differences in the Old Babylonian period. To-day, since we know more about the text, the whole discussion seems pointless. THUREAU-DANGIN was the first to point out that the distances in the text could very well be radial distances, if the text is taken literally. If this interpretation is correct, then the numbers in the text were, of course, not measured, but pure speculation. The pythagorean 'Harmony of the Spheres' also assumes that the distances between individual planetary spheres are proportional to simple integers. These speculations might well be connected with Babylonian cosmology.

After HOMMEL's partial publication, the text was lost for some time, until in 1931 O. NEUGEBAUER rediscovered it in HILPRECHT's collection in Jena and published the remainder of the text. It is clear from this publication that, whether they signify radial or transverse distances, the numbers in the text can in neither case have been the result of accurate measurement, as Weidner had supposed, but that the distances were assumed to be proportional to simple integers (19 : 17 : 14 : 11 : 9 : 7 : 4), and that the sexagesimal fractions that had created the impression of great accuracy were simply the result of a division.

HS 229 is basically a mathematical problem text of the same kind as many others; the only difference is that stellar distances are used instead of the usual sums of money that are to be divided among seven brothers. The problem was: Given, that it is

19 from the Moon to MUL.MUL (the Pleiades),
17 from MUL.MUL to SIBA.AN.NA (Orion),
14 from SIBA.AN.NA to KAK.TAG.GA (Sirius?),
11 from KAK.TAG.GA to BAN (the 'bow' consisting of δ Canis maioris and neighbouring stars),
9 from BAN to SHU.PA (Arcturus),
7 from SHU.PA to GIR.TAB (Scorpio)
4 from GIR.TAB to the star AN.TA.GUB (the 'Outermost').

and given that the sum of all these distances is 2,0 (= 120) *bēru*, what are the individual distances? The solution naturally runs as follows: the sum 2,0 *bēru* = 1,0,0,0 GAR is divided by 19+17+14+11+9+7+4 = 1,21; the result is 44,26;40 GAR. This is multiplied successively by 19, by 17, by 14, etc., and thus the distances from the Moon to the Pleiades, from the Pleiades to Orion, etc., are found.

THUREAU-DANGIN and NEUGEBAUER concluded from the style of the cuneiform symbols that the text was probably written in the 12th or 11th century B.C. The scribe ERIBA-MARDUK himself states that the text is a copy, so the original might be older.

In any case, as THUREAU-DANGIN rightly remarks, the text represents a pre-scientific stage of Babylonian astronomical speculation, not the beginning of scientific astronomy.

II. 'The three stars each'

In Chapter 1 we became acquainted with HESIODOS' popular rules for determining the time for sowing and so on. Naturally, the demand for such rules was just as great in ancient Babylon as elsewhere. Under the HAMMURABI dynasty, the official New Year was subject to substantial variations owing to the irregular insertion of the intercalary month. The farmers had therefore to rely on the weather and the stars for determining the correct times for their work.

This explains why the scribes took the trouble, after the introduction of the names for the months in the uniform Babylonian calendar, to connect these months with the risings of stars. This relation found its literary expression in the fifth table of the Creation Epic (line 3):

> He (Marduk) made the year, divided its boundaries, (For the) 12 months three stars each he set.

Several lists of these 12 times 3 stars have been preserved, with few deviations from one another. The present custom is to call these texts 'Astrolabes'. The Assyrian scribes had a better name for them: 'The three Stars each'[1]).

Table 1. Astrolabe B (SCHROEDER, Keilschrifttexte aus Assur No. 218)

Month	Stars of Ea	Stars of Anu	Stars of Enlil
I. Nisannu	IKU	DIL.BAT	APIN
II. Aiaru	MUL.MUL	SHU.GI	*A-nu-ni-tum*
III. Simānu	SIBA.ZI.AN.NA	UR.GU.LA	MUSH
IV. Dūzu	KAK.SI.DI	MASH.TAB.BA	SHUL. PA.E
V. Abu	BAN	MASH.TAB.BA.GAL.GAL	
			MAR.GID.DA
VI. Ulūlu	*ka-li-tum*	UGA	SHU.PA
VII. Tashrītu	NIN.MAH	*zi-ba-ni-tum*	EN.TE.NA.MASH. .LUM
VIII. Araḫsamna	UR.IDIM	GIR.TAB	LUGAL
IX. Kislīmu	*sal-bat-a-nu*	UD.KA.DUḪ.A	UZA
X. Tebētu	GU.LA	*al-lu-ut-tum*	A^mushen 2)
XI. Shabatu	NU.MUSH.DA	SHIM.MAH	DA.MU
XII. Addaru	KUA	^dMarduk	KA.A

[1]) A. SCHOTT, Z. d. deutschen Morgenl. Ges., 88 (1934), p. 311, note 2.
[2]) The word mushen means bird, and A^mushen (or more precisely A₂^mushen) means Eagle.

The earliest of the surviving texts, the so-called Berlin Astrolabe or Astrolabe B, is from Assur and was written about 1100 B.C. The text arranges the stars in three parallel columns of 12 stars each (see Table 1). Besides the list of stars, the text also contains a commentary on the relative position of the stars, their rising and setting, and their significance for agriculture and mythology.

The word mul = star in front of the names in the original text has here been omitted for brevity (except for MUL.MUL, where it is part of the name). The predicates 'of Ea', 'of Anu' and 'of Enlil' which appear after the single names in the original are here set at the top of the columns.

In reproducing the star names we follow GÖSSMANN's Sumerian Lexicon[1]), with some simplifications. The phonetically written Accadian words are shown, as usual, in italics, Sumerian words and ideograms in capitals. In the case of the ideograms the pronunciation is known to us in only a few cases from cuneiform glosses.

The rectangular shape of the list of stars in Astrolabe B is probably not the original one. From the Library of ASSURBANIPAL (669-630) we have a fragment of a circular table (see Fig. 5), and there are strong arguments, which we shall examine presently, for the round form being earlier.

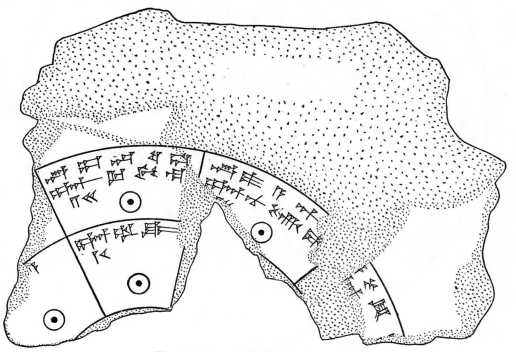

Fig. 5. Fragment of a Circular Astrolabe.

[1]) Sumerisches Lexikon, Part IV, Vol. 2: Planetarium Babyloniacum, by P. GÖSSMANN, Rome 1950.

As can be seen from the fragment reproduced in Fig. 5, the circular table was divided into sectors, each bearing, in clockwise order, the name of a month. In addition there are two other concentric circles drawn in such a way that the disk is divided into three rings and each sector into three parts. Each of the resulting 36 parts contains one star name and one number, with the stars of Ea in the outer ring, those of Anu in the middle and those of Enlil in the inner ring. So far as can be judged from the fragment, the distribution. of the stars over the months coincided with the astrolabe B.

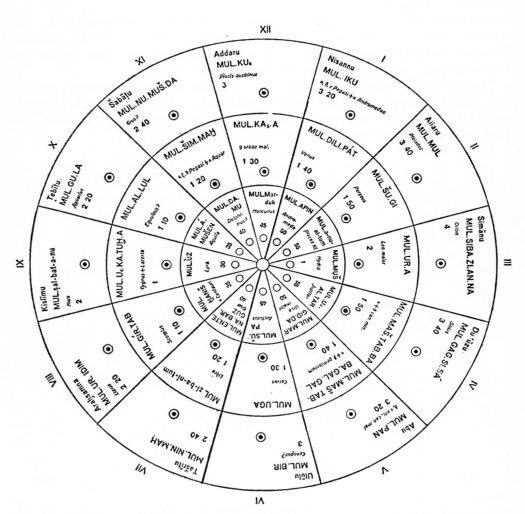

Fig. 6. Reconstruction of a Circular Astrolabe according to A. Schott, Zeitschrift Deutsche Morgenl. Ges. *88*, p. 302.

Another text in rectangular form, which we shall call Astrolabe P, was copied by T. G. PINCHES and published by A. SACHS in his collection 'Late Babylonian astronomical and related texts copied by PINCHES and STRASSMAIER', Providence 1955, No. 1499. Still another rectangular list was published in 1918 by A. ZIMMERN (Zeitschr. f. Assyriologie *32*, p. 72).

Comparison of the texts shows that in P the stars of Anu and Enlil with the relevant numbers have all been erroneously displaced by one month. An error of this kind can arise only when a circular astrolabe is being copied. Copying from a list, a scribe is not going to transcribe the twelfth line first by oversight and then return to the first line. This confirms the conjecture made long ago by A. SCHOTT, that the astrolabes were originally circular, and that they were only later transposed into rectangular lists, for convenience in writing.

Immediately after the lists of the 'Three Stars Each' in astrolabe B it is explicitly stated that their heliacal rising occurs in the relevant month. When, however, the text goes on to assert that their heliacal setting takes place exactly six months later, it oversimplifies the position: indeed, the assertion is not even approximately true for the majority of stars.

As we shall see later, the stars of Anu were taken to be in the neighbourhood of the celestial equator, and those of Ea and Enlil to the South and North of it respectively.

The circular and rectangular astrolabes achieved a widespread distribution. We have texts from Assur, Nineveh, Uruk and Babylon, covering between them a period of almost 1000 years.

III. The stars of Elam, Akkad and Amurru

There are two texts containing lists of twelve stars of Elam, twelve stars of Akkad and twelve stars of Amurru (published in Cuneiform Texts British Museum 26, Pl. 40-41 and 44). The stars contained in these lists are collected in Table 2.

The one new star in these lists is $^{mul}nibirum$, which, however, is identical with $^{mul\ d}Marduk$ and means Jupiter. This is clearly expressed in the first Table of the series $^{mul}APIN$ (BM 86 378, col. 1 36-38):

> When the stars of Enlil have disappeared the great, faint star, which bisects the heavens and stands, is $^{mul\ d}Marduk-nibiru$, $^{mul}SAG.ME.GAR$; he (the god) changes his position and wanders over the heavens.

The predicate 'faint' appears to contradict the name 'great star', but the following explanation of the complete sentence has been suggested by SCHAUMBERGER. 'In the morning, when the stars of the northern sky have disappeared, the great Jupiter, stationary in the middle of the sky (i.e. on the meridian), is still faintly visible.'

Table 2. Stars of Elam, Akkad and Amurru

No.	Stars of Elam	Stars of Akkad	Stars of Amurru
1	. . .	APIN	IKU
2	. . .	*A-nu-ni-tum*	SHU.GI
3	. . .	SIBA.ZI.AN.NA	MUSH
4	. . .	UD.AL.TAR	KAK.SI.DI
5	. . .	MAR.GID.DA	MASH.TAB.BA.GAL.GAL
6	. . .	SHU.PA	BIR
7	. . .	*zi-ba-ni-tum*	NIN.MAḪ
8	GIR.TAB	UR.IDIM	LUGAL
9	. . .	UZA	*sal-bat-a-nu*
10	GU.LA	A ^{mushen}	AL.LUL
11	N[U.MUSH.DA]	DA.MU	SHIM.MAH
12	. . .	*ni-bi-rum*	KA.A

Almost the same sentence occurs already in astrolabe B (col. II 29-32):

> The red star which, when the stars of the night are finished, bisects the heavens and stands there whence the south wind comes, this star is the god *Nibiru-Marduk*.

We can therefore conclude that the identity $^{mul\ d}Marduk$ = $^{mul}nibiru$ = Jupiter is valid for our texts.

We now see that the stars of Elam, Akkad and Amurru are identical with the stars of the astrolabe, and that their order in each case corresponds exactly with the order of the twelve months in the astrolabe. Thus, the stars of Elam, Akkad and Amurru are month-stars, corresponding to the twelve months of the year and they were supposed to have their Morningfirst just in the months to which they were assigned.

The names Elam, Akkad and Amurru reflect the political situation in Old Babylonian times. It may therefore be assumed that these lists are old.

There is no astronomical principle to be found in the distribution of the stars over the three countries. On the other hand, the division into 'stars of Ea, Anu and Enlil', that is into zones parallel to the equator, is definitely scientific in character. It may therefore be assumed that the Astrolabes represent an improvement upon an earlier stage in the development, in that they recast the old lists which had been arranged according to countries.

The numbers on Pinches' astrolabe

The numbers appear on the circular astrolabe K (Fig. 5) and on the rectangular astrolabe P. In the outer ring of the circular astrolabe (see fig. 6) and in the first column of the tabular form the numbers rise from 2 to 4 by equal increments of 0;20 and then decrease again by equal amounts. The numbers in the middle ring are half, and those in the inner ring a quarter, of those in the outer ring. From the fact that the maximum 4 is reached in month III, i.e. in early summer, we may conclude that the numbers have something to do with the length of the day.

This is confirmed by a comparison with ^{mul}APIN, a text which we shall discuss in detail later: the same numbers appear here too, inserted in a list of heliacal risings. The text says: '(Duzu 15) 4 mana is a day watch, 2 mana is a night watch'.

It is known that day and night were each divided into three watches, and that one mana is a weight of about one pound. Hence, as O. NEUGEBAUER was the first to see, this sentence means: 'To establish the length of a day or night watch at the time of the summer solstice, put four or two mana in a water clock; when it is empty, that will be the end of the watch.'[1])

If the numbers on the astrolabe are to be interpreted similarly, the numbers of the outer ring must signify day watches, the middle ring half watches and the inner quarter watches. Thus the Babylonians divided each watch into four equal parts, which means that they divided the whole duration of daylight into twelve equal parts, just as the Greeks did. HERODOTOS was therefore right in saying that the Greeks learned about 'the twelve parts of the day' from the Babylonians (HERODOTOS, Histories II 109).

Which stars were meant?

Some stars on the astrolabes are not fixed stars, but planets:

DIL.BAT	= Venus,
sal-bat-a-nu	= Mars,
UD.AL.TAR	= ^{d}*Marduk* = Jupiter.

This is very curious, for planets do not appear in a fixed month of the year.

Several other stars are easy to identify because they are zodiacal stars or constellations, which frequently occur in connection with planets in later observational texts:

[1]) O. NEUGEBAUER: The water clock in Babylonian astronomy. Isis 37 (1947) p. 37.

ḪUN.GA	= Aries (not on the astrolabes)
MUL.MUL	= Pleiades
MASH.TAB.BA.GAL.GAL	= Gemini
NANGAR	= Cancer, especially Praesepe
UR.GU.LA	= Leo
LUGAL	= Regulus
zibanītu	= Libra
GU.LA	= Aquarius
GIR.TAB	= Scorpio

Another means of identifying constellations is the star catalogue with which the ^{mul}APIN series begins. It is this important text which we must now consider in detail.

THE SERIES ^{mul}APIN

According to an oral communication of E. F. WEIDNER, the series ^{mul}APIN, so called after its opening words, consists of three tablets. The principal copy of the first tablet, the text BM 86 378, was published by L. W. KING in Cuneiform Texts 33, plates 1-8. It dates from approximately the third century B.C. The text can be completely restored with the aid of five copies – one Neo-Babylonian, two from ASSURBANIPAL's library (hence written before 612 B.C.), two from Assur.

The principal copy of the second tablet is VAT 9412 from Assur, dated 687 B.C. All in all, seven copies are known: three from Assur, three from ASSURBANIPAL's library and one Neo-Babylonian[1]. In addition, there are texts in which the two tablets are combined in one large one. Of the third tablet, only a small part has been published as yet.

The oldest of these texts, the one dated 687 B.C., comes from Assur, but various facts make a Babylonian origin of the series probable. One of our texts bears on the back the remark 'Copy from Babylon'[2]).

The first tablet contains the following sections:

    I. List of 33 stars of Enlil, 23 stars of Anu and 15 stars of Ea.

    II. Dates of Morning Rising of 36 fixed stars and constellations.

    III. Stars that are rising while others are setting.

    IV. Differences between the Morning Rising dates of some selected stars.

    V. Visibility of the fixed stars in the East and West.

    VI. List of 14 *ziqpu*-stars.

    VII. Relation between the culmination of *ziqpu*-stars and their Morning Rising.

    VIII. The stars in the path of the Moon.

[1]) E. F. WEIDNER, Ein babyl. Kompendium d. Himmelskunde, Am. J. of Sem. Lang. and Lit. 40 (1924), p. 186.

[2]) Cuneiform Texts British Museum 26, Table 47, Line 3.

The second tablet deals with:

   IX. Sun, planets and the 'Path of the Moon'.
    X. Sirius and the equinoxes and solstices.
   XI. The risings of some further fixed stars.
  XII. The planets and their periods.
 XIII. The four corners of the sky.
 XIV. The astronomical seasons.
  XV. Babylonian intercalary practice.
 XVI. Gnomon tables.
XVII. Length of a night watch on the 1st and 15th day of the month, period of visibility of the Moon.
XVIII. Omens connected with fixed stars and comets.

To all appearances, the series ^{mul}APIN is a compilation of nearly all astronomical knowledge of the period before -700. Everything we know about the astronomy of that time is in some way related to the series ^{mul}APIN.

We shall consider the individual sections more or less in order. In so doing we shall also come to a better understanding of the older astrolabe texts. We shall not, unfortunately, be able to study the second and third table completely, because some sections have not yet been published.

The star catalogue

As A. SCHOTT noticed, the beginning of the series ^{mul}APIN follows the astrolabe system very closely, but at the same time it makes some substantial improvements. First of all it replaces the rigid scheme of the twelve-times-three stars by two separate lists: on the one hand a list of the stars of Enlil, Anu and Ea, on the other a list of the heliacal risings.

The first list contains 33 stars of Enlil, 23 stars of Anu and 15 stars of Ea. While the data in the text about the relative positions of these stars are not usually sufficient to enable us to identify them, they nonetheless give worthwhile clues. For example, the enumeration of the stars of Anu begins as follows:

— ^{mul}IKU, the dwelling-place of Ea, the first of the stars of Anu,
— the star that stands opposite ^{mul}IKU: ^{mul}shi-nu-nu-tum (= ^{mul}SHIM.MAḪ).
— the stars that stand behind ^{mul}IKU: ^{mul}LU.ḪUN.GA, the God Dumuzi,
— MUL.MUL, the sevenfold divinity, the great Gods, etc.

Both of the last named constellations, LU.ḪUN.GA and MUL.MUL, are well known from later texts: they are Aries and the Pleiades. The first two must therefore belong to the same area, with Aries following IKU in the order from right to left. From

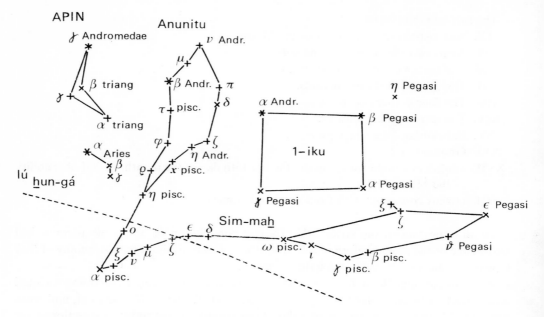

Fig. 7. IKU = Pegasus and its surrounding.

section II of the same text we obtain a further piece of information, the date of the morning rising of IKU. Hence one can infer that IKU must be the rectangle of Pegasus. By similar methods we find that *shinunutum* = SHIM.MAH, the constellation 'opposite IKU' must be the southern Fish of the zodiac with the stars ϑ and ε of Pegasus (see Fig. 7).

The identification of the constellations of ^{mul}APIN was carried out primarily by BEZOLD and KOPFF and by KUGLER in the 'Ergänzungshefte' to his 'Sternkunde und Sterndienst'. Their results were substantially confirmed by later scholars, though isolated points were refined and improved[1]. Taken together, these researches enable us to identify with certainty the following constellations, in addition to those mentioned earlier:

IKU ('Field') = Rectangle of Pegasus
SHIM.MAH ('Great Swallow') = south-west part of Pisces (+ stars up to ε Pegasi),
Anunītu ('Lady of the Heavens') = north-east part of Pisces + central part of Andromeda,
APIN ('Plough') = Triangulum + γ Andromedae
SHU.GI ('Old Man' or 'Charioteer') = Perseus

[1] See my paper 'The thirty-six stars' in Journal of Near Eastern Studies *8*, p. 6 (1949).

SIBA.ZI.AN.NA ('True Shepherd of the Sky') = Orion,
MUSH ('Serpent' or 'Snake-dragon') = Hydra + β Cancri,
KAK.SI.DI or GAG.SI.SA ('Arrow') = Sirius,
BAN ('Bow') = Parts of Canis Maior and Puppis
MAR.GID.DA ('Wagon') = Ursa maior
UGA^{mushen} ('Raven') = Corvus
SHU.PA = Arcturus,
EN.TE.NA.MASH.LUM = Centaurus,
UR.IDIM ('Mad Dog') = Serpens or Caput serpentis,
UD.KA.DUH.A ('Panther-griffin') = Cygnus + parts of Cepheus,
UZA ('Goat') = Lyra,
AL.LUL = Procyon,
A^{mushen} ('Eagle') = Aquila,
KUA ('Fish') = Fomalhaut or Piscis Austrinus.

We see that a large number of the Babylonian constellations correspond exactly to classical Greek ones. Thus, MASH.TAB.BA. GAL.GAL means 'the Great Twins': our constellation Gemini. It is not quite clear whether UR.GU.LA means 'Great Dog', 'Lion' or 'Lioness', but UR.A means probably 'Lion'. LUGAL (Regulus) means 'King', MUSH means 'Serpent', UGA^{mushen} 'Raven'. The Babylonian 'Serpent' held its head somewhat higher than our Hydra (see Fig. 8). Similarly Libra *(zibanītu)* and Eagle (A^{mushen}) correspond to our constellations of the same name, and the Fish (KUA) to

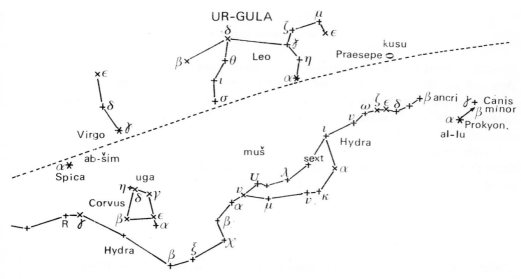

Fig. 8. Leo and Hydra.

our southerly Fish. Furthermore, we find a scorpion (GIR.TAB) and a Bull of Heaven (GUD.AN.NA) that correspond respectively to our Scorpio and Taurus. The Wagon (MAR.GID.DA) is naturally Ursa Maior, the Great Bear or Great Wagon.

In other cases the Babylonian conception differs from the Greek. Cygnus and the lower part of Cepheus form a storm-demon or griffin (UD.KA.DUḪ.A). APIN means 'plough', and the configuration Triangulum + γ Andromedae does in fact have the form of a plough (see Fig. 7). *Anunītu* and SHIM.MAḪ = shinuntu ('the Great Swallow') were much larger and more impressive than our two little Fishes.

In the region of our Canis major the Babylonians had an Arrow (KAK.SI.DI) and a Bow (BAN). Fig. 9 shows the most probable reconstruction of these constellations. Instead of our Lyra the Babylonians had a Goat (UZA). Hercules was a dog (UR.KU), Aries a hired labourer (LU.ḪUN.GA). The bright southerly star Canopus was the celestial likeness of 'Ea's city Eridu' (NUN^{ki} ^{d}E-a).

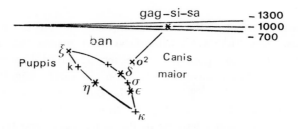

Fig. 9. KAK.SI.DI = Arrow and BAN = Bow.

The three paths in the sky

Next we must consider the significance of the division of the stars into those of Enlil, Anu and Ea. BEZOLD and SCHAUMBERGER have shown that the 23 stars of Anu are all within a girdle that reaches from about 17 degrees North of the equator to about 17 degrees South, and that the 33 stars of Enlil are all North of this 'path', while the 15 starts of Ea are South of it.

Comparing the list from ^{mul}APIN with the Astrolabes, SCHAUMBERGER found that no fewer than fourteen constellations were differently allocated. In most cases the Astrolabes are wrong. The star catalogue of ^{mul}APIN is definitely better than the Astrolabes.

The 36 morning risings

Section II of ^{mul}APIN contains a list of dates of first visibility (Morning Rising) of stars and constellations, as follows:

Month	I.,	day 1	LU.ḪUN.GA rises,
		day 20	GAM rises.
Month	II.,	day 1	MUL.MUL rises,
		day 20	*is li-e* rises.
Month	III.,	day 10	SIBA.ZI.AN.NA and MASH.TAB.BA.GAL.GAL rise.
Month	IV.,	day 5	MASH.TAB.BA.TUR.TUR and AL.LUL rise,
		day 15	KAK.SI.DI, MUSH and UR.GU.LA rise.
Month	V.,	day 5	BAN and LUGAL rise.
Month	VI.,	day 10	NUN^ki and UGA rise,
		day 15	SHU.PA rises,
		day 25	AB.SIN rises.
Month	VII.,	day 15	*zibanitu*, UR.IDIM, EN.TE.NA.MASH.LUM and UR.KU rise.
Month	VIII.,	day 5	GIR.TAB rises,
		day 15	UZA and GAB.GIR.TAB rise.
Month	IX.,	day 15	UD.KA.DUḪ.A, A^mushen and PA.BIL.SAG rise.
Month	X.,	day 15	SHIM.MAḪ, *shi-nu-nu-tum*, IM.SIS rises.
Month	XI.,	day 5	GU.LA, IKU and LU.LIM rise,
		day 25	*Anunītu* rises.
Month	XII.,	day 15	KUA and SHU.GI rise.

The list contains 36 names of stars and constellations, just as the Astrolabe lists. The ^mulAPIN-list and the Astrolabes have 24 constellations in common. Of these, eleven rise in the same month according to both lists, while in seven cases the difference is only one month. In all cases in which the texts disagree, the text ^mulAPIN gives the correct date on which one star of the constellation in question becomes visible for the first time in the morning sky, with deviations of 10 days at most from modern calculation. The best fit is obtained if the calculation is made for Babylon between 1300 to 1000 B.C., provided the rising of LU.ḪUN.GA is taken as the beginning of the stellar year and the rising of a constellation is defined as the day on which its first star becomes visible.

Section IV of ^mulAPIN contains a list very closely related to this one, giving the differences between the heliacal risings of the brightest stars as follows:

From the rising of KAK.SI.DI 55 days to the rising of NUN^ki;
from the rising of KAK.SI.DI 60 days to the rising of SHU.PA;
from the rising of SHU.PA 10 days to the rising of AB.SIN; etc.

The differences are in agreement with the list of heliacal risings, if it is assumed that the year contains exactly 12 months of 30 days each. In my paper 'The thirty-six stars' in J. Near Eastern Studies *8* I have shown that both lists were probably derived from an original list of observed date differences, starting with the Morningfirst of Sirius. This original list can be reconstructed unambiguously from the text. The reconstructed

Table 3

Babylonian Constellation	Day	Modern First star	Day	Error
KAK.SI.DI	0	Sirius	0	—
MUŠ	0	β Cancri	8	−8
UR.GU.LA	0	ε Leonis	8	−8
BAN	20	δ Can. mai.	18	2
LUGAL	20	Regulus	19	1
NUN^{ki}	55	Canopus	50	5
UGA	55	γ Corvi	—	—
ŠU.PA	60	Arcturus	62	−2
AB.SIN	70	Spica	70	0
zibanītu	90	α Librae	95	−5
UR.IDIM	90	δ Serpentis	—	—
EN.TE.NA.MAŠ.LUM	90	γ Centauri	89	1
UR.KU	90	η Herculis	—	—
GIR.TAB	110	γ Scorpii	104	6
UZA	120	Vega	121	−1
GAB.GIR.TAB	120	Antares	117	3
UD.KA.DUḪ.A	150	δ Cygni	140	10
A^{mushen}	150	ζ Aquilae	146	4
PA.BIL.SAG	150	γ Sagittarii	144	6
ŠIM.MAḪ	180	ε Pegasi	186	−6
GU.LA	200	β Aquarii	190	10
IKU	200	β Pegasi	199	1
LU.LIM	200	γ Cassiopeiae	193	7
A-nu-ni-tum	220	β Andromedae	229	−9
KUA	240	Fomalhaut	234	6
ŠU.GI	240	γ Persei	238	2
LU.ḪUN.GA	260	α Arietis	262	−2
GAM	280	Capella	277	3
MUL.MUL	290	Pleiades	297	−7
is li-e	310	Aldebaran	314	−4
SIBA.ZI.AN.NA	330	γ Orionis	339	−9
MAŠ.TAB.BA.GAL.GAL	330	Castor	336	−6
MAŠ.TAB.BA.TUR.TUR	355	ι Geminorum	—	—
AL.LUL	355	Procyon	361	−6

list is reproduced in the first two columns of Table 3. The next two columns give the time when the first star of the Babylonian constellation will be visible according to modern calculations, and the last column contains the error 'Babylonian minus modern'. The date of rising is given in days from the rising of Sirius, which we know with great accuracy from ancient observations.

The errors could be reduced somewhat by making a slight reduction in the arc of visibility during the dry part of the year and a slight increase during the rainy part (from NUN^{ki} to GAM).

The modern calculations in the above list relate to the year -1000 and the latitude of Babylon. This is because the figures show that the observations were probably not made in Assyria, but rather in the latitude of Babylon and probably between -1400 and -900. In this period the deviations between text and calculation are so small that we must assume that the observations were made with great care, probably over a number of years.

Further sections of the text ^{mul}APIN

Section III contains a list of simultaneous risings and settings, like the following examples:

— ^{mul}SIBA.ZI.AN.NA rises and ^{mul}PA.BIL.SAG sets.
— ^{mul}KAK.SI.DI, ^{mul}MUSH and ^{mul}UR.GU.LA rise and ^{mul}GU.LA and ^{uul}A^{mushen} set.[1]

Of even greater interest are sections VI and VII, which deal with the so-called *ziqpu*-stars.

Ziqpu stars[2]

The observation of the rising and setting of stars near the horizon is very easily disturbed by the varying condition of the atmosphere. We learn from ^{mul}APIN that the Babylonians got over this difficulty to a certain extent by observing, instead, the simultaneously occuring culmination of other stars, the so-called *ziqpu*-stars.

Thus we read (^{mul}APIN, BM 86 378, Col. IV 1ff.):

The *ziqpu*-stars, which stand in the path of Enlil in the middle of the sky across from the chest of the observer of the sky, and by means of which the risings and settings of the stars are observed by night:

[1] The determinative 'mul' means star. It has generally been omitted in our transcriptions, but it is hardly ever missing from the cuneiform inscriptions.
[2] For this section see J. SCHAUMBERGER, Zeitschrift für Assyriologie *50* (1942), p. 42.

SHU.PA, BAL.UR.A, AN.GUB.BA^{mesh}, UR.KU, UZA, UD.KA.DUH.A, LU.LIM, SHU.GI, GAM, MASH.TAB.BA.GAL.GAL, AL.LUL, UR.GU. LA, ERU, HE.GAL.A.A.

The procedure is explained as follows:

> To observe the *ziqpu*, set yourself in the morning of 20 Nisannu before sunrise, the West to your right, the East to your left, your eyes to the South: then *kumara sha* ^{mul}UD.KA.DUH.A is to be found in the middle of the sky across from your chest and ^{mul}GAM is rising;
> — On 1 Aiaru *irtu sha* ^{mul}UD.KA.DUH.A is to be found in the middle of the sky across from your chest, and MUL.MUL is rising; etc.

This description makes it clear beyond any possible doubt that *ziqpu* is the Babylonian technical term for culmination. This fits the etymology of the word, too: it belongs to the verb *zaqāpu* 'to erect'. When, therefore, bad atmospheric conditions prevented the direct observation of the rising of GAM, it was possible to observe instead the simultaneous culmination of *kumara sha* ^{mul}UD.KA.DUH.A, which means 'shoulder (or the like) of the griffin', and so on.

There was another purpose, for which the *ziqpu*-stars were employed, namely for telling the time at night.

Water-clocks, which were in general use, were inaccurate instruments. They were quite handy for measuring short time intervals, but they were inadequate when it was a question of determining the exact time of an astronomical phenomenon occurring during the night.

In reports of lunar eclipses, therefore, from -620 at the latest, the moment when the eclipse began was related not only to the rising or setting of the sun, but to the culmination of a *ziqpu*-star as well. The time interval that had to be measured with the water-clock could thereby be reduced to fewer USH (1 USH = 4 minutes), and now and then could be dispensed with altogether. According to SCHAUMBERGER, the resultant determinations of time are among the most accurate achieved in all antiquity. By modern calculations their margin of error is from 1 to 2 USH.

Thus, in the letter HARPER 1444 (discussed by SCHAUMBERGER, Z. f. Assyriol. 47 (1941), p. 127) we read:

> ... The Moon was eclipsed in the morning watch, beginning from the South (?), from the South brightening (again), darkened on the right, darkened in the constellation Scorpio; the star *kumara sha* ^{mul}UD.KA.DUH.A culminated; it was a 2-finger eclipse ...

According to SCHAUMBERGER, this text relates to an eclipse in the year −620.

One might say that the moment of an eclipse was expressed in sidereal time. In order to determine the difference in time between two such moments, one needs a further list giving the time differences between the culminations of the individual *ziqpu*-stars.

Such lists have in fact been preserved; the oldest fragment comes from the library of ASSURBANIPAL. Another, better preserved text AO 6478 belongs to the Seleucid period, but is an exact parallel. It begins almost word for word in the same way as the already quoted passage from ^{mul}APIN:

> Distance between the *ziqpu*-stars which stand in the path of Enlil in the middle of the sky across from the chest of the observer of the sky, by means of which the risings and settings of the stars can be observed by night:
> —$1\frac{1}{2}$ mana weight, 9 USH on the earth, 16200 *bēru* in the sky from ^{mul}SHU-DUN to ^{mul}SHUDUN ANSHE EGIR-*ti*;
> —2 mana weight, 12 USH on the earth, 21600 *bēru* in the sky from ^{mul}SHU-DUN ANSHE EGIR-*ti* to ^{mul}GAM-*ti* (= *kippati*); etc.

The 'weight' is the weight of water that runs out of the water-clock, the 'USH on the earth' are time intervals of 4 minutes, and the '*bēru* in the sky' evidently relate to some speculation about the size of the fixed star sphere. The conversion rules are as follows: 1 *mana* = 6 USH, 1 USH = 1800 *bēru*. Hence, according to the Babylonian conception, the circumference of the fixed star sphere amounted to 360 × 1800 = 648 000 *bēru*, or about 7 million kilometres.

Twenty-siz *ziqpu*-stars in all are enumerated, the distances between them varying from 5 to 30 USH. For the complete list and the identification of the *ziqpu*-stars the reader is referred to the article by SCHAUMBERGER already mentioned.

The significance of this *ziqpu*-text lies principally in the fact that, in SCHAUMBERGER's words, 'the mere existence of *ziqpu*-time determinations means that endeavours were made as early as in Assyrian times to achieve the most accurate time-determination possible, i.e. that one of the essential requirements of good astronomical observation was appreciated and relatively well satisfied'.

The constellations in the path of the moon

Various evidence makes it likely that the twelve signs of the zodiac were still unknown when the text ^{mul}APIN was written. On the other hand, ^{mul}APIN appears to represent the last stage in the development of Babylonian astronomy before the introduction of the zodiacal signs. This view is supported by Section VIII of the text, a list of the con-stellations in the path of the Moon:

The Gods who stand in the path of the Moon, and through whose domain the Moon each month moves and touches them:

MUL.MUL, ^{mul}GUD.AN.NA, ^{mul}SIBA.ZI.AN.NA, ^{mul}SHU.GI, ^{mul}GAM, ^{mul}MASH.TAB.BA.GAL.GAL, ^{mul}AL.LUL, ^{mul}UR.GU.LA, ^{mul}AB.SIN, ^{mul}zi.ba.ni.tum, ^{mul}GIR.TAB, ^{mul}PA.BIL.SAG, ^{mul}SUHUR.MASH, ^{mul}GU.LA, zibbāti^{mesh}, ^{mul}SIM.MAH, ^{mul}A-nu-ni-tum and ^{mul}LU.HUN.GA.

It is immediately apparent from the fact that 18 constellations are named, rather than 12, that the writer is thinking in terms of constellations and not zodiacal signs. The number 18 is not quite certain, because the 'tails' zibbāti^{mesh} are probably to be taken together with both the following names ('tails of SHIM. MAH and Anunītum'). The part of the sky in question is reproduced in Fig. 7.

If we omit the six names GUD.AN.NA (Taurus), SIBA.ZI.AN.NA (Orion), SHU.GI (Perseus + northern part of Taurus ?), GAM (Auriga or Capella), SHIM.MAH (southwest part of Pisces) and Anunītum (north-east part of Pisces), those remaining are exactly the Babylonian names of the later signs of the zodiac, beginning with Taurus (MUL. MUL, actually Pleiades) and continuing in sequence to Aries (LU.HUN.GA).

In later times the zodiacal signs were named after the constellations they contained. In the beginning there were certain variations: the sign of Taurus could be denoted equally well by the names MUL.MUL (Pleiades), GUD.AN.NA (Taurus) or is li-e (Hyades - Aldebaran); it was only later that the names became standardized.

The four astronomical seasons

The second tablet of the ^{mul}APIN series contains in section XIV (Text Sm 1907) the following remarkable statement:

From XII 1 to II 30 the sun is in the path of Anu:

Wind and storm.

From III 1 to V 30 the sun is in the path of Enlil:

Harvest and heat.

From VI 1 to VIII 30 the sun is in the path of Anu:

Wind and storm.

From IX 1 to XI 30 the sun is in the path of Ea: Cold.

This sections shows that the solar year was divided into twelve schematic months during which the sun dwelt in different parts of the sky.

Plate 11a: VAT 7 851. Moon, Pleiades and Taurus.

Plate 11b: VAT 7 847. Jupiter, Leo and Hydra.

Plate 11c: VAT 6 448. Mercury, Virgo and Corvus.

Plate 11. Engraved drawings with names of stars, Seleucid period. Plate 11c is highly remarkable, because it shows the virgin with the corn ear, who is represented on Egyptian pictures too (see Plate 15). The name AB.SIN engraved on the drawing (above the star to the left) denotes either the zociacal sign Virgo or the brightest star Spica in the constellation Virgo. The Greek word Spica signifies corn ear. The drawing seems to indicate that the image of the virgin with the corn ear was of Babylonian origin.
Reproduced from E. F. WEIDNER, Archiv für Orientforschung 4, Plate V.

Plate 12. Boundary stone from the Kassite period (14th century B.C.) with Scorpion, Moon and Stars.
Photo Musée du Louvre.

The first question is, whether the Babylonians thought of the motion of the sun simply as a North-South movement which caused the four seasons, or whether they knew that the sun moves in an inclined circle.

The answer is: they did know that the sun moves in an inclined circle, for immediately after the enumeration of the constellations in the path of the Moon, the text explicitly states that not only the Moon, but also the Sun and the other five classical planets move along the same path.

The path of the sun was therefore thought of as an inclined circle through the zodiacal signs, this circle being divided into four equal parts by the zones of Ea, Anu and Enlil, so that the sun remained just three months in each sector (see Fig. 10).

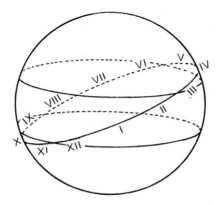

Fig. 10. The zones of Ea, Anu, and Enlil and the path of the sun according to ᵐᵘˡAPIN.

According to this scheme, the equinoxes and solstices must occur in the middle of months I, IV, VII and X. This is in fact just what ᵐᵘˡAPIN states, once in the first tablet and twice in the second.

In the Babylonian scheme the year was divided into four astronomical seasons corresponding to the four parts into which the ecliptic was divided by the zones of Enlil, Anu and Ea. These four seasons were further subdivided into three solar months, but there were no twelve parts of the ecliptic to correspond to these months, or at least the text makes no mention of this. The correspondence between the division of the year and the division of the zodiac was incomplete: the solar year was divided into 12 parts, but the zodiac into only four parts. To reach complete agreement each of the four parts of the zodiac had to be subdivided into three parts of equal length, as indicated in Fig. 10. This subdivision, which gave rise to the *signs of the zodiac*, was not made until somewhat later, in the Neo-Babylonian or Persian period.

Gnomon Tables

The Greeks gave the name 'gnomon' to a vertical rod on a horizontal base that was used to tell the time of day by the measurement of the length of the shadow. DIOGENES LAERTIOS informs us that ANAXIMANDROS set up a gnomon in Sparta which also indicated the equinoxes and solstices.[1]

We have already quoted HERODOTOS' remark that the Greeks learned of 'Polos and Gnomon' from the Babylonians. His statement about the gnomon is confirmed by our cuneiform texts, for the second table of ^{mul}APIN contains in Section XVI a list which gives for the various seasons the time when the shadow of a rod one cubit height is one, two, . . . cubits long[2]. This list is reproduced in Table 4.

This list is based on the following assumptions:

1. The time after sunrise when the shadow length is 1 cubit, is 2 *bēru* (= 4 hours) at the summer solstice, 3 *bēru* (= 6 hours) at the winter solstice and 2½ *bēru* (= 5 hours) at the equinoxes.

2. The ratio of gnomon length to shadow length is proportional to the time elapsed since sunrise.

The resulting approximation is quite good during the summer; in winter too the agreement from the second line on is not too bad, but the first line is plain nonsense. In the month of Tebetu the shadow length of 1 cubit is never attained, not even at noon.

DURATION OF THE NIGHT AND VISIBILITY OF THE MOON[3]

The first astronomical phenomena which the Babylonians found out how to calculate were:

(a) rising and setting of Venus;
(b) the length of day and night;
(c) the rising and setting of the moon.

The Venus calculations, which are contained in a copy of the 63rd Table of the great Omen Series Enuma Anu Enlil, have already been discussed in Chapter 2.

Of great interest are the calculations of the length of the day and night. We can distinguish two systems in our texts.

According to the *earlier system*, which we encountered in the Astrolabes, the spring

---

[1] See G. S. KIRK and J. E. RAVEN: The presocratic philosophers, p. 99.
[2] E. F. WEIDNER, Amer. J. of Semitic Languages *40* (1924), p. 198.
[3] VAN DER WAERDEN, J. of Near Eastern Stud., *10* (1951), p. 20

Table 4

Date	15. Nisannu	15. Duzu	15. Tashritu	15. Tebetu
Day-watch	3 mana	4 mana	3 mana	2 mana
Night-watch	3 mana	2 mana	3 mana	4 mana
Shadow length (cubits)				
1	2½ bēru Day	2 bēru Day	2½ bēru Day	3 bēru Day
2	1 bēru 7 USH 30 GAR Day	1 bēru Day	1 bēru 7 USH 30 GAR Day	1½ bēru Day
3	⅔ bēru 5 USH Day	⅔ bēru Day	⅔ bēru 5 USH Day	1 bēru Day
4		½ bēru Day		⅔ bēru 2 USH 30 GAR Day
5		12 USH Day		18 USH Day
6		10 USH Day		½ bēru Day
8		7 USH 30 GAR Day		11 USH 15 GAR Day
9		6 USH 40 GAR Day		10 USH Day
10		6 USH Day		9 USH Day

equinox falls on XII 15, the longest day is III 15, and the ratio of the longest day to the shortest night is 2 : 1. The year is divided into twelve schematic months of thirty days each. The months are connected with the heliacal risings of certain stars; the zodiac is not mentioned.

According to the *later system* (exemplified by ^{mul}APIN, Section XVII) the spring equinox falls on I 15 and the longest day on IV 15. The ratio of the longest day to the shortest night is 2 : 1, but sometimes — in the same text — it is assumed to be 3 : 2. This second and improved value is, however, only mentioned and is not used in calculations.

In both systems the length of the day varies by linear increments for six months, followed by linear decrements for six months. On the basis that the longest day is 2/3 and the shortest day 1/3 of a full 24-hour day, the length of any day or night can easily be calculated.

In the Seleucid period these simple rules were replaced by more accurate ones. The length of the day is no longer made dependent on the schematic division of the year, but on the actual position of the sun in the zodiac. The variation in its length is still linear, but the rate is slower near the solstices and quicker near the equinoxes. We shall return to this point in Chapter 6.

Already in the earliest texts we find, in connection with the length of the night, a method for calculating the times of rising and setting of the moon. This method is based on the following assumptions:

1. In the last night before the New Moon the moon sets just before sunset and remains invisible.

2. For each following day until the fifteenth night the setting of the moon is retarded by 1/15 of the night.

3. In the fifteenth night the moon rises at sunset and sets at sunrise; it shines the whole night.

4. For each following day until the thirtieth the moon's rising is retarded by 1/15 of the night.

5. Consequently the moon is invisible on the thirtieth day, when its rising coincides with that of the sun.

As we shall see in Chapter 8, VETTIUS VALENS and PLINIUS used the same rules for calculating the rising and setting of the moon.

For a detailed discussion of these rules and the texts in which they are applied see my paper in J. of Near Eastern Studies *10* (1951) quoted before, or the German edition of this book.

The British museum ivory prism

The ivory prism BM 56-9-3, 1136, found by LOFTUS in the central part of the ruins of Niniveh, remained a riddle for a long time. LENORMANT described it as 'rules of a game'.

The four sides of the prism contain predominantly numbers. Sides A and B are still unexplained, but FOTHERINGHAM succeeded in deciphering and completing sides C and D. Only the lower halves of these sides are preserved, of which the uppermost lines explain in very few words the significance of the numbers. Here we reproduce the top lines of side C and all that is preserved of side D.

Side C

Day Aiaru Ululu	Night Aiaru Ululu
Night Arahsamna Adaru	Day Arahsamna Adaru
6 2/3 *(bēru)* Day	5 *(bēru)* 10 (USH) Night
. . .	. . .

Side D

Day Duzu		Night Duzu	
Night Tebetu		Day Tebetu	
8 *(bēru)* Day		4 *(bēru)* Night	
	20 (USH)		10 (USH)
1 *(bēru)* 10			20
2		1	
2 2/3		1	10
3	10	1	20
4		2	
. . .		2	10
		. . .	

The units of measure *bēru* and USH are not named in the text, but they can be deduced as follows. First, the regular formation of the arithmetical sequence on the right shows that the larger unit is 30 times the smaller one. This is the case for *bēru* and USH, but no other known units. Second, if the units are *bēru* and USH, then the indicated length of the daytime and the night is in complete agreement with all the other texts of the later system. Now we can complete the scheme of sides C and D of the ivory prism as follows (the Roman figures denote the months):

Day IV Night X	} 8 *bēru*
Day III and V Night IX and XI	} 7 *bēru* 10 USH

Day II and VI Night VIII and XII	} 6 2/3 *bēru*
Day I and VII Night I and VII	} 6 *bēru*
Night II and VI Day VIII and XII	} 5 *bēru* 10 USH
Night III and V Day IX and XI	} 4 2/3 *bēru*
Night IV Day X	} 4 *bēru*

The numbers in lines 4 to 10 of side D obviously represent one, two, three, four, five, six and seven twelfths of the day or night. The same is true for side C.

Popular and astronomical time units

The ivory prism shows us that the Babylonians divided the day and night each into 12 equal parts, like the Greeks. This confirms the report of HERODOTOS (II 109) already quoted: 'From the Babylonians the Greeks learned Polos and Gnomon and the twelve parts of the day'.

We have seen that the Astrolabes already divided the day into twelve equal parts. The three day-watches were halved and the halved again, thus giving 6 half-watches, or 12 quarter-watches.

It seems clear that these watches, half-watches and quarter-watches were *popular* time units in Babylon, just as were the twelfths of the day and night in Greece and Rome. Astronomers such as PTOLEMY used 'equinoctial hours' of exactly equal length, and to-day we follow this usage. The Babylonian scientific units were *bēru* and USH. No other time units are found in the astronomical texts of the Persian and Seleucid periods.

On the other hand, the earlier astrological texts used the popular division of day and night. The omen of an eclipse depends on the watch in which it occurs.

It is now easy to guess the purpose of the ivory prism. It can be used for converting *bēru* and USH into popular time units. For example, after the moment of an eclipse had been measured in *bēru* and USH by means of a water clock, this time had to be converted into watches and quarter watches to make it suitable for astrological prediction.

A lucky chance enables us to confirm this conjecture, for we have two reports of one and the same eclipse observed in Babylon, one using popular hours and the other scientific

E R R A T A

to:

B.L. van der Waerden, SCIENCE AWAKENING II
The birth of astronomy

Correction to page 89. Lines 3-5 should read:

Year 7, Duzu 14, at night, $1\frac{2}{3}$ *bēru* after sunset,
the moon made an (almost) total eclipse, (but) a
little was left over. North (wind) went.

units. The scientific report is in line 19 of the reverse of the text 'STRASSMAIER KAM-
BYSES 400' and reads, according to PETER HUBER:

> Year 7, Duzu 14, at night, 1 2/3 bēru after sunset, a lunar eclipse, visible from
> beginning to end; it extended over the northern half of the lunar disc; the moon
> was (nearly) totally eclipsed, (but) a little was left; (the eclipse) went north.
>
> (KUGLER, Sternkunde I, p. 71).

The other report is to be found in PTOLEMY (Almagest V, Ch. 14) and reads:

> In the seventh year of KAMBYSES, on the night after the 17th Egyptian
> Phamenoth, one hour before midnight, a lunar eclipse was observed in Babylon,
> extending from the North over half of the diameter.

PTOLEMY's immediate source may have been HIPPARCHOS. Now it could be assumed
that HIPPARCHOS or some other Greek astronomer had converted the Babylonian 1 2/3
bēru into Greek hours, and that PTOLEMY quoted this Greek report. But this explanation
does not work. For if we take the given time '1½ bēru after sunset' and use reasonably
accurate astronomical tables to convert this into hours before midnight, we obtain
10h25m, i.e. more than 1½ equinoctial hours or 1¾ temporal hours before midnight,
whereas PTOLEMY gives 'one hour before midnight'.

A good explanation was given by FOTHERINGHAM. The 1 2/3 bēru were converted
into temporal hours not by the correct Greek methods, but by the very inaccurate method
of the Assyrian ivory prism. According to side D of this prism, 1 2/3 bēru in the month
Duzu correspond to exactly 5 twelfths of the night. So a Babylonian astronomer would
report to his King, using his table to convert the observed time of 1 2/3 bēru, that the
eclipse began 5 temporal hours after sunset, or one hour before midnight. Finally, the
astrological report somehow came into PTOLEMY's hands, while the scientific version
remained in Mesopotamia until it was brought to London and copied by STRASSMAIER.

We shall now look more closely at these astrological reports with the principal ob-
jective of finding what, in the way of astronomical science, lies behind them.

The reports of the astrologers

The Assyrian King ASSARHADDON (681-669) must have been unusually superstitious.[1]
Perhaps he was an accomplice to the murder of his father SANHERIB and was thereafter
haunted by fear and a guilty conscience. At any rate no king has bequeathed to us so
many oracular enquiries as he did. To the king's urgent interest in the will of the Gods

---

[1] W. VON SODEN, Herrscher im alten Orient, Springer Verlag (1954) p. 118.

is to be attributed the fact that we have a considerable number of reports[1]) and letters[2])
from the Court Astrologers principally addressed to him and to his son and successor
ASSURBANIPAL (669-630). Both kinds of texts are basically the same, except that the letters
begin with a salutation to the King, while the reports are merely signed with the name of
the astrologer.

The way these reports are built up is best explained by an example (Report No. 207):

> Venus has become visible in the West in the path of the (stars) of Enlil. The
> following is the interpretation thereof: If Venus was visible in the month
> Simanu, overthrow of the enemy. If Venus was visible in the path of the (star)
> of Enlil, the King of Akkad will have no worthy foe, etc.

The first sentence reports the observation which has just been made. The attached
'interpretation' is, as a rule, quoted verbatim from the series Enuma Anu Enlil.

The reports of the astrologers enable us to make deductions about the astronomical
knowledge of those who wrote them. The interpretation is not always easy. For example,
MÂR-ISHTAR writes as follows to ASSARHADDON[3]):

> On the 27th the Moon stood (for the last time in the sky). On the 28th, 29th,
> 30th we prepared for the observation of the solar eclipse: (the Sun-God) let it
> go by, arranged no eclipse. On the 1st the Moon was (again) visible.

In KUGLER's opinion the fact of MÂR-ISHTAR spending three days on the look-out
for a problematical solar eclipse really elicited no very high regard for his knowledge.
SCHOTT, however, made it seem plausible that MÂR-ISHTAR carried out his observations
for this solar eclipse by royal command — in the first of the four letters he promises the
King expressly that he will keep a look-out for the eclipse of the sun about which the
King had written to him.

SCHOTT also refers to a letter of the Court Astrologer BALASI containing a fairly tart
reply to a similar request of the King's, presumably because it got on his nerves to spend
endless days on the look-out for an eclipse of the sun which he was sure would not take
place.

We cannot, therefore, draw many legitimate conclusions from an astronomically
senseless activity of an astronomer of that time. Valid inferences about the extent of
astronomical knowledge can be obtained only from positive facts.

---

[1]) R. C. THOMPSON, The reports of the magicians and astrologers of Nineveh and Babylon, London (1900)
[2]) Published in Harper, Assyrian and Babylonian Letters. In 1970 a new publication has appeared:
SIMO PARPOLA: Letters from Assyrian Scholars to the Kings Esarhaddon and Assurbanipal I. Verlag
Butzon & Bercker, Kevelaer.
[3]) A. SCHOTT and J. SCHAUMBERGER, Vier Briefe Mâr-Ishtars an ASARHADDON. Zeitschr. f. Assyriologie *47*
(1941), p. 89.

The most important of these positive facts is the successful prediction of a lunar eclipse by the astrologer NADINU. It seems that we have both NADINU's report predicting the eclipse and also that in which he proudly confirms its occurrence. Report No. 273 reads as follows:

> On the 14th an eclipse of the moon will take place: woe for Elam and Amurru, good for my Lord the King. Let the heart of my Lord the King rejoice. It will be seen without (?) Venus. To my Lord the King have I spoken as follows: an eclipse will take place.
> From *Irassi-ilu*, the servant of ⟨*Na-di-*⟩*nu-u*.

Report No. 274 F contains the confirmation of the prediction:
> ... To my Lord the King have I written: 'An eclipse will take place'. Now it has not gone by, it has taken place. In the occurrence of this eclipse lies happiness for my Lord the King. The month Aiaru is Elam, the 14th day is Elam, the morning watch is ... When ⟨Ven⟩us (?) set ..., Amurru ... Amurru is met with Elam ...
> ⟨From ..., the Servant⟩ of *Na-di-nu*.

To be sure, it cannot be proved that both reports relate to the same eclipse; it is not even quite certain that both reports emanate from NADINU, because the signatures of the writers have been damaged. The restorations of the signatures were suggested to P. HUBER by D. J. WISEMAN, who was so kind as to check the original tablets in the British Museum. He takes IRASSI-ILU to be a scribe writing at the instructions of the astrologer NADINU.

We shall return in the next chapter to the question of how such predictions could possibly have been made at so early a date, when there was as yet no theory of the moon's motion. The only explanation I can find is that recurrence-periods for eclipses were used.

SUMMARY

It is difficult to follow in detail the development of astronomy in the Assyrian period. Most of the texts come to us in versions which stem from the seventh century B.C., or later still, and it is therefore impossible to assign a specific astronomical discovery to a definite century; often even the millenium is uncertain. What little can be said about the temporal succession of the stages of development is as follows.

Between -1400 and -900 the following things happened:

1) composition of the great Omen Series 'Enuma Anu Enlil';

2) exact observations of the heliacal risings of the fixed stars;

3) observations of daily risings, settings and culminations;

4) composition of the circular and rectangular Astrolabes before −1100.

With less certainty we may also ascribe to this period:

5) a very primitive representation of the Venus phenomena by arithmetical sequences (Table 63 of the great Omen Series);

6) calculation of the lengths of day and night by increasing and decreasing arithmetical series based on an inaccurate ratio of 2 : 1 between the extreme values;

7) calculation of the rising and setting of the moon by increasing and decreasing arithmetical series (14th Table of the great Omen Series);

8) speculations about the distances of the fixed stars (HILPRECHT's text).

From the same period we also have boundary stones with symbols of gods, the purpose of which was to call down the wrath of those gods upon anyone who might venture to remove the boundary stone or otherwise infringe the rights of the proprietor. Some of the symbols certainly represent stars; with others the interpretation is uncertain. On one boundary stone of the 14th century there is a scorpion (Plate 12); perhaps this was intended to be the zodiacal constellation Scorpio. If only the authentic texts of the Cassite period were more numerous!

The series ^{mul}APIN, probably assembled shortly before −700, and the related texts show significant advances, namely:

9) the better ratio 3 : 2 of longest day to shortest night;

10) primitive calculation of the shadow length of an upright rod (Gnomon);

11) first steps towards the introduction of the zodiacal signs: constellations in the path of the moon and astronomical seasons;

12) determination of the time intervals between the culminations of various stars.

In the middle of the 8th century astronomy seems to have received a new impetus, as shown by:

13) systematical observations of eclipses from the time of NABONASSAR (747-735) on;

14) successful predictions of lunar eclipses in the Seventh Century B.C.

The last two points indicate the beginning of a new line of development which was to be continued in the Neo-Babylonian and Persian period, namely the systematic observation and prediction of lunar, solar and planetary phenomena.

CHAPTER IV

THE NEO-BABYLONIAN AND PERSIAN PERIOD

A considerable part of this chapter is due to PETER HUBER (Federal School of Technology, Zürich).

General review

After the collapse of the Assyrian hegemony, Babylonian civilization experienced a brilliant renaissance under the Chaldaean rulers NABOPOLASSAR and NEBUCHADNEZZAR II. There was a conscious attempt to continue the glorious traditions of the HAMMURABI era. Numerous cuneiform legal deeds and business documents survive, which enable us to follow in detail the affairs of individual families, the rise and fall of banks and great business houses, their commerce and litigations during the Neo-Babylonian and the subsequent Persian period. Astronomical observation texts, preserved in later copies, testify to intensive scientific activity, which had already begun in the Assyrian period, and continued, ever more systematically, down to the 1st century A.D.

The Persian hegemony had little effect upon Babylonian religion and civilization. The Persian Kings were rather tolerant in religious matters, as long as the priests of the subject peoples were not rebellious. Once, however, when XERXES was in Egypt, there was an uprising in Babylon, led by a certain SHAMASH-ERIBA. XERXES hurried back with an army, besieged the city and took it. Thereupon he confiscated the treasure of Marduk, carried away the pure gold statue of the god and killed the priest who tried to prevent the ravishing of the temple. (HERODOTOS, Histories I 183).

The languages of the cuneiform texts were Sumerian and Akkadian. In the course of the first millenium, however, the Akkadian language was increasingly superseded by the Aramaeic idiom, and cuneiform script by the Aramaeic alphabet. However, in the temple schools the old languages and cuneiform script were still fostered for a long time. Astronomical texts were written in cuneiform right down to the first century A.D.; this is why so many have survived.

After ALEXANDER conquered the Persian kingdom in 331 B.C., the Babylonian temples were restored and the priests reestablished in their offices. Under his successors, the Seleucids, the temple scribes in Babylon and Uruk were extremely active. Eclipses and lunar phenomena were predicted, planetary tables were computed. The latest cuneiform text that can be dated is an astronomical almanac of the year +75.

At the same time astrology flourished, attaining unprecedented authority in the whole ancient world. The older astrology, as represented principally by the great Omen Collection 'Enuma Anu Enlil', was superseded in the Persian period by a new prophetic art, horoscope astrology, which is still in use to-day. The earliest horoscopes that survive are from Babylon; the oldest is ascribed by SACHS[1]) to the year −409. From Babylon horoscopy spread to the West (through Asia Minor and Syria to Egypt, Greece and Rome) and to the East (to Persia and India). In its train astrology carried with it astronomical calculating procedures, which are indispensable for any caster of horoscopes.

Chronology

In this chapter we shall often be dealing with observational texts dated according to kings, so we reproduce below a list of the Babylonian and Persian kings from NABOPOLASSAR on. For each king we give the year of his accession (more precisely, the year B.C. in which the 1st Nisannu of his accession year occured). By Babylonian usage, this year was counted as the year 0 of the king in question.

Year 0 of Nabopolassar is thus, according to the table, the Babylonian year which began in the spring of 626 B.C. Year 1 of NABOPOLASSAR began in 625 B.C., etc.

Chaldaean kings of Babylon

NABOPOLASSAR	626 B.C.
NEBUCHADNEZZAR II	605
AMEL-MARDUK	562
NERGAL-SHAR-USUR	560
LABASHI-MARDUK	556
NABUNAID	556

Persian kings

CYRUS	539
CAMBYSES	530
DARIUS I	522
XERXES	486
ARTAXERXES I	465
DARIUS II	424
ARTAXERXES II	405
ARTAXERXES III	359
ARSES	338
DARIUS III	336

[1]) A. SACHS, Babylonian Horoscopes, Journal of Cuneiform Studies 6 (1952), p. 49.

The characteristics of the astronomy of this period

The astronomy of the New-Babylonian and Persian period has the following typical features:

1. Systematic, dated and recorded observations of eclipses and lunar and planetary phenomena,
2. Calculation of Periods,
3. Prediction of eclipses,
4. Division of the zodiac into 12 signs of 30° each,
5. Rise of horoscope astrology,
6. Development of mathematical astronomy.

This period cannot be separated from the preceding one at any particular point in time: they overlap. For, as we have already seen, observations and predictions of eclipses had already begun in Assyrian times.

OBSERVATIONAL TEXTS

Observations and predictions

Since A. SACHS published in 1955 the astronomical cuneiform texts copied by PINCHES, it has been possible to form a fairly representative picture of Babylonian observational astronomy. Above all, the descriptive catalogue prefacing this publication[1]), which includes all the datable texts known up to 1955, is highly informative. In his 'Sternkunde und Sterndienst' I, KUGLER had already published and edited one or more examples out of each category, but it was only with SACHS' publication that it became clear how the mass of texts is distributed among the individual categories. We can now state with certainty that the systematic observation of celestial phenomena began in the Assyrian period and continued without a break into late Seleucid times.

The observational texts fall into two categories:

I. Diaries, mostly covering one year or half a year;
II. Collections of similar phenomena from several years.

As a rule these texts contain only observations, though occasionally a remark such as 'An eclipse that failed' is encountered. Such a remark obviously refers to a calculated eclipse.

---

[1]) A. SACHS, Late Babylonian astronomical and related texts copied by PINCHES and STRASSMAIER, Providence (1955).

We have two texts related to the diaries, which contain, besides observations, a relatively large number of predictions, namely the text 'STRASSMAIER KAMBYSES 400' for the year −522 and CBS 11901 for the year −424. We shall return to these texts later when we have discussed the observational texts proper.

The scantiness of the surviving ancient predictions becomes intelligible when we remember that almost all our texts come from Seleucid archives. The Seleucid astronomers collected, copied or excerpted those of the ancient observations that were important to them, and thus insured their preservation; but they had hardly any use for the old calculations, so that these have almost all been lost.

Astronomical diaries

The term 'diaries' was first applied to these records by A. SACHS. Among astronomical texts, the diaries form by far the largest group. They give a full report, in chronological order, of astronomical and meterological observations, water levels and market prices, epidemics, earthquakes and other unusual events. We have diaries for the years −567. −453, −440, −418, −417 and so on. From −384 down to the first century B.C. nearly half of the years are represented by diaries in SACHS' collection. We may assume that diaries were kept continuously from −567 onwards. The later texts from −384 were almost all found in a single archive in Babylon, whereas the earlier chance finds are mostly of unknown origin. This explains the large gaps in our material before −384. Quite recently, SACHS discovered a diary for −650, as P. HUBER informed me.

The earliest preserved diary

The text VAT 4956, dating from year 37 of NEBUCHADNEZZAR II (−567), was published in 1915 by P. V. NEUGEBAUER and E. F. WEIDNER[1]). It is preserved only in a copy of much later date, but that appears to be a faithful transcript (orthographically somewhat modernized) of an original of NEBUCHADNEZZAR's time. At the end the text contains as a catch-line the beginning of a corresponding table for the next year 38 of NEBUCHADNEZZAR.

The text begins:

> Year 37 of NEBUCHADNEZZAR, King of Babylon. Nisannu 30: the Moon became visible behind GUD.AN (= Hyades); 14 (?) USH (= 56 minutes) period of visibility [. . .]

---

[1]) Berichte Kön. Sächs. Ges. Wiss. Leipzig (phil.-hist.) *67* (1915) p. 29. For a copy of the cuneiform text see E. F. WEIDNER, Archiv f. Orientforschung *16* (1953), Plate XVII after p. 424.

'Nisannu 30' here means 1st Nisannu, thus simultaneously giving notice that this day coincides with the 30th day of the preceding month, i.e. that the preceding month contained only 29 days. Similarly, 'Aiaru 1' below at the beginning of the next month means that the preceding month Nisannu had 30 days. This elegant practice of giving the length of the month by implication continued until late hellenistic times.

The text continues:

> Saturn opposite SHIM (= SHIM.MAḪ, south-west part of Pisces). On the morning of the 2nd a rainbow formed an 'obstruction' in the west. In the night of the 3rd the Moon was 2 cubits (1 cubit = 2°) before [. . .]. At the beginning of the night of the 9th the moon was 1 cubit in advance of the star at the hind foot of Leo (= β virginis). On the 9th the sun was surrounded by a halo in the west. ⟨On the 11th⟩ or 12th Jupiter's evening rising took place. On the 14th the God was seen with the God (i.e. sun and moon stood in opposition at evening, the sun on the western horizon, the full moon in the east). 4 USH (= 16 minutes) passed between sunrise and the setting of the moon on the next morning . . . On the 15th it was cloudy. On the 16th Venus [. . .]. On the morning of the 20th the sun was surrounded by a halo. From noon till evening rainstorm. A rainbow formed an 'obstruction' in the east. From the 8th intercalary Adaru to the 28th the flood rose 3 cubits 8 fingers (1 cubit = 24 fingers ≈ 50 cm). 2/3 cubit to a flood [. . .]. At the King's command a sacrifice (was made). In this month a fox forced his way into the city. Coughing and [. . .].
>
> On the 1st Aiaru, while the sun was still visible, the moon was seen 4 cubits below the western posterior star of the Great Twins (= β Geminorum); it was broad, wore the tiara [. . .]. Saturn opposite SHIM.MAḪ. Mercury, whose heliacal setting had taken place, was not visible. In the night of the 1st a violent (?) south-east storm. On the 1st. [cloudy] all day. Venus reached the greatest elongation in the west (?). On the 2nd a violent (?) north wind blew. On the 3rd Mars entered NANGAR (= Praesepe), on the 5th he emerged again. On the 10th Mercury had his [heliacal rising] behind the twins. On the 18th Venus was 1 cubit 4 fingers above LUGAL (= Regulus). On the 26th the moon was still visible for 23 USH (= 92 minutes). On the 27th [. . .].

The text reports similarly on the observations of months III to XII. On the 15th Simanu we find the interesting remark: 'Eclipse of the moon, which failed to occur'. This refers to the eclipse of the moon of 4th July −567, which was invisible in Babylon because the full moon occured there shortly after noon.

On the basis of this text and the later diaries we can form a very good idea of Babylonian observational practice, as carried out from −567 or even from −650.

The 'Lunar six'

Six lunar phenomena, called by A. SACHS the 'Lunar Six', were regularly observed and recorded. In our texts, the six observed time intervals are denoted by standard cuneiform signs, which may be read as

NA, SHU, ME, NA, MI = ge, KUR.

The first of these was observed just after New Moon, on the evening of first visibility of the crescent. The next four were observed just before and after Full Moon. Finally, KUR was observed on the day of last visibility of the moon in the morning. The meaning of the terms is:

NA = time between setting of sun and moon on the evening of first visibility of the crescent,

SHU = time between the last setting of the moon before sunrise and sunrise,

ME = time between the last rising of the moon before sunset and sunset,

NA = time between sunrise and the first setting of the moon after sunrise,

MI (or ge) = time between sunset and the first rising of the moon after sunset,

KUR = time between the rising of the moon and sunrise on the morning of last visibility of the moon just before New Moon.

All these time intervals are expressed in USH, and their dates are also recorded. In earlier texts only USH (= 4minutes) and half USH are recorded, whereas the later texts use smaller fractions of USH down to $\frac{1}{6}$. Perhaps the recording of smaller fractions was made possible by a technical advance in the construction of water clocks.

The course of the moon in the zodiac

The observational texts often report conjunctions of the moon with bright stars in the zodiacal belt. The texts give us the date and the approximate time of the conjunction, using expressions like 'at the beginning of the night', and also the difference in latitude, measured perpendicular to the zodiac, expressed in 'fingers':

1 cubit *(ammatu)* = 24 fingers = 2 or $2\frac{1}{2}$ degrees.

If the measurement was not made at the moment of conjunction, the difference in longitude between the moon and the fixed star was also given. In the Seleucid period, a standard list of nearly 30 bright stars near the ecliptic was used. PETER HUBER has found that very small angles are usually accurate to 1 finger, larger ones to 2 fingers, angles from about 1 cubit to 4 fingers, and from 3 cubits upwards to $\frac{1}{2}$ cubit. This fall in accuracy seems to indicate that the angles were estimated rather than measured.

If these observations are to be used for calculating tables of the motion of the moon and the planets, the measured distances must be converted into longitudes. For instance, if a planet is observed 2 cubits behind Spica, the longitude of the planet would be the longitude of Spica plus 4°. But what is the longitude of Spica? What is needed, is a catalogue of longitudes of bright stars in the zodiacal belt. In fact, a fragment of such a catalogue has survived: it was published by A. SACHS in Journal of Cuneiform Studies 6, p. 146 (1952). The fragment gives the longitudes of the following stars:

Loin (?) of Leo (θ Leonis)	20° Leo
Hindfoot of Leo (β Virginis)	1° Virgo
Root of the corn-stalk (γ Virginis)	16° Virgo
Bright star of the corn-stalk (α Virginis)	28° Virgo
Southerly scale (α Librae)	20° Libra
Northerly scale (β Librae)	25° Libra.

Although the terminology of the fragment appears to be pre-Seleucid and the longitudes are pretty inaccurate (the standard error of the individual longitudes is over 1°), they were still in use as late as the year 111 B.C.

The catalogue was used by P. HUBER in a paper in Centaurus 5, p. 192 (1958) to determine the origin of the Babylonian zodiac. He found the mean difference between the Babylonian and modern longitudes for the year −100 to be 4.4°.

Nearly the same value had been found by KUGLER and myself earlier from Babylonian lunar and planetary tables[1]).

Collections of ancient eclipse and planetary observations

The texts to which we now turn became available for the first time in 1955, when SACHS published the transcriptions made by PINCHES, with an extremely valuable Descriptive Catalogue.

We find in these texts:

a) Detailed reports on successive lunar eclipses, arranged in 18-year groups. We have several fragments from a large text, which covered at least the years from −730 to −316 (SACHS-PINCHES No. 1414ff.).

b) Dates (year and month) of successive lunar eclipses, arranged in 18-year groups, at least for the years from −646 to −271 (Nos. 1418, 1422ff., 1428ff.).

c) Dates (year and month) of successive solar eclipses, arranged in 18-year groups, at least for −347 to −285 (No. 1430).

d) Observations of Jupiter, arranged in 12-year groups, at least from −525 to −489 (No. 1393).

---

[1]) For details see VAN DER WAERDEN: History of the Zodiac, Archiv für Orientforschung, Vol. 16.

e) Observations of Venus, arranged in 8-year groups, from −463 to at least −416 (No. 1387).

f) Observations of Venus and Mercury, the former, according to SACHS, from the year −586/585 (No. 1386).

g) Observations of Mars and Saturn from −422 to −399 including their conjunctions with the moon (No. 1411, 1412).

In addition, we have a considerable number of fourth century observational texts relating to the planets.

The Greek astronomer PTOLEMY chose for the starting point of his calendar the year of accession of the Babylonian king NABONASSAR (−747), because 'from this time on the old observations too have generally been preserved down to the present day' (PTOLEMY, Almagest III 7). This statement is fully confirmed by the text-group a), b) and c).

In the observational texts for Venus we may observe the gradual improvement of the observational technique. Right from the beginning the texts give the duration of the month, and tell us how long the crescent was visible on the first night of each month. There is also a full report on the morning and evening risings and settings of Venus. On the other hand, conjunctions with normal stars are at first recorded only sporadically, at most twice or three times a year. It is only from −430 that conjunctions appear to be observed with some completeness.

As an example of the stenographic brevity of such a table we reproduce a small part of the Venus text mentioned under e) in transliteration and translation (No. 1387, Rev. III, lower panel):

> *Text:* 23 bar 30 15 6 *ina* shu
> ⟨*ina*⟩ lu igi nim *ina* 3 ki 4
> igi gu₄ 1 24 sig 30 16
> 22 (?) *e* lugal $\frac{2}{3}$ kùsh lal

Translation by PETER HUBER (with explanations in brackets):

> Year 23 (of ARTAXERXES I, month) Nisannu 30 (i.e. the preceding Adaru had 29 days. The New Moon was visible for) 15 (USH. On the) 6th at evening (Venus was) visible (for the first time) in Aries. (She already stood) high, (she) could have been already) visible around 3rd or 4th. (Month) Aiaru 1st (i.e. Nisannu had 30 days. The new moon was visible) 24 (USH. Month) Simanu 30 (i.e. Aiaru had 29 days. The new moon was visible) 16 (USH On the) 22nd (?) (Venus stood) $\frac{2}{3}$ cubits a(bove) Regulus, balancing (i.e. having the same longitude).

The text STRASSMAIER KAMBYSES 400

This text was published by KUGLER (Sternkunde I, p. 61). It is a late and inaccurate copy which must, however, relate to an original of the Persian period. The front side contains calculations of lunar phenomena for year 7 of KAMBYSES ($-522/21$), namely the month lengths and the six time intervals between the rising and setting of moon and sun at the new moon, full moon and last visibility, which we have just discussed in the case of the observation texts. These must (at least in part) be calculations, because there are none of the meterological remarks which we otherwise find inserted in the observation texts (compare the text PINCHES-SACHS No. 1431, which assembles the corresponding observations for the years -322ff). Further, the text contains all the time intervals, whereas the unfavourable conditions caused by rain would probably have made it impossible to observe every single one. It is not known how the calculations were made.

The reverse contains observations from the 7th and 8th year of KAMBYSES. The first section contains, by planets, the dates and constellations in which the following events occurred:

> Jupiter EL, MF, MSt, ESt, EL;
> Venus EL, MF, ML, EF;
> Saturn EL, MF, EL;
> Mars   EL, MF, MSt, EL;

(EL = Eveninglast, MSt = Morning Stationary Point, etc.). It is possible that these observations served as a basis for the planetary theory of System A, which was invented not long after the date of the text (see chapter 7).

The second section contains observations of the positions of planets relative to other planets and the moon. The third section contains two eclipse observations, one of which is found in PTOLEMY too. These have already been quoted in our discussion of the temporal hours in Chapter 3.

Very often it is difficult to decide whether text data were observed or calculated. We know from the diaries of later times that missing observations were filled in by calculation, sometimes without explicit indication of the fact, sometimes with the note 'not observed', sometimes with a note that the observation gave a different result. In the case of Sirius phenomena an investigation by A. SACHS[1]) has shown that calculation was the rule, even when the statement 'not observed' is missing.

The text CBS 11 901

The text CBS 11 901 belongs to the year -424 and gives with laconic brevity the dates of New Moon, Full Moon and last visibility of the Moon, one lunar and one solar eclipse, the summer solstice and the autumnal equinox, the heliacal rising of Sirius and the heliacal rising and setting of all planets.

---

[1]) A. SACHS, J. of Cuneiform Stud., 6 (1952), p. 112.

KUGLER, who edited the text completely (Sternkunde 2. Ergänzungsheft, p. 233), believed he could conclude that all the dates were calulated, because there is a complete absence of meteorological observations and because the text shows an eclipse not visible in Babylon without the comment, customary in the observation texts, 'It was missing'. It seems probable, however, that the text mainly records observations: SCHOCH[1]) pointed out that the Mars and Mercury dates coincide much better with modern tables than is otherwise normal in the case of Babylonian calculations. The lunar eclipse too coincides with modern calculation to within a few minutes.

CALCULATION OF PERIODS

Everybody knows that the visible shape of the moon changes periodically, the period being one month. Just so, the equinoxes and solstices return every year. The fact that the heliacal risings and settings of the fixed stars recur annually is explicitly stated in [mul]APIN. The schematic calculation of the Venus phenomena in the Venus tablets of Ammizaduga is based, as we have seen, on the assumption of the periodic repetition of the appearance and disappearance of Venus. Hence the periodicity of celestial phenomena was known long before the Neo-Babylonian period. Yet, accurate period relations are not to be found in the earlier texts. For example, the [mul]APIN compendium does not give a single period for the sun, moon or planets, apart from the schematic year of 12 months of 30 days each.

The situation changed rapidly during the Persian period. More and more accurate periods were found and used as tools for predicting lunar and planetary phenomena.

We may distinguish two kinds of periods: *short periods*, ranging from 8 years for Venus to 83 years for Jupiter, which were used for easy and not very accurate predictions, and *long periods*, ranging from 265 to 1151 years, on which more accurate calculations were based.

We shall first discuss the short periods.

The 'Saros'

As we have seen, lunar eclipses were arranged in 18-year groups. An eclipse period of 18 years is mentioned in many cuneiform texts from the Persian to the Seleucid reign. Modern authors call this period 'Saros'. We shall also use this expression, but we must warn the reader that the Babylonian word SAR, from which the Greek word Saros is

---

[1]) Astronomische Abhandlungen, Ergänzungshefte zu Astron. Nachrichten *8*, No. 2.

derived, denotes a period of 3 600 years. In our cuneiform texts, the period of 18 years is sometimes called 'the eighteen', but never SAR.

The 'Saros' contains exactly 223 synodic months, approximately 239 anomalistic periods of the moon, and approximately 242 draconitic months. The duration of the period is 6 585$\frac{1}{3}$ days. The period is particularly suitable for predicting the time of the day or night at which an eclipse will take place, because it contains, in a good approximation, an integer number of anomalistic months. The time of an eclipse is strongly influenced by the anomalistic motion of the moon, but this influence is largely eliminated by taking together 223 months.

The 'Saros' period can be made still more useful by multiplying it by 3; for then we obtain an integer number of days. This means that eclipses which are 669 months apart take place at nearly the same time of the day or night. Greek authors call this period of 669 months 'Exeligmos', which means 'full rolling-off'. The Greek author GEMINOS (Isagoge, ed. MANITIUS, Chapter 18) acribes this period to the Chaldaeans, and in fact the period of 54 years is mentioned in a cuneiform text from Uruk (F. THUREAU-DANGIN, Tablettes d'Uruk, Paris 1922, Text no. 14). This text will be quoted in the sequel as 'Tabl. d'Uruk 14'.

Intercalation periods

As we know, many Babylonian years contained 13 months. After 500 B.C. the intercalary month was usually a second Adaru (A), but sometimes a second Ululu (U). Between 700 and 500 B.C. U-years are found almost as often as A-years.

All reported intercalary years have been collected and tabulated by R. A. PARKER and W. A. DUBBERSTEIN in their 'Babylonian Chronology' (Brown Univ. Press, Providence, 1956). Their table shows that there is no regularity to be detected in the intercalary years before CAMBYSES. From 529 to 503 B.C. we observe a regular intercalation. In 8 years there are three intercalary years, namely one U-year and two A-years, as the following list shows (the dashes indicate normal years):

$$
\begin{array}{llll}
- & 527U & - & 525A & - & - & 522A & - \\
- & 519U & - & 517A & - & - & 514A & - \\
- & 511U & - & 509A & - & - & 506A & - \\
- & 503U & -
\end{array}
$$

The regular recurrence, especially of the U-years, is so striking that it can hardly be just a coincidence. This eight-year intercalary cycle was recognised as such by KUGLER.

The next intercalary year 500 does not fit into the 8-year cycle, nor into the 19-year cycle which begins in the next year 499. In the following table we give the year numbers of the first and last years of a 19-year period; the years between are represented simply by an A, U or dash. The letter a signifies that a second Adaru is probable but not recorded.

```
500 A  − A  − − A  − a  − − A  − − A  − − U  − A 482
481 −  − a  − − a  − A  − − A  − − A  − − U  − A 463
462 −  − A  − − a  − A  − − A  − − A  − − A  − A 444
443 −  − A  − − a  − A  − − A  − − A  − − A  − A 425
424 −  − A  − − A  − A  − − A  − − A  − − U  − A 406
405 −  − A  − − A  − A  − − A  − − a  − − U  − A 387
```

Here we have, starting from 499 B.C., six whole periods in which the sequence of intercalary years is exactly the same, with the sole exception that twice we have an A where we should expect a U (towards the end of the third and fourth lines). The regularity is so marked that coincidence can be completely excluded. A probability calculation confirms this intuitively evident conclusion, as it also does in the case of the 8-year period above.

The intercalary year 385 A is irregular, but thereafter the series continues regularly down to + 73 A:

```
386 − A  − − − A  − A  − − A  − − A  − − U  − A 368
367 − − A  − − A  − A  − − A  − − A  − − U  − A 349
348 − − A  − − A  − A  − − A  − − A  − − U  − A 330 and so on to
```

+ 71 − − A − − (after +75 the cuneiform texts cease).

Who determined the intercalation? From the reign of NABUNAID we have a royal decree stating that the current year 15 (= 541 B.C.) has a second Adaru. We have two similar decrees from the Persian period, except that these emanate not from the King, but from the officials of the great temple Esagila in Babylon[1]). It would appear, therefore, that in the Persian reign intercalation was controlled centrally from Esagila.

Why are there exceptions from regular intercalation in the Persian period, but not under the Seleucids? Maybe the reason is that in the Seleucid period we are no longer dealing with the civil calendar, but with one designed by astronomers for their own professional use. They compiled planetary tables which were calculated for considerable periods in advance (up to 71 years). The scribes could not know beforehand what the state would prescribe, but for their own purposes they used a regular calendar.

The relation year: month

The 8-year intercalary period which the Babylonians employed from 528 to 503 contains 96 + 3 = 99 months. The corresponding figure for the 19-year period is 228 + 7 =

---

[1]) PARKER and DUBBERSTEIN. Babyl. Chronol., p. 1—2.

= 235 months. Hence we obtain the following approximate period relations:

$$8 \text{ years} = 99 \text{ months}$$
$$19 \text{ years} = 235 \text{ months.}$$

The second relation was used, according to GEMINOS, by the Greek astronomers METON and EUKTEMON (about 430) and KALLIPPOS (about 330). The 8-year period, again according to GEMINOS, was known before METON. As far as we know, these periods are of theoretical significance only: they were not used as the basis for intercalation in the Greek cities.

The 8-year period is not accurate: the 19-year period is much better. Intermediate between them in accuracy is a 27-year period, record of which has also come down to us. In the text SH 135, line 15, we read:

'The phenomena of Sirius recur on the same day after 27 years'.

This means that 27 Sirius years (calculated e.g. from one Morningfirst of Sirius to the next) contain an integral number of months. The number can be found directly by addition of the numbers for the 8- and 19-year periods, i.e.

$$27 \text{ years} = 334 \text{ months.}$$

To test these relations for accuracy and to compare them with later Babylonian results, we calculate the ratio of months to years on a sexagesimal basis, as follows:

(1)   from the 8-year period: 1 year = 12;22,30 months
(2)   from the 27-year period: 1 year = 12;22,13,20 months
(3)   from the 19-year period: 1 year = 12;22,6,19 months.

From the Seleucid period we have a set of rules for calculating the phenomena of Sirius and the solstices and equinoxes[1]), which is based on the following ratio:

(4)   1 year = 12;22,6,20 months.

NEUGEBAUER and SACHS suppose that this relation is derived from the 19-year period by rounding off. The rules based on relation (4) were used possibly as early as -322, but certainly from -232, for calculating the Morning Rising, Evening Rising and Evening Setting of Sirius.

---

[1]) O. NEUGEBAUER, Solstices and Equinoxes, Journal of Cuneiform Studies 2, p. 209. A. SACHS, Sirius dates, J. of Cuneiform Studies 6, p. 105.

In a procedure text for Jupiter, published by KUGLER (Sternkunde I, p. 147), we find an even better ratio. In this text SH 279 it is stated that the sun requires 12 months and 11;3,20 days for a complete circuit. Here, as almost always in Babylonian planetary calculations, 'days' means thirtieths of the mean synodic month. This gives the ratio:

(5)   1 year = 12;22,6,40 months.

In Babylonian lunar calculations there are, as we shall see, two systems A and B. In the older system A the ratio used is:

(6)   1 year = 12;22,8 months.

In system B, where the period ratios are generally more accurate, the mean monthly motion of the sun is 29;6,19,20 degrees. The annual motion is of course 360°. Dividing and rounding off to the third sexagesimal place, we have:

(7)   1 year = 12;22,7,52 months.

This ratio is still better than (6). Hence we see that in the course of time the Babylonian astronomers achieved ever more accurate values for the ratio year: month.

How were these values obtained from observations?

In principle, there are two means of determining the length of the year, namely:
a) from observations of the stars, or
b) from observations of equinoxes and solstices.

Method b) was that mostly used by the Greek astronomers. METON and EUKTEMON observed the summer solstice of the year −431 (= 432 B.C.) on the 27th June in the morning[1]). Starting from this date, EUKTEMON composed his astronomical calendar, fixing the dates of the equinoxes and solstices and also the annual risings and settings of the most important fixed stars by their distance from the summer solstice[2]). KALLIPPOS, HIPPARCHOS and PTOLEMY also determined the solar year on the basis of observations of the equinoxes and solstices.

The Babylonians bothered themselves much less about an accurate determination of these seasonal points. They calculated them schematically, working from the summer solstice and simply making the interval between successive seasonal points equal to 3 months and 3 days. Very often we find at such points the note 'nu PAP', i.e. not observed. Although the dates have errors of up to 5 days, we nowhere find the remark that observation gave a different day from calculation.

---

[1]) PTOLEMY, Almagest III 1, p. 205 Heiberg.
[2]) A. REHM, Griechische Kalender III, Sitzungsber. Heidelberger Akad. (phil.-hist.) 1913, 3. Abh. See also VAN DER WAERDEN, Greek astronomical calendars, Journal of Hellenic Studies, 80, p. 168.

If one wishes to compare such ratios as (6) and (7) with modern calculation, the sidereal and tropical years must be distinguished. The *sidereal year* is the time in which the sun returns to the same fixed star; this is somewhat more than $365\frac{1}{4}$ days. The *tropical year* is the time in which the sun returns to the same equinox; this is less than $365\frac{1}{4}$ days.

It turns out that both estimates (6) and (7) give a duration of the year which is somewhat larger than the sidereal year, and considerably larger than the tropical. This seems to indicate that the Babylonians derived their values not from the observation of equinoxes and solstices but from the fixed stars. As far as we know, the Babylonians used observations of equinoxes or soltices only incidentally, in complete contrast to the Greeks.

Planetary periods

The following set of planetary periods was used for predictions in the Seleucid era:
Saturn:

> 59 years = 2 revolutions = 57 synodic periods.

Jupiter:

> 71 years = 6 revolutions = 65 synodic periods, or, alternatively
> 83 years = 7 revolutions = 76 synodic periods.

Mars:

> 47 years = 25 revolutions = 22 synodic periods, or, alternatively
> 79 years = 42 revolutions = 37 synodic periods.

Venus:

> 8 years = 8 revolutions = 5 synodic periods.

Mercury:

> 46 years = 46 revolutions = 145 synodic periods.

Some of these periods were known long before the Seleucid era. This is proved by a Text SH 135, published by F. X. KUGLER in Vol. I of his Sternkunde, p. 45. KUGLER's commentary is still useful, but he did not succeed in interpreting every detail. Since NEUGEBAUER's clarification of the terminology of the mathematico-astronomical texts, the important text SH 135 can be better understood. The text contains the ancient names of planets, which were in use before the fourth century, and some periods which were definitely out of date in the Seleucid period.

The following translation of the fragmentary text is due to P. HUBER, who has made the translation as literal as possible:

Line 1. [. . .] you return behind yourself
       2. [. . .] (heliacal) setting . . .
       3. [. . .] . . . year, which in the year . . .
       4. ⟨. . . moon: in⟩ 27 days it returns (to its) position (?).

5. ⟨... appearance⟩ of Venus: for 8 years you return behind yourself,
6. [...] 4 days you subtract, (and) you see (i.e.: have the result).
7. ⟨... appearance of⟩ Mercury: 6 years you return behind yourself.
8. [...] you add,
9. [...] you add to the appearance, (and) you see.
10. ⟨... appearance⟩ of Mars: 47 years
11. you return behind yourself, 12 days [...]
12. [...] 12 days you add to the appearance, and you see.
13. [...] appearance of Saturn: 59 years
14. you return behind yourself, day for day you see.
15. [...] appearance of Sirius: 27 years
16. you return behind yourself, day for day you see.

It is clear from this translation that the text does not merely enumerate the periods of the planets: it also gives the detailed procedure for calculating planetary phenomena by means of periods. In the cases of Saturn and Sirius the date of the previous phenomenon, preceding the calculated one by 59 and 27 years respectively, can be retained (i.e. these periods contain a whole number of synodic months), while for Venus, Mercury and Mars some corrections must be made. The terminology coincides largely with that of the later 'procedure texts', although with a marked preference for the phonetic as against the ideographic script.

The way in which these periods were used for predicting planetary phenomena is made clear by a class of texts which A. SACHS has called Goal-Year Texts.

Goal-year texts

The earliest goal-year texts that have come down to us derive from the Seleucid period, but the basic idea may well be older and go as far back as the Persian epoch. The goal-year texts are collections of observations from years which precede the 'goal-year' by a planetary or lunar period, as the case may be. The purpose of such a text is clear: it must have been used, together with the period relations, to produce astronomical predictions. In detail, a goal-year text for year X contains observations from the following years:

Saturn: year X-59;

Jupiter: cardinal points for the year X-71, conjunctions with normal stars for the year X-83;

Mars: cardinal points for the year X-79, conjunctions for the year X-47;

Venus: year X-8;

Mercury: year X-46;

Moon: Lunar Six and eclipses for the year X-18, and sums SHU + NA and ME + MI for the second half of the year X-19.

The term 'cardinal points' calls for some explanation. In the planetary tables of the Seleucid era five or six phenomena are calculated for each planet, which recur in every synodical period. NEUGEBAUER denotes the phenomena by Greek letters, whereas I prefer notations like MF, ML, etc. In the following list both notations will be used. For the upper planets Saturn, Jupiter and Mars the five cardinal points are

Γ = MF = Morningfirst = First Visibility in the Morning
Φ = MSt = Morning Station = First Stationary Point
Θ = Op = Opposition (or Evening Rising just before Opposition)
Ψ = ESt = Evening Station = Second stationary point (end of retrograde motion)
Ω = EL = Eveninglast = Last Visibility in the Evening.

For the lower planets Venus and Mercury, which always remain near the sun and never come into position, the cardinal points are:

Γ = MF = Morningfirst = First Visibility as Morning Star
Φ = MSt = Morning Station = Second Stationary Point (end of retrograde motion)
Σ = ML = Morninglast = Last Visibility as Morning Star.
Ξ = EF = Eveningfirst = First Visibility as Evening Star
Ψ = ESt = Evening Station = First Stationary Point
Ω = EL = Eveninglast = Last Visibility as Evening Star

How can we explain that in the case of both Jupiter and Mars observations of the cardinal points and conjunctions from two different years were used? The most probable answer is that the calculation of the cardinal points for Jupiter, for example, is made more easily from the observations of Year X-71, while the conjunctions are better based on the observations of X-83. A glance at Table ACT[1]) No. 611, which contains the cardinal points for the years 180 to 251 of the Seleucid era as calculated in accordance with the Babylonian A' Jupiter theory, confirms this. According to this text, in year 180 the morning rising takes place at date VI 13 at 10° Virgo, 71 years later again at date VI 13 but this time at 5° Virgo. The date of a cardinal point can therefore be simply repeated after 71 years. However, the −5° displacement of its position is so large that in the neighbourhood of the stationary points the dates of the conjunctions with the same normal stars can hardly be related to one another any more. If, however, we go on another 12 years, we see that in 83 years the position of a cardinal point is displaced by a mere −0° 50', the date changing by roughly half a month. This explanation is due to P. HUBER.

If one wants to make predictions for Venus for the year X from observations made in the year X-8, one has to subtract 4 days from the date, as stated in SH 135. In fact,

---

[1]) ACT always means the standard edition of O. NEUGEBAUER, Astronomical Cuneiform Texts.

5 synodic periods of Venus are 8 years minus 2½ days, or 99 synodic months minus 4 days. Similar corrections for Mercury and Mars are also indicated in SH 135.

The 18-years' period for the moon is, as we have seen, 6 585⅓ days. The Babylonian astronomers knew this, for GEMINOS informs us that the triple Saros or Exeligmos contained, according to the 'Chaldaeans', 19 756 days. Therefore, if they wanted to predict the 'Lunar Six' for the year X from the observed Lunar Six for the year X-18, they had to add ⅓ of a day to every rising or setting time of the moon.

Why did the Babylonians also record the sums SHU + NA and ME + MI for the second half of the year X-19? Well, it often happens that because of bad weather the time of rising or setting of the moon is not observable. In the first half of the Babylonian year the sky is usually clear, but the second half is the rainy season. The sum SHU + NA is just the daily retardation of the setting of the moon in the middle of a month, and ME + MI is the daily retardation of the moon's rising. This daily retardation depends mainly on the sun's position in the zodiac. Now 19 years contain, in a good approximation, an integral number of months, hence at the end of this number of months the daily retardation of the moon's rising or setting repeats itself.

Long periods

According to KUGLER (Sternkunde I, p. 48), the text Sp. II 985 contains the old planet names that were in common use before the fourth century. The text mentions the following 'long periods':

Saturn	589 years
Jupiter	344 years
Mars	284 years
Venus	6 400 years
Moon	684 years.

On the other hand, the Seleucid calculation tables make use of the following periods:

Saturn	265 years =	9 circuits =	256 synodic periods
Jupiter	427 years =	36 circuits =	391 synodic periods
Mars	284 years =	151 circuits =	133 synodic periods
Venus	1151 years =	1151 circuits =	720 synodic periods
Mercury	480 years =	480 circuits =	1513 synodic periods.

Exactly the same periods occur in Greek astrological texts. In an extract from AN-TIOCHOS[1]), RHETORIOS writes:

[1]) Catalogus codicum astrologorum Graecorum I (Brussels, 1898) p. 163.

'Saturn completes the greatest return in 265 years, Jupiter in 427 years, Mars in 284 years, Helios in 1461 years, Venus in 1151 years, Mercury in 480 years, the Moon in 25 years'.

The period of the sun (Helios) mentioned here is the well-known Sothis period of the Egyptians. After the passage of this amount of time the rising of Sirius (and hence the summer solstice too, by a fair approximation) falls on the same date in the Egyptian calendar.

The 25-year lunar period is also a calendar period: 25 Egyptian years are approximately 309 months[1]). The other periods mentioned by RHETORIOS are all Babylonian, as comparison with the cuneiform texts shows.

It is not to be supposed that the large periods result from direct observation. For in that case Venus observations, for example, would have been needed for 1151 or even 6400 years. A better explanation of the 1151-year Venus period can be found if we start with the 8-year period, which requires, according to the Babylonian Venus tables, a correction of $2\frac{1}{2}$ degrees, to be subtracted from the longitude of Venus. Now at the time of its appearance or disappearance Venus is always near the sun and, according to the Babylonians, always at the same distance from the sun. Hence it follows that in 5 synodic periods of Venus the sun completes exactly 8 revolutions less $2\frac{1}{2}$ degrees. Multiplying by 144, we find that the sun completes 1151 revolutions in 720 synodic periods, i.e. we have the relation:

$$720 \text{ synodic Venus periods} = 1151 \text{ solar years.}$$

This relation was continually used in the tables of the Seleucid period.

KUGLER has given a similar explanation for the 6400-year Venus period. See F. X. KUGLER, Sternkunde I, p. 50.

The periods of Saturn can be explained analogously. In 59 years Saturn completes two circuits and a small additional arc, which, by modern calculation, amounts to nearly 1°. The Babylonians apparently overestimated this arc somewhat and made it 1°20'. Saturn's average annual movement is 12 to 13 degrees, which is equal to 9 or 10 times the additional arc of 1°20'. If we take the factor as 10, we have 590 − 1 = 589 years as the period for exactly 20 complete circuits. If we take the factor as 9, we have 9 × 59 − 1 = 530 years for 18 circuits, or 265 years for 9 circuits.

In the case of Jupiter, the basis is the 71-year period in which Jupiter completes 6 circuits minus 5 or 6 degrees. Multiplying by 6 and adding a further synodic period in which Jupiter travels 30 to 36 degrees according to the tables, we obtain the relation 427 years = 36 circuits. According to KUGLER, the 344-year period can similarly be obtained by summing smaller periods, namely 344 = 4 × 83 + 12 = 4 × 71 + 5 × 12.

Likewise, KUGLER explains the 284-year Mars period by the formula

---

[1]) O. NEUGEBAUER and A. VOLTEN: Ein demotischer astronomischer Papyrus (Carlsberg 9). Quellen u. Studien Gesch. Math. B4, p. 383.

$$284 = 3 \times 79 + 47.$$

The greatest difficulties are presented by the 684 year lunar period. The number cannot be explained away as a copying error, for, as KUGLER has pointed out (Sternkunde, I, p. 53), it occurs several times in astrological texts. In Sp. I 184 (line 3) we read: 'In 684 years eclipses of sun and moon recur'.

KUGLER established that this figure cannot have been obtained by direct observation of eclipses separated by 684 years, for the simple reason that there is in fact no eclipse period of about 684 years. Nor was he able to reach the figure 684 as a multiple of the 18-year eclipse period or by a combination of other lunar periods known to us. The figure presented a real puzzle.

Analysis of earlier eclipse predictions led me to a possible solution of the puzzle. I found that, though the 18-year periods could not provide the explanation, there was a shorter and less accurate eclipse period of 47 months which could. The argument runs as follows.

The path of the moon intersects the ecliptic at the *nodes*: the ascending and the descending node. The time taken by the moon to return to the same node is called the *draconitic month*. Lunar and solar eclipses occur only when the full or new moon is in the neighbourhood of a node. It is an idea common to many peoples that a dragon who has his abode in the nodes swallows the moon or the sun: hence the name 'dragon month' or 'draconitic month'.[1]) The dragon month is almost two days shorter than the normal synodic month, which is calculated from one full (or new) moon to the next. 47 synodic months are about equal to 51, or more exactly to $51\frac{1}{237}$ draconitic months. Thus, if the full moon is in the vicinity of a node, it will be near the same node 47 months later; hence 47 months make up a (not very accurate) eclipse period.

If now it is assumed that the Babylonians underestimated the fraction $\frac{1}{237}$ as $\frac{1}{180}$, which is not at all a bad approximation, we obtain on multiplying by 180 the period relation

$$8460 \text{ synodic months} = 9181 \text{ dragon months.}$$

Thus we have obtained an apparently accurate 684-year eclipse period which is in fact very inaccurate, because 180 times $\frac{1}{237}$ is not nearly an integer.

The 'great year'

In considering the large periods, we have mentioned a Greek astrological text (an excerpt from ANTIOCHOS transmitted by RHETORIOS), in which long periods of the planets, the sun and the moon are recorded. The last sentence of this excerpt reads:

---

[1]) The Arabs call the ascending node the 'dragon's head' and the descending the 'dragon's tail'. See W. HARTNER, Le problème de la planete Kaid, Conférences du Palais de la Découverte D 36 (Paris, 1955).

'The cosmic recurrence takes place in 1 753 005 years; then all the stars come together in the 30th degree of Cancer or the first degree of Leo, and a complete fulfilment occurs; but when they meet in Cancer, there will be a flood in one part of the Universe'.

RHETORIOS' long periods are, as we have seen, derived from Babylonian astronomy. But the legend of the Great Deluge is Babylonian too; hence we may suppose that the whole doctrine of 'cosmic recurrence' is of Babylonian origin.

This suggestion is in fact confirmed by a fragment of BEROSSOS. BEROSSOS was priest of Bel, who migrated from Babylon to Ionia and about 280 B.C. founded an astrological school on the island of Kos. The fragment is to be found in SENECA, Quaestiones naturales III 29:

'Berossos . . . states that the course of the stars determines a conflagration and a flood. For a conflagration will rage over the Earth when all the stars which now wander in various paths assemble in Cancer . . .; but a flood is imminent when the same band of stars meets in Capricorn. The former is caused by the summer solstice, the latter by the winter solstice.'

The fragment probably belongs to BEROSSOS' 'Babyloniaka'. In this fragment the flood plays a central role, hence it seems natural to suppose that the whole doctrine to which Berossos refers is Babylonian in origin. The correctness of this supposition is confirmed by the fragments of the second book of the 'Babyloniaka' which EUSEBIOS and SYNKELLOS have preserved (SCHNABEL, BEROSSOS Fr. 28-29 and 29b). In these fragments BEROSSOS enumerates the 'Kings of the Assyrians', from ALOROS, the first King of Babylon, to XISUTHROS, in whose reign the greatest and first flood was supposed to have occurred. The reigns of the kings are expressed in Sar, Ner and Sos, a Sar being 3600 years, a Ner 600 years and a Sos 60 years. The word Sar is in fact Akkadian and signifies the number 3 600. The whole method of counting corresponds exactly to the Babylonian number system; so that there can be no doubt that Berossos drew his material from Babylonian traditions.

The total reigns of all the Kings amount, according to Berossos, to 120 Sars or 432 000 years. These 120 Sars in turn form a part of a period five times larger. For BEROSSOS speaks of 'records which were kept with great care in Babylon and which cover a period of about 2 150 000 years'. These records concerned 'the sky, the sea, the creation, the Kings and the events of their reigns'. By a careful analysis of the figures given by BE-ROSSOS, SCHNABEL[1]) has shown that the framework of BEROSSOS' chronology was as follows:

from the creation to the time of ALEXANDER the Great	2 148 000 years
from ALEXANDER to an expected universal catstrophe	12 000 years
Total 600 sar =	2 160 000 years

[1]) P. SCHNABEL, Die babyl. Chronologie in Berossos' Babyloniaka, Mitteil. Vorderas. Ges. (1908), No. 5.

From at least 500 A.D. on, the Hindu astronomers worked with a world period that is just twice as long as that of BEROSSOS:

$$1 \text{ Mahâyuga} = 4\ 320\ 000 \text{ years}^1).$$

The divisibility of this number by 60^3 is a clear sign that this world-period ultimately derives from Babylon; for the Indian number system is purely decimal. The coincidence with BEROSSOS becomes still more striking when we take note of the division of the Mahâyuga by the Indians into four parts in the ration 4 : 3 : 2 : 1, so that the last partial period, the Kaliyuga, contains exactly as many years as BEROSSOS' 120 Sars, namely 432 000.

Other figures that again are divisible by high powers of 60 are to be found in a report by AETIOS (Diels, Doxographi Graeci p. 363):

> The so-called *Great Year* occurs when all (planets) return to the same place from which their motions began . . . According to Herakleitos, the Great Year consists of 18 000 years, while Diogenes the Stoic makes it 360 such years as that of Herakleitos.

DIOGENES the Stoic is also known as Diogenes of Babylon. His 'Great Year' consists of

$$360 \cdot 18\ 000 = 30 \cdot 60^3 \text{ years.}$$

Here again we have a high power of 60, which can only be explained as stemming from the Babylonian number system. Many other 'Great Years' have come down to us, e.g. those of ORPHEUS and KASSANDROS with lengths of 120 000 and 3 600 000 years respectively. An astronomical inscription from KESKINTO in Rhodos (P. TANNERY, Mém. Sc. II, p. 487) gives a Great Year of 291 400 years. In this time, according to the inscription, each of the planets completes a whole number of sidereal and synodic circuits.

The mention of the names ORPHEUS and HERAKLEITOS indicates that the idea of the Great Year was known to the Greeks before BEROSSOS. In fact, the 'Great Year' or 'Perfect Year' is mentioned by PLATON, ARISTOTELES and EUDEMOS. PLATON's 'perfect year' is simply an astronomical period, after which all the planets return to the point where they started. ARISTOTELES mentions a flood in the winter of the 'Great Year' and a conflagration in the summer. EUDEMOS relates: 'If we are to believe the Pythagoreans, I shall in the future, even as everything recurs according to the Number, again tell you tales here, holding this little stick in my hand, while you will sit before me as you do now; and likewise everything else will be just the same.'

With this we go as far back as the Pythagoreans, i.e. at least to the fifth century.

---

[1]) See e.g. W. E. CLARK: The Aryabhatiya of Aryabhata, Chicago 1930.

It appears that PYTHAGORAS himself, who lived in the sixth century, believed in the perpetual recurrence of all events. In a short and generally reliable excerpt from PYTHAGORAS' teaching which has come down to us through DIKAIARCHOS, we read: 'Pythagoras says . . ., that everything that has once happened, will recur after a certain period, and that nothing is really new' (PORPHYRIOS, Vita Pyth., 19, p. 26 NAUCK).

We shall return later to the astrological fatalism which finds expression in the doctrine of the predestined recurrence of everything. What concerns us here is the very close connection between the doctrine of the Great Year and Babylonian period calculations. For what else is the Great Year than a common multiple of all the planetary periods? And the idea of such a common multiple that can actually be calculated could only have occurred to someone who, like the Babylonians, was profoundly interested in planetary periods and the assessment of their ratios in numerical terms.

Close ties between Pythagorean and Babylonian teachings can also be detected in their geometry and arithmetic (see VAN DER WAERDEN, Science Awakening I, p. 124). The astrological fatalism of the Pythagoreans certainly stems from Babylon, the classical country of astrology. The knowledge that the heavenly phenomena are comprehensible in terms of number must also have come to the Pythagoreans from Babylon; for it was only much later that the Greeks learned how to calculate the heavenly phenomena numerically.

PREDICTION OF ECLIPSES

In Chapter II we have already discussed two reports of Assyrian astrologers predicting eclipses. We shall now consider some other reports.

The following translation is based on that of R. C. THOMPSON: The Reports of the Magicians, but improved by E. F. WEIDNER (oral communication). The reports are numbered according to THOMPSON:

272 B. A lunar eclipse occurs on 14th Adar . . . When the eclipse occurs, the King, my Lord, might send out (messengers) . . .

274. An eclipse has taken place, but it was not visible in the Residence (Nineveh). This eclipse has thus gone by. The Lord of the Kings might send (messengers) to Assur, to Kalakh, to Babylon, Nippur, Uruk and Borsippa. What was seen in these cities, the King will certainly learn . . . The Great Gods in the city in which the King lives have hidden the sky and not shown the eclipse; the King may therefore know that the eclipse is not directed against him or his land[1]).

---

[1]) R. F. HARPER: Assyrian and Babylonian Letters, Nr. 895.

These prophecies cannot be dated, but, as the letters were found in Assurbanipal's library, they must be older than 612 B.C., the year of the library's destruction. On the other hand, the prediction of eclipses undoubtedly requires the availability of serial observations. As far as we know the first systematic collection of eclipse observations began after 750, so we may assume that the predictions first became possible after 700. Probably the majority of the astrologers' reports and letters belong to the period from 681 to 630 B.C., that is, to the reigns of Asarhaddon and Assurbanipal.

The premature eclipse Thompson 271

One report can be dated with reasonable certainty, namely Thompson 271. This records an eclipse that occured 'prematurely' *(ina lā mināti-shu)* on the 14th of the month. The relevant omen from the great omen series Enuma Anu Enlil, giving the consequences of such an eclipse, is quoted in the text. A commentary on this omen, throws some light on the meaning of the expression 'premature'. The commentary says:

> If the Moon is eclipsed too early *(ina lā mināti-shu)* — this happens when six months have not yet passed, and similarly, if an eclipse takes place on the 12th or 13th day, . . .[1])

According to this commentary, the expression 'premature' would be applicable when an eclipse occurs less than 6 months after the previous one, or when it occurs on the 12th or 13th day of the month. The translation 'premature' is certain, for the word is also applied to full moon phenomena: on the 12th and 13th day of the month the full moon counts as 'premature', on the 15th and 16th day as 'retarded' *(ina lā adanni-shu)*. Literally, the two expressions mean something like 'not in its number, or period' and 'not in its appointed time' respectively.

In our case the eclipse took place on the 14th; so the second alternative given in the omen commentary does not apply. The first, namely that there had been another eclipse less than 6 months previously, is however equally inapplicable; for according to the tables of Neugebauer and Hiller[2]) there was not a single pair of lunar eclipses visible in Babylon between the years − 750 and − 600 having a separation of less than six months.

P. Schnabel suggested (Zeitschr. für Assyriol. 35, p. 306) that in this case 'premature' means simply that an eclipse happened before one was expected. We shall see presently that such an explanation is indeed possible.

Schnabel fixed the date of this 'premature' eclipse as 10/11 June, − 668. This dating

---

[1]) J. Schaumberger, drittes Ergänzungsheft to Kugler's Sternkunde, p. 251.
[2]) P. V. Neugebauer and O. Hiller, Spezieller Kanon d. Mondfinsternisse, Astronomische Abhandlungen (Ergänzungshefte zu Astron. Nachrichten) 9, No. 2 (1934).

was made possible by the fact that the same report mentions a Jupiter phenomenon: 'Jupiter stood in the place where the sun rises'. The phenomenon referred to is, most probably, the morning rising of Jupiter. If we now assume (as SCHNABEL did) that the text, having been found in Nineveh, belongs to the period −705 to −612, when the Sargonids resided in Nineveh, the only possibility is the eclipse of June, −668.

Eclipse that failed

The text VAT 4956 from year 37 of NEBUCHADNEZZAR II, which we have already discussed above, reports an 'eclipse that failed' for 4th July, −567. An eclipse was expected, but none occurred. The prediction was certainly not made by means of the 18-year 'saros' or the triple period, the 54-year 'Exeligmos'. These periods are, to be sure, Babylonian and were used for eclipse prediction by the Babylonians of later times; but there was no eclipse visible in Babylon either 18 or 54 years before that of 4th July, −567.

The solar eclipse in October, −424

The text CBS 11 901 reports a solar eclipse for Tishritu 28. This refers to the eclipse of

23rd October, −424,

which, according to KUGLER's calculation, was not visible in Babylon. There can be no question of a prediction on the basis of the Saros period, because the eclipse has no precursor in the Saros cycle. Our conclusion must be the same as in the preceding case, namely: in the period from −700 to −400 there were Babylonian methods for predicting solar and lunar eclipses which were not based on the 'Saros' of 18 years.

Methods of prediction

What methods are possible for the prediction of an eclipse? Only three possibilities are known to me.

1°. The first method is, to make use of an observed regularity in the occurence of eclipses. The time between two successive lunar eclipses is always an integer number of lunar months, because such eclipses are possible only at Full Moon. Very often the time is a multiple of six months, such as

6 or 12 or 18 months

but it also happens that the interval is 6n + 5 months, e.g.

5 or 11 or 17 or 23 months.

More precisely, lunar eclipses occur in sequences. Within a sequence the distances are multiples of 6 months, and two successive sequences are separated by an interval of 6n + 5 months. In the middle part of a sequence there may be one or two total eclipses, but at the beginning and end of a sequence only partial eclipses are possible.

As an example, let us consider the eclipses during a period of 15 years just before the 'premature' eclipse of − 668. From the 'special canon' of R. HILLER and P. V. NEUGE-BAUER we can draw a list of all lunar eclipses visible at Babylon between − 683 and − 668. We shall arrange the eclipses in 3 sequences and denote the partial eclipses by p, the total eclipses by t. Between the lines we shall note the number of months between successive eclipses.

1st sequence	2nd sequence	3rd sequence	4th sequence
−681 Aug p			−670 Jan p
6			6
−680 Jan t	−678 June p		−670 July p
6	12		6
−680 July t	−677 May t	−673 Sep t	−670 Dec t
6	18	6	12
−679 Jan p	−676 Nov p	−672 Feb p	−669 Dec p
6	35	23	6
−679 July p			−668 June p
11			17

The first sequence is an exceptionally complete one. In the middle we have two total eclipses, preceeded by one and followed by two partial eclipses. In the next three sequen-ces we have only one total eclipse, in the 2nd and 4th case preceeded by one or two partial eclipses, and in all cases followed by one or two partial eclipses. In the first sequence the distances are all 6 months; in the other three sequences the distances are 6 or 12 or 18 months. After the end of each sequence there is an interval of 11 or 17 or 23 or 35 months, during which no lunar eclipses are observed. The same kind of regularity can be observed through the whole table of HILLER and P. V. NEUGEBAUER.

I think the Babylonian scribes had an idea of this regularity, for they called an eclipse 'premature' if it occured less than 6 months after another eclipse. This means: they knew that a normal time distance between two lunar eclipses is 6 months, and that a distance of less than 6 months occurs only in exceptional cases.

The Babylonian scribes had records of solar and lunar eclipses observed during many years, so it is quite possible that they knew about the sequences and used them for predictions. The method is very simple: If a sequence of eclipses is observed, one may expect a similar sequence 41 or 47 months later.

If the Babylonians used this method, we can explain why they called the eclipse of June 10/11, −668 'premature', and also why they predicted an eclipse for July 4, −567. The eclipse of −668 was the last one of the fourth sequence in our list. The preceeding eclipse, of December −669, had a magnitude of only 2 digits, which means that only 2 twelfths of the moon's diameter were eclipsed. Therefore it would be reasonable to expect that this eclipse would be the last one of the sequence, and that a period without eclipses of at least 11 months would follow. But no, the next eclipse came after only 6 months. Therefore the scribe called the eclipse 'premature'.

Next we consider the predicted eclipse of July, −567, which was reported as 'an eclipse that failed'. In fact, according to the Canon of NEUGEBAUER and HILLER, no eclipse was visible at Babylon in that month. Let us consider the five or six predecessors of this predicted eclipse!

	1st sequence		2nd sequence	
	−572 Apr t		−568 Jan t ?	
		12		6
	−571 Mar p		−568 July t ?	
		6		6
	−571 Sep p		−567 Jan p	
		29		

The two eclipses of −568 were total, but the totality could not be seen at Babylon. It is even questionable whether the eclipses were visible at all: the January eclipse ended near sunset, and the July eclipse began near sunrise. Anyhow, during the years −568 and −567, 47 months after the first sequence, a new sequence was to be expected. Especially in July −567, six months after the visible partial eclipse of January, which had a magnitude of 7 digits, one might expect another partial eclipse. This explanation is due to M. SCHRAMM (unpublished).

2°. Another method of predicting eclipses is by means of periods. All possible approximate eclipse periods of less than 30 years were calculated by E. DITTRICH (Das Weltall 30, p. 33). He found periods of

6, 41, 47, 88, 135, 223, 358 months.

The Saros has 223 months. We have already seen that the eclipse predictions of −567 and −424 cannot be explained by means of the Saros. The only periods that would explain the prediction of −567 are the periods of 6 and 47 months. To apply either one of these periods would amount to just the same thing as to use the sequences of eclipses considered before, for 47 months before the eclipse of −567 July we have the eclipse of −561 September, the last one of our first sequence, and 6 months before July we have the eclipse of January, −567, the last one of the second sequence. Just so, the prediction of the solar eclipse of −424 could be explained by the use of the period of 47 months, for just 47 months before this eclipse there was a solar eclipse (May 31, −435) that was almost total in Babylon.

The theoretical reason why the period of 47 months is often successful lies in the fact that 47 synodic months are nearly equal to 51 draconitic months. It is quite possible that the Babylonians knew this period relation. As we have seen before in the section 'Long Periods', the period of 684 years mentioned in our texts can be explained, starting with the period of 47 months and multiplying it by 180.

The period of 47 months also gives us a possible explanation why MAR-ISHTAR kept watch for a solar exlipse on Abu 28, 29 and 30 in the year −632. From modern calculation we know that there was a solar eclipse on June 17, −632, but it was not visible at Babylon. Preceding this there was a solar eclipse 47 months earlier (August 29, −636) and another 47 months earlier again (November 11, −640). The 47-months period may well have led to the expectation of an eclipse at the end of the month Abu in −632. This explanation was suggested by SCHAUMBERGER.

3°. The third method to predict eclipses is, to calculate the time and magnitude of an expected eclipse by means of lunar tables. We shall see in Chapter 6 that these methods of calculation were developed during the Persian reign, probably as early as −500. This method of calculation is excellent for lunar eclipses, but not very good for solar eclipses, because the Babylonians had no means of calculating the lunar parallax, which has a considerable influence on the magnitude of a solar eclipse.

I suppose that at the time of the lunar eclipses of −668 and −567 lunar tables were not yet available. At the time of the solar eclipse of −424 they were available, but we do not know whether these tables were used for the prediction of solar eclipses.

The eclipse of THALES

In the 'Histories' of HERODOTOS I 74 an account is given of an eclipse which was predicted by THALES for the very year in which it actually took place. The account runs thus:

I 74. After this there was war between the Lydians and the Medes for five

years; each won many victories over the other, and once they fought a battle by
night. They were still warring with equal success, when it chanced, at an encounter which happened in the sixth year, that during the battle the day was suddenly turned to night. Thales of Miletus had foretold this loss of daylight to the
Ionians, predicting it for the year in which the change did indeed happen. So
when the Lydians and Medes saw the day turned to night they ceased from
fighting, and both were the more zealous to make peace.

Modern calculations show that the most probable date of the eclipse is May 28, −584.
This solar eclipse was total at the place of the battle in Northern Turkey.

HERODOTOS wrote more than a century after the event, but XENOPHANES, who lived
only half a century after Thales, also knew about this prediction. It is recorded that
XENOPHANES 'admired THALES for his prediction'. Thus it seems to me that the forecast
is well attested.

At this time, Greek methods for predicting eclipses were not available, but the Babylonians did predict lunar and solar eclipses even much earlier. Therefore it seems reasonable to suppose that THALES used Babylonian methods.

In the preceding section three prediction methods were described. The third method,
by means of tables, was hardly available at the time of THALES. The second method, by
means of periods, would lead to a prediction of an eclipse at the end of a certain month,
at New Moon. Now a curious feature about the forecast of THALES was that it was given
not for a certain date, but for a certain *year*. How is it possible to predict an eclipse for a
certain year?

The following solution to this problem was proposed by M. SCHRAMM in lectures given
at Zurich University in 1965.

SCHRAMM's first point is political. He noted that it was very important for kings and
generals to know beforehand that in a certain year or years no eclipse was to be expected.
We have seen from the story of HERODOTOS that a whole military enterprise was upset
by an eclipse: the leaders were forced to make peace because the soldiers were scared.
Another famous example is that of XERXES, whose march to Greece came to a stop
because of an eclipse. The story is told by HERODOTOS VII 37:

The army then wintered, and at the beginning of spring was ready and set
forth from Sardis to march to Abydos. When they had set forth, the sun left his
place in the heaven and was unseen, albeit the sky was without clouds and very
clear, and the day was turned into night. When Xerxes saw and took note of
that, he was moved to think upon it, and asked the Magians what the vision
might signify. They declared to him, that the god was forecasting the Greeks
the vanishing of their cities; for the sun (they said) was the forecaster of the
Greeks, as the moon was theirs. Xerxes rejoiced exceedingly to hear that, and
kept on his march.

Now is it possible to make a prediction that in a certain year eclipses can or cannot be expected?

Let us first consider lunar eclipses. We have seen that they occur in sequences of two, three, four or even five eclipses, the duration of such a sequence being $2\frac{1}{2}$ years at most. After each sequence there is a period of one or two years during which no lunar eclipse is possible, because during this period the Full Moon is always too far from the node.

Solar eclipses are less frequent than lunar ones and show much less regularity, but still it is true that every four years there is a period of one or two years during which no solar eclipse is possible, because the New Moon is too far from the node during such a period. The argument is just the same for New Moon as for Full Moon. It is true that there are many disturbing circumstances such as the lunar parallax which influence the occurrence of Solar Eclipses, but still: if the moon is too far from the ecliptic at the time of New Moon, no solar eclipse is possible.

Summing up, we see that there are periods of one or two years during which no solar eclipse is possible, and in between there are periods of 2 or $2\frac{1}{2}$ years during which solar eclipses are more frequent. In the middle part of such a period solar eclipses are even more probable than at the beginning or end. Therefore, if THALES knew of these periods, he might have told his Delian friends: 'Take care, in this year it is well possible that the sun will be eclipsed'. In fact this happened, and THALES was afterwards praised for his prediction[1]).

THE ZODIAC

We have seen in the preceding chapter, that at the end of the Assyrian period the Babylonian and Assyrian scribes had not yet divided the zodiacal circle into 12 zodiacal signs. Still, at that time this division must have been 'in the wind'. The Babylonians had divided the year into 12 solar months of equal duration, and they had also divided the zodiacal circle into 4 parts corresponding to 4 seasons of 3 months each, such that the sun dwelt just 3 months in every part. What was more natural than to divide each of the 4 parts of the circle into 3 sections such that the sun dwells just 1 month in every section? Thus, one would have 12 sections of the zodiacal circle corresponding to the 12 months of the solar year.

---

[1]) SCHRAMM also noted that periods of one or two years with lunar eclipses alternate with periods, just $23\frac{1}{2}$ months later, in which solar eclipses are possible. In −586 two total lunar eclipses, in January and July, were visible at Miletus. If Thales observed these, he might predict the possibility of solar eclipses, say between the summer of −585 and the summer of −584.

Perhaps in the New-Babylonian, but certainly in the Persian period this division of the circle into 12 'zodiacal signs' of equal length was actually carried out. The names of the signs are enumerated in a text from Uruk published by THUREAU-DANGIN (Tablettes d'Uruk, No. 14):

LU.ḪUN.GA	= Aries
MUL	= Taurus
MASH	= Gemini
NANGAR	= Cancer
UR.A	= Leo
AB.SIN	= Virgo
zi-ba-ni-tu	= Libra
GIR.TAB	= Scorpio
PA	= Sagittarius
SUḪUR	= Capricornus
GU	= Aquarius
zib	= Pisces

The signs of the zodiac are named after constellations in their sector, so that it is often hard to tell whether, for example, MUL is intended to mean the sign Taurus or the constellation Pleiades. Strict attention must be paid to the formulation. For example, if in a table of Venus observations (PINCHES-SACHS, Late Babyl.astr.texts, No. 1387) we read that in the year −445 the evening setting of Venus took place 'in the end of Pisces' *(ina til kun-me)*, this must mean the zodiacal sign and not the constellation Pisces, in agreement with the later terminology. When, however, the same text reports that in the year −454 the evening rising of Venus took place 'behind Praesepe', this must mean the group of stars Praesepe and not the sign of Cancer which is denoted by the same name.

A diary, VAT 4924 from the year −418, uses both the signs and the constellations of the zodiac for determining the position of planets. As A. SACHS[1] remarked, the text says in four places that planets stand 'before' or 'behind' a certain zodiacal constellation. On the other hand, there are places in the same text where only the zodiacal signs can be meant, e.g.:

Nisannu: Jupiter and Venus in the beginning of Gemini.
Adaru II: Jupiter in the beginning of Cancer[2].

---

[1]) In O. NEUGEBAUER, The Exact Sciences in Antiquity, 2nd ed., p. 140.
[2]) See B. L. VAN DER WAERDEN, History of the Zodiac, Archiv f. Orientforschung *16*, p. 220 (1953).

The boundaries of the signs

The Greek astronomers used to identify the first point of Aries with the vernal point, i.e. with one of the two intersections of the ecliptic with the equator. The Babylonian astronomers and some Greek astrologers followed a different practice, relating the origins of the signs not to the vernal point, but to the fixed stars. This is quite clear from cuneiform lunar tables in which the vernal point is put at 10° or 8° of Aries, but never at 0° Aries.

The reasons which induced the Babylonians to relate the signs to the fixed stars are not hard to find. First, the stars are easy to observe, while the equinoxes are not. Second, the zodiacal signs derive their names from constellations in them. They correspond approximately to the months of the year (whence the number 12 and the division of each sign into 30 degrees, corresponding to the 30 days of the month), but this approximate requirement is not as yet sufficient to fix them accurately. They are more closely determined by the two following requirements: first, the signs must be of equal length, and second, they must enclose the constellations after which they are named. How strong this requirement is can be seen in the case of the star Spica (AB.SIN). The Babylonian sign Virgo is named after this star, but in the Babylonian division of the ecliptic Spica is right at the end of Virgo at 28° or 29°. A small backward displacement of the boundaries — and the star AB.SIN would no longer be within the sign AB.SIN.

The division of the zodiac into 12 signs of 30 degrees each is essential for mathematical astronomy. Without such a system of coordinates no lunar or planetary tables are possible. Now AABOE and SACHS[1]) recently discovered a lunar table calculated for the year 475 B.C. Hence the division of the zodiac into 12 signs of equal length must have existed at that time. There are even reasons to suppose that it was known and used for astrological predictions even earlier, in the 6th century, in the time of NEBUCHADNEZZAR. These reasons will be explained in the next chapter.

Mathematical astronomy

The greatest achievement of Babylonian astronomy during the Persian reign was the development of mathematical methods for the calculation of solar, lunar and planetary positions, of eclipses and of other celestial phenomena. An account of these methods will be given in Chapters 6 and 7. The next Chapter 5 deals with the religious background of astronomy and its relation to astrology.

---

[1]) ASGER AABOE and ABRAHAM SACHS: Two Lunar Texts of the Achaemenid Period from Babylon. Centaurus *14*, p. 1 (1969).

CHAPTER V

COSMIC RELIGION, ASTROLOGY AND ASTRONOMY

SUMMARY OF THIS CHAPTER

In the evolution of Babylonian astronomy we may distinguish three major stages:

1. *Astronomy of* ^{mul}APIN, late Assyrian reign (1000-612 B.C.). The main achievements of this period are:
   a) Detailed study of the fixed stars, their risings, culminations, and settings.
   b) Calculation of the duration of daylight and the rising and setting of the moon by 'linear methods'.
   c) Recognition of the zodiac as path of the Moon, the Sun and the planets. Zodiacal constellations. Position of the zodiac with respect to the zones of Enlil, Anu and Ea. The seasons of the year.
   d) Systematic observation and prediction of eclipses.

2. *Zodiacal Astronomy*, Chaldaean reign (612-539 B.C.). Main features:
   a) Division of the Zodiac into 12 signs of 30 degrees each.
   b) Systematic observation of the Moon and the planets, their positions with respect to the fixed stars, their first and last visibility, stationary points, conjunctions etc.

3. *Mathematical Astronomy*, Persian reign (539-331 B.C.). The most important achievements of this period are
   a) Determination of accurate periods for the Sun, the Moon and the planets (see Chapter 4).
   b) Calculation of the motion of the Sun, the Moon and the planets, of eclipse magnitudes and other lunar and planetary phenomena. These calculations were based upon an admirable mathematical theory, which will be explained in Chapters 6 and 7.

These three major steps in the evolution of astronomy are closely related to three distinct types of astrology, viz.

1. *Omen Astrology*. This is the type of astrology we find in the omen series Enuma Anu Enlil and in the reports of the royal Assyrian astrologers. Omen Astrology is not concerned with birth horoscopes and it does not use zodiacal signs. For the application to Omen Astrology the astronomy of ^{mul}APIN is perfectly sufficient.

2. *Primitive Zodiacal Astrology*. This kind of astrology is known from texts ascribed to 'Orpheus' and 'Zoroaster', which will be discussed later in this chapter. There are some reasons to assume that this type of astrology was already in use under the Chaldaean reign. Essential for this kind of astrology is the use of the twelve zodiacal signs, but it has nothing to do with birth horoscopes. For its application, systematic observations of the kind mentioned under 2 b) are necessary, but a mathematical theory of planetary motion is not needed. Therefore, astronomy of type 2 seems to be connected with astrology of type 2.

3. *Horoscopic Astrology*. This is the kind of astrology we all know. It makes use of zodiacal signs and of birth horoscopes. It originated in the Persian reign. The mathematical tools necessary for casting horoscopes are just the methods of Mathematical Astronomy. Therefore, Type 3 Astronomy and Type 3 Astrology belong together: the latter cannot exist without the former.

Connections between religion and astrology

In Chapter 2, I have already pointed out that the fundamental idea of astrology is a religious idea. The stars were supposed to influence our fate, because they were regarded as mighty gods.

We have just seen that three kinds of astrology, very different in character, succeeded each other. The main purpose of this chapter is, to show that these three types of astrology were related to contemporary religious currents. More precisely, there are close connections

1) between Omen Astrology and Old-Babylonian polytheism,

2) between Primitive Zodiacal Astrology and Zervanism, the fatalistic worship of Infinite Time,

3) between Horoscopic Astrology and Zoroastrism, the religion of ZARATHUSTRA.

We shall first investigate the religious currents which manifested themselves in the Old-Babylonian and Persian Empires and in Greece between −700 and −300. Next we shall consider the various types of astrology connected with these new religions. Finally we shall show that each of these types of astrology required a quite definite kind of astronomy. Thus, our excursion into the history of religion and astrology will shed more light upon the evolution of scientific astronomy.

TRADITION AND NEW RELIGIOUS CURRENTS

If we compare the religious attitude of the period before −700 with the period after −300, we detect a tremendous difference. No matter whether we direct our attention to

Greece, Egypt or Asia, the differences are everywhere of the same kind. The triumphal advance of cosmic religion and its attendant astrology is an international phenomenon.

The polytheism of earlier times

In what follows, we shall use the words 'heaven' and 'sky' indiscriminately. For the Persians, Greeks and Romans there is no distinction between the two: heaven is the place where the Sun, the Moon and the other celestial gods are.

The great Gods of the Greeks dwelt on mount Olympus, not in heaven. Helios (the Sun), Selene (the Moon) and Uranos (the Sky) are numbered among the gods, but they are not the greatest of them. The Thunderer, Zeus, may originally have been a sky god, but in classical times he was not identified either with the sky or with the universe. According to the Theogony of HESIODOS (about −700) his reign began long after the creation of the earth and the sky.

A similar polytheism is to be found in Babylon. It is true that from ancient times the stars were worshipped as 'gods of the night', and that Sun, Moon and Venus had the standing of a trinity of great gods. The sky god Anu was likewise held in high repute, but the greatest god, the creator, was Marduk, the state god of Babylon.

In Egypt IKHNATON (−1370) proclaimed the sun god Aton as the only god, but after his death the old polytheism was reintroduced. In this polytheistic system there was a sun god, a moon god and a sky goddess; Sothis = Sirius was also worshipped, but the sky gods were not the highest nor the mightiest gods.

New religious currents

After 600 B.C. we can observe the invasion of the Greek world by new ideas and the onset of doubts about the traditional gods. The new ideas induced powerful reactions, such as the condemnation of ANAXAGORAS for atheism and the execution of SOKRATES for 'worship of new gods'.

In the Persian kingdom and in Egypt too there were serious religious crises, leading to violent conflict. KAMBYSES derided the cult of Apis by the Egyptian priests (HERODOTOS III 28). XERXES killed the high priest of MARDUK and confiscated the golden statue of the god (HERODOTOS I 183). He also destroyed a place of worship and commanded that thenceforth only Ahura Mazda was to be honoured in that place.

Unfortunately, our information about all these events is limited to reports of the events themselves: the interplay between political and religious motives is not always clear. It is quite possible that political motivation was the main driving force behind the trial of ANAXAGORAS or the actions of XERXES. Still, the spread of the worship of Ahura Mazda under DARIUS and XERXES is an indubitable fact, clearly attested by their own

inscriptions, some of which will be quoted below. The Persian kings promoted everywhere in their empire the cult of the sky god and monotheism: examples of this will be
found below.

We are better informed about the time after 400 B.C., because we have the dialogues
of PLATON and other Greek sources. We see how the flood of Cosmic Religion sweeps
over the Greek world. The belief that the soul is immortal and has its home in the sky
takes ever greater hold. PLATON is the great prophet of the new faith[1]). The Stoic KLE-
ANTHES (3rd century B.C.) described the sun as animate fire and as the leading power in
the cosmos. The Stoics CHRYSIPPOS and POSEIDONIOS (2nd and 1st centuries B.C.)
taught, as PLATON did, that the cosmos is an animate, rational, living being and that our
soul takes part in the cosmos[2]).

Shortly after 300 B.C. astrology began its triumphal procession through the ancient
world. In the Ptolemaeic era it advanced from Babylonia and Syria to Egypt. In 139 B.C.
astrology already had so many adherents in Rome that an edict was passed expelling
from Rome the astrologers together with the worshippers of Jupiter Sabazios[3]). By the
time of Augustus and even earlier the walls and ceilings of Egyptian temples were covered
with pictures of the starry sky, the zodiac and the star gods (Plates 7 and 8). The doctrine
of the inescapability of Fate and the eternal recurrence of all things became an obsession.
Mithras, the Iranian sun god, was worshipped throughout the Roman empire as Sol
invictus and as the Saviour of Mankind. Other mystery religions too, such as that of Isis,
were everywhere winning adherents[4]). Religions were amalgamated, old myths were
reinterpreted. The Gnosis taught that the powers of the Cosmos are malevolent and that
the Soul can free itself from them and become one with the highest god, who is pure
spirit[5]). It was in this atmosphere that the Christian religion of salvation originated.

We shall now attempt to unravel the first beginnings of this complex web. The Babylonian and Egyptian texts for the period from − 700 to − 300 desert us almost completely,
so we must rely principally on Persian and Greek sources.

Of the Persian texts the most important are the inscriptions of the Persian kings and the
Avesta, the holy scripture of the Zoroastrians. In the Avesta we find in particular the
Gathas or hymns of ZARATHUSTRA. Apart from these ancient texts, we shall also, with
necessary caution, adduce later Pahlevi writings such as the Bundahishn.

[1]) PLATON: Phaidon, Timaios, Laws. FESTUGIÈRE, La révélation d'Hermès II: Le dieu cosmique (Paris, 1949).
[2]) For the teachings of the Stoics about the Gods and the Cosmos see principally CICERO: De natura deo-
rum II. Also DIOGENES LAERTIOS: Lives of the Philosophers VII 134—149. On POSEIDONIOS see
K. REINHARDT: Kosmos und Sympathie.
[3]) F. H. CRAMER, Astrology in Roman Law and Politics (Amer. Phil. Soc., Philadelphia, 1954) p. 58.
[4]) F. CUMONT, Les religions orientales dans le paganisme romain, Paris, 1929 (3rd edition).
[5]) H. JONAS: Gnosis und spätantiker Geist, Göttingen, Vandenhoeck, 1954 (2nd edition). FESTUGIÈRE:
La révélation d'Hermès Trismégiste III: Les doctrines de l'âme (1953); IV: Le dieu inconnu et la gnose
(1954); Gabalda et Cie., Paris.

Plate 15. Sacrifice to an astral god. Illustration in an Arab manuscript Bodleian Or. 133 in Oxford, Folio 29. This picture shows that even in the Islam Cosmic Religion still had a mighty influence. See also P. CHWOLSON: Die Ssabier und der Ssabismus (St. Petersburg 1856, reprinted by Oriental Press, Amsterdam 1965). Photo Bodleian Library, Oxford.

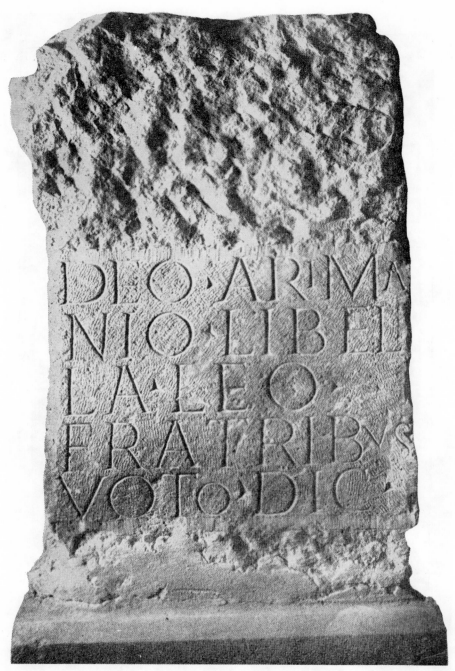

Plate 16. Inscription from a sanctuary of Mithras at Altofen near Budapest (M. J. VERMASEREN, Corpus inscript. et mon. rel. Mithriacae II, Fig. 461). From the words DEO ARIMANIO we may conclude that the followers of Mithras in the Roman Empire worshipped the evil spirit Ahriman (Greek: Areimanios) as a god, just as the Magi did according to PLUTARCHOS (Isis and Osiris 369 E, Loeb Classical Library 306, p. 113). This worship of two gods, Ormuzd and Ahriman, is compatible with Zervanism, but not with orthodox Zoroastrianism.

THE RELIGION OF ZARATHUSTRA

The polytheism of the Aryan peoples is known from very old sources. When the Mitanni king MATTIWAZA, who reigned in Asia Minor about −1400, concluded a treaty with the Hittite king SHUPPILULIAMA, he called as witnesses the great gods '*Mitra, Uruna, Indara* and *Nashatia*'. The same gods were worshipped in India: their Sanskrit names are *Mitra, Varuna, Indra* and the *Nasatyas*. Among the Persians too, whose language is closely related to Sanskrit, we find the names *Mithra, Indra* and *Nahaithya*[1]).

The reform of ZARATHUSTRA considerably reduced this pantheon. Ahura Mazda was raised high above all the other gods. Indra, Nahaithya and many other 'Daevas' were condemned. The cult of Mithras was also opposed at first, but later Mithras was taken up into the Pantheon of the Zoroastrians.

In classical and hellenistic times we find four forms of Persian religion.

1) *The orthodox Zoroastrianism* worships Ahura Mazda as the highest god, but it also venerates Fire, Earth, Moon, Mithras etc.

2) A later variety is the '*religion of two gods*', which PLUTARCHOS in 'Isis and Osiris' describes as the cult of the Magi[2]). Besides Ormuzd the Magi worshipped the evil spirit Ahriman and brought him offerings, which was strictly forbidden to orthodox Zoro-astrians.

3) *Zervanism* considers the God of Time *Zervan* or *Zurvan* as father of the twins Ormuzd and Ahriman and as creator of all things. In late antiquity Zervanism was widespread in Cilicia and Syria among the Magi; it is also traceable in the Sassanid kingdom[3]).

4) Finally the *Mithras cult* must be mentioned. The god Mithra or Mithras was at all times a mighty rival of Ahura Mazda. In Roman times his cult spread from Cilicia over all the Roman empire.

Only one of these four forms of religion is well known from authentic sources, namely orthodox Zoroastrianism. It is therefore in this direction that we shall first turn.

The Gathas of the Avesta

The oldest part of the Avesta is formed by the Gathas, the Hyms of ZARATHUSTRA. The Gathas have a very personal, unmistakeable style: the unanimous opinion of all commentators ascribes them to ZARATHUSTRA himself.

The first expert translation of the Gathas was made by C. BARTHOLOMAE: Die Gathas

---

[1]) See J. DUCHESNE-GUILLEMIN: La religion de l'Iran ancien (Presses Universitaires, Paris 1962).
[2]) See especially K. BIDEZ et F. CUMONT: Les mages hellénisés, Paris 1938.
[3]) R. C. ZAEHNER: Zurvan, a Zoroastrian Dilemma. Oxford, Clarendon Press 1955.

des Avesta, Strassburg 1905. An interpretation deviating in many points from that of Bartholomae was given by H. S. NYBERG: 'Die Religionen des alten Iran' (Leipzig, 1938) to be cited as NYBERG, Religionen. A completely different interpretation can be found in E. HERZFELD's two-volume work 'Zoroaster and his World' (Princeton Univ. Press 1947). The Gathas are indeed very difficult. New translations into French and German are offered by:

> J. DUCHESNE-GUILLEMIN: Zoroastre, Paris 1948.
> H. HUMBACH: Die Gathas des Zarathustra, Heidelberg 1959.
> W. HINZ: Zarathustra, Stuttgart 1961.

In the following review we shall confine ourselves to a few principal points that are relevant to the present enquiry and that can be traced back to the Gathas without dispute. Naturally, I also have an opinion on the contested points; thus I hold with HERZFELD and ALTHEIM[1]) that ZARATHUSTRA probably lived in the 6th century B.C., but that does not affect the following discussion.

The ethics of ZARATHUSTRA

The principal purpose of ZARATHUSTRA is ethical. The soul is placed before a choice between Good and Evil, between Truth and Falsehood. If it chooses the Good, it will be rewarded on the last day by the 'Wise Lord' Ahura Mazda; but if it chooses the Evil, it will at the end be judged by fire. The Daevas, i.e. the evil gods, from whom mankind should turn away, have chosen the 'most evil design' and the 'desire for murder'[2]).

The meaning of the expression 'desire for murder' requires some elucidation. It does not mean common murder or war, for it is Daevas, Gods, who have chosen this desire. In all probability the expression refers to the slaying of the Bull that was customary in the cult of Mithras. In the famous 'Gatha of the Bull' (Yasna 29) ZARATHUSTRA declares that Ahura Mazda appointed him as protector of the bull. He most emphatically forbids his followers to slay bulls.

Similarly, PYTHAGORAS, EMPEDOCLES and the later Pythagoreans emphatically condemned the sacrifice of cattle[3]). Hence at about the same period (before 500 B.C.) there were similar religious tendencies in evidence in the Persian empire and in the Greek world, tendencies to depart from the ancient tradition of blood offerings and to develop religious doctrines, in which the notions *good* and *bad* play a central role.

---

[1]) F. ALTHEIM und R. STIEHL: *Supplementum Aramaicum* (Grimm, Baden-Baden 1957). Appendix: Das Jahr Zarathustras, p. 21.

[2]) These words appear in Yasna 30, Strophe 6. The Gathas form Sections 28—34, 43—51 and 53 of the Yasna in the Avesta: they will therefore be cited as 'Yasna 28' etc.

[3]) See DIELS, Fragmente der Vorsokratiker, EMPEDOKLES B 128, 136, 137. OVIDIUS, Metamorphoses XV, 75—142. Further evidence in A. ROSTAGNI, Il Verbo di Pitagora, Torino 1924.

The judgement by fire at the end of time

In his great visionary hymn (Yasna 43) ZARATHUSTRA connects the creation of life with the last ordeal, when Ahura Mazda judges Good and Evil:

> As beneficient I recognized thee, O Mazda Ahura, when I saw thee as the first at the birth of the world, when thoud didst make deeds and words yield their reward, an evil for evil, a good reward for good, by thy power at the last turning-point of the creation[1]).

According to the immediately preceding strophe 4 the distribution of the rewards to the good and evil men will take place 'through the heat of thy fire, mighty in justice'. The judgement by fire is impressively described in another hymn of ZARATHUSTRA (Yasna 34, Strophe 4):

> Then thy fire, O Ahura, mighty through justice, we desire to be for the faithful man manifestly pleasant, O Mazda, but for the hostile man visibly painful, according to the sign of thy hand.

ZARATHUSTRA's eschatology made a very deep impression. In the writings of the stoics, in the gnostic book 'Pistis Sophia', in apocryphal apocalypses, in the middle Persian treatise Bundahishn, everywhere we find the judgment by fire, with many gruesome details. Thus in the Bundahishn we read that a river of molten metal burns up the evil with a stench, but that the good go about therein as in warm milk. In the 'Testament of Isaak' it is said that the fire is intelligent and does the righteous no harm, but burns up the evil with a great stench[2]).

The idea of the judgement by fire and of 'wise fire' reached Greece very early. HERAKLEITOS of Ephesus (about 500 B.C.) says in a passage perserved in verbatim quotation: 'Fire in its advance will judge and convict all things'. He also says that the Fire is 'gifted with reason and cause of the whole world government'[3]).

HERAKLEITOS' judgement by fire probably goes back to Iranian ideas; but it also contains a new element. In the Avesta the fire annihilates only the evil, not the earth and certainly not the whole universe. ZARATHUSTRA's outlook is on the human, not the cosmic, level. But in HERAKLEITOS the event is cosmic. Further, the last judgement in the Avesta is *unique*: afterwards there is only eternal bliss for the righteous. But in HERAKLEITOS the conflagration is a *recurrent* event:

---

[1]) Yasna 43, Strophe 5, translated into English from the German translations of BARTHOLOMAE, NYBERG, and HUMBACH, making use of the English translation of M. W. SMITH: Studies in the Syntax of the Gathas, Univ. of Pennsylvania Dissertation 1929.

[2]) For further testimonies see C. M. EDSMAN: *Ignis divinus*, Skrifter Vetensk.-Soc. Lund 34 (1949).

[3]) H. DIELS, *Fragmente der Vorsokratiker*, HERAKLEITOS B 63—66.

This cosmos, the same for all, was not made by god or man, but ever was and is and shall be, ever-living fire, being kindled and quenched in due measure.

HERAKLEITOS' fire is wise and ever living, i.e. divine. The judging, divine fire is good Zoroastrian doctrine, but the idea of universal conflagration and of the periodic recurrence are additions. These ideas are Babylonian, as we have seen in Chapter 4. BEROSSOS, the priest of Bel, who founded an astronomical school on the isle of Kos around 300 B.C., reported in his 'Babyloniaka' on the doctrine of periodic catastrophes (deluge and universal conflagration) in connection with the chronology of the Babylonian kings[1]).

We must therefore assume that the Iranian idea of the judgement by fire was transmitted to Babylon before the end of the sixth century and was there combined with old Babylonian ideas about deluge and world periods. It was from Babylon that the doctrine of periodically recurrent cosmic fire catastrophes was transmitted to Greece.

Greek tradition knows of a man who travelled to Egypt and Babylon at just this time in the sixth century and who then lived in Greece and South Italy as a religious prophet and sage, namely PYTHAGORAS. If it was in fact he who was the intermediate, we should expect to find traces of the same doctrine in the Pythagorean tradition. This expectation is thrice fulfilled.

First, we have a fragment of DIKAIARCHOS, which has already been quoted in Chapter 4 in the section on 'The Great Year': 'PYTHAGORAS says that all things that have once happened will recur after certain periods'.

Second, EUDEMOS, a pupil of ARISTOTELES, testifies that, according to the teachings of the Pythagoreans, 'everything recurs in conformity to number'. The full text of his statement was given in Chapter 4.

Thirdly, there is a doxographical tradition about the Pythagorean HIPPASOS, a contemporary of HERAKLEITOS. AETIOS reports:

> HERAKLEITOS and HIPPASOS say that the beginning of everything is fire.
> For from fire the universe sprang and in fire will the universe end, so they say.
>
> (DIELS, Fragmente der Vorsokratiker, Herakleitos A 5)

SIMPLIKIOS reports more fully:

> HIPPASOS of Metapontum and HERAKLEITOS of Ephesos also say, that the One is in motion and limited; yet they make fire the beginning and would have all else springing from fire . . . and in fire do they dissolve all things again: . . . for all is exchanged for fire, says HERAKLEITOS. This latter also assumes an order and a finite time for the change of the cosmos according to some destined necessity.
>
> (DIELS, Fragmente der Vorsokratiker, HERAKLEITOS A 5)

---

[1]) See P. SCHNABEL: *Berossos* (Leipzig 1923).

According to DIELS, this report comes from THEOPHRASTOS' 'Opinions of the Physicists'. From the same source there is a report of DIOGENES LAERTIOS (VIII 84):

> HIPPASOS of Metapontum, likewise a Pythagorean, asserts that the time of the change of the cosmos is limited . . .

The expression 'finite time for the change of the cosmos' must refer to the 'Great Year'. This interpretation is confirmed by the fact that there is a tradition of a 'Great Year' in connection with both HERAKLEITOS and HIPPASOS.

HIPPASOS' Great Year was, according to CENSORINUS (De die natali XVIII 8) a relatively short period of 59 years. This 'great year' is obviously not a period of all the planets. However, Saturn and Jupiter return to nearly the same place in the sky after 59 years, and a 59-year period for Saturn is regularly used in the cuneiform texts.

CENSORINUS says that the Great Year of HERAKLEITOS contained 10 800 years, but AETIOS makes it 18 000 years. Both figures are divisible by 3 600; and 3 600 years make one Babylonian Sar. The origin of HERAKLEITOS' great year, as of the doctrine of recurrent cosmic conflagrations, may thus be presumed to be Babylonian.

The importance of the doctrine of cosmic catastrophes for our purposes is that we can in this case see clearly how an Iranian doctrine, which in itself has nothing to do with astrology, is combined in Babylon with astrological fatalism and astronomy. The judging fire stems from Iran, the deluge and period calculation from Babylon. The combination of all these elements gave rise to the doctrine of the great year with universal winter and summer, with catastrophe by fire and by deluge. In this case we can also follow the transmission of the doctrine to Greece and its further development there.

In other cases, where the chain of ideas cannot be followed so well, we may assume a similar development. The Persians and Magi reached Babylon before the end of the sixth century B.C. and there they became acquainted with Babylonian astrology and astronomy[1]. From this contact of two cultures something new sprang: an astrological doctrine of fate, closely related to science on the one hand and religion on the other, which spread from Babylon over the whole ancient world.

THE SKY-GOD

The second volume of A. J. FESTUGIÈRE's great work on Hermes Trismegistos[2]) bears the title: Le dieu cosmique. In this volume FESTUGIÈRE followed the development of the

---

[1]) J. BIDEZ et F. CUMONT: Mages hellénisés I, Paris 1938.
[2]) A. J. FESTUGIÈRE: La révélation d'Hermès Trismégiste (Paris, Gabalda et Cie). I: L'astrologie et les sciences occultes (1950). II: Le dieu cosmique (1949). III: Les doctrines de l'âme (1953). IV: Le dieu inconnu et la gnose (1954). To be cited as: FESTUGIÈRE I, II, III, IV.

doctrine of the cosmic god from PLATON and XENOPHON right up to late Hellenistic and Roman times. But we can go further back in time, in Greece to the Orphic sect and the Pythagoreans, in Persia at least to ZARATHUSTRA.

Ahura Mazda as the highest god

Opinions differ on the question whether ZARATHUSTRA's teaching is to be described as monotheism; but this much is certainly clear, that ZARATHUSTRA elevated his god Ahura Mazda high above all others.

The great inscription of DARIUS at Naksh i Rustam begins as follows:

> A Great God is Ahuramazda, who created the earth here, who created the sky there, who created man, who created happiness for men, who made DARIUS to be king, the one to be king over many.

Ahura Mazda is thus, according to DARIUS, the creator. He is the highest, but not the only, god. In an inscription from Persepolis we read:

> The great Ahura Mazda, the greatest of the gods, made DARIUS to be king.

The picture which HERODOTOS (I, 131) paints of the Persian religion agrees well with these inscriptions:

> As to the usages of the Persians, I know them to be these. It is not their custom to make and set up statues and temples and altars, but those who make such they deem foolish, as I suppose, because they never believed the gods, as do the Greeks, to be in the likeness of men; but they call the whole circle of heaven Zeus, and to him they offer sacrifice on the highest peaks of the mountains. They sacrifice also to the sun and moon and earth and fire and water and winds.

Many of the gods of the Avesta are abstract, spiritual beings such as Vohu Mana (good purpose), Daena (wisdom or religion), Haurvatat (health), Ameretat (immortality), which cannot easily be imagined in human shape. This shows the accuracy of HERODOTOS' observation. The highest god, whom he calls Zeus, can only be Ahura Mazda; for in the inscriptions of the kings DARIUS and XERXES Ahura Mazda is the highest god, and HERODOTOS lived not much later than XERXES. The other gods named by HERODOTOS almost all appear in the Avesta as well: fire (Atar), earth (Armaiti), wind (Vata) and the waters, which are extolled in Yasna 38 as 'living mother'.

Syncretism and monotheism

The religious policy of the Persian kings followed two main lines. On the one hand the subject peoples were allowed to keep their gods and priests, so far as they did not call in question the authority of the Great King and the highest god. On the other, monotheism was everywhere promoted, and the highest god of the people in question was always identified with the Persian sky-god.

When CYRUS conquered Babylon, he took the right hand of the Marduk statue, thereby winning the god's recognition of him as king of Babylon. DARIUS too left Babylonian religion in peace. But when the city of Babylon revolted against XERXES, he confiscated the treasury of Marduk and the golden statue and killed the high priest (HERODOTOS I, 183). Wherever polytheistic religion came into conflict with imperial policy, it was mercilessly persecuted.

In an inscription of XERXES there is a passage which illustrates his religious policy well. XERXES says:

> Within these lands was a place, where formerly the Daevas were worshiped. Following Ahuramazda's will I overthrew the Daeva nest and commanded: The Daevas you shall not worship. Where formerly the Daevas were worshiped, there I worshiped Ahuramazda and the holy Arta.

NYBERG suggests that XERXES here refers to the events in the temple of Marduk. But HERZFELD is more probably correct in saying that the reference is to the pre-zoroastrian Persian gods, as it is in the Avesta. Be that as it may, at any rate the monotheistic tendency of the inscription is clear. Instead of many gods only one shall be worshipped in future, says XERXES.

The contribution made by the Persian kings to the advance of Jewish monotheism is generally known. In 538 B.C. CYRUS permitted the Jews to return to Jerusalem. His edict is reproduced in the Book of Ezrah, Chapter I:

> Thus saith KORES, king of Persia, The Lord God of heaven hath given me all the kingdoms of the earth; and he hath charged me to build him an house at Jerusalem, which is in Judah.

This KORES is CYRUS, the founder of the Persian empire. EZRAH was a royal scribe in the service of ARTAXERXES I. I assume that the edict of which CYRUS 'made a proclamation throughout his kingdom' is correctly reproduced in the Book of EZRAH. Similar expressions to 'He hath given me all the kingdoms of the earth' are to be found in the inscriptions of the Persian kings. The name 'God of heaven' for the highest god agrees with HERODOTOS' statement: 'They call the whole circle of heaven Zeus'. We may safely conclude that CYRUS identified the Lord of the jews with the Persian sky-god.

The passage of HERODOTOS just quoted indicates that the Persians also indentified their sky-god with the Greek Zeus; for HERODOTOS' principle is, to reproduce faithfully what his informants tell him. In this case his informants were certain Persians. The identification of Zeus with Ahura Mazda is also found in an inscription of ANTIOCHOS I of Commagene (69-34 B.C.) from the east terrace of Mount Nemrud-Dagh[1]).

In all this the policy of the Persian kings comes out clearly: the promotion of monotheism and the identification of the principal alien gods with the Persian sky-god. Even as the whole earth is, or at least should be, subject to the Great King, so all gods are made subordinate to the sky-god. This is the doctrine proclaimed by DARIUS in his inscriptions.

Monotheistic tendencies in Greece

An Orphic saying which has come down to us in various forms reads as follows in its oldest formulation:

> Zeus was the First, Zeus the Last, Splendour of the Thunderbolt; Zeus is the Head, Zeus the middle, out of Zeus is all perfected. Zeus is the foundation of the earth and the starry sky.

The saying is is really old, because PLATON in his Laws (715E) alludes to this 'ancient logos'. The 'Orphic books' containing these sayings mostly originated in the sixth century. According to the unanimous verdict of all philologists, they contain oriental elements.

In the verses just quoted Zeus is extolled as the creator of the earth and the sky, just like Ahura Mazda in the inscription of DARIUS quoted earlier.

XENOPHANES, who left his home town Colophon in Asia Minor around 540 B.C. to travel around the cities of southern Italy as a singer, wrote:

> 'One god, the greatest among gods and men, neither in form like unto mortals nor in thought'.
> 'But without toil he swayeth all things by the thought of his mind.'
> 'Yes, and if oxen and horses or lions had hands, and could paint with their hands, and produce works of art as men do, horses would paint the forms of the gods like horses, and oxen like oxen, and make their bodies in the image of their several kinds.'[2])

The resemblance to Persian ideas is striking. 'Ahura Mazda, the greatest of the gods', writes DARIUS. 'The greatest among gods and men', writes XENOPHANES. Both

---

[1]) M. VERMASEREN: Corpus inscr. mon. relig. Mithriacae I (Nijhoff, The Hague 1960) p. 54.
[2]) Translation by BURNET: Early Greek Philosophy, Chapter II.

have a strong tendency towards monotheism, but both admit other gods as well, though exalting the one god high above them. It is ridiculous to think of gods in human form, so say both XENOPHANES and HERODOTOS' Persian informants.

The highest god of the Persians was, according to HERODOTOS, the sky, and XENOPHANES' one god was likewise heaven or the universe. This at any rate is the way PLATON and ARISTOTELES understood XENOPHANES' teaching, PLATON writes (Sophistes 242 d): 'The Eleatic school among us, from XENOPHANES on and beginning even earlier, speaks of that as being One which is called All'. And ARISTOTELES (Metaphyscis A 5, 968 b): 'XENOPHANES says, looking upon the whole heaven, that God is One'.

EMPEDOKLES expresses himself about the deity very much like XENOPHANES:

> Fragment 134: He boasts not a human head upon his body, two branches spring not from his shoulders, no feet has he, no swift knees, no shaggy parts; rather is he only a holy, unspeakable Mind, darting with swift thoughts over the whole cosmos.[1])

XENOPHANES and EMPEDOKLES both bring into prominence the contrast between corporeal, visible and tangible things and the realm of mind, which is to be encompassed only in thought. Both stress that the divine belongs whole and entire to the realm of mind. In PLATON's doctrine this idea was carried further. Here we shall only briefly note that the distinction between the realm of mind (menok) and the corporeal (getik) also plays an important part in the theology of the Zoroastrians[2]). The distinction is found as early as the Gathas (Yasna 28).

The cosmos as living being

In PLATON's dialogue 'Timaios' the cosmos is conceived as a living being with soul and understanding: 'God created a single visible living being, containing within itself all animals that are by nature akin to it' (Timaios 30 d).

In 'the Laws', PLATON developed further the concept of a living, reasonable, divine cosmos. A soul of blameless excellence, or perhaps several of that kind, direct the revolution of the sky (Laws 898 c and 899 b). PLATON here cautiously leaves two possibilities open: the traditional view, that sun, moon and the other heavenly bodies are gods, and the other that a *single* cosmic god governs them all. As we see from the Timaios, PLATON himself inclines towards the latter view.

FESTUGIÈRE has already remarked that PLATON was not the first to advocate the doctrine of the divine mind governing the cosmos. Many of the arguments for the thesis that

---

[1]) E. S. KIRK and J. E. RAVEN: *The presocratic philosophers* (Cambridge Univ. Press 1966), p. 349.
[2]) H. LOMMEL, *Die Religion Zarathustras*, Tübingen 1930. See also NYBERG, *Religionen*, p. 21.

the cosmos has a soul which appear in PLATON's dialogues appear in almost the same form in XENOPHON's 'Memorabilia Socratis'. Comparison of the Memorabilia with passages such as Phaidon 97b-98c, where PLATON makes SOKRATES bear a very personal testimony, give the definite impression that SOKRATES himself was of the opinion that the universe is ordered according to reason.

The Pythagoreans were of the same opinion. They assumed that, on account of their divine nature, the heavenly bodies moved with the most perfect of all motions: uniform circular motion. They also assumed that all motions in the sky are comprehensible in terms of number and harmonically ordered, or, in their own expression: 'The whole heaven is harmony and number'[1]).

It is to be assumed that PYTHAGORAS himself held the sky to have soul, but we have no direct proof of this. It is, however, certain that he believed in the immortality of the soul. Both these doctrines are closely related. No better expression for this relation is to be found than the words of ALKMAION, who was close to the earliest Pythagoreans. The relevant passage comes from ARISTOTELES, De anima A2, 405a:

> Alkmaion too seems to have held much the same view about the soul as these others; for he says that it is immortal owing to its similarity to the immortals; and it has this quality because it is always in motion; for everything divine is in continual motion — the sun, the moon, the stars and the whole heaven.

As proof that the stars have soul, PLATON adduces the fact that their motion follows mathematical laws. Thus astronomy provides a logical justification for his religious doctrine. He was anxious to prove that the belief in the star gods is a reasonable belief. But the origin of the cosmic mysticism which PLATON professes does not lie in science. People worshipped the sky, the sun and the moon as gods long before they had a scientific astronomy.

IMMORTALITY AND TRANSMIGRATION OF SOULS

The immortality of the soul in the Avesta

A central position in the ideas about death contained in the Avesta is occupied by the Cinvat bridge, the bridge to the sky over which the souls of the dead must pass. The top of the bridge is quite narrow like the edge of a sword. The evil souls fall from this

---

[1]) ARISTOTLE: Metaphysics A5, 986 A. Loeb Classical Library.

Plate 17. Mosaic showing the bird Phoenix rising from its ashes, a symbol for the immortality of the soul, from Daphne. The myth of Phoenix is also connected with the veneration of the divine Fire (see C. M. EDSMAN: Ignis divinus, Lund 1949). Photo Musée du Louvre, Paris.

narrow edge into hell, but for the righteous the bridge widens, so that they can pass over unharmed[1]).

The Cinvat bridge appears as early as the Gathas (Yasna 46 and 51). In the Vendidad there is a description of a young maiden conducting the soul over the Cinvat bridge and before Vohu Mana. Vohu Mana rises from his golden throne and greets the soul. Then the soul goes on to Ahura Mazda.

In another passage in the later Avesta (Vendidad VII 52) we read: 'When the souls of the pious pass over into the other world, the stars, moon and sun will bless them'. Hence we may conclude that the last home of the good souls was thought to be exactly where the stars, moon and sun are, i.e. in the sky.

All this has as yet nothing to do with astrology. In the Avesta the soul rises through the three regions Humat (good thought), Hukht (good words) and Hvarest (good action) to the light-world of Ahura Mazda. Similarly in the original version of the middle Persian book of Arda Viraf, the soul rises through these three regions. In the later versions, the three regions are replaced by the seven heavens or planetary spheres. In CICERO's Somnum Scipionis souls must pass through the seven planetary spheres in order to reach the sphere of the fixed stars, the abode of the blessed[2]). In Servius' commentary on Aeneid VI 714, the souls before birth go down through the planetary spheres, acquiring thereby from Saturn inertia, from Mars wrath, from Venus lust, from Mercury avarice, from Jupiter ambition. All that seems to be later astrological adaptation. BOUSSET assembled all the evidence about the soul's journey to the sky and came to the conclusion that it all began with a Persian myth, in which the planets played as yet no part.[3])

I believe that this Persian myth had a decisive influence on the rise of birth horoscopy. To explain this in more detail we must first consider the Greek evidence.

Greek ideas about the soul

HOMEROS supposes that the souls in Hades are no longer conscious. Only a few elect are 'removed' to the Elysian fields and so escape death[4]). The 'Homeric hymn' to Demeter, which was presumably composed about 600 B.C., promises those initiated into the mysteries a better lot after death, but it seems that this promise was not yet developed into a coherent doctrine of immortality.

The position changed completely in the 6th century, when the Orphic and Pythagorean teachers proclaimed their new, orient-inspired beliefs.

---

[1]) The evidence from the Gathas, Vendidad, Hadhôcht-Nask, Mênôke chrat, Bundahishn and Arda Viraf is assembled in NYBERG, *Religionen*, p. 180—186.
[2]) P. BOYANCÉ: Etudes sur le songe de Scipion.
[3]) W. BOUSSET: Die Himmelsreise der Seele, Archiv f. Religionswiss. 4 (1901), p. 136 and 229.
[4]) For the evidence the reader is referred once and for all to the fundamental work by ERWIN ROHDE: Psyche (1st ed. 1893, 4th ed. 1907).

Unfortunately, almost nothing is known of the doctrine taught by PYTHAGORAS himself to his disciples. DIKAIARCHOS tells us[1]:

> What he said to his associates, nobody can say for certain; for silence with them was of no ordinary kind. None the less the following became universally known: first he says that the soul is immortal; next, that it changes into other kinds of living beings; also that all events recur in certain cycles, and that nothing is really new; and finally, that all living things should be regarded as akin. PYTHAGORAS seems to have been the first to bring these things to Greece.
>   (KIRK and RAVEN, The presocratic philosophers, p. 221 and 223).

This dry summary is elaborated with more substance and form in later Pythagorean fragments. Thus the Pythagorean SOTION, Senaca's tutor, tells why PYTHAGORAS abstained from animal food:

> PYTHAGORAS held that all beings were interrelated, and that there was exchange between souls who transmigrated from one shape into another. If one may believe him, no soul perishes or ceases from its functions at all, except for a tiny interval — when it is being poured from one body into another. We may question at what time and after what seasons of change the soul returns to man when it has wandered through many a dwelling-place; but meanwhile, he (Pythagoras) made men fearful of guilt and parricide, since they might be, without knowing it, attacking the soul of a parent and injuring it with knife or with teeth — if, as is possible, a related soul be dwelling in this bit of flesh.
> (SENECA, Epistolae morales, Liber 18, Epistle 108; Loeb Classical Library, Vol. 77, p. 241).

In the final book XIV of his Metamorphoses OVIDIUS lets PYTHAGORAS give a splendid speech about abstinence from flesh, transmigration of souls and immortality. The genuine antiquity of the lines of thought developed by SOTION and OVIDIUS is attested by their appearance in the extant fragments of EMPEDOKLES[2]. There is also contemporary evidence (Xenophanes B 7 and Ion of Chios B 4 in DIELS, Fragmente der Vorsokr.) confirming that PYTHAGORAS taught the transmigration of souls.

PINDAROS, whose famous odes were composed between −500 and −450, held the same views about the transmigration, immortality and divinity of the soul as PYTHAGORAS, EMPEDOKLES, ALKMAION and the Orphic school. He says that, to expiate an

---

[1] DIKAIARCHOS was a contemporary of ARISTOTLE. He studied the history of the Pythagorean order. The fragment quoted comes from *Porphyrios*, Vita Pythag. 19.
[2] DIELS, Fragmente der Vorsokr., Empedokles B 117, 128, 136 and 137. Interpretation see especially A. ROSTAGNI, Il Verbo di Pitagora, Torino 1924.

'ancient sin', the soul must wander from one body to another. Only after the soul has completed its third faultless life on earth can Persephone release it from the cycle of rebirths[1]).

On the divinity and immortality of the soul PINDAROS says:

> While the body of all men is subject to over-mastering death, an image (eidolon) of life (aionos) remaineth alive, for it alone cometh from the gods. It sleepeth while the limbs are yet active; yet, to them that sleep, in many a dream it giveth presage of a decision of things delightful or doleful.

This 'eidolon' is obviously not what we to-day call soul. It is not that element in us which feels, thinks and makes resolutions; for 'it sleepeth while the limbs are yet active'. The eidolon plays no part in the activity of wakeful and fully conscious man. Nonetheless, we shall in future call the eidolon soul, because PINDAROS himself in other passages calls that which is left over from a dead man 'psyche'.

According to PINDAROS (Ol. II, 57-60), the soul after the death of the body comes into Hades, where 'One' passes stern sentence on the deeds of its life. The lot of the damned is 'unimaginable toil' in the depths of Tartaros. The good go to the subterranean seat of bliss, where the sun shines upon them when it sets on the earth, and where in flowery meadows they enjoy a life of noble ease.

Thus PINDAROS. We are here very far from the Homeric doctrine of the soul, but quite close to the teaching of the Gathas.

Similar ideas about the fate of the soul after death are found on the golden plates from Crete and Southern Italy. There is an English translation in W. K. C. GUTHRIE, Orpheus and Greek Religion (Methuen, London 2nd ed., 1952) p. 172-175. We see from these tablets that the Orphic and Pythagorean ideas about the immortality and heavenly origin of the soul met with agreement in widely scattered places.

Heaven as the Home of Souls

The Avesta teaches not only that good souls are rewarded after death, but also that they ascend to heaven. The same teaching is also found in Greece.

EPICHARMOS, the Sicilian comic poet, wrote: 'If you are good at heart, no ill will befall you in death. In the heights of heaven the spirit will live forever.' Similarly the inscription for the fallen of the battle of Potidea (−431) says: 'The aether will receive their souls, as the earth receives their bodies'.

---

[1]) See E. ROHDE, Psyche, p.502 (1st ed.). The page numbers of the first edition appear in the margin of the later editions.

PLATON too teaches that the soul is immortal, and that the righteous will enter heaven. His great dialogue, the 'Republic', ends with a grand myth, in which it is described how the souls of the dead come into a mysterious region, where there is one way down and one up: the righteous ascend to heaven, and the unrighteous descend beneath the earth, where they are punished tenfold for the evil they have done. All this is very strongly reminiscent of the judgement of Ahura-Mazda over souls and the Cinvat bridge, over which the righteous pass into heaven, while the unrighteous fall into the abyss. PLATON's 'daemonic meadow' where the unborn souls assemble to choose their lot recalls the flowering meadow in the Hadocht-Nask, where the dead meet their immortal souls[1]).

PLATON himself points to the oriental origin of this myth, by presenting it as the vision of a Pamphylian whose body lies as though dead on the field of battle, while his soul views the splendours of the cosmos and the fate of souls.

According to PLATON, the soul has its true home in heaven. In the dialogue Phaidros SOKRATES speaks ecstatically and says

> Soul, considered collectively, has the care of all that is soulless, and it traverses the whole heaven, appearing sometimes in one form and sometimes in another. Now when it is perfect and fully winged, it mounts upward and governs the whole world; but the soul which has lost its wings is borne along until it gets hold of someting solid, when it settles down, taking upon itself an earthly body, which seems to be selfmoving, because of the power of the soul within it. The whole, compounded of body and soul, is called a living being, and is further designated as mortal
>
> (Phaidros, 246 b-c, Loeb Classical Library, Vol. 36, p. 473).

It seems to me that we are here touching upon the deepest religious root of horoscope astrology. The soul comes from the heavens, where it partook of the circulation of the stars. It unites itself with a body and forms with it a living being. This explains how human character comes to be determined by the heavens.

This is exactly PLATON's opinion. In the 'Phaidros' he describes how Zeus and the eleven principal gods drive their war-chariots in the heavens; the twelfth, Hestia, stays in the house of the gods. With them goes the heavenly host: the gods and demons, accompanied by all souls that wish to follow the gods. When the souls later lose their wings and fall to the earth, they follow in the conduct of their lives, as far as they can, the god whom they followed in heaven. To those who were in the train of Ares in heaven, murder will come easily, and similarly for the other gods. Is not this pure astrology?

Let us now compare what the middle Persian text Dînkard (9-10 cent.) says about the birth of ZARATHUSTRA:

---

[1]) J. BIDEZ, Eos ou Platon et l'Orient, Brussels 1945.

As revelation mentions it: When Aûharmazd had produced the material of
Zaratûst, the glory then, in the presence of Aûharmazd, fled on towards the
material of Zaratûst, on to that germ, from that germ it fled on . . .; from the
endless light it fled on, on to that of the sun; from that of the sun it fled on,
on to the moon; from that moon it fled on, on to those stars; from those stars
it fled on, on to the fire in the house of Zôish; and from that fire is fled on, on to
the wife of Frâhîmvana-zôish, when she brought forth that girl who became
the mother of Zaratûst

(translation by WEST, Sacred Books of the East 47, p. 17).

This legend presents a very primitive picture of the universe, in which the moon and
sun are more distant from us than the fixed stars, whereas according to the astrologers
the fixed stars are above the sun. Clearly we are here dealing not with ideas derived from
astrology, but with original religious ideas. The soul of ZARATHUSTRA is of celestial
origin: it descends from the highest heaven down to the earth. These religious conceptions originally had nothing to do with the zodiac or the rest of Babylonian science,
but it was the later combination of this science with those religious conceptions that
made possible the birth and development of horoscope astrology.

This is confirmed by closer consideration of what HERODOTOS says about the transmigration of souls. He mentions a cycle of souls with a period of 3000 years. It seems to
me that this period should be regarded as a cosmic period. The soul wanders through
the whole cosmos (HERODOTOS himself mentions as stations of this wandering the earth,
the sea and the heaven) and returns into a human body after 3000 years. If, with ALK-
MAION, we make an analogy between the perpetual motion of the soul and the perpetual
circling of the stars, then the migration period of 3000 years is on the same footing as the
planetary periods of the astronomers and the world periods of the cosmologists.

In middle Persian texts there is frequent mention of a world period of 9000 or 12000
years, divided into three or four periods of 3000 years each[1]). I conjecture that the Egyptian soul-period is connected with this.

Be that as it may, it does not seem too risky to assume that the Egyptian ideas about
the circulation of souls and the circulation of the heavenly bodies formed a single,
coherent complex of ideas that was taken over by PYTHAGORAS and further developed
by him.

To determine the origin of this complex of ideas let us consider more closely the
astronomical and cosmological elements in it: the doctrine of astronomical and world
periods. Systematic collections of earlier and more recent observations, which are an
essential prerequisite for the calculation of planetary periods, are to be found only in
Babylon. The doctrine of world periods and world catastrophes is likewise Babylonian.
Thus the astronomical and cosmological part of the doctrine can be ascribed with cer-

---

[1]) H. S. NYBERG: La cosmologie Mazdéenne, Journal asiatique 214 and 219.

Plate 18. Monumental horoscope for the coronation of king ANTIOCHOS I of Commagene (69 to 34 B.C.). According to O. NEUGEBAUER and H. B. VAN HOESEN: Greek Horoscopes (Philadelphia 1959), the date of coronation was July 7th, 62 B.C., when the Sun stood in Leo. For a description of the whole monument on mount Nemrud Dagh see HUMANN und PUCHSTEIN: Reisen in Kleinasien und Nordsyrien (Berlin 1890). Photo Staatliche Museen, Berlin.

tainty to Babylon. The establishment of this fact suggests the hypothesis that the doctrine of transmigration of souls was transmitted from India or Iran to Egypt *via Babylon*.

As regards the time of this transmission, the Assyrian period is out of question. Assurbanipal's Library, which was destroyed in −611, has yielded a mass of texts, none of which contains the slightest intimation of the complex of ideas under consideration. The sole remaining possiblity is the period of the Chaldaean kings (−625 to −539).

At the court of NEBUKADNEZAR II (−604 to −561) there were Egyptians, Greeks, Medes and Persians[1]). Two observational texts have been preserved which testify to the astronomical activity of the men working at this court. Here there were all the prerequisites for the fusion of Iranian ideas with Babylonian scientific doctrines. We shall later adduce still further arguments favouring just this period as the time of origin of the new outlook upon the world that we find in the Orphic and Pythagorean schools.

THE CULT OF MITHRAS AND SOLAR THEOLOGY

Mithras as Sun-god

The god Mithras belongs, as we have seen, to the general pantheon of the Aryans in the Mittani kingdom, in Iran and India.

In a text from Assurbanipal's Library 'Mitra' is given as one of the many names of the sun-god Shamash[2]). Thus as early as the Assyrian period Mithras was regarded a sun-god.

In later times Mithras was always treated as a sun-god. On a monument of ANTIOCHOS I of Commagene (see Plate 19, 20 and 22), one of the four gods portrayed is identified as

'Apollon Mithras Helios Hermes'[3]).

In inscriptions of the Roman period Mithras is called 'Deus Sol invictus' (Plate 23). In middle Persian 'Mihr u Mâh' (Mihr = Mithra) is a common expression for 'sun and moon'.

The Mithras cult with its animal sacrifice and emphasis on blood was violently rejected by ZARATHUSTRA. Later, however, Mithras was taken up into the Zoroastrian pantheon. In Yasht 10, the 'Mithra-Yasht' of the Avesta, Ahura Mazda expressly confirms that he had given Mithras the same titles to offering and worship as he had himself[4]).

---

[1]) E. F. WEIDNER, Mélanges Syriens offerts à Dussaud II (Paris, 1939), p. 923.
[2]) JENSEN, Z. f. Assyriol., 2, p. 195.
[3]) F. CUMONT: *Textes et monuments rel. aux mystères de Mithra II* (Paris, Leroux 1896), p. 187.
[4]) I. GERSHEVITCH, The Avestian Hymn to Mithra, Cambridge 1959.

Plate 19a. Antiochos I of Commagene (left) and Apollon-Mithras-Helios with Phrygian cap and sun-rays. Relief on the West-Terrace of mount Nemrud Dagh (see also Plate 18). Photo Theresa Goell, Director of the Nemrud Dagh excavations.

Plate 19b. Head of a statue on the West-Terrace of Mount Nemrud Dagh. Possibly Apollon-Mithras-Helios.

Plate 20. Mithras killing the divine Bull. From Circus Maximus in Rome. Note the inscription DEO SOLI INVICTO MITHRAE (To the god Invicible Sun Mithras). See M. J. VERMASEREN: Corpus Inscr. Mithriacae I, Fig. 122. Photo Ernest Nash.

Plate 21. Mithraeum under the church San Clemente in Rome (VERMASEREN, Corpus inscr. I, Fig. 95). In the middle Mithras, killing the bull.

Photo Anderson

The principal part of the Mithra-Yasht is a magnificent hymn to Mithras that is probably older than Zoroastrianism. The hymn mentions the country around Sogdiana and Chwarism with its deep lakes, navigable rivers, rich meadows and high mountains, thus indicating as its origin the north-eastern part of the Persian kingdom, the region between Samarkand and the Aral Sea. Here Mithras appears not as sun-god, but as god of the bright daytime sky. He comes 'over the Harâ range, before the immortal sun with swift steeds'. He sets himself 'first upon the gold-decked splendid heights and thence, full of power, looks out upon the whole Aryan domain' (NYBERG, Religionen, p. 53).

According to this Yasht and other texts, Mithras is a god of justice, of contract, and as such he was at all times honoured. According to PLUTARCHOS (Vita Artaxerx. 4, Vita Alex. 3) and XENOPHON, the Persian kings' oaths were sworn by Mithras.

The spread of the Mithras cult

By the time of the Roman Emperors we find the cult of the bull-slaying Mithras established in the whole Roman empire, from Britain to Syria[1]. The earliest inscription from Rome (VERMASEREN, Corpus I, No. 594) can be dated to the period around +100.

By what route did the cult come to Rome? PLUTARCHOS in his 'Vita Pompei' tells us that the Cilician pirates held secret mysteries on Olympus in Lycia (in the south of Asia Minor) and that the cult of Mithras was first spread by these pirates. According to APPIANUS (Mithridates, 63 and 92) these pirates came into contact with people from Syria, Cyprus, Pamphylia and Pontus, from whom they then took over the Mithras-mysteries.

In fact Mithras had been worshipped for centuries in the East of Asia Minor. Several kings of Pontus (from −280 to −62) were called MITHRIDATES. On plate 19a we see Mithras-Helios extending his hand to king ANTIOCHOS of Commagene (−68 to −33).

The worshippers of Mithras in Asia Minor were mainly the magi, who arrived there as early as about −500. They were called 'Maguseans'[2]) According to the testimony of bishop BASILIOS of Caesarea, the ancestors of the Maguseans came from Babylon (Bidez-Cumont I, p. 68). The most plausible hypothesis is that the Mithras cult came from Persia or Media via Babylon to Asia Minor and thence to Rome.

This hypothesis is confirmed by further evidence. In a Latin inscription a priest of Mithras calls himself 'Babylonian priest of the Persian temple of Mithras'. This inscription shows that the worshippers of Mithras knew that Persian and Babylonian elements are fused together in his cult.

The Babylonian elements can also be clearly discerned in the sanctuaries of Mithras.

---

[1] M. J. VERMASEREN: Mithra, Ce dieu mystérieux (ed. Sequoia, Paris-Brussels 1960).
[2] J. BIDEZ and F. CUMONT: Les mages hellénisés I (Paris, Les belles lettres 1938), p. 5—55.

Everywhere we find the symbols of the zodiacal signs and the planets (Plates 22 and 23). A priest of Mithras calls himself 'studiosus astrologiae' (Bidez-Cumont I, p. 67).

In the Mithras hymn of the Avesta (Yasht 10) the zodiacal signs and astrology are not yet mentioned. We must therefore suppose that the Magi became acquainted with astrology in Babylon and that it was there that the ancient Mithras cult was infiltrated by astrological ideas.

The three worlds of Julianus

The Roman emperor JULIANUS the Apostate, who reigned from 361 to 363 A.D., composed a 'Hymn to King Helios', in which the following somewhat enigmatical words appear:

(148A)

It were better indeed to keep silence; but yet I will speak.

Some say then, even though all men are not ready to believe it, that the sun travels in the starless heavens far above the region of the fixed stars. And on this theory he (Helios) will not be stationed midmost among the planets but midway between the three worlds: that is, according to the hypotheses of the mysteries, if indeed one ought to use the word 'hypothesis' and not rather say 'established truths', using the word 'hypothesis' for the study of the heavenly bodies. For the priest of the mysteries tell us what they have been taught by the gods or mighty daemons, whereas the astronomers make plausible hypotheses from the harmony that they observe in the visible spheres . . .

(148C)   Now besides those whom I have mentioned, there is in the heavens a great multitude of gods who have been recognised as such by those who survey the heavens, not casually, nor like cattle. For as he (Helios) divides the three spheres by four through the zodiac, which is associated with every one of the three, so he divides the zodiac also into twelve divine powers; and again he divides every one of these twelve by three, so as to make thirty-six gods in all. Hence, as I believe, there descends from above, from the heavens to us, a three-fold gift of the Graces: I mean from the spheres, for this god (Helios), by thus dividing them by four, sends to us the fourfold glory of the seasons, which express the changes of time.

(Translated by W. C. WRIGHT: The Works of the Emperor Julian, Vol. I, Loeb Classical
                                                                                 Series).

JULIANUS here tells us a secret that was revealed 'by Gods or mighty daemons'. He constrasts this secret doctrine with the hypotheses of the astronomers, which are taken

Plate 22a. Mithras killing the bull, surrounded by Zodiacal Signs and other symbols, from a Mithraeum in Sidon (Phoenicia). Musée du Louvre, Collection Leclerq (VERMASEREN, Corpus inscr. I, Fig. 26.)

Plate 22b. Gem from Udine. Mithras and Bull surrounded by sun, stars and other symbols (VERMASEREN, Corpus inscr. II, Fig. 654).

Plate 23. Mithras killing the bull, from Osterburken (Germany). On the arc above the god the 12 zodiacal signs (VERMASEREN, Corpus inscr. II, Fig. 340). Photo Badisches Landesmuseum, Karlsruhe.

as only probable, because they agree with the phenomena. He speaks of 'mystical hypotheses' or rather 'dogmas'. All these expressions indicate that the doctrine which JULIANUS partially discloses in obscure words, was handed down as a secret doctrine in a mystery cult. Now we know that JULIANUS was initiated into the Mithras mysteries. So we may conjecture that this secret doctrine belongs to the mysteries of Mithras.

JULIANUS first says that the sun moves not in the middle of the planets, but 'in the starless space far above the fixed stars'. This, as we shall shortly see, is an Iranian idea. Next he says that the sun moves in the 'three worlds'. The doctrine of the 'three worlds' is developed in the last part of the passage quoted, and related to the division of the zodiac into twelve parts and to the four seasons. This doctrine, as we shall see, is Babylonian.

All the Greek astronomers assume that the fixed stars are farther from us than the sun and the planets. The normal sequence of the planets in the writings of the astrologers and astronomers is: Moon, Mercury, Venus, Sun, Mars, Jupiter, Saturn, fixed stars. The sun here stands 'in the middle of the planets'. This view is rejected by JULIANUS. According to his 'mystical hypotheses' the sun moves far above the fixed stars.

The same idea can be found in the Avesta and in middle Persian books. Here the subject is the journey of the soul to heaven, which takes it via a series of intermediate stations from the Cinvat bridge to Garôdemâna, the house of Ahura Mazda. Among the stations there are in turn stars, moon and sun, always just in this order in the ascent and in inverse order in the descent of the soul. The principal sources are quoted by BOUSSET in Archiv f. Religionswiss. 4, pp. 155-169. BOUSSET also proves that the soul's ascent through the heavenly spheres plays an important role in the Mithras mysteries. 'The Mithras religion was the bridge, whereby those ideas were transported to the West', says BOUSSET in conclusion.

We now come to the three Worlds or Orders (Kosmoi). The zodiac, says JULIANUS, is related to these three. Hence the sphere, as the last sentence says, is divided into four, the division being connected with the four seasons. Immediately before this he mentions the division of the zodiac into twelve. It may be assumed (though JULIANUS does not say this) that the twelve parts are derived from the four parts by trisection, in other words, that each of the four parts consists of exactly three signs. If this be accepted, it follows that the sun spends roughly three months in each of the four parts of the zodiac, and that the year consequently divides into four seasons of three months each.

JULIANUS calls the four seasons 'a threefold gift of the Graces'. This is readily intelligible, because there is one cold and one hot season and two intermediate periods (spring and autumn) which are similar in temperature; hence there are essentially only three different seasons or gifts of the graces.

The fourfold division originates, in JULIANUS' account, from the fact that the zodiac is related to the 'three worlds'. This can be explained as follows: the three worlds are three zones of the heaven, the northern part of the zodiac lying in the first zone, the southern part in the third zone, and the two remaining parts in the middle zone. In summer the sun is in the northern zone, in winter in the southern, in spring and autumn in the middle zone.

If this explanation of JULIANUS' words is accepted, his account not only makes reasonable sense, but also agrees exactly with the Babylonian theory of the seasons as we find it in the text ^{mul}APIN. There the sun spends 3 months in the path of Anu (middle zone), 3 months in the path of Enlil (northern zone), again 3 months in the path of Anu, and finally 3 months in the path of Ea (southern zone). In the path of Anu there is wind and storm, in Enlil harvest and heat, in Ea cold. The 4 sectors of the zodiac, in each of which the sun spends 3 months, each consists of 3 zodiacal signs. The Babylonian theory of seasons and zodiacal signs agrees with JULIANUS' words, if the 'three worlds' are interpreted as the paths of Enlil, Anu and Ea.

By further trisection of the 12 signs JULIANUS obtains 36 'powers of gods'. In fact, the astrologers divide each zodiacal sign into three parts, called decans, and consider the 36 decans as divine powers[1]).

This trisection of the zodiacal signs is at the same time the only point at which the secret doctrine disclosed by JULIANUS coincides with the doctrines of the Hellenistic astrologers. The astrologers place the sun in the middle of the planets. Nowhere in the astrological literature have I been able to find mention of the 'three worlds'. The astrologers place the spring equinox at 8° or 0° Aries, not at 15°, as the ^{mul}APIN theory demands. Therefore the secret doctrine of JULIANUS cannot derive from hellenistic astrology. It must have sprung from a fusion of Iranian ideas with Babylonian doctrines, and then been handed down in the Mithras cult.

The sun as highest god

It is known that the sun was greatly honoured in late antiquity as Sol invictus. In the hymn quoted above, the emperor JULIANUS glorifies the sun as King of the universe. Several centuries earlier CICERO wrote (Somnium Scipionis 4): 'The Sun resides in the middle, being Leader, King and Governor of the other lights, the Reason and Ordering Principle of the universe'. CUMONT[2]) has collected numerous passages from Greek and Roman authors where the Sun is celebrated as king or as 'Director in the dance of the planets'.

Some of these authors give a learned justification of the great importance assigned to the sun. There are three principal arguments which are continually advanced, namely:

1) The sun gives us not only, as everybody knows, the day-light, but also by its course in the zodiac it causes the change of the seasons.

[1]) W. GUNDEL: Dekane und Dekansternbilder Studien (Bibl. Warburg 1936).
[2]) F. CUMONT: La théologie solaire, Mémoires présentés par divers savants à l'acad. des Inscr. 12 (1919), p. 447.

2) The planets conform to the sun in their motions. Venus and Mercury never go far from the sun and always return to it again. The superior planets stand still and turn retrograde, as soon as they have reached a certain elongation from the sun. In this sense the sun indeed directs the dance of the planets.

3) The moon obtains its light from the sun.

What is the origin of these arguments?

1) Whereas the dependence of the seasons on the position of the sun is regarded as self-evident to-day, in antiquity it was not so. Many believed that the warmth of the 'dog days' was caused by Sirius, the principal star of the 'Great Dog', whose morning rising takes place at the end of July. That seasonal warmth derives from the position of the sun is a scientific discovery, made in Babylon: as we have seen, it is clearly expressed in ^{mul}APIN.

2) The Babylonians also knew that the planets appear and disappear, turn retrograde and forwards again, all at certain definite elongations from the sun. This 'sun-distance principle' is, as we shall see in Chapter 7, the basis of the calculation of all time intervals in Babylonian planetary calculations.

3) The fact that the moon has its light from the sun is a Greek discovery. The Babylonians had a different theory. Their doctrine, as we know from a fragment of BEROSSOS, was that the moon is a ball with a bright and a dark half, the bright half always being turned towards the sun[1]. This theory explains the phases of the moon just as well as the Greek theory and can be used equally well as an argument for the superiority of the sun.

It thus appears that the learned solar theology which we find in Greek and Latin authors goes back to the Babylonians.

ZERVANISM AND ASTRAL FATALISM

Zervanism is a Persian religious doctrine, according to which Zervan or Zurvan, the God of Time, is the highest god and the progenitor of all things.

By *Astral Fatalism* I understand the astrological doctrine: 'Everything depends on the stars'. Astral fatalism teaches that we are in the fetters of an inevitable destiny. When the stars return to the same place at the end of the 'great year', everyting on earth, down to the minutest detail, will be repeated. We have met this idea among the Pythagoreans and even in the teaching of PYTHAGORAS himself, for he taught that 'all things that once happen recur after a certain period, and nothing is really new'. The Stoics held the same opinion: NEMESIOS (Anthrolopogia 38) writes:

[1] P. SCHNABEL: Berossos (Leipzig 1923), p. 211.

The Stoics explain: the planets return to the same celestial sign, where each individual planet originally stood . . .; in certain times the planets bring conflagration and annihilation of all things; then the world starts again anew from the same place, and while the stars again turn the same way as before, each individual thing will . . . be restored unchanged; then will there again be a Socrates and a Platon . . . everything will be the same and unchanged down to the minutest details.

PLATON did not adopt this fatalistic doctrine. For him the soul is free from birth to choose its own lot. It can choose the fate of a tyrant, an athlete or an ordinary citizen, a lion or a nightingale (Republic 617e-620d).

Astral fatalism is also found in middle Persian sources from the Sassanid period, i.e. between 220 and 650 A.D. For example, in the book Maînôg-i Khirad (or Mênôk î Khrat)[1]) we read:

All fortune, good and ill, that befalls man, comes from the twelve (zodiacal signs) and the seven (planets).

In Chapter 27 of the same book we read:

. . . For at the appointed time that will happen, which must . . .

The fatalism of Mênôk î Khrat is combined with a definite Zervanistic outlook. Quite generally in our middle Persian sources Zervanism and astral fatalism always appear together. In the Mênôk î Khrat, chapter 27, Fate (Bakht), the Moment and the Decision are named as essential attributes of Zurvân. In Chapter 8 we read that Ormuzd created all things with the consent of boundless Zurvân.

Zervanism and astral fatalism stand in sharp contrast to orthodox Zoroastrianism. Zarathustra's ethics are based on the freedom of the individual's will. According to the orthodox doctrine Ahura Mazda is the highest God and the Creator: he has no God of Time above him. In certain middle Persian sources Zervanism is condemned as heresy[2]).

We shall now attempt to learn something of the beginnings of Zervanism.

The time-god Zervan

The name of the god: Zervan Akarana, i.e. boundless time, appears in the Avesta, though not in the Gathas, but in the later Yasna and in the Vendidad. *Space* and *Time*,

---

[1]) Maînôg-i Khirad VIII 8, ed. WEST, Sacred Books 24, p. 32. NYBERG, J. Asiatique 214, p. 199.
[2]) R. C. ZAEHNER: Zurvan, a Zoroastrian Dilemma (Oxford, Clarendon Press 1946), p. 26. To be quoted as ZAEHNER, Zurvan.

Thwâsha and Zurvân, are named together in Yasna 72 : 10 as divine powers. According to BIDEZ and CUMONT, Thwâsha means 'space', according to NYBERG 'atmosphere', according to DARMESTETER 'heaven'. Zurvân is mentioned in the Avesta only quite incidentally, neither as a mighty god, nor as father of the twins 'good spirit' and 'evil spirit'.

For fixing the date of Zervanism a fragment of EUDEMOS[1]) regarding the Magi is important. EUDEMOS speaks of a being 'that some call *place*, some *time* and that unites in itself all intelligible things'. From this 'sprang the good god and the evil demon or, as some say, light and darkness'.

Topos and Chronos, Place and Time, this pair corresponds exactly to the pair Thwâsha and Zurvân in the Avesta. The doctrine of the good god and the evil demon, who sprang from the time-god, agrees with the ideas of the Magi, as we shall see presently. EUDEMOS' testimony tells us that these views were held by certain Magi as early as the fourth century B.C.

Of the classical authors who have described the religion of the Persians and Magi, EUDEMOS is the only one to mention the time-god. In the inscriptions of the Persian kings, Ahura Mazda is the highest god; Zervan does not appear.

The myth of the twins

The twins whom EUDEMOS calls 'the good god and the evil demon' already appear in ZARATHUSTRA's Gathas, viz. in Yasna 30 : 3-5 and 45 : 2. The meaning of the latter passage is not contested:

> I will speak of the two spirits at the beginning of life, of which the more benificient spake thus to the evil one: . . .

The 'evil spirit' is called *anghra mainyu*, or in middle Persian *Ahriman*. The good one is called in 30 : 5 'most beneficient spirit'. Later (not in the Gathas) he was identified with Ahura Mazda and called Ormuzd.

In Yasna 30 : 3, where the two spirits are mentioned for the first time, they are described as twins.

The language of this passage is rather difficult. Three essentially different translations have been offered:

1 (Bartholomae). The two spirits in the beginning, who revealed themselves as twins in a dream vision, (are) the better and the evil in thought and word and deed . . .

---

[1]) See e.g. BIDEZ et CUMONT: Les mages hellénisés I, p. 62 and II, p. 69. EUDEMOS, a pupil of ARISTOTELES, lived around 320 B.C.

2 (M. W. Smith). Now these two spirits at the beginning, the twins, by a vision, revealed themselves in thought, and in word, and in deed, (as) these-two, the better and the bad . . .

3 (H. Humbach). These are the two fundamental intentions, the twins, who became known as the two dreams, as the two kinds of thought and word and work, the better and the worse[1]).

No matter which translation is more correct, most authors agree on one point. Zarathustra supposed his audience to know about the twins already. He referred to an old myth or tradition about the twins, and he gave this tradition a new, moral sense. In his re-interpretation the twins represented the better and the bad, between which everyone has to choose. 'Between these two the wise have chosen rightly, not the foolish'.

Nyberg, in his Religionen des alten Iran (p. 103-107), stresses the point that Zarathustra refers to an already existing twin-myth. Herzfeld and Humbach agree. Widengren advances several arguments in favour of this hypothesis[2]). In particular, he refers to an Indian myth, which has several details in common with the Zervanistic twin myth.

Other sources can be adduced to tell us more about the twin myth. According to Eudemos, the twins spring from a Being which some call Place, others Time. The twins themselves are called 'the good god and the evil demon' or 'light and darkness'.

The myth reported by Eudemos cannot be derived from Zarathustra's vision. In the Gathas there is no mention of Space and Time. According to Yasna 44 : 5 Light and Darkness are creations of Ahura Mazda; they cannot, therefore, stem from an original god 'Time' or 'Space'. Nowhere in the Avesta are light and darkness identified with the twins.

That Light and Darkness, or Day and Night, are creations of Time is a very natural thought, but not one that can in any way be deduced from the Vision of Zarathustra. Rather can we imagine that Zarathustra knew about an older twin myth and that he re-interpreted the twins as the good and the evil, using this to bring out the full force of his doctrine of the incompatibility of good and evil and of the choice that faces each one of us. In Yasna 45 : 2 he makes the Holy one speak to the Evil one as follows:

> Of us two neither the thoughts, nor the commandments, nor the wills, nor the decisions, nor the words, nor yet the deeds, nor the characters, nor the souls agree.

---

[1]) Humbach gives the reasons for his interpretation in Zeitschr. der deutschen Morgenl. Ges. 107, p. 262 and 370.

[2]) G. Widengren in Numen *1* (1954), p. 17. See also Duchesne-Guillemin: La religion de l'Iran ancien, p. 187.

Detailed reports on the Zervanistic version of the twin myth are to be found in the writings of Christian authors of the fifth century A.D. The Armenian father EZNIK and the Syrian author THEODOR BAR KONAI report[1]) how, according to the shocking doctrine of ZERDUSHT (ZARATHUSTRA), Zruan or Zervan made offerings for a thousand years in order to obtain a son and then had doubt about the result. Finally two sons were begotten, the one (Ormizd or Hormizd) as a result of the offerings, the other (Ahriman) in consequence of the doubt. This part of the myth is very ancient, for the offering and the doubt are found in the legend of the Indian creator-god Prajâpati[2]). Then it is told how Ahriman by a trick obtained dominance for nine thousand years.

The general source of these reports is perhaps a polemic 'On the Magi in Persia' by bishop THEODOROS OF MOPSUESTA (around 400), of which PHOTIOS gives a résumé. The Cilician bishop inveighs against the 'abominable doctrine of the Persians which was introduced by ZARADES (= ZARATHUSTRA), of *Zuruam* (= Zurvan), the creator of all things, whom he also calls *Tyche*' (BIDEZ-CUMONT, Mages hellénisés II, fragment D 14).

The identification of the god Zurvan with Fate (Tyche) is very remarkable. It shows that not only in the East under the Sassanids, but also in the West, Zervanism and fatalism go hand in hand[3]).

The Magi in Cilicia, against whom the bishop of Mopsuesta's polemic was directed, spoke Aramaic and were called Maguseans (BIDEZ-CUMONT I, p. 35). The bishop BASILIOS of Caesarea (died 379) assures us that their predecessors came from Babylon and that they traced their descent back to the god Zurvan.

The male-female god

Allusions to the twins Hormizd and Ahraman (or Hormuz and Ahriman), which were begotten by Zurvan in the same maternal womb, are also to be found in the Acts of the Persian martyrs[4]). These martyrs were Christians who wanted to show their Sassanid judges the inconsistencies of the Persian religion. The myth to which they refer is in general the same as that reported by EZNIK and THEODOR, but in the Acts of the Martyrs there are two different versions of the myth. According to one version the twins had (as in EZNIK's account) a mother. In the other version Zurvan was hermaphrodite and begot the twins in his own womb. The expression 'male-female' appears in Anâhêdh's testimony with express reference to Zurwân, while Âdhurhormizd declares:

---

[1]) The texts are given in ZAEHNER: Zurvan, A Zoroastrian Dilemma, p. 419.
[2]) J. DUCHESNE-GUILLEMIN: La religion de l'Iran ancien, p. 187.
[3]) See H. S. NYBERG: Cosmologie Mazdéenne, J. Asiatique 214, p. 193—310 and 219, p. 1—134.
[4]) The texts are in ZAEHNER, Zurvan, p. 432—437. Commentary p. 74.

... so Zurwân too showed himself far from having the qualities of a god;
for he never even knew what was formed in his womb

(ZAEHNER, Zurvan p. 435).

A male-female Supreme God, who produces all out of himself, is also found in
Pythagorean and Orphic sources, which have been collected by FESTUGIÈRE (Révélation
d'Hermès IV, p. 43). FESTUGIÈRE first quotes from the Theologumena Arithmetika of the
neo-Pythagorean IAMBLICHOS (about 320 A.D.):

> The Pythagoreans call the Unity (Monas) not only God, but also Reason and
> male-female . . . In so far as the Unity is the germ of all things, the Pythagoreans
> regard it as male-female, not only because they consider the odd as male, being
> difficult to divide, the even as female, being easily divided, and the unity is both
> even and odd, but also because it is considered as father and mother, since it
> contains in itself the reason (Logos) for matter and form . . .

We see how IAMBLICHOS or his source tries to explain the male-female nature of the
unity on a philosophical basis, by using the concepts of Form (Eidos) and Matter (Hyle).
The original thought, however, was not, in my opinion, philosophical, but rather mythol-
ogical. The concepts mother and father have no relevance in a philosophical discourse on
principles, but they have in a theogony. When EZNIK and THEODOR BAR KONAI say that
in the beginning Zervan was all alone and nothing besides him existed, and when in the
continuation of the myth they make mention of a mother, a disturbing inconsistency
results, which, it seems, some Zervanists resolved by the explanation that Zervan begot
the twins in his own womb and was thus father and mother simultaneously. The mytho-
logical foundation of the male-female nature of the creator-god seems to me to be the
original, the philosophical one only a subsequent reshaping.

In fact, the idea that the creator-god must be male-female can be traced in Greek sources long before IAMBLICHOS. FESTUGIÈRE shows that the concepts Unity, male-female, god,
etc. were developed in the same sequence as in IAMBLICHOS by NIKOMACHOS OF GERASA
(2nd century A.D.). Further, he points to verses by VALERIUS SORANUS (about −100),
in which Jupiter is addressed as 'Progenitor genetrixque deum, deus unus et omnes'.
According to FESTUGIÈRE, the Latin poet was imitating an orphic hymn, in which Jupiter
was called both 'male' and 'immortal nymph'. This hymn contains very ancient verses,
to which PLATON already alludes.

DIOGENES of Babylon, the Stoic (about −200) quotes the saying 'Zeus male, Zeus
female'. Perhaps he had in mind the same Orphic verse. At any rate he represents the
saying as being generally known.

The fact that the idea of the male-female creator-god appears in Pythagorean and
Orphic writings, where we can trace many other strong oriental influences, speaks very
much in favour of the oriental origin of the idea.

Plate 24. The winged god Aion = Zervan with lion's head, human body and snake, standing on a World-globe. From a stanctuary of Mithras in Rome, now in Museo Torlonia (VERMASEREN, Corpus inscr. I, Fig. 152). DUCHESNE-GUILLEMIN identified the winged god with Ahriman, but it seems to me that CUMONT had good reasons for his identification with Aion. See VERMASEREN: Mithra, ce dieu mystérieux. Photo ALINARI.

Chronos Apeiros

About 60 B.C., in Commagene on the Euphrates, King ANTIOCHOS I erected a monument with a Greek inscription, in which Persian gods were identified with Greek gods (Oromazdes with Zeus, Mithras with Helios and Apollo, etc.) The inscription also mentiones 'Infinite Time'. The relevant section reads:

> May the Holy Law be set as the rule for all generations of men, which Infinite Time will destine for the succession in this country, each with his particular fate in life.

SCHAEDER[1]) identified the 'chronos apeiros' (Infinite Time) here mentioned with Zervan akarana, in which CUMONT and NYBERG follow him. In the inscription Time appears as the god of fate, who allots to each man his portion in life. We recall that THEODOROS of Mopsuesta and EZNIK of Kolb also equate Zurvan with Fate.

The god with the lion-head

In some sanctuaries of Mithras there are pictures of a winged god with a lion's head and a human body, round which a snake twines itself (Plate 24). Who is this god?

Such a figure is mentioned in several magic papyri, where he is called *Aion*, i.e. life, life-time or eternity[2]). In one of these papyri Aion is called 'God of Gods' and 'boundless'. The lion-headed god is thus Boundless Time, Zervan akarana[3]).

The magic papyri and the pictures of the lion-headed god show how far the influence of Zervanism reached in late antiquity. In the texts ascribed to 'Hermes trismegistos', too, the god Aion plays a major role. According to FESTUGIÈRE IV, p. 152-175, Aion in these texts is both boundless space and boundless time and creator of the world.

The exact date of the books of Hermes is not known, but there are two texts from the 1st century B.C. that also describe Aion as creator of the world. The one is a fragment of the Roman augur MESSALA (53 B.C.), who identifies Aion with Janus[4]). It begins as follows:

> Janus, who creates all and rules all . . .
>
> (FESTUGIÈRE IV, p. 176).

---

[1]) H. H. SCHAEDER: Urform und Fortbildungen des manichäischen Systems, p. 138.
[2]) R. P. FESTUGIÈRE: La révélation d'Hermès Trismégiste IV, p. 182.
[3]) On the lion-headed god see also J. DUCHESNE-GUILLEMIN, La Nouvelle Clio 10 (1960) and M. J. VERMASEREN: Mithra, ce dieu mystérieux, p. 98.
[4]) LYDOS, De mensibus IV 1, p. 64 (Wachsmuth).

The other text is an inscription on a statue of Aion in Eleusis, dedicated by a Roman named QUINTUS POMPEIUS, who lived in the reign of AUGUSTUS. It reads:

> Aion, who remains ever unchanged by virtue of his divine nature, who is one with the one world, who likewise has neither beginning nor middle nor end, who partakes of no change, who created the whole of divine, living nature
>
> (FESTUGIÈRE IV, p. 181).

We can, however, trace the lion-headed time-god much further back: he appears in a theogony which is ascribed to ORPHEUS.

The theogony of ORPHEUS

The neo-platonist DAMASKIOS reports a 'theogony according to HIERONYMOS and HELLANIKOS'. The Christian apologist ATHENAGORAS gives a description of the same theogony, ascribing it to ORPHEUS[1]). Hence we may assume that it appeared in certain 'Books of ORPHEUS'.

According to this theogony, the first two principles were Water and Earth, from them being born a third principle. 'It was a snake with the heads of a bull and a lion, between which was the face of a god. On his shoulders he had wings, and his name was *Chronos ageraos* (unaging time) or also Herakles. Together with him was Ananke (Necessity), of the same nature as Adrasteia, extended incorporeally throughout the whole cosmos and touching its boundaries'.

In another theogony, the 'theology of the so-called Orphic rhapsodies', which DAMASKIOS calls 'the normal Orphic theology', *Chronos* is actually the first god, who produces everything out of himself. In the enumeration of the generations of the gods after Chronos the two theogonies closely resemble one another.

The date of the 'Books of ORPHEUS' is not known. It is, however, certain that by the time of PLATON there was already 'a whole bundle of books by Musaios and Orpheus', in which the genealogy of the Gods was described (PLATON, Republic 364e and Timaios 40d). The information that PLATON gives us about this genealogy agrees well with the Orphic theogonies that have come down to us. These therefore certainly go back to a source of considerable antiquity.

It was ARISTOTLE's opinion that the verses known as Orphic were composed not by ORPHEUS, but by ONOMAKRITOS. This ONOMAKRITOS, who is also mentioned in HERODOTOS VII 6, lived in the 6th century B.C. Some Pythagoreans of that century were also named as authors of Orphic verses. We thus need have no hesitation in assuming that

---

[1]) W. K. C. GUTHRIE: *Orpheus and Greek Religion* (2nd ed., London 1952), Ch. IV.

'Books of Orpheus' existed as early as the 6th century, containing a genealogy of the gods which agrees in its essentials with the late excerpts that have come down to us.

Since a god Chronos appears in *both* the theogonies handed down, it seems reasonable to assume that this time-god was already mentioned in the orphic writings of the sixth century.

Independently of all this, we can point to a god called Chronos in the theology of PHEREKYDES of Syros, who lived around the middle of the 6th century B.C. PHEREKYDES wrote a prose theogony, from which some verbatim quotations have been preserved. The first fragment begins as follows:

> Zas and Chronos ever were, as was also Chthonie

> (DIELS, Fragmente der Vorsokratiker, PHEREKYDES B 1).

DAMASKIOS quotes this sentence and reports further that Chronos caused fire, air and water to come forth from his seed. The omission of the earth from the list of created elements is quite in order, for Chthonie, the earth, was ever there.

Comparing now the doctrines of 'ORPHEUS' and PHEREKYDES with Zervanism, we find:

1) In the theogony of HIERONYMOS and HELLANIKOS the name 'chronos ageraos' corresponds exactly to the old Persian 'Zervan akarana'. The winged beast with snake's body and lion's head is indubitably a fabulous beast of the orient. Lion's head, wings and snake are also seen in the pictures of Aion in the Mithras mysteries. The connection between this theogony and oriental Zervanism is thus demonstrated beyond doubt.

2) In the rhapsodical theogony, Chronos is the first god who produces all out of himself, like the oriental Zervan.

3) In the theogony of PHEREKYDES Chronos is a god who ever was and a creator god producing everything from his seed, like the god Zervan of the Magi.

Zervan akarana is mentioned in the Avesta. The suggestion that PHEREKYDES or the Orphic writers influenced the Avesta will surely find no support in any quarter. Only one possibility then remains, that it was Zervanism that influenced both PHEREKYDES and the Orphic writers.

The dating of Zervanism

Various dates have been handed down for PHEREKYDES. According to DIOGENES LAERTIOS I 121 he was in his prime in 544 B.C. Other dates are even earlier. If Zervanism influenced PHEREKYDES, it must have existed earlier than −550.

For ZARATHUSTRA too a variety of dates has been reported, the latest possible being

Plate 25. Bronze plate from Luristan (probably 8th or 7th century B.C.), explained by R. GHIRSHMAN in Artibus Asiae 21, p. 37. In the middle a winged god with two faces, a male face above and a female face on the breast. Two little men seem to come forth from his shoulders. They can well be interpreted as twins. On the left three youths (below) and three mature men, on the right three old men. We may conclude that the god is a god of the ages of mankind, a god of Time. The bronze plate can be understood as an illustration to the pre-Zoroastrian myth of the twins. Photo Cincinnati Art Museum.

around 540 B.C. We have given reasons for supposing that ZARATHUSTRA found the myth of the twins already in existence and gave it a new, moral interpretation. In the version, which EUDEMOS has preserved for us, there was an original being 'Time' or 'Space', the father of the twins. If ZARATHUSTRA found this version in existence, it must have existed by about −550 at the latest.

These two independent arguments give each other mutual support. They both lead to a time before the conquest of Babylon by CYRUS (539 B.C.), i.e. to the Neo-Babylonian period.

In EUDEMOS and all later reports the adepts of Zervanism were the Magi, whom HE-RODOTOS declares to be of Median origin. We may thus assume that the Zervanistic twin myth originated in Media.

This section had already been written when I caught sight of a bronze from Luristan which provides striking confirmation of my early dating of Zervanism (Plate 25). The scene depicted on it was most illuminatingly interpreted by R. GHIRSHMAN in Artibus Asiae 21, p. 37. In the middle we see a winged god, from whose shoulders the twins appear to proceed. The god has a man's head on top and a woman's face on his breast. When we recollect that, in one of the versions handed down by the Syrian authors, the father of the twins, the time-god Zurvan, was male-female and begot the twins in his own womb, we see that the Luristan bronze can be considered as an illustration of this version of the myth.

The god on the bronze has wings. The time-god of the Orphic theogony also had wings, as did the lion-headed god in the mysteries of Mithras (Plate 24).

According to EZNIK's report, Zruan (Zurvan) gives his son Ormizd the sacrificial branch. The twins on the bronze plaque also hold a kind of branch in their hands.

On the bronze we see youths, mature men and old men; they obviously represent the three ages of man. This too fits in well with a time-god.

According to GHIRSHMAN the bronze plaque belongs to the 8th or 7th century B.C. Luristan lies in the southern part of ancient Media. Thus, our conclusion that the myth of the twins stems from Media and existed before −550 is strikingly confirmed by the Luristan bronze.

STAGES IN THE DEVELOPMENT OF COSMIC RELIGION AND ASTROLOGY

In the foregoing we have made the acquaintance of a number of religious movements, which we have followed to a certain extent separately. It is time now to draw the threads together and look at the relations between the individual trends. At the same time we shall consider the development of astrology and its relation to cosmic religion.

Plate 26. Relief in white marble, perhaps from Rome, new in a museum in Modena (VERMASEREN, Corpus inscr. I, Fig. 197). The orphic god Phanes is born from an egg. The 12 zodiacal signs surrounding it show that the egg represents the Cosmos. The two halves of the broken egg are pictured once more at the top and bottom. The snake winding itself around the body is a common attribute of the Time-God Aion. Apparently Phanes was identified to a certain extent with Aion. Photo Bandieri.

Plate 27. Sculpture from a sanctuary of Mithras in Chapel Hill (the ancient Borcovicium) in England. The sculpture represents the god Phanes just born from the world-egg. In an inscription from Rome (see page 176) Mithras is identified with Phanes, hence it is possible that this sculpture represents Mithras appearing as Phanes. Photo Museum of Antiquities, The University, Newcastle upon Tyne.

The development of cosmic religion

The religious trends which we have considered individually above can be put together in groups in the following temporal sequence:

First group: Babylonian-Assyrian astral religion

Second group: Mithras cult
              Zervanism
              Orphism

Third group: Zoroastrianism
              Worship of the Heaven (as highest god)
              Monotheistic tendencies
              Spiritualization of the concept of God

The dating of the Babylonian-Assyrian astral religion presents no difficulty. We have an old Babylonian 'Prayer to the Gods of the Night' and other evidence from the time of HAMMURABI.

The continued vitality of this astral religion even in late Assyrian times is attested by a passage in the Bible. In the Second Book of Kings (Ch. 21, v. 5-6), we have the following report of MANASSE, who was King of Judah around −670:

> And he built altars for all the host of heaven in the two courts of the house
> of the LORD. And he made his son pass through the fire, and he observed
> times, and used enchantments, and dealt with familiar spirits and wizards ...

'Observing times' is just what astronomers and astrologers do. Astrology was flourishing at the Assyrian court at just this time.

In the second group only Orphism can be dated with certainty: it flourished in Greece in the sixth century B.C.

In the case of Zervanism we have given reasons for supposing that it was also already in existence in the sixth century. Further, we have seen that Zervanism and Orphism are closely connected. In Plate 27 we show a picture of a god who combines certain attributes of the time-god (human body with a snake twined around it) with those of the Orphic god Phanes, who sprang from the egg.

Mithras, as we have seen, was an Aryan god, who was worshipped in Aryan countries long before the sixth century. By chance we can demonstrate his worship in Persia just around the middle of the sixth century. According to the Bible (Ezrah 1, 8) the treasurer of the king KORES = CYRUS was called MITHREDATH.

The connection between the cult of Mithras and Zervanism is shown by the many pictures of the time-god that have been discovered in Mithraic sanctuaries (Plate 24). The principal proponents in late antiquity of Mithraism and Zervanism were the Magi in the region of Taurus.

We can also prove a direct connection between Mithraism and Orphism. In Rome at the foot of the Aventine three Greek inscriptions were discovered[1]), of which the first two were dedicated 'to the god Helios Mithras', the third 'to the god Helios Mithras Phanes'. In this inscription, the Orphic god Phanes is clearly identified with Mithras. Further, in a British Mithras sanctuary (Borcovicium, Chapel Hill) a portrayal of Phanes (or Mithras) was discovered showing him just emerging out of the divided egg shell.

Thus there is a close connection between Mithraism, Zervanism and Orphism, all three being closely connected with astrology. All three existed at the same time in the sixth century. We can therefore confidently put them together in one group.

Mithraism and Zervanism have this further feature in common, that both are incompatible with orthodox Zoroastrianism. Zarathustra condemned the sacrifice of the bull in the cult of Mithras. Zervan is not mentioned in the Gathas at all, and in the later Yasna only incidentally. If Ahura Mazda is the highest god and the creator, Zervan cannot occupy this position.

Opinions vary about the date of ZARATHUSTRA, but it was certainly only after −540 that Zoroastrianism reached the West of the Persian empire. Darius proclaimed in his inscriptions that Ahura Mazda is the highest god and the creator, and Xerxes referred expressly to Zoroastrian teaching, in that he condemned the Daevas and enjoined that only Ahura Mazda was to be worshipped. Zoroastrianism is therefore later than the religious movements of the second group.

The connection between Zoroastrianism and the worship of the sky-god as the supreme god was demonstrated at the beginning of this chapter. Other tendencies in Zoroastrianism were found to be an inclination towards monotheism and the spiritualisation of the concept of god. The same tendencies can be shown in XENOPHANES and EMPEDOKLES. PYTHAGORAS and HERAKLEITOS too proclaimed doctrines showing many points of contact with Zoroastrian doctrines.

Thus cosmic religion flooded in three great waves from Iran and Babylon to the West. The first wave spread from Babylon: in Juda it came into conflict with Jewish religion. The second and third waves came from Iran via Babylon: they reached Greece in quick succession in the sixth century.

Three stages of astrology

The old omen astrology, well known to us from the collection 'Enuma Anu Enlil' and the reports of the Assyrian court astrologers, differs from the later horoscope

---

[1]) M. VERMASEREN, Corpus Inscr. Mithr. 1, Mon 472—475.

astrology in two respects. First, the signs of the zodiac, which play the principal role in horoscope astrology, do not appear in the earlier kind of astrology at all. Second, the older astrology deals principally with events of *general* interest. It prophesies good or bad harvests, war or peace. It is true that some birth omina have come down to us from the second millenium, such as:

> If in the 12th month a child be born, this child will grow old and will produce many children.

However, these omina are completely different in character from the rules of horoscopy, which tell how to predict the destiny of an individual from the state of the planets at the moment of his birth.

Between the old and the new astrology there is another intermediate stage, in which the zodiacal signs appear, but birth horoscopes are not yet cast. To this stage belong certain astrological fragments of 'ZOROASTER', which are preserved in the compilation 'Geoponica' of CASSIANUS BASSUS[1]). The Greek treatise 'On Nature' by Pseudo-ZOROASTER, from which these fragments presumably derive, originated in pre-Christian times, probably between -350 and -250 according to BIDEZ and CUMONT.

Among these fragments there is a 'Dodekaeteris of Zeus'. The planet Jupiter ($=$ Zeus) has a sidereal orbital period of almost 12 years; it thus stays about one year in each of the twelve signs of the zodiac. The Dodekaeteris gives for each of the 12 signs a prediction of the weather and the crops for the year in question. So at this stage we have general prognoses which make use of the zodiacal signs, but have as yet nothing to do with birth horoscopy.

Several such Dodekaeterides have been handed down in the astrological literature[2]). According to BOLL, one comes from the Syria of the Augustan period. Another is ascribed to ORPHEUS[3]). Thus there appears to be a connection between this kind of zodiacal astrology and Orphism.

Connections with Babylon can also be shown. First, the Dodekaeteris is several times described in the astrological literature as a 'Chaldaean period'. Then there is a Geoponica fragment of 'ZOROASTER'[4]) which explains a method of calculating the setting and rising of the moon. This method rests on the assumption that the daily retardation of the moon's setting after new moon is exactly $\frac{1}{15}$ of the night and the daily retardation of the rising is likewise $\frac{1}{15}$ of the night. The same assumption is, as we have seen, the basis of a Babylonian procedure that was already known in Assyria by about -700. Pseudo-Zoroaster thus had a more than passing acquaintance with old Babylonian astronomy.

---

[1]) For an edition of these fragments see BIDEZ et CUMONT: Mages hellénisés II, *0* 37 to *0* 52; commentary in I, p. 107—127.

[2]) See art. Dodekaeteris by F. BOLL in PAULY-WISSOWA, Realenzyklopädie (neue Bearbeitung).

[3]) O. Kern, Orphicorum Fragmenta, p. 267—296.

[4]) BIDEZ-CUMONT II, p. 174, Fragment *0* 39.

By comparison with horoscope astrology, the astrology of the ZOROASTER fragments creates a decidedly primitive impression. We are thus justified in placing this as a 'second stage' between the old omen astrology and the later horoscope astrology.

In our discussion of stellar religion we likewise discerned three stages. The first, old Babylonian religion, is obviously closely connected with omen astrology, One manifestation of the second stage is Orphism, whose connection with the astrology of the second stage we have just seen. To the third stage of stellar religion belongs the doctrine of the celestial origin of the soul, and this gives the religious basis of horoscope astrology. Thus we can present the development in the following schematised form:

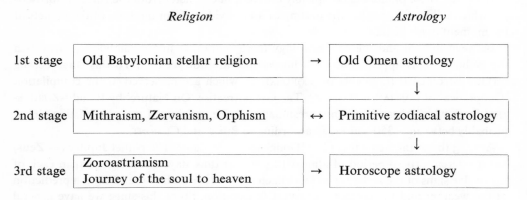

	Religion		*Astrology*
1st stage	Old Babylonian stellar religion	→	Old Omen astrology
2nd stage	Mithraism, Zervanism, Orphism	↔	Primitive zodiacal astrology
3rd stage	Zoroastrianism Journey of the soul to heaven	→	Horoscope astrology

It should be remarked that the left half of this scheme is oversimplified. The multiplicity of religious tendencies in the Near East, Egypt and Greece cannot be compressed into a three-part scheme without distortion. The boundary between the second and third stages is not at all sharp. However, the division of astrology in the right half of the scheme is quite clear and sharp and the interaction with cosmic religion well attested in all three cases.

Sirius and the harvest

The Roman astrologer MANILIUS[1]) reports that the priests in the region of Taurus used to observe the rising of Sirius from a mountain top and accordingly predict the weather, illnesses, alliances, war and peace.

How observations of the rising of Sirius can be used as a basis for predicting the harvest and other events of the coming year is explained in two astrological fragments of ZORO-ASTER, preserved in the Geoponica of CASSIANUS BASSUS[2]). The zodiacal sign must be observed, we read in fragment *0* 40, in which the moon stands at the morning rising of

---

[1]) MANILIUS, Astronomica I, 401—406.
[2]) BIDEZ et CUMONT: *Mages* I, p. 123—127 and II, p. 179—183, Frag. *0* 40 and 41.

Sirius. If the moon is in Leo, there will be corn, oil and wine in abundance, there will be battles, a king will appear, etc. According to the second fragment 0 41, the zodiacal sign to observe is the one in which the moon stands at the first thunder after the morning rising of Sirius. Again, the forecast varies according to the zodiacal sign. F. BOLL has published another fragment[1]) from Syria in which the same method is taught as in the ZOROASTER Fragment 0 40.

An indication that the rising of Sirius has something to do with the harvest is found in the Avesta. Yasht 8 of the Avesta is dedicated to the star-god Tishtrya. As we shall see later, Tishtrya is probably Sirius. Strophe 36 of this Yasht reads:

> We offer to Tishtrya . . . for according to the way he rises the year be good for the land. Will the Aryan lands have a good year?

> (DARMESTETER, Zend-Avesta II, p. 424).

Strophe 44 reads:

> We offer to Tishtrya, the magnificent, triumphant star, whom Ahura Mazda has set as *Lord* and *Overseer* of all the stars

> (ibid, p. 426).

With this we must now compare the evidence of PLUTARCHOS (Isis and Osiris, 47):

> Hereupon Horomazes increased himself three times in size, placed himself as far from the sun as is the earth from the sun, and adorned the heaven with stars. He set one star, Sirius, before all the rest as *watchman* and *lookout*.

The almost literal coincidence between Plutarchos and Strophe 44 enables us to conclude that Tishtrya means Sirius. On this assumption, the statement in Strophe 36: 'According to the way he rises, so will the year be good for the land', fits exceptionally well with the harvest predictions based on the rising of Sirius which have been handed down to us by MANILIUS and the fragments of 'ZOROASTER'.

The connection between the Tishtrya cult and that of Mithras is shown by the fact that the Tishtrya-Yasht contains a Mithras myth. The same people that worshipped Tishtrya also worshipped Mithras. Where did this people live?

In Strophe 36 of the Tishtrya-Yasht mention is made of the 'Aryan countries', an expression which also occurs in the Mithra-Yasht. Ariana, the land of the Aryans, coincides for the most part with modern Iran. This then was the home of the Tishtrya cult.

---

[1]) Catalogus codicum astrologorum graecorum VII, p. 183, and BIDEZ-CUMONT, Mages II, p. 181.

The geographical horizon of the Mithra-Yasht is, as we have seen, the region between Samarkand and the Lake Aral. In the Tishtrya Yasht a certain *Vouru-kasha Lake* plays a part. According to NYBERG and others, this is the Lake Aral (NYBERG, Religionen des alten Iran, p. 251 and 402). Another possibility, which NYBERG considers less likely, is the Caspian.

Like the Mithra-Yasht, the Tishtrya Yasht has a strong feeling for nature. The god Tishtrya comes in the form of a horse to the Vouru-kasha Lake and conquers the Pairikâs, who move about between heaven and earth preventing the rain from falling. The star-god Satavaêsa scatters the clouds, and, thank to Tishtrya, they unload themselves of the rain and cause a good harvest.

We are clearly dealing here with a North Iranian nature myth, in which the zodiacal signs and astrological science as yet play no part. Tishtrya is the bright star Sirius, which becomes visible in the morning sky in high summer, which then climbs ever higher and finally in the autumn brings the longed-for rain.

The Mithras cult is found later among the Maguseans in the Taurus region in an altered form, mixed up with Babylonian astronomy. We can assume that a similar admixture took place in the Sirius cult. The old Irian idea, that Sirius brings the rain and assures the outcome of the harvest, is mixed up with Babylonian ideas about the influence of the moon and the zodiacal signs. This seems to me to be the origin of the rules for harvest prediction which the Magi ascribed to their prophet ZOROASTER.

The dating of primitive zodiacal astrology

The astrology of ZOROASTER, which we have outlined in the two preceding sections, belongs to the second stage in our scheme of development. It makes use of the zodiac, but is otherwise of a decidedly primitive nature, very close to the old omen astrology.

The numerous astrological texts of the Assyrian period belong in character to the old omen astrology. No mention is made in any of them of the twelve-part zodiac. The transition to the second stage must therefore have taken place after the Assyrian period.

On the other hand, we shall see that in the period after -450 horoscopy, i.e. the astrology of the third stage, became ever more predominant. The time limits for the second-stage astrology are thus -630 to -450.

We can, I believe, go somewhat further and conjecture that this intermediate astrology originated at the time of the Chaldaean kings (-625 to -538).

This hypothesis is supported above all by the relation between the second-stage astrology and Orphism. For there is a 'Dodekaeteris of Orpheus' and a 'Great Year of Orpheus'. Orphism flourished in Greece in the time of PHEREKYDES and ONOMAKRITOS, i.e. between -570 and -510.

Horoscopy

The oldest cuneiform horoscope which has come down to us can be ascribed, according to SACHS[1]), to the year −409. It comes from the archives of a temple in Babylon. Other horoscopes belong to the years −287, −262, −257, −234, and so on.

Babylonian horoscopes contain as a rule the birth date of the child, the positions of the moon, sun and planets (mostly only the zodiacal sign, but sometimes also the longitude in degrees within the sign), the duration of visibility of the new moon and the full moon in the morning after sunrise, and also the last visibility of the moon. The prediction derived from this information is usually rather summary; but sometimes details are given about the significance of individual planets.

Greek sources also confirm the existence of horoscopy before −400, the principal astrologers being called 'Magi' or 'Chaldaeans'. DIOGENES LAERTIOS (Vitae philosophorum II 45) writes:

> Aristotle reports that a Syrian Magus came to Athens and predicted to Sokrates among other ills even his violent death.

SOKRATES died by the cup of hemlock in −398. If there is any truth in our report, horoscopy must have reached Greece by about −400.

Furthermore CICERO (De divinatione II, 87) has preserved for us an opinion expressed by EUDOXOS (around −370):

> Eudoxus wrote that not the least credence should be given to the Chaldaeans in their predictions and assertions about the life of a man based on the day of his birth.

From a still earlier time there is a report of GELLIUS (Noctes Atticae XV 20):

> A Chaldeaean predicted to his father from the stars the brilliant future of Euripides.

The mention of a 'Chaldaean', the predictions relative to an individual and the phrase 'from the stars', all point unmistakeably to horoscopy. EURIPIDES won his first prize for tragedy at the age of 40 in −441. Since the prediction was made to his father, he must still have been young and as yet unknown. Thus, if made at all, the prediction must antedate −445.

The Babylonian texts also lead us to much the same date. The text no. 1387 from −445 already mentioned and VAT 4924 from −418 give positions of the planets with respect

---

[1]) A. SACHS, Babylonian Horoscopes, J. of Cuneiform Studies 6 (1952), p. 49.

to zodiacal signs (Venus at the end of Pisces, Jupiter and Venus in the beginning of Gemini, etc.). These data are not direct observations: the end of Pisces and the beginning of Gemini are not marked in the sky. Direct observations of distances between planets and fixed stars from a good basis for astronomical calculations, but data such as 'Venus stood at the end of Pisces' are of little value for astronomy. Why did the texts contain such statements? To me, the explanation is clear: it was horoscope astrology that required just such positions of the planets in relation to the signs of the zodiac.

Thus we come to the conclusion that horoscopy originated in Babylon before −450 and was already known in Greece before −440.

Horoscopes for conception and birth

We have already mentioned that the Babylonian BEROSSOS, a priest of Bel, founded an astrological school on the Greek island of Kos about −300. His pupil ARCHINOPOLOS applied the methods of birth horoscopy to the moment of conception (VITRUVIUS IX 4). The same idea is found in a Babylonian horoscope for the year −257, which KUGLER (Sternkunde II, p. 558) published. This interesting text (Rm IV 224) reads:

> (Obverse) Year 53 ⟨Addaru II⟩ at night on the 1st day (= −257, March 17) the moon below the front star at the beginning of Aries (= γ Arietis, according to an unpublished study by Dr. TEUCHER).
> On the 12th equinox.
> On the 1st day the Moon ... Pisces[1]) ...
> (Reverse) Year 54 Kislinnu 1 (i.e. the preceding month has 30 days) at night on the 8th at the beginning of the night below the Fish (= η Piscium) 1½ cubits. The Moon had already moved 0 cubit towards the East.
> On the 20th solstice.
> On the 13th (= −257, Dec. 20) ... of the moon.
> At this time Jupiter was in Capricorn, Venus in Scorpio, the moon in Gemini, Mercury had set heliacally in the East in Sagittarius, Saturn and Mars in Libra.

The date 17th March −257, the first day of Addaru II of the year 53, is mentioned twice, the second time out of chronological order, namely after the mention of the equinox on the 12th. On the second occasion Pisces is mentioned.

The date 20th Dec. −257, the 13th Kislimu of the year 54, is likewise out of chronolo-

---

[1]) According to KUGLER, this is a copyist's error. It should read: Sun in Pisces; for the moon must have stood in Aries according to line 1.

gical order in the text. For this date the positions of the planets in the zodiacal signs are given, as in other horoscopes of this period.

KUGLER has further remarked that the two dates, 17th March and 20th Dec., are just 279 days apart. Since the purpose of compiling the planetary positions for these dates can only have been astrological, we may suppose that the first date relates to the conception, the second to the birth of a child. Now CENSORINUS tells us (De die natali 8) that, in the Chaldaean view, the position of the sun in a certain degree of a zodiacal sign denotes the place of conception. In fact, if KUGLER's correction is right, our text mentions the position of the sun, in the sign of Pisces, for the first date.

Thus we have here a conception-and-birth horoscope for the year −257.

THE DEVELOPMENT OF ASTRONOMY IN THE SIXTH CENTURY

Summary of previous results

We have seen that, after the fall of the Assyrian empire (−611) the old polytheism was being pushed aside by a new religious movement which flooded in two mighty waves from Iran to the West. The first wave was that of Zervanism, which reached Greece about −550. The second was the worship of Ahura Mazda, which was proclaimed around −500 as the official religion of the Persian empire. Connected with this was the doctrine of the celestial origin and immortality of the soul.

We have also seen that the old Omen astrology was replaced, about the same time or somewhat later, by a new zodiacal astrology, within which we have to distinguish two further stages: *primitive zodiacal astrology* and *horoscopy*. The first is connected in the sources with Orphism, which in its turn is most closely tied up with Zervanism. On the other hand, horoscopy is closely connected with the doctrine of the celestial origin of the soul; its existence can be demonstrated in Babylon about −450 and in Greece about −440.

Relations between astrology and astronomy

It is to be expected *a priori* that there were two stages in the development of astronomy, corresponding to the two stages of astrology. Zodiacal astrology, even of the most primitive kind, requires astronomical concepts and observations, and horoscopy requires an even more highly developed astronomy. We shall now examine this point more closely.

In order to predict the events of the coming year from the Dodekaeteris of ORPHEUS or that of ZOROASTER it is necessary to know the zodiacal sign in which Jupiter stands. For this a single observation at the beginning of the year generally suffices; sometimes a further observation in the course of the year is required. For ZOROASTER's method of predicting the harvest in a given year one must know the sign in which the moon stands in the morning of the first visibility of Sirius. This is already more difficult, because the moon moves fast and can be invisible on this morning. In the 14 days from new moon to full moon the moon is visible only in the evening. The most natural procedure then would be to observe the moon in the evening and deduce from its position among the stars its position relative to the zodiacal signs. The morning position is then obtained by interpolation between two evenings.

Therefore zodiacal astrology (at least in the beginning, as long as there was no satisfactory theory of lunar motion available) required *systematic observational activity*.

All the more does horoscopy call for regular observation of the moon and planets. A child is frequently born in the daytime, when the stars are not visible. In the relevant night the sky may be overcast. Or the approach to the astrologer may be made some time after the birth. The astrologer then requires either a continuous record of observations or theoretically calculated tables.

We must therefore assume that there must have been systematic lunar observations at the time of primitive zodiacal astrology, and that by the time horoscopy came into use (i.e. in the early Persian period) systematic observations had been extended to all the planets.

The observational texts confirm our expectations. While only a few observational texts have been preserved from the new Babylonian and early Persian periods, these few have exactly the character expected. We shall now consider this more closely.

Observational texts from the 6th Century

Let me first recall that the eclipse observations, which started in the Assyrian period, were continued on a regular basis in the neo-Babylonian and Persian periods. Official observers and scribes had the job of carrying out these observations.

At the beginning of the reign of NEBUCHADNEZZAR II we encounter a new form of observational text. One text, which possibly stems from this time, contains observations of the course of the planet Venus[1]). From the year −567 (year 37 of the reign of NEBUCHADNEZZAR) we have an astronomical diary, containing lunar and planetary observations[2]). Unfortunately, the part of the text relating to the end of the month Sivan, where the morning rising of Sirius must have taken place, is lost; but at the beginning of the same month note is made of the lunar positions for the evenings of the 5th (perhaps also 6th), 8th, 9th and 10th Sivan, e.g.:

---

[1]) PINCHES-SACHS, Late Babyl. Astron. Texts (Providence 1955), Text 1386, p. xviii and 214.
[2]) P. V. NEUGEBAUER and E. F. WEIDNER: Ein astronomischer Beobachtungstext, Ber. Sächs. Ges. Wiss. Leipzig 67 (1915), p. 29.

At the beginning of the night of the 5th the moon overtook by 1 cubit eastwards the northern star at the foot of the Lion.

Observations of this kind are exactly what is required for an approximate calculation
of lunar positions. With these observations and a fixed star catalogue giving the longitudes of the major zodiacal stars the observed lunar positions can be converted into
longitudes, and the longitudes for intermediate positions can be interpolated. The lack
of precision in the calculation does not matter, because all that was needed for the
prognoses of primitive zodiacal astrology was the zodiacal sign in which the moon stood.

We therefore suppose that the observations of year −567 served among other purposes
to provide the lunar and planetary positions necessary for the predictions of primitive
zodiacal astrology. But in that case this astrology must already have been in existence
by about −570, and the division of the zodiac into twelve signs even earlier.

The art of soothsaying at the court of the Chaldaean kings

The learned men at the Assyrian court were not only astronomers, but also astrologers
and in general soothsayers. The situation was probably the same at the court of the
Chaldaean kings. We know from two texts that astrological dreams were interpreted at
the court of NABUNAID.[1]) It may therefore be assumed that the lunar and planetary
observations found in the texts served the purposes not only of science, but also, and
perhaps principally, of astrology.

This assumption is confirmed by ISAIAH, who predicts the coming fall of the Babylonian
kingdom and derides the 'daughter of Babylon' in the following words:

Let now the astrologers, the star-gazers, the monthly prognosticators, stand
up and save thee from these things that shall come upon thee (Isaiah, 47:13).

Besides Egyptians and others there were at the Chaldaen court both Medes and Persians
(see E. F. WEIDNER in Mélanges syriens offerts à Dussaud II, p. 930). NEBUCHADNEZZAR'S
wife was a Median princess. Now we have seen earlier that the doctrine of world periods
and catastrophes, which we find in Greek texts from −500 on, originated from a fusion
of Iranian ideas with Babylonian doctrines. I imagine that this fusion took place in the
Neo-Babylonian period.

After −530, under KAMBYSES and his successors, Babylonian astronomy begins to
flower afresh, as we shall see in the next chapter. This period saw the development of
lunar and planetary theory, the organisation of the intercalary system and the intensi-
fication of observational activity.

[1]) E. F. WEIDNER: Studien zur babyl. Himmelskunde. Rivista degli Studi Orientali 9 (1922), p. 297.

I suppose that this renewed vigour is closely connected with the rise of horoscopy. Astrologers who want to cast horoscopes need methods for calculating planetary positions.

In order to obtain more information about the astrological activity in the Persian period, let us consider the divine names of the planets, which came into use, at least in Greece, during just this period.

DIVINE NAMES OF PLANETS

Up to the present day, we give the planets names of Roman gods. Just so, the Greeks called the planets after the gods Kronos, Zeus, etc. We find divine names of planets also in Hellenistic Egypt, Syria, Minor Asia, Armenia, Babylonia, Persia and elsewhere. Because these divine names play an important role in horoscopic astrology, it is interesting to trace their history as far back as possible.

Greek and Latin names of planets

The history of the Greek names of the planets was investigated by FRANZ CUMONT in a fundamental paper in l'Antiquité classique 4 (1935). I shall give a summary of his results.

HOMEROS has names only for Venus, not for the other planets. Venus as Morning Star was called Eosphoros, and as Evening Star Hesperos.

DEMOKRITOS, who lived about −430, does not give the planets names: he even says that he does not know how many planets there are. However, at about the same time or even earlier, the Pythagoreans asserted that there are exactly seven planets, including Sun and Moon, and they established a definite order of the planets according to their distances, as we know from EUDEMOS[1]).

After −430 the following names were in use:

Time of Platon (after 430 B.C.)	Hellenistic (after 330 B.C.)	Late Antiquity (after 200 B.C.)	Latin name (after 100 B.C.)
Star of Kronos	Phainon	Kronos	Saturnus
Star of Zeus	Phaeton	Zeus	Jupiter
Star of Ares	Pyroeis	Ares	Mars
Star of Aphrodite	Phosphoros	Aphrodite	Venus
Star of Hermes	Stilbon	Hermes	Mercurius

[1]) SIMPLIKIOS, Commentary to De Caelo, ed. Heiberg, p. 471.

According to CUMONT, it is probable that the Pythagoreans already used the divine names. In any case, PLATON and his contemporaries never used any other names than these. In the dialogue Epinomis, written by PLATON or his pupil PHILIPPOS of Opus, it is said that the divine stars have no names, but only surnames: they are called after the gods Aphrodite, Hermes, Kronos, Zeus and Ares. According to the author, these surnames are due to the 'Barbarians', who first made observations of the 'cosmical gods'. The Epinomis expressly mentions the countries Egypt and Syria, in which these observations have been made.

This passage shows clearly that the divine names were the earliest Greek names of planets, except in the case of Venus.

The names in the second column of our table are scientific names, which were used in the astronomical and astrological writings of the Hellenistic age. After 200 B.C. they gradually went out of use and were replaced by the simpler denominations Kronos, Zeus, etc. The Romans replaced the Greek divine names by the names of the corresponding Roman gods.

Babylonian names of planets

In Babylonia just as in Greece, two sets of names were in use, one scientific and one divine. In astronomical cuneiform texts we find the scientific names, mostly in abbreviated form. The divine names were names of gods whose characters were similar to those of the Greek and Roman planetary gods. Thus, the highest god Marduk corresponds to Zeus or Jupiter. Ishtar, the goddess of love, was identified with Aphrodite or Venus. Nergal was a warrier god, like Ares or Mars, etc.

The divine names are very old. All scholars agree that the custom to associate planets with gods originated in Babylonia and was subsequently adopted by other nations.

The names were:

Scientific name	Name of God	Latin name
Kaimânu	Ninib	Saturnus
Mulu-babbar	Marduk	Jupiter
Sal-bat-a-ni	Nergal	Mars
Dili-pat	Ishtar	Venus
Gu-utu	Nabu	Mercurius

Persian names of planets

Unfortunately, the old-Persian names of the planets are not known. However, we are pretty well informed about divine names of planets which were in use in different parts of the Persian empire: in Egypt, Syria, Babylonia and Minor Asia, and we also have a complete list of middle-Persian names that were in general use under the Sassanid reign (AD 226-640). Most of these names are names of Persian gods whose old-Persian names are also known; only the name of the planet Saturn goes back to the Babylonian name Kaimânu. In the following list, the middle-Persian or Pahlavi names are taken from J. DUCHESNE-GUILLEMIN: La religion de l'Iran ancien, Paris 1962. The oldest source in which they appear seems to be the Bundahishn, Chapter V.

Planet	Babylonian name	Old-Persian God	Pahlavi name
Saturn	Kaimânu	—	Kaivân
Jupiter		Ahura Mazda	Ohrmazd
Mars		Verethragna	Varhrân
Sun		Mithra	Mihr
Venus		Anâhitâ	Anâhît
Mercury		Tîra[1])	Tîr
Moon		Mâh	Mâh

DUCHESNE-GUILLEMIN remarks that it is difficult to date the Pahlavi names of planets accurately. Still, he feels that the use of divine names for the planets cannot well be an invention of the Sassanid era, because in the sacred books of that era all planets were condemned as creatures of the devil. The identification of the planets with great gods must be a relict from an earlier period, in which at least three of the planets (Jupiter, Venus and the Sun) were regarded as benevolent.

As we have seen, the identification of planets with gods is fundamental for horoscopic astrology. Now this kind of astrology originated in the Achaemenid period (539-331 B.C.) and spread over the whole ancient world during the Hellenistic period (after 330 B.C.). Therefore it seems reasonable to assume that the identification of planets with Persian gods took place during the Achaemenid or early Hellenistic period.

In favour of this assumption we may, once more, quote the dialogue Epinomis, in which the divine names of the planets are ascribed to 'the barbarians' in general, including, of course, the Persians. The Syrians, who are expressly mentioned, lived within the Persian

---

[1]) According to A. GOETZE (Zeitschr. für vergleichende Sprachforschung indogerm. Sprachen *51*, p. 146, footnote[5]), the Pahlavi form Tîr is not derived from Avestian Tishtrya, but from old-Persian Tîra.

empire. Quite a number of astronomers and astrologers, living in Babylon, in the very heart of the empire, were busy making observations, calculating planetary positions and casting horoscopes. The Babylonians, Greeks, Egyptians and Syrians all used the divine names of the planets and based their horoscopes on the assumption that the planets are mighty divine powers. So why should the Persians, who ruled over all these nations and who certainly were influenced by the Babylonian civilization, make an exception to the general rule?

As we have seen, the Achaemenid kings had a strong tendency to identify foreign gods with their own gods. The astrologers too identified the great gods of all nations with planets. The Persian kings had every reason to propagate these identifications and to persuade their subjects to accept them. One universal cosmic religion was much better for them than several conflicting religions.

Beside these general considerations, there are quite a number of specific arguments, all pointing into the same direction. Let us consider the single planets one after the other.

The sun

In Roman texts Mithras is called 'Sol invictus'. In an inscription of ANTIOCHOS of Commagene, dated 62 B.C. (see Plate 19 and 20) Mithras is identified with Helios. In a text from the library of ASSURBANIPAL 'Mitra' is mentioned as one of the many names of the Sun-God. Hence the identification Mithra = Sun is very old.

The moon

In the case of Mâh, the god of the Moon, there is no problem at all. In all countries the Moon and the Moon-God are called by one and the same name.

Mars

On the monumental horoscope of ANTIOCHOS of Commagene (62 B.C.) thee large planets are pictured, just above the lion (see Plate 18). Their names are given as

> [Mars:] Pyroeis, (Star) of Herakles
> [Mercury:] Stilbon, (Star) of Apollon
> [Jupiter:] Phaeton, (Star) of Zeus.

The designation of Jupiter as Star of Zeus is the usual one, but the other two differ from general Greek usage. The usual name of Mars in the time of ANTIOCHOS was

'Star of Ares', and of Mercury 'Star of Hermes'. ANTIOCHOS reconciled his designations with the usual ones by just identifying Herakles with Ares, and Apollon with Hermes. His identifications, inscribed below the statues of the gods, were:

$$Zeus = Oromasdes$$
$$Artagnes = Herakles = Ares$$
$$Apollon = Mithras = Helios = Hermes$$

Oromasdes is, of course, the Persian god Ahura Mazda. Mithras is Mithra, the Persian sun god. But who is Artagnes?

The original Persian name of this god is Verethragna, the mighty warrior, the dragon-killer. In middle-Persian texts he was called *Varhrân*, in Armenia *Vahagn*, in Syria *Wahrâm*. Armenian authors regularly translate Herakles as Vahagn. The Greek version Artagnes is not derived from the Syriac or Armenian name, but directly from the old-Persian *Verethragna*.

ANTIOCHOS identified Artagnes with Herakles and called Mars 'Star of Herakles'. Hence the association of Mars with Verethragna was not a Sassanid invention: it was established already in the time of ANTIOCHOS.

We can even go back in time to the second or third century B.C. CUMONT, in his article on the names of planets in l'Antiquité classique 4, has given a list of divine names of planets which were in use in Hellenistic Egypt. The names are quoted by late astrologers from astrological books ascribed to 'the Egyptians' or to 'NECHEPSO and PETOSIRIS[1]).' According to F. BOLL, the books ascribed to PETOSIRIS were written before −150. In these Hellenistic Egyptian books, the planets were usually called by their scientific Greek names, but their divine names were also mentioned. The names are:

Planets	Scientific names	Divine names
Saturn	Phainon	Star of Nemesis
Jupiter	Phaeton	Star of Osiris
Mars	Pyroeis	Star of Herakles
Venus	Phosphorus	Star of Isis
Mercury	Stilbon	Star of Apollon

Another set of astrological books was ascribed to the 'Chaldaeans', i.e. to the Babylonian astronomers and astrologers. From these books we have numerous quotations by Greek authors; obviously they were written in Greek or available in Greek translations.

---

[1]) See VAN DER WAERDEN: Die „Aegypter" und die „Chaldäer". Sitzungsber. Heidelberger Akad. (Math. Kl.) 1972, 5. Abhandlung, p. 201.

In two of these quotations[1]) it is said that the Chaldaeans called Pyroeis 'Star of Herakles', and the Greeks 'Star of Ares'.

We can now put the evidence together. The planet Mars was called after the god Verethragna = Artagnes = Herakles in several countries which once belonged to the Persian empire: in Egypt, in Minor Asia and in Sassanid Persia. The identification can be traced back to the early Hellenistic reign (-200 or even ealier). It is ascribed to the 'Chaldaeans', i.e. to Babylonian astrologers, by authors like EPIGENES[2]), who claim to have studied cuneiform texts. Now, Verethragna was an old-Persian god. Hence it seems probable that the old-Persian name of Mars was 'Star of Verethragna'.

Jupiter

In the Armenian version of the Romance of Alexander the Great (the so-called Pseudo-Callisthenes) the name *Zeus* is consistently translated as *Auramazd*, no matter whether the god or the planet is meant[3]). The text was probably written in the fifth century A.D., long after the christianization of Armenia, which took place early in the third century. The name Auramazd (derived, of course, from Ahura Mazda) must have been a relict from an earlier period, just as our name of the planet Jupiter is a relict from the Roman period.

According to GELZER[4]), the Persian gods Ahura Mazda, Verethragna etc. were introduced in Armenia during the Arsacid reign in Persia. So we may suppose that during this reign the identity

$$\text{Ahura Mazda} = \text{Zeus} = \text{Planet Jupiter}$$

was generally recognized.

In the Syriac version of the romance of Alexander, which derives from a middle Persian original, the planet is called *Hörmizd*, which corresponds to middle Persian *Ohrmazd*. In the Bundahisn the planet was also called *Ohrmazd*. The whole evidence points towards the conclusion that the usual middle Persian name of the planet was *Ohrmazd*, not only under the Sassanids, but already under the Arsacids, who reigned in Persia from about -250 to $+226$.

ANTIOCHOS of Commagene calls Jupiter 'Star of Zeus', and he identified Zeus with *Oromasdes*. Hence, in Minor Asia, the identity of Ahura Mazda with Zeus and his relation to the planet Jupiter was recognized as early as 62 B.C.

[1]) See F. CUMONT: Les noms des planètes. L'antiquité classique *4* (1935), p. 20, footnote (1).

[2]) About EPIGENES see A. REHM: Das 7. Buch der Nat. Quaest. des Seneca, Sitzungsber. Bayer. Akad. München 1921 (1. Abh.), and also the article Epigenes in PAULY-WISSOWA's Real-Enzyklopädie.

[3]) A. M. WOLOHOJIAN: The romance of Alexander the Great. Columbia Univ. Press New York 1969.

[4]) H. GELZER: Zur armenischen Götterlehre. Berichte sächs. Ges. Wiss. Leipzig 1896, p. 100.

As we have seen, HERODOTOS and his Persian informants already identified Ahura
Mazda with Zeus. Eighty years later, PLATON and his friends called Jupiter 'Star of
Zeus', and asserted that 'the Barbarians' did the same thing. Hence, it seems very probable
that already during the Achaemenid period the Persians called Jupiter 'Star of Ahura
Mazda'.

Venus

HERODOTOS tells us (Histories I 131) that the Persians worshipped Aphrodite as
'Urania', that is, as a celestial goddess. He has misunderstood her name as 'Mithra'.
In the Avesta, the name of the goddess is Ardvî Sûrâ Anâhitâ. From this name are derived
the middle Persian name Anâhît and the late Syriac name Anahîd, which names were
used for the goddess as well as for the planet Venus.

By analogy with Mars and Jupiter, we may conjecture that already under the Achaemenids the planet Venus was called 'Star of Anâhitâ'. Fortunately, we have a confirmation from a genuine old text: the Anâhitâ-Yasht of the Avesta.

The Yashts of the Avesta are hymns to the gods and divine powers. Yasht 1 is devoted
to Ahura Mazda, yasths 2, 3, 4 and 11, 12, 13 to typical Zoroastrian divinities. Most
important for our investigation are the Yashts 5-8, 10 and 14, which are devoted to pre-
Zoroastrian gods, namely:

                        5 to Ardvî Sûrâ Anâhitâ,
                        6 to the Sun,
                        7 to the Moon,
                        8 to Tishtrya (= Sirius),
                       10 to Mithra,
                       14 to Verethragna.

As we see from this list, Mithra was distinguished from the sun. Mithra was the god
of Daylight: he was said to rise over the mountains before sunrise. In any case, Mithra
was a celestial god, and so are the Sun, the Moon and Tishtrya. Therefore, and because
of HERODOTOS' designation 'Urania', we may expect Anâhitâ to be a celestial goddess
as well. This expectation is confirmed by the text itself. I quote:

85. Geh herzu, komm wieder her, o gewaltige, makellose Ardvî, von jenen
Sternen dort zu der ahurageschaffenen Erde.

90. O gewaltige, makellose Ardvî! Mit welchem Opfer soll ich huldigen,
dass dir Mazda eine Bahn bereite, nicht eine Bahn diesseits, sondern über dem
Sonnenball . . .

96. Ich will den allgefeierten goldenen Berg Hukairya verehren, von dem
mir aus einer Höhe von tausend Männern die gewaltige, makellose Ardvî
herankommt . . .

132. . . . Komm wieder her, o gewaltige, makellose Ardvî, von jenen Sternen dort zu der ahurageschaffenen Erde, zu dem opfernden Zaotar . . .

(Translation by F. WOLFF: Avesta, first ed. 1910, reprint 1924, p. 182).

Anâhitâ, Mithra and Verethragna were popular gods, who were worshipped in the east of Iran before ZARATHUSTRA. The present redaction of the hymns was made by a Zoroastrian, but their main contents is pre-Zoroastrian.

ZARATHUSTRA introduced several abstract notions of divine powers such as Vohu Mana (Good Mind), Asha (Truth or Right Order), etc. These names are completely absent from the Mithra- and Anâhitâ-Yasht. The god Mithra 'rises over the mountains', Anâhitâ becomes visible 'at a height of 1000 men', she is depicted as a beautiful girl, who girdles herself in order to make the view of her breasts more pleasant, etc. These Yashts are eminently visual, not abstract. For the author of the Yashts, the beauty of girls, of rivers and mountains, and of the bright morning sky means quite a lot.

In the Gathas, the beauty of Nature is hardly ever mentioned. ZARATHUSTRA is more interested in people and cattle, in right and wrong, in immortality and the exaltation of the soul. It is quite a different type of religion.

NYBERG (Religionen des alten Iran, p. 262) calls Ardvî Sûrâ Anâhitâ 'a celestial Aphrodite in the full sense of the word'. Yet he does not identify her with the planet Venus, the Anahîd or Anâhît of the Syriac and middle Persian texts. He supposes that the Anâhitâ of the Yasht was identified with the Milky Way, which the people of eastern Iran might have considered as the celestial representation of the river Jaxartes.

It seems to me, that the text of the Yasht is more easily understood if we identify Anâhitâ with the planet Venus. In the Yasht, Anâhitâ is called mighty and splendid. Do these epitheta fit the faint Milky Way? It is said that Anâhitâ has her orbit above the sun, but that she may leave the region of the stars and come nearer to us. For Venus, this makes sense, but not for the Milky Way. In verse 96 a king or a priest is said to have climbed the mountain Hukairya in order to worship the goddess. He saw her come from a height of 1000 men. Can one say of the Milky Way that it appears at a definite height over a mountain?

For these reasons, the most plausible hypothesis seems to be that the author of the Yasht identified Anâhitâ with the planet Venus. Together with the Sun and the Moon, Venus formed a triad of great celestial gods, in the Avesta as well as in Old-Babylonian texts. The Yashts 5, 6 and 7 were devoted to this Triad, and Yasht 8 to the brightest fixed star, Tishtrya = Sirius.

Mercury and Sirius

The middle Persian name of Mercury was *Tîr*, which comes from old Persian *Tîra*. In the Bundahish, *Tîr* is distinguished from *Tîshtar*, which is the name of a fixed star or constellation, most probably Sirius. The middle Persian star name Tîshstar is derived from Avestian *Tishtrya*.

As we have seen, one of the Yashts of the Avesta was devoted to Tishtrya. On the other hand, Tîr or Tîra occurs already under the Achaemenid reign as a component of theophoric names such as TIRIDATES, TIRIPIRNA and TIRIBAZOS. A person named TIRIDATA lived under ARTAXERXES I (465-424 B.C.). It follows that the names *Tîra* and *Tishtrya* both existed as names of gods in the Achaemenid age. More specifically, Tishtrya = Sirius was venerated in the Eastern part of the Persian empire, and Tîra or Tîr was worshipped in the West.

The two gods were closely related, for in the Persian calendar the fourth month was called *Tîr*, and in the Avesta the same month is called *Tishtrya*. The relation between the two is explained in the middle-Persian Bundahish as follows:

> Seven chieftains of the planets have come unto the seven chieftains of the constellations, as the planet Tîr (Mercury) under Tîshtar (Sirius), . . .

(Bundahish, Chapter V, 1, translated by E. W. WEST. Sacrec Books of the East V:
Pahlavi Texts).

To understand this, we must recall that in the Bundahish the planets were supposed to be evil powers. To prevent them from doing harm, they were placed under the supervision of benevolent constellations.

In analogy to the other planets, we may say that it is not unreasonable to assume that Tîr or Tîra was the name of the planet Mercury already during the Achaemenid reign.

Saturn

In our middle-Persian texts Saturn is the only planet that has no divine name. The planet is called *Kaivân*, which is derived from the Babylonian scientific name *kaimânu*. How can we explain this anomaly?

A clue is given by Armenian texts, in which Saturn is called *Zruan*, which means Zurvan or Zervan[1]). So the divine name of Saturn seems to have been *Zervan*.

We have seen that Zervan was also called Tyche or (in middle-Persian) bakht, which means Fate. This accords well with the Egyptian designation of Saturn: 'Star of Nemesis'. Nemesis, the divine revenge, is a form of Fate.

---

[1]) M. HUBSCHMANN: Armenische Grammatik, p. 94, Footnote. In the Armenian version of the romance of ALEXANDER the name of the god Kronos is nearly always translated as *Zruam*. The Armenian historian MOSES OF KHOREN also translates Kronos as Zruan.

If we translate the equation Saturn = Zervan into Greek, we obtain

$$\text{Kronos} = \text{Chronos}.$$

In fact, several Greek authors state that Kronos is Chronos, or Time. In an inscription from Elateia[1]), dating from the fifth or fourth century B.C., Poseidon is called 'Son of Chronos', which means that Poseidon's father Kronos is here called Chronos. PLUTAR-CHOS gives a fuller account:

> These men are like the Greeks who say that Kronos is but a figurative name
> for Chronos (Time), Hera for Air, and that the birth of Hephaistos symbolizes
> the change of Air into Fire
>
> (PLUTARCHOS, Isis and Osiris 32, transl. by F. C. BABBITT).

Among the Greek authors who asserted that Kronos is only a figurative name for Chronos, we must include PHEREKYDES of Syros, who said that Zeus (whom he called Zas) is the aether, Chtonie the earth, and Kronos Time (Chronos). See DIELS, Fragmente der Vorsokratiker, PHEREKYDES A 9.

As we have seen, PHEREKYDES was influenced by Zervanism, for he held Chronos to be the first god and the creator. Hence we may conjecture that the identification Kronos = Chronos was a Zervanist doctrine.

Now the question arises: How can Chronos, the never-ageing, infinite Time, the first of the gods, who ever existed, be identical with Kronos, the old man, the son of Uranos, the ruler of the Golden Age? In the theogonoy of PHEREKYDES and the Orphics, the two play a completely different role: Chronos stands at the beginning of the series of successive rulers and Kronos comes much later. What does PHEREKYDES mean when he says that Kronos is Time?

In the Avesta (Yasna 72,10) two Zervans appear:

Zrvan-akarana = 'Boundless Time'
Zrvan-dareyô-χvaδâta = 'Time whose autonomous sway lasts for a long time'[2]).

In the Pahlavi books, the distinction between the two Zervans is further elaborated. A particularly clear explanation is given in Chapter 26 of the Greater Bundahish:

> This is the operation of Time, that it was infinite but was made finite for the

---

[1]) See E. HOFFMANN: Sylloge epigrammatum Graecarum 174.
[2]) See R. C. ZAEHNER: Zurvan, a Zoroastrian Dilemma (Oxford, Clarendon Press 1955) p. 57 and 275.

act of creation until the consummation, that is when the Destructive Spirit is
made powerless: then it mingles with that same infinity for ever and ever

(translated by ZAEHNER: Zervan, p. 338).

Chronos ageraos, the Never-Ageing Time of the Orphic texts is, of course, the Greek
equivalent of Zrvan akarana. On the other hand Kronos, the ruler of the Golden Age,
is more similar to 'Time whose reign lasts for a long time'. Zrvan akarana, the creator of
everything, cannot be identified with just one planet, but the finite Zrvan, the equivalent
of Kronos, could well be the god of the planet Saturn.

We can now understand why the name Zervan was eliminated from the Persian list
of planets and replaced by the neutral name Kaimânu. DARIUS was strongly opposed to
Zervanism. In his inscriptions, he calls Ahura Mazda 'the greatest of the gods' and 'the
creator of heaven and earth and men', whereas the Zervanists considered Zervan as the
highest god and the creator. In the Achaemenid inscriptions, Zervan is never mentioned,
nor does HERODOTOS mention the God of Time in his account of Persian religion. Zervanism led a hidden existance under the Achaemenids.

Two systems of gods

As we have seen, the Yasths 5-8, 10 and 14 of the Avesta are devoted to the following
pre-Zoroastrian gods:

        5. Anâhitâ
        6. Sun
        7. Moon
        8. Tishtrya
      10. Mithra
      14. Verethragna.

On the other hand, in the Bundahish, we find a system of six planetary gods corresponding to the seven planets of the astrologers with the exception of Kaivân = Saturn:

        Ohrmazd
        Varhrân
        Mihr
        Anahît
        Tîr
        Mâh.

The gods of the first list are popular gods: in the Yashts they are depicted just as they lived in the imagination of the people. Of course, there may have been more pre-Zoro-astrian popular gods, e.g. a god of the sky and a goddess of the earth.

The second list has a semiscientific character: it was developed under the influence of Babylonian astronomy and astrology. The Babylonians had a list of gods corresponding to the seven planets, including the Sun and the Moon. Therefore, when the Medes and Persians came into contact with Babylonian astrology, they dressed up a list of Iranian divinities corresponding in character to the Babylonian planetary gods. The people who concocted this list were probably the Magi, the 'great syncretists of Persian religion', as NYBERG says. They came to Babylon during the reign of CYRUS or even earlier.

In order to adapt the popular list of Gods to the doctrine of the astrologers, the Magi had to identify Mithra with the Sun. In a system of planetary gods, whose positions can be calculated, there is no place for a god of Dawn, who rises before the Sun. Also, they had no use for the fixed star Tishtrya = Sirius. Therefore, they replaced him by the arrow-god Tîra, but they also retained the great god Tishtrya, for they placed the planet Mercury = Tîra under the supervision of Sirius = Tishtrya. For Jupiter = Marduk, their only possible choice was Ahura Mazda, and for Mars = Nergal the most natural choice was Verethragna = Varhran. Thus, they obtained a list of six planetary gods, which was retained in the Arsacid and Sassanid era.

For Saturn the magi were in a dilemma. One possibility was, to identify Saturn = Ninib with 'Zervan of the long dominion'. This was done by some, as the Armenian name Zruan for Saturn shows. The other possibility was, to call the planet Saturn by its neutral name Kaimânu = Kaivân, and thus to avoid any allusion to Zervanism.

It is possible that the association of Saturn with the finite Zervan was current in Media as early as 550 B.C. This would explain the statement of PHEREKYDES: 'Kronos is Time'. Probably the system was changed in the time of DARIUS. Because DARIUS was opposed to Zervanism, the planet Saturn was henceforth just called *Kaivân*.

THE INSCRIPTIONS OF THE ACHAEMENIDS

The conclusion to be drawn from the preceding investigation is: probably, the Persian divine names of the planets originated in the Achaemenid period (539-331 B.C.) or even earlier. We now ask: Is this conclusion consistent with the inscriptions of the Achaemenid kings?

Decrees and inscriptions of CYRUS

As we have seen, the first Achaemenid king CYRUS tried to unify the religions in his empire by identifying foreign gods with the Persian 'God of Heaven'. In a decree, which is preserved in the book of Ezra, he ordered the Jews to erect a temple for the 'God of Heaven'. This designation of the God of Israel seldom occurs in the Bible, except in this particular decree: the term was probably dictated by KORES = CYRUS himself.

The same CYRUS also wrote an inscription in which he called Marduk 'the King of the Gods'. How could he do this without provoking a conflict whith his own countrymen who venerated their own God of Heaven as the highest god? I suppose he identified Marduk with the Persian God of Heaven, just as the Persian informants of HERODOTOS identified their own God of Heaven with the Greek Zeus.

In Babylon, the planet Jupiter was called 'Star of Marduk'. I suppose CYRUS knew this. Therefore, let us make the hypothesis that CYRUS too regarded Jupiter as the star of the highest god Ahura Mazda = Marduk, and let us have a closer look at his inscription from this point of view.

> He (Marduk) scrutinized every land, his glance fell everywhere, seeking a just prince after his heart's desire, that he might grasp his hands. Cyrus, King of Anshan, whose name He pronounced, He called to the overlordship of the world . . .
>
> Marduk, the Great Lord, the protector of his people, looked joyfully upon his pious deeds and his just heart, commanded him to move to His City of Babylon, caused him to set forth upon the road to Babylon, whereon He went along by his side like a friend and comrade. As uncountable as the waters of the river, his far-flung troops with their ready weapons strode by his side.
>
> Without battle or strife He caused him to enter into Babylon, His City. He protected Babylon from affliction. And the King Nabu-na'id, who had not worshipped Him, Marduk delivered into the hands of Cyrus.
>
> The people joyously blessed the Lord who by His might had turned death into life and had spared them annihilation and woe, and they chereished His name . . .
>
> When I entered peacefully into Babylon, and amidst jubilation and festivity established the residence of command in the palace of the princes, Marduk the Great Lord inclined the generous heart of the Babylonians towards me, and I ever daily concerned myself with His worship.

I think these words of praise to Marduk were not just vague phrases, but had a quite realistic meaning. When CYRUS marched toward Babylon, the planet Jupiter went alongside as a friend and helper at the southern sky, and with the god went his innumerable troops, the fixed stars.

It is well known that the Babylonian priests were not satisfied with their king NABU-NAID. I suppose they saw that the mighty stars, especially the star of Marduk, were favourable to CYRUS, and for this reason they persuaded the people of Babylon to give up the town without resistance. In return for this help, CYRUS confirmed the priests in their offices, took the hands of the statue of Marduk and declared that Marduk should be worshipped as the highest god.

This, to say the least, is a possible interpretation of the clay cylinder inscription of CYRUS.

KAMBYSES *and* DARIUS

Under KAMBYSES careful observations of the moon and the planets were made. The text 'STRASSMAIER KAMBYSES 400', which contains the records of these observations, also contains calculations of the rising and setting of the moon.

A series of observations of Jupiter was started under KAMBYSES and continued under DARIUS. Based upon these observations, a theory of the motion of Jupiter was developed under the reign of DARIUS, as we shall see in Chapter 7. Theories of Saturn and Mars followed, but Jupiter was studied most carefully: more than half of the extant planetary tables are devoted to Jupiter. I guess the motion of Jupiter was considered highly important for astrological predictions. This is confirmed by the existence of several 'Dodekaeterids' of the planet Jupiter, ascribed to ORPHEUS and to ZOROASTER.

It seems to me that the importance of the star Jupiter = Marduk = Ahura Mazda is reflected in the inscriptions of DARIUS, especially in the great Behistun inscription, in which DARIUS describes his victories over his ennemies.

Right at the beginning of the inscription DARIUS says that Ahura Mazda made him king, and he repeats it over and over again. DARIUS knew perfectly well that he made himself king by his victories over the magi and his other adversaries. Yet in all his reports about these victories he says: 'Ahura Mazda gave me help', and 'According to the will of Ahura Mazda I have won this battle'. And every time, immediately after having asserted that Ahura Mazda helped him, he gives the date of the battle. Why did he give these dates, and what exactly did he mean by saying that Ahura Mazda helped him?

I suppose he meant plainly and simply that Jupiter's position at the sky was favourable at all these dates.

To check this hypothesis, I have calculated the positions of Jupiter at the dates of the battles.

The first battle was on December 13th, 522 B.C. According to TUCKERMAN's tables[1]) Jupiter's longitude was 204°. At the time of DARIUS, the difference between the Babylonian and modern longitudes was just 10°, so the Babylonian longitude was 214°, or Scorpio 4°.

The last battle was on December 28 or 29, 521 B.C. The modern longitude of Jupiter was nearly 233°, hence the Babylonian longitude was slightly less than 243°, i.e. Jupiter stood between 2° and 3° of the sign Sagittarius.

[1]) BRYANT TUCKERMAN: Planetary, Lunar and Solar Positions 601 B.C. to A.D. 1 Amer. philos. soc. Philadelphia 1962.

It follows that the decisive battles all took place while Jupiter was within or just beyond Scorpio. DARIUS repeats three times that the whole campaign took place in one year:

> This is what I did during one and the same year after I became king.

This 'one year' was certainly not a solar year: it lasted longer. Some authors have supposed that by 'one year' DARIUS meant a calendar year of 13 months, but I know of no calendar year that begins and ends in December. It seems more probable that DARIUS meant a year of Jupiter in the sense of the 'Dodekaeterid of Zeus', i.e. the time during which Jupiter dwelt in one zodiacal sign, in this case in Scorpio.

New let us see what predictions the 'Dodekaeteris of Zeus' gives for a year in which Jupiter dwells in Scorpio. I take the version ascribed to ZOROASTER, published as Text *0* 42 by BIDEZ and CUMONT, Les mages hellénisés, Vol II:

> When Zeus is in Scorpio, *in the house of Ares*, the beginning of the winter will be cold, with hail; the middle part will be warm, and the end mild. The spring will be like winter up to the summer solstice; there will be rain and thunder. The sources will lack water. The grain will be medium, wine and oil plenty . . .

When Jupiter, the Royal Star, stands in the house of the war god Ares, it seems pretty clear that the time for a military campaign of the king would be considered favourable. So we can understand DARIUS well when he says in § 62 of his inscription

> This, what I did, I did it according to the will of Ahura Mazda in one and the same year.

Just after this sentence DARIUS also mentions the other gods:

> Ahuramazda brought me help and the other gods that are.

Among the 'gods that are' DARIUS must have included the Sun and the Moon. I suppose he also included the other planetary gods. They plainly 'are': they exist beyond any doubt, everybody can see them. PLATON calls them 'visible gods'. The words of DARIUS may well mean that Jupiter and the other planets brought him victory. I feel that many people in his empire, especially the Babylonian priests and astrologers, would interpret his words just as I do, and that this was DARIUS' intention.

In a letter to GADATES, a royal official in Magnesia on the Maeander in Ionia, DARIUS writes

> . . . But because you ignore my policy towards the gods, I will give you, if you do not change, proof of my wronged feelings, for you exacted tribute from the

sacred cultivators of Apollo and commanded them to dig unhallowed ground, not knowing the mind of my ancestors toward the god, who spoke the whole truth to the Persians.

(translation by C. J. OGDEN in A. T. OLMSTEAD: History of the Persian Empire, p. 156)

The ancestors of DARIUS did not reign over Ionia, so if DARIUS says that Apollon 'spoke the truth to the Persians', he probably identified Apollon with a Persian oracle god who spoke the truth to his ancestors. It is possible that he meant Mithra, but it seems even more probable that he identified Apollon, the god of the planet Mercury, with the Persian god Tîra.

Inscriptions of XERXES

The inscriptions of XERXES closely follow the model of his father DARIUS:

A great god is Ahuramazda, who created this earth, who created man, who created peace for man, who made Xerxes king, one king of many, one lord of many.

That which I did, all I did by the favour of Ahuramazda. Ahuramazda brought me aid until I finished this work.

XERXES also mentions the other gods:

May Ahura Mazda and the other gods protect me and my empire and what I have built.

Inscriptions of ARTAXERXES II

ARTAXERXES II MNEMON, the thoughtful, as he was called by the Greeks, reigned from 404 to 359 B.C. At this point, I must remind the reader that the oldest known horoscope was cast for the year 410 B.C. Of course, it is possible that the calculation was made in a later year, when the child had reached a certain age. In any case we may be sure that horoscopes were cast as early as the reign of ARTAXERXES II. This is also confirmed by PLATON's allusions to horoscopy and to the celestial origine of souls in Phaidros 246 a - 256 e.

A fundamental assumption in horoscopy is that three of seven planets are benevolent: Jupiter, Venus and the Sun. According to our hypothesis, the Persian gods of these three stars were *Ahura Mazda*, *Anâhitâ* and *Mithra*. Therefore, if ARTAXERXES II believed, as his contemporary PLATON did, in the power of the planetary gods, it would be natural for him to place himself and the buildings he erected under the protection of just these three gods.

Now this is exactly what he did. In an inscription in Susa we read:

> Says Artaxerxes the king: By the favour of Ahuramazda this is the hadish palace which I built in my lifetime as a pleasant retreat. May *Ahuramazda*, *Anahita* and *Mithra* protect me and my hadish from all harm!

> (Translation by OLMSTEAD, History of the Persian Empire, p. 423).

Also in other inscriptions ARTAXERXES II invoked the protection of just these three gods. He erected temples for Mithra and Anâhitâ. He indeed needed the help of the Goddess of Love and Fertility, for he had 360 concubines and 115 sons!

The interpretation of the inscriptions of the Achaemenids presented here has the advantage that all inscriptions, from CYRUS to ARTAXERXES II, are in accordance with each other. There is continuity in the religious policy of the inscriptions. They all propagate the worship of Marduk = Ahura Mazda and the other planetary gods (with the exception of Zervan, who is never mentioned).

If the traditional interpretation is accepted, there are two discontinuities: one between CYRUS and DARIUS, the other between XERXES nad ARTAXERXES II. The first king CYRUS is supposed to have venerated Marduk and to have ignored the Persian gods altogether in his inscriptions. DARIUS, on the other hand, is supposed to have proclaimed Ahura Mazda as the highest god, ignoring Marduk's claim to the same title. A century later came ARTAXERXES II, who propagated the cult of Mithra and Anâhitâ. Thus, one gets the impression that there were two complete breaks in the tradition. In my opinion, there was no break at all: all Acheamenid kings paid homage to the same cosmic gods, and the only innovation of ARTAXERXES II was that the stressed the importance of the cult of Mithra and Anâhitâ more than his predecessors did. All Achaemenids tried to establish a kind of unified cosmic religion, which would be acceptable for all peoples in their empire.

However, there was one mighty god that could not so easily be integrated in the system: *Zervan akarana*, the highest god of the Magi.

Darius and the Magi

In his 'Histories' III 78-79 HERODOTOS tells us how DARIUS and his friends made an end to the reign of the 'false Smerdis' by forcing their way into the palace and killing the leading Magi. The story continues thus:

79. Having killed the Magians and cut off their heads, they left their wounded where they were . . . The other five took the Magians' heads and ran with much shouting and noise, calling all Persians to aid, telling what they had done and showing the heads; at the same time they killed every Magian that came in their way. The Persians, when they heard from the seven what had been done and how the Magians had tricked them, *thought it right*[1]) to follow the example set, and drew their daggers and slew all the Magians they could find; and if nightfall had not stayed them they would not have left one Magian alive. This day is the greatest holy day that all Persians alike keep. They celebrate a great festival on it, which they call Massacre of the Magians. While the festival lasts no Magian may come abroad, but during this day they remain in their houses.

This is a curius story indeed. DARIUS and his friends not only killed the leaders, but 'every magian that came in their way', and the other Persians did the same thing and 'thought it right' to do so. Moreover, the day of the killing was celebrated as the greatest holy day of the Persians. On this day all Magi had to hide in their houses, which means that they had to be ashamed. Ashamed of what? What was their sin?

In the whole story of HERODOTOS, the magi are represented not only as vanquished enemies, but as liars and impostors. Just so, in the Behistun inscription, DARIUS condemns all his enemies as liars and evildoers. DARIUS clearly implies that the Magi and all their adherents were opponents of Ahura Mazda, who helped DARIUS because he was on the side of Truth and Righteousness. Once more we may ask: What was the sin of the Magi against Ahura Mazda?

MESSINA, in his book 'Der Ursprung der Magier', expressed the opinion that the Magi were adherents of ZARATHUSTRA, and that DARIUS was opposed to the religion of ZARA-THUSTRA. This seems improbable. It is true that DARIUS was not a Zoroastrian in the strict sense of the word: he did not mention Vohu Mana and the other Amesha Spentas in his inscriptions. However, he did say that Ahura Mazda is the highest god and the creator, and so did the Zoroastrians. Hence it was impossible for DARIUS to regard the Zoroastrians as opponents of Ahura Mazda. Also, DARIUS laid great stress on the op-position between good and bad, between truth and falseness, just as ZARATHUSTRA did. One of the main points in the teaching of ZARATHUSTRA is the struggle of Righteousness against Falseness, and in the inscriptions of DARIUS the same attitude prevails.

It seems to me that the solution of the riddle must be sought in another direction. A main point in the religion of DARIUS was the supremacy of Ahura Mazda, hence we may suppose that the Magi did not acknowledge this supremacy. Now if Ahura Mazda is not highest god and creator, who is? In my opinion, the answer can only be: Zervan akarana.

[1]) Literal translation. For the rest I followed the translation of GODLEY in Loeb's Classical Library.

ZAEHNER has shown in his book 'Zervan, a Zoroastrian Dilemma', that during the Sassanian reign there was a permant struggle between Zervanism and orthodox Zoroastrism. A times Zervan was regarded as the mightiest god, at other times Zervanists were prosecuted, and at still other times a compromise was attempted. Now I suppose that this struggle began already at the time of DARIUS or even earlier, and that the Magi were Zervanists.

In favour of this hypothesis I can adduce two more arguments. First, we have seen that Zervanism came from Media. The Magi too came from Media, as HERODOTOS tells us. Secondly, our earliest literary testimony about Zervanism is that of EUDEMOS, who says that the Magi venerated a god called Space or Time, father of the twins Good and Evil, or Light and Darkness. Hence at the Time of EUDEMOS the Magi were Zervanists. Therefore they may well have been Zervanists at the time of DARIUS.

From the story of HERODOTOS we see that DARIUS oppressed the Magi, but his successor XERXES needed their help at a critical point of his expedition against Greece. As HERODOTOS reports (VII 37), the heir was about to march from Sardes to Abydos, when the sun suddenly darkened: 'the day was turned into night', says HERODOTOS. XERXES was frightened; we may suppose that his officers and soldiers were frightened too. Maybe some of them refused to march on. XERXES now asked the Magi what the eclipse might signify. They declared that the god was showing to the Greeks the disappearance of their cities; for the sun (they said) was the forecaster of the Greeks, as the moon was theirs. 'XERXES rejoiced exceedingly to hear that, and kept on his march'.

It seems that at this occasion (or even earlier) XERXES made his peace with the Magi. From now on they were no longer oppressed, but recognized as respectable people. HERODOTOS reports (I 132) that at every sacrifice a Magian had to be present and to chant a song of the birth of the gods. For 'no sacrifice can be offered without a Magian', says HERODOTOS. This means that the Magi had obtained an official status within the Persian cult. In the sequel they were eager to prove that they were, and ever had been, good Zoroastrians[1]).

---

[1]) See E. BENVENISTE: The Persian Religion according to the chief Greek texts, Paris 1929. Also G. MESSINA: Der Ursprung der Magier, Rome 1930.

CHAPTER VI

THEORY OF THE MOON

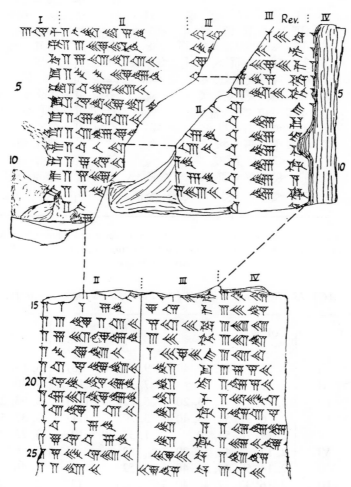

Fig. 11 a. PINCHES' copy of the reverse of a Lunar Table, ACT 13 (O. NEUGEBAUER, Astronomical Cuneiform Texts I, p. 97), consisting of 3 parts:

upper left Sp II 80 = BM 34 604 = PINCHES-SACHS 34,

upper right Sp III 175 = BM 35 661 = PINCHES-SACHS 36,

lower part Sp II 110 = BM 34 628 = PINCHES-SACHS 33.

Reproduced from A. SACHS: Late Babylonian Astronomical Texts copied by PINCHES and STRASS-MAIER (Brown Univ. Press, Providence 1955).

Over 300 cuneiform texts are extant which contain calculations of lunar and planetary phenomena by mathematical methods. In some of these, the 'procedure texts', the methods of calculation are explained. The majority of these texts is in the British Museum (BM), other tablets are in the Louvre (Paris) and in other collections.

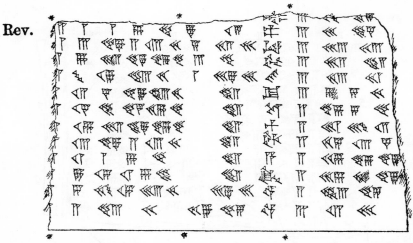

Fig. 11 b. STRASSMAIER's copy of sp II 110 = BM 34 628, Reverse, reproduced from KUGLER: Babylonische Mondrechnung, Tafel VII. To be compared with PINCHES' copy, lower half of fig. 11 a, and with the transcription below.

ACT 13 (Reverse) = Sp II 110. Full Moons for the year 195

Col. T		Col. Φ	Col. B		Col. C
195	I	1, 58, 15, 11, 6, 40	9, 7, 30	(8)	3, 19, 25
	II	2, 1, 1, 6, 40	7, 15	(9)	3, 30, 54
	III	2, 3, 47, 2, 13, 20	5, 22, 30	(10)	3, 33, 23
	IV	2, 6, 32, 57, 46, 40	3, 30	(11)	3, 32, 52
	V	2, 9, 18, 53, 20	1, 37, 30	(12)	3, 23, 21
	VI	2, 12, 4, 48, 53, 20	52	(1)	3, 6, 5, 20
	VII	2, 14, 50, 44, 26, 40	52	(2)	2, 46, 5, 20
	VIII	2, 16, 32, 57, 46, 40	52	(3)	2, 31, 39, 12
	IX	2, 13, 47, 2, 13, 20	52	(4)	2, 25, 13, 4
	X	2, 11, 1, 6, 40	52	(5)	2, 26, 46, 56
	XI	2, 8, 15, 11, 6, 40	52	(6)	2, 36, 20, 48
	XII	2, 5, 29, 15, 33, 20	37, 30	(7)	2, 53, 45
196	I	2, 2, 43, 20	28, 45	(7)	3, 12, 30

All these texts were excavated in Babylon and Uruk; they probably stem from only two archives. The Babylon texts were excavated between 1870 and 1890, the Uruk texts between 1910 and 1914. The tablets from Babylon are far more numerous.

Between 1880 and 1893, the Jesuit Father STRASSMAIER copied many tablets in the British Museum, mostly from the collections Sp (SPARTOLI), Rm (RASSAM), and SH (SHEMTOB), and made his copies available to the Jesuit Fathers EPPING and KUGLER. After STRASSMAIER came T. G. PINCHES, who made numerous careful copies between 1895 and 1900, but did not make them available to others.

To a considerable extent, STRASSMAIER and PINCHES copied the same tablets. The PINCHES copies were buried in the British Museum for half a century, until A. SACHS got permission to study and to publish them, together with a few STRASSMAIER copies, in his 'Late Babylonian Astronomical and Related Texts', Brown University Press, Providence 1955, to be quoted as PINCHES-SACHS.

According to SACHS, the copies drawn by PINCHES are superior to STRASSMAIER's in almost all respects. They are 'finished products, executed with the consummate skill and craftsmanship so familiar to Assyriologists'. Aside from their higher accuracy, the PINCHES copies have a decided advantage over STRASSMAIER's because of the hundreds of joins made by PINCHES. Additional joins were made by O. NEUGEBAUER in the category of mathematical astronomy, and about 150 more were made by A. SACHS in 1954 in all categories of texts. In the publication of SACHS, joins made by NEUGEBAUER and SACHS are indicated by dotted lines (see fig. 11a).

The reader may compare the copies of one text made by STRASSMAIER and by PINCHES by looking at fig. 11 a and 11 b. Just below fig. 11 b, a transcription of the text in modern notation is given.

The first contributions towards the interpretation of the texts were made by EPPING and STRASSMAIER. Next came Father F. X. KUGLER, who succeeded in explaining the main points of the methods of calculation, first of the Lunar Tables[1]), and seven years later of the Planetary Tables for Jupiter, Saturn, Mercury and Venus[2]). The Theory of Mars was not reconstructed until much later.

KUGLER's fundamental investigations formed the starting point of all further research Without KUGLER's work, all subsequent investigations would have been inconceivable, said NEUGEBAUER[3]) in 1937.

In the beginning, KUGLER's work received little attention. Before 1937, only two papers by P. SCHNABEL (Zeitschr. fur Assyriol. *35* and *37*) and one by A. PANNEKOEK (Proceedings Akad. Amsterdam *19*) contributed to a better understanding of Babylonian mathematical

---

[1]) F. X. KUGLER: Die babylonische Mondrechnung. Herder, Freiburg im Breisgau 1900.

[2]) F. X. KUGLER: Sternkunde und Sterndienst in Babel I (Aschendorff, Münster in Westfalen 1907). Volume II and three Ergänzungshefte were published later, the third by J. SCHAUMBERGER in 1935, but the work was never finished.

[3]) O. NEUGEBAUER: Untersuchungen zur antiken Astronomie I. Quellen und Studien Gesch. Math. B *4*, p. 32 (1937).

astronomy. Also the publication of an important set of texts from Uruk by THUREAU-DANGIN[1]) must be mentioned.

The decisive new impulse came from O. NEUGEBAUER. He started investigating the Babylonian theory of the Moon in 1935, just after having finished Volumes 1 and 2 of his monumental publication of mathematical cuneiform texts[2]). In his paper of 1937 quoted before[3]), he announced his decision to prepare a complete edition of all known cuneiform texts in the category of mathematical astronomy.

It took NEUGEBAUER twenty years of hard work to bring out this edition. It appeared in 1955 in three Volumes under the title Astronomical Cuneiform Texts (Lund Humphreys, London). This standard publication will be quoted as NEUGEBAUER, ACT or just as ACT. Texts will be quoted by their ACT-Numbers.

In his 1937 paper, NEUGEBAUER also developed a program for futher research. Step by step, this program was realized by NEUGEBAUER himself, VAN DER WAERDEN, PETER HUBER, ABRAHAM SACHS, ASGER AABOE and others. By our joint efforts, we now have reached a nearly complete understanding of the Babylonian theory of the motion of the Moon and the Planets.

In this book I shall present only the basic ideas of the Babylonian theories. For greater detail, the reader is here once and for all referred to NEUGEBAUER's ACT and to his book The Exact Sciences in Antiquity (Providence, 1957).

The systems A and B

In Babylon as well as in Uruk two systems of lunar calculation were used side by side. KUGLER called them I and II, though he himself recognized that system II is probably the older. NEUGEBAUER changed the names from II and I to A and B respectively. The principal difference is that in System A the sun moves with a constant velocity (30° per month) in one part of the zodiac and with a different constant velocity (28°7'30'') in the remainder, whereas in system B the distance covered each month by the sun increases or decreases from month to month by constant differences.

Later on we shall discuss the question, when and by whom these systems were discovered. The texts of system A reproduced in ACT belong to the years −262 to −13, those of system B to −251 to −68. Thus both systems were used side by side for two centuries at least.

The texts mostly contain data for the New Moon and Full Moon in one or two years. There are also eclipse texts which cover a larger number of years.

[1]) F. THUREAU-DANGIN: Tablettes d'Uruk. Paris, Geuthner 1922.
[2]) O. NEUGEBAUER: Mathematische Keilschrifttexte. Quellen und Studien Gesch. Math. A3, Teil 1 and 2 (1935), Teil 3 (1937).
[3]) O. NEUGEBAUER: Untersuchungen zur antiken Astronomie I. Quellen und Studien Gesch. Math. B 4, p. 32 (1937).

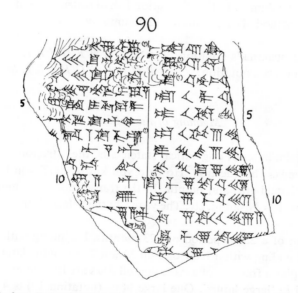

Plate 28. Text 200 h, from Babylon. The oldest known lunar table belonging to system B, calculated for the years 60 and 61 of the Seleucid Era (—251 and —250) Museum number BM 35 203. Above a photograph, made in the British Museum, below the copy of PINCHES, reproduced from A. SACHS: Late Babyl. Astron. and related Texts (Brown Univ. Press, Providence 1955) No. 90.

SYSTEM A

The lunar table ACT 13, from Babylon, gives information about New Moons on the obverse and about Full Moons on the reverse for the years 194 and 195 of the Seleucid Era, i.e. for the years −117 and −116. Three fragments (PINCHES-SACHS, nos 34, 36 and 33) have been preserved; they were joined by SACHS. Their reverse is reproduced in fig. 11 a, as copied by PINCHES. The lower piece 33 (old Museum number Sp II 110), was also copied by STRASSMAIER: this copy is reproduced in fig. 11 b.

The whole text contained 26 lines. The first line applies to the last month of the year 193, the following ones to the 13 months of 194 and the 12 months of 195. The numbers are arranged in four columns; the other columns are lost. Every line on the obverse contains the results of calculations for the New Moon at the end of the month in question, and every line on the reverse refers to the Full Moon in the middle of the month.

Just below fig. 11 b, a transcription of the reverse of Sp II 110 (= PINCHES-SACHS no. 33) is given. Missing numbers have been restored, following KUGLER and NEUGEBAUER. Whenever their transcriptions disagreed, I have consulted the copies of STRASSMAIER and PINCHES.

KUGLER denoted the four columns of the text by letter A B C D. NEUGEBAUER changed the notation into T Φ B C. Here I shall follow NEUGEBAUER's notation.

The original text probably contained several more columns. All in all, we find in texts of System A fourteen columns. In this exposition I shall restrict myself to the explanation of the meaning and method of calculation of 12 columns, which will be denoted as follows:

NEUGEBAUER's notation: T Φ B C E Ψ F G J K L M
(KUGLER's notation: A B C D E F G H I K L M).

Meaning of the columns

Let me first explain, in short dogmatical statements, the astronomical meaning of the figures in the columns. The question 'How do you know that?' will be answered later.

Col. T: Year (Seleucid era) and month. In the transcription the months are denoted by Roman numbers: I = Nisannu, etc. The year x in the Seleucid Era begins in the spring of $-331+x$.

Col. Φ: Duration of a Saros period of 223 months, beginning with the present New or Full Moon and ending with a New or Full Moon 223 months later. The duration is always 6 585 days plus a fraction of a day; the full days are left out and only the fraction is given, expressed in 'large hours'. One large hour (notation 1^H) is 4 of our hours, or 60 USH:

$$1^H = 60° = 4 \text{ hours},$$
$$1° = 1 \text{ USH} = 4 \text{ minutes}.$$

Col. B: Longitude of Moon in signs and degrees.

Col. C: Duration of Daylight, in large hours.

Col. E: Latitude of Moon, in 'barleycorn'. The unit še (še means barleycorn) is $\frac{1}{6}$ of a finger, and 1 finger is $\frac{1}{12}$ of a degree, hence

$$1 \text{ še} = 1 \text{ barleycorn} = \tfrac{1}{6} \text{ finger} = \tfrac{1}{72} \text{ degree.}$$

Col. Ψ: Eclipse magnitude, in fingers.

Col. F: Daily motion of the Moon, in degrees per day.

Col. G: Duration of the preceding month. The duration is always 29 days plus a fraction of a day. The full days are left out, and the fraction is expressed in 'large hours'.

Col. J: Correction, to be subtracted from G.

Col. K: Difference in time of sunset from the day of the preceding New Moon (or Full Moon) to the present day.

Col. L: Corrected duration of the month, calculated by means of the formula

$$L = G - J + K.$$

Col. M: Date and time of New Moon or Full Moon, the time being reckoned from sunset and expressed in 'large hours'.

Some texts contain two more columns P_1 and P_3. Their meaning is

P_1 = Time form sunset to the setting of the moon on the evening of first visibility of the crescent.

P_3 = Time from rising of the moon to sunrise on the morning of last visibility of the moon before New Moon.

We shall not go into details concerning the calculation of these two additional columns, but refer the reader to NEUGEBAUER's ACT I, p. 65, 208 and 230.

Calculation of Column Φ

Column Φ contains values of a '*Lineair Zigzag Function*', as NEUGEBAUER calls it. Such a function increases by a constant monthly increment d to a maximum M and then decreases again by equal amounts d to a minimum m (see fig. 12). In our case the values are

$$d = 0; 2, 45, 55, 33, 20$$
$$M = 2;17, 4, 48, 53, 20$$
$$m = 1;57, 47, 57, 46, 40.$$

As NEUGEBAUER has shown, the values of $Φ$ are times, expressed in 'large hours' or in USH (degrees of time). For the reader's convenience, I have chosen the large hour

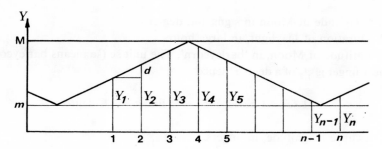

Fig. 12. Graph of a Linear Zigzag Function. At the maximum we have
$$(M - y_3) + (M - y_4) = d$$
and at the minimum
$$(y_{n-1} - m) + (y_n - m) = d.$$

(= 4 hours) as unit. If the USH is taken as unit, the semicolon has to be shifted one place to the right.

The rules for computing the value Φ_n from the preceding value Φ_{n-1} are:

    if Φ is increasing:

(1) $$\Phi_n = \Phi_{n-1} + d,$$

    if Φ is decreasing:

(2) $$\Phi_n = \Phi_{n-1} - d,$$

    if Φ passes through its maximum M:

(3) $$(M - \Phi_{n-1}) + (M - \Phi_n) = d,$$

    if Φ passes through its minimum m:

(4) $$(\Phi_{n-1} - m) + (\Phi_n - m) = d.$$

Calculation of Column B

The reverse of our text ACT 13 gives in Col. B the longitudes of the moon at Full Moon. The longitudes of the sun differ from these by just 6 signs, hence they are:

195	I	9°7′30″	(2)
	II	7°15′	(3)
	III	5°22′30″	(4)
	IV	3°30′	(5)
	V	1°37′30″	(6)
	VI	52′	(7)
	VII	52′	(8)
	VIII	52′	(9)
	IX	52′	(10)
	X	52′	(11)
	XI	52′	(12)
	XII	37′30″	(1)
196	I	28°45′	(1)

We see that in the signs (7), (8), (9), (10), (11) the sun moves through 30° each month, while in signs (1), (2), (3), (4), (5) it moves through only 28°7′30″. The ecliptic thus appears to be divided into a 'fast arc' and a 'slow arc'. KUGLER found that the boundary points between these two arcs are 13°(6) and 27°(12), i.e. 13° Virgo and 27° Pisces. If, for example, the sun is at 52′(12) in month XI and if it moved on at the same speed of 30° per month, then in month XII it would be at 52′ (1). But from 27° (12) the velocity is reduced by $\frac{1}{16}$. Hence, from the length of the stretch from 27° (12) to 52′ (1), one sixteenth must be subtracted:

$$\tfrac{1}{16} \cdot 3°52' = 14'30''.$$

Hence the position of the sun will be 37′30″ (1) and of the moon 37′30″ (7), which is the figure the text gives.

Just so, the sun is at 1°37′30″ (7) in month V. If it would move on at the same speed of 28°7′30″, then in month VI it would be at 29°45′ (6). But from 13° (6) the velocity is increased by $\frac{1}{15}$, so we have to add

$$\tfrac{1}{15} \cdot 16°45' = 1°7',$$

hence the position of the sun is 52′ (7), in accordance with the text.

If one wants to pass from a Full Moon to the New Moon of the same month, the calculation is very easy on the fast arc, where the sun covers 15 degrees in half a month. Thus we have:

Longitude of Sun in Month VI at Full Moon	52′ (7)
Motion in ½ month	15°
Hence Longitude of New Moon	15°52′ (7).

This is in accordance with the obverse of our text. The accordance proves that KUGLER's interpretation of the numbers in Column B as longitudes of the Full and New Moon was correct.

The fast arc from 13° (6) to 27° (12) contains 194 degrees, hence the sun, travelling 30° per month, needs

$$\tfrac{194}{30} = 6;28 \text{ months}$$

to cover the fast arc. Just so, the sun needs

$$\frac{166}{28;7,30} = 5;54, 8 \text{ months}$$

to cover the slow arc. Hence the sun makes one complete revolution in

$$6;28 + 5;54, 8 = 12;22, 8 \text{ months.}$$

Thus the solar year of System A is

$$1 \text{ solar year} = 12;22, 8 \text{ months.}$$

As we have seen in Chapter 4, this figure is too large. The value of System B

$$1 \text{ solar year} = 12;22, 7,52 \text{ months}$$

is slightly better.

Calculation of Column C

In System A as well as in System B, the duration of daylight is assumed to depend on the longitude of the sun. If this longitude is 10° Aries, day and night are both 3^H (this means: 3 large hours, or 12 hours). Hence, the spring equinox was taken at 10° (1). From 10° (1) to 10° (2) the duration of daylight increases by 40′ for every degree of solar longitude, from 10° (2) to 10° (3) by 24′ for each degree, from 10° (3) to 10° (4) by 8′ per degree. The longest day thus has

$$3^H + 20° + 12° + 4° = 3^H 36°.$$

After the maximum the duration of daylight decreases first by 8′, then by 24′, then by 40′ and once more by 40′, then by 24′ and 8′ per degree of solar longitude down to the minimum $2^H 24°$. Finally it increases again by 8′, 24′ and 40′ per degree up to the spring equinox.

In fig. 13 we show the duration of daylight as a function of solar longitude. The function is 'piecewise linear'.

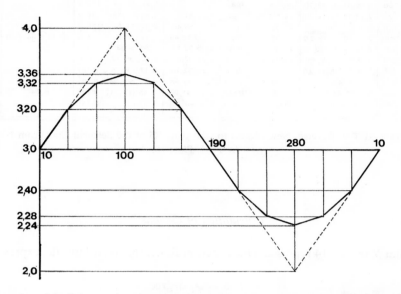

Fig. 13. Duration of daylight as a function of the longitude of the sun. Dotted line: Calculating scheme of the Assyrian period.

The steepest parts of the graph have a slope of 40' per degree of solar longitude. The dotted line in fig. 13 represents a simple linear zigzag function having just this slope. This type of function was used in the Assyrian period, as we have seen in Chapter 3. System A is an improvement on the older system in three respects. First, the maximum and minimum fit Babylon much better. Second, the piecewise linear function of System A yields a much better approximation to the true wave-like function. Third, whereas the duration of daylight was a function of the *date* in the earlier texts, it is now made a function of the *solar longitude*.

The precession of the equinox is not recognized in either system A or B. The equinoxes are fixed on the ecliptic, namely at 10° of Aries and Libra in system A, at 8° in system B. For the time of our text ACT 13 the assumption of 10° for the equinox is quite wrong: for −500 it would be correct.

Before passing to Column E, we first show in fig. 14a transcription of a text containing seven columns

$$I = T, \ II = \Phi, \ III = B, \ IV = C, \ V = E, \ VI = \Psi, \ VII = F.$$

Rev.	I	II	III	IV	V	VI	VII	Rev.
1.	[3,5] bar	2,[2,23,42,13,20]	[22,30 gír-tab]	3,[1]3,35	1, 7,43,12 lal lal	28,41,1[2 hab]	[12, 8]	1.
	gu₄	2, 5,[9,37,46,40]	[28,30 gír-tab]	3,27,24	3,44,37,18 lal lal		[12,50]	
	sig	2, 7,55,[33,20]	[26,37,30 pa]	3,34,14	5,43,23 lal lal		13,[32]	
	šu	2,10,41,28,[53,20]	[24,4]5 máš	3, 34, 2	6,41,51,18 lal u		1[4,14]	
5.	izi	2,13,27,24,[26,40]	[22,5]2,30 gu	3,26,51	4,43, 5,36 lal u		[14,56]	5.
	kin	2,16,[13,20]	21,32 zib-me	3,12,18,40	2,42,11,54 lal u		[15,38]	
	[du₆]	[2,15,10,22,13,2]0	21,32 hun	2,[5]2,18,40	1,12, 7,36 u u	2[9,]2[5,1]6 hab	[15, 34]	
	[apin]	[2,12,24,26,4]0	21,32 múl	2,35,23,12	3,54,19,30 [u] u		14, 52	
	[gan]	[2, 9,38,31,6,4]0	21,32 maš	2,26.27,44	6, ., 35,12 u u		14, 10	
10.	[ab]	[2, 6,52,35,33,2]0	21,32 kušú	2,25,32,16	6,17, 9, 6 u lal		13, 28	10.
	[zíz]	[2, 4, 6, 4]0	21,32 a	[2]32.36.48	4,10, 5[3,24] u lal		12,46	
	[še]	[2, 1,20,44,26,]40	21,32 a[bsin]	[2,4]7,41,20	1,45,[15,24] u lal	8,34 be	12, 4	
	[3,6 bar]	1.58,34,48,5[3,20]	20 [rín]	[3,]6,40	2.1[5] lal lal		11,22	

Fig. 14. Text ACT 9, Reverse. New Moons for the year 185 of the Seleucid Era. From Neugebauer, ACT III, Plate 18.

Calculation of Column E

Column V in Fig. 14 represents the function E, i.e. the lunar latitude, expressed in še:

$$1 \text{ še} = \tfrac{1}{72} \text{ degree.}$$

The general behaviour of this function is that of a piecewise linear function, as shown in fig. 15. The maximum of E is

$$7,12 \text{ še} = 6°,$$

which is a reasonable value for the maximal latitude of the Moon. At the 'nodes' the latitude is zero. In the neighbourhood of the nodes, when E lies between $+2,24$ and $-2,25$ the slope of the function is twice as large as outside the nodal zone. This too is reasonable.

If we look at Column V of fig. 14, we see in every line a number followed by two cuneiform signs lal or u, which mean 'minus' and 'plus'. Thus we read in the first line

$$1, 7;43,12 \quad \text{lal} \quad \text{lal}$$

The first lal means: the latitude is negative. Northern latitudes were counted as positive, southern latitudes as negative. The second sign lal means 'decreasing'. Thus, we may read the first line as

$$-1, 7;43,12 \quad \text{decreasing.}$$

We now consider the values of E outside the nodal zone, i.e. those that are larger than

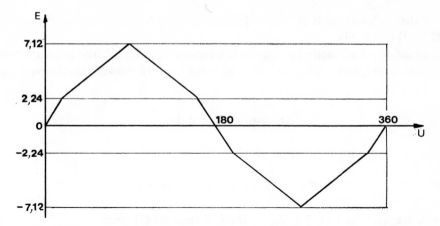

Fig. 15. Lunar latitude E as a function of u = λ—Ω, the elongation of the moon from the lunar node.

2,24, and calculate the differences δ between successive entries. On the increasing and on the decreasing branch these differences are calculated from

(5) $E_n - E_{n-1} = \pm \delta.$

For the passage through the maximum or minimum we use a rule like our earlier formulae (3) and (4), e.g. for the maximum $M = 7,12$:

(6) $(M - E_{n-1}) + (M - E_n) = \delta.$

Using these formulae, we find between the lines 2, 3, 4 and 5 a constant difference, which we shall call d:
$$d = 1,58;45,42.$$

Between lines 5 and 6 we find a slightly larger difference
$$\delta = 2, 0;53,42.$$

Between lines 6, 7 and 8 we find much larger differences, because we are in the nodal zone. Between the lines 8, 9, 10 and 11 the differences are again constant, but they have a larger value than before:
$$D = 2, 6;15,42.$$

KUGLER has found that the months in which δ has the larger value D are just the months in which the monthly motion of the sun is 30°, whereas δ has the smaller value d

whenever the sun's motion is $28°7'30''$. This is the case when the sun is on the 'slow arc' from $27°$ (12) to $13°$ (6).

Quite generally, if the motion of the sun in a certain month is $\Delta\lambda$, and hence the motion of the moon in longitude $360 + \Delta\lambda$, the difference $\delta = \Delta E$ between successive E-values is given by

(7) $\Delta E = 6;15,42 + 4\,\Delta\lambda.$

For $\Delta\lambda = 30$, this formula yields

$$\Delta E = 6;15,42 + 2,0 = 2,6;15,42,$$

in accordance with the text. For $\Delta\lambda = 28; 7,30$ formula (7) gives

$$\Delta E = 6;15,42 + 1,52;30 = 1,58;45,12$$

in agreement with the text. Between lines 5 and 6 we have

$$\Delta\lambda = 28;39,30$$

and hence

$$E = 6;15,42 + 1,54;38 = 2,0;53,42$$

which again agrees with the text.

Formula (7) may be written as

(8) $\Delta E = 4(\Delta\lambda + k)$

with

$$k = 1;33,55,30.$$

In the nodal zone, the slope of E is twice that of E', hence we have in the zodal none

(9) $\Delta E = 8(\Delta\lambda + k)$

What is the astronomical signification of formulae like (8) and (9)?

First we may remark that the right side of (9) depends only on the longitude of the moon, not on the time the moon needs to cover the distance $360 + \Delta\lambda$. The time Δt depends on the varying velocity of the moon, but the motion in latitude depends only on $\Delta\lambda$. This means: the moon moves with varying velocity in a fixed orbit.

However, this orbit is not completely fixed: it changes its situation with respect to the ecliptical circle from one month to the next. This is due to the small correction term $+ k$ in (9). The correction term is in fact the monthly motion of the node.

This may be seen as follows. The quantity E is the moon's latidute in še:

$$1 \text{ še} = \tfrac{1}{72} \text{ degree.}$$

Hence, to obtain the latitude β expressed in degrees, we have to calculate

$$\beta = \tfrac{1}{72} E.$$

Dividing both sides of (9) by 72, we obtain

$$\Delta\beta = \tfrac{1}{9}(\Delta\lambda + k)$$

or

(10) $$\beta_1 - \beta_0 = \tfrac{1}{9}(\lambda_1 - \lambda_0 + k).$$

This means: the point (λ_1, β_1) representing the position of the moon in month no. 1 lies on the straight line

(11) $$\beta - \beta_0 = \tfrac{1}{9}(\lambda - \lambda_0 + k).$$

This straight line gives us the orbit of the moon in month no. 1, as long as it lies within the nodal zone. The slope of this line is $\tfrac{1}{9}$. The node, i.e. the intersection of the orbit with the ecliptic, is found by putting $\lambda = 0$ in equation (11). This gives us

$$- 9\beta_0 = \lambda - \lambda_0 + k,$$

and hence

$$\lambda = \lambda_0 - 9\beta_0 - k.$$

If the longitude of the node is denoted by Ω, we thus find for month no. 1

(12) $$\Omega_1 = \lambda_0 - 9\beta_0 - k.$$

In the same way, we can calculate the position of the node in month no. 0. The orbit now passes through the point (λ_0, β_0), and it has the same slope $\tfrac{1}{9}$, hence its equation is

(13) $$\beta - \beta_0 = \tfrac{1}{9}(\lambda - \lambda_0).$$

Putting $\lambda = 0$, we find the position of the node in month no. 0:

(14) $$\Omega_0 = \lambda_0 - 9\beta_0.$$

Subtracting (14) from (12), we find

(15) $$\Omega_1 - \Omega_0 = -k$$

which means: *the node moves backward (i.e. in the direction of decreasing longitudes) over a distance*

$$k = 1°33'55''30'''$$

every month.

Formula (13) may now be written as

$$\beta_0 = 9(\lambda_0 - \Omega_0)$$

and formula (11) as

$$\beta_1 = 9(\lambda_1 - \Omega_1).$$

The same holds, of course, for all successive months, as long as we are in the nodal zone. Hence we may write, quite generally

(16) $$\beta = \tfrac{1}{9}(\lambda - \Omega)$$

in the nodal zone.

In the modern theory, $\lambda - \Omega$ is called the *argument of the lunar latitude.* If we put

(17) $$u = \lambda - \Omega$$

we can write (16) as

(18) $$\beta = \tfrac{1}{9}u.$$

Outside the nodal zone, the slope of the function β is halved. Hence we obtain for β as a function of u just the graph shown in fig. 15.

All formulae in this section are elementary. The clever astronomer who invented System *A* could easily have made all these calculations for himself. Hence it is not unreasonable to suppose that he knew about the backward motion of the lunar nodes and that

$$k = 1°33'55''30'''$$

was just the amount he assumed for this backward motion.

Column Ψ: Magnitudes of eclipses

The eclipse magnitude E is calculated only for values of E inside the nodal zone, i.e. for $|E| < 2{,}24$. If two successive values of E are both within the nodal zone, one takes the smaller one of the two. The latitude E is first converted into fingers by dividing E by 6, for 1 finger = 6 še. Now there are two cases:

1) E is decreasing. In this case we are in the neighbourhood of the 'descending node', where the moon passes from positive into negative latitudes. In this case one puts

$$17{;}24 - \frac{E}{6} = \Psi.$$

2) E is increasing; we are in the neighbourhood of the 'ascending node'. In this case the formula for Ψ is

$$17{;}24 + \frac{E}{6} = \Psi.$$

In the case of Full Moon, where a lunar eclipse is possible, Ψ is the number of fingers the moon is immersed in the shadow zone. If $\left|\dfrac{E}{6}\right|$ exceeds $17{;}24$, there is no immersion and no eclipse is possible.

Calculation of Column F

Column F gives the velocity of the moon, expressed in degrees per day. According to the procedure texts, F is a linear zigzag function with

difference $d = 0{;}42$
maximum $M = 15{;}56,54,22,30$
minimum $m = 11{;}\ 4,\ 4,41,15$
amplitude $\Delta = M - m = \ 4{;}52,49,41,15.$

In one month the velocity of the moon passes once through its maximum and once through its minimum, completing one oscillation plus d. The total variation of F in one month is therefore $2\Delta + d$. In an *anomalistic period* the velocity goes once from minimum to maximum and back again: the total variation of F in this period is thus 2Δ. Hence

$$1 \text{ anomalistic period} = \frac{2\Delta}{2\Delta + d} \text{ months.}$$

The calculation gives

6695 anomalistic periods = 6247 months.

The periods of column Φ coincide exactly with those of column F. The maxima and minima too are reached at the same time. F can be calculated from Φ by a simple formula

$$F - 15 = 0;15,11,15\ (\Phi - 2;13,20),$$

which is given in the procedure text ACT 200, section 5.

It is curious that the mean value of F, viz.

$$\mu = 13;30,29,31,52,30 = \tfrac{1}{2}(M + m)$$

is too large: it should be 13;10,35, as in system B.

In many texts, abbreviated values for the maximum and minimum of F are used, viz.

$$d = \ \ 0;42$$
$$m = 15;57$$
$$M = 11;\ 4.$$

This simplifies the calculation, but it gives rise to an additional inaccuracy. In the course of years, F gets out of step with Φ.

Calculation of Column G

Column G gives the excess of the month (from New Moon to New Moon or from Full Moon to Full Moon) over 29^d on the assumption that the sun moves through $30°$ in a month. The moon then moves through $390°$, and the question is, how long it takes to do this.

This time interval depends on the velocity of the moon at the end of the month, and also on whether this velocity is increasing or decreasing. Now the lunar velocity F is a function of Φ, hence we may expect that G depends on Φ and also on whether Φ is increasing or decreasing.

This expectation is confirmed by our texts. In several procedure texts, including the important text ACT 200, G is defined as a piecewise linear function of Φ.

Let us introduce the following notation. If y is a linear function of x defined in an interval from x_0 to x_1, we may write

$$y - y_0 = s(x - x_0)$$

and call s the slope of the function. As soon as the initital value y_0 and the slope s are given, the function y is completely determined in the interval from x_0 to x_1.

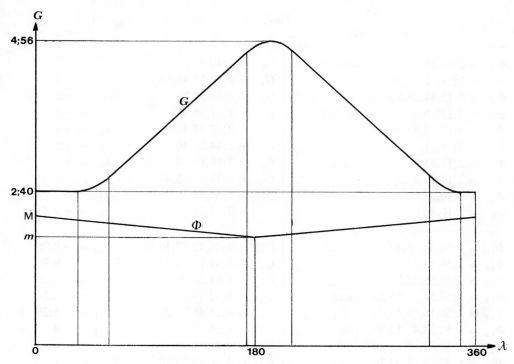

Fig. 16. Φ and G as functions of the longitude λ of the moon, reckoned from the point in the lunar orbit where the lunar velocity is maximal.

G is now a piecewise linear function of Φ, defined as follows. To Φ_0 belongs the value G_0. From Φ_0 to Φ_1 the function is linear with slope s_1. To Φ_1 belongs the value G_1. From Φ_1 to Φ_2 the slope is s_2, etc. The values Φ_n, G_n and s_n are given by the following table (see next page). The explanation of this complicated prescription for computing G will be given later.

Calculation of Column J

Column G gives the duration of any month under the assumption that the sun moves through 30° in that month. If the motion of the sun is less than 30, say $30 - x$ degrees, the moon needs less time to overtake the sun, hence a correction term has to be subtracted from G. This correction term is J. As might be expected, J is proportional to x:

$$J = x \cdot 0;30,26^{\text{H}}.$$

Table for G

Φ_0	= 2;13,20	decreasing	G_0	= 2;40	
Φ_1	= 2;13, 2,13,20	,,	G_1	= 2;40,17,46,40	s_1 = -1
Φ_2	= 2;12,44,26,40	,,	G_2	= 2;40,53,20	s_2 = -2
Φ_3	= 2;12,26,40	,,	G_3	= 2;41,46,40	s_3 = -3
Φ_4	= 2;12, 8,53,20	,,	G_4	= 2;42,57,46,40	s_4 = -4
Φ_5	= 2;11,51, 6,40	,,	G_5	= 2;44,26,40	s_5 = -5
Φ_6	= 2;11,33,20	,,	G_6	= 2;46,13,20	s_6 = -6
Φ_7	= 2;11,15,33,20	,,	G_7	= 2;48,17,46,40	s_7 = -7
Φ_8	= 2;10,57,46,40	,,	G_8	= 2;50,40	s_8 = -8
Φ_9	= 2;10,40	,,	G_9	= 2;53,20	s_9 = -9
Φ_{10}	= 1;58,31, 6,40	,,	G_{10}	= 4;46,42,57,46,40	s_{10} = $-9;20$
Φ_{11}	= 1;58,13,20	,,	G_{11}	= 4;49,11, 6,40	s_{11} = $-8;20$
Φ_{12}	= 1;57,55,33,20	,,	G_{12}	= 4;51,21,28,53,20	s_{12} = $-7;20$
Φ_{13}	= 1;57,58, 8,53,20	increasing	G_{13}	= 4;53,14, 4,26,40	s_{13} = $6;20$
Φ_{14}	= 1;58,15,55,33,20	,,	G_{14}	= 4;54,48,53,20	s_{14} = $5;20$
Φ_{15}	= 1;58,33,42,13,20	,,	G_{15}	= 4;56	s_{15} = 4
Φ_{16}	= 1;58,37, 2,13,20	,,	G_{16}	= 4;56	s_{16} = 0
Φ_{17}	= 1;58,54,48,53,20	,,	G_{17}	= 4;56,35,33,20	s_{17} = 2
Φ_{18}	= 1;59,12,35,33,20	,,	G_{18}	= 4;56,35,33,20	s_{18} = 0
Φ_{19}	= 1;59,30,22,13,20	,,	G_{19}	= 4;56	s_{19} = -2
Φ_{20}	= 1;59,48, 8,53,20	,,	G_{20}	= 4;54,48,53,20	s_{20} = -4
Φ_{21}	= 2; 0, 5,55,33,20	,,	G_{21}	= 4;53,14, 4,26,40	s_{21} = $-5;20$
Φ_{22}	= 2; 0,23,24,13,20	,,	G_{22}	= 4;51,21,28,53,20	s_{22} = $-6;20$
Φ_{23}	= 2; 0,41,28,53,20	,,	G_{23}	= 4;49,11, 6,40	s_{23} = $-7;20$
Φ_{24}	= 2; 0,59,15,33,20	,,	G_{24}	= 4;46,42,57,46,40	s_{24} = $-8;20$
Φ_{25}	= 2;13, 8, 8,53,20	,,	G_{25}	= 2;53,20	s_{25} = $-9;20$
Φ_{26}	= 2;13,25,55,33,20	,,	G_{26}	= 2;50,40	s_{26} = -9
Φ_{27}	= 2;13,43,42,13,20	,,	G_{27}	= 2;48,17,46,40	s_{27} = -8
Φ_{28}	= 2;14, 1,28,53,20	,,	G_{28}	= 2;46,13,20	s_{28} = -7
Φ_{29}	= 2;14,19,15,33,20	,,	G_{29}	= 2;44,26,40	s_{29} = -6
Φ_{30}	= 2;14,37, 2,13,20	,,	G_{30}	= 2;42,57,46,40	s_{30} = -5
Φ_{31}	= 2;14,54,48,53,20	,,	G_{31}	= 2;41,46,40	s_{31} = -4
Φ_{32}	= 2;15,12,35,33,20	,,	G_{32}	= 2;40,53,20	s_{32} = -3
Φ_{33}	= 2;15,30,22,13,20	,,	G_{33}	= 2;40,17,46,40	s_{33} = -2
Φ_{34}	= 2;15,48, 8,53,20	decreasing	G_{34}	= 2;40	s_{34} = -1
Φ_{35}	= 2;13,20	,,	G_{35}	= 2;40	s_{35} = 0

E.g. if the motion of the sun is $28°7'30''$, we have

$$x = 1;52,30$$
$$J = 1;52,30 \times 0;30,26 = 0;57, 3,45$$

in accordance with the text.

Calculation of Columns K, L and M

At the day of New Moon (or Full Moon) in month number n, D_n is the duration of daylight, hence $\frac{1}{2}D_n$ is the time from noon to sunset. Just so, in the preceding month, $\frac{1}{2}D_{n-1}$ is the time from noon to sunset. The difference is

$$K_n = \tfrac{1}{2}D_{n-1} - \tfrac{1}{2}D_n.$$

This time has to be added to the duration of the month, if the time of each New Moon (or Full Moon) is reckoned not from noon but from sunset. The first correction J was subtractive. Hence the corrected duration of the month is 29 days plus

$$L = G - J + K$$

large hours. Since G lies between 2;40 and 4;57 and since J and K are small correction terms, L always lies between 2 and 5.

The exact time of New Moon or Full Moon, reckoned from sunset, is now given by

(19) $$M_n = M_{n-1} + L_n$$

or, if this sum exceeds 6^H, by

(20) $$M_n = M_{n-1} + L_n - 6.$$

In the first case, the date of sunset in question is 29 days after the date of the sunset in the preceding month. In the second case, it is 30 days after this date. Thus, if one knows whether the preceding month had 29 or 30 days, one can calculate the date and time of the present New Moon (or Full Moon).

We have first explained the astronomical meaning of the columns, and next their calculation. The order of discovery of these explanations was just opposite. KUGLER and his successors first found out from the numerical tables and the procedure texts, how the numbers in the tables were calculated, and next they could guess what might be their astronomical meaning. In some cases this meaning was fairly obvious, but in other cases it was very difficult to find it. The most difficult case was that of Column Φ. I shall now describe how the riddle was finally solved, 66 years after the publication of KUGLER's Babylonische Mondrechnung, by the combined efforts of KUGLER, NEUGEBAUER, myself and AABOE.

Column Φ and the Saros

KUGLER proposed, with some hesitation, to interpret Φ as the apparaent diameter of the moon. This interpretation rested on the fact that the numerical values of Φ increase and decrease with the moon's velocity F. However, KUGLER's interpretation had to be abandoned when NEUGEBAUER[1]) found a Procedure Text consisting of fragments of BM 36 705 and BM 36 725, from which it became clear that Column Φ has something to do with the Saros Period of 223 months, and that the Φ-values are times, expressed in large hours.

The procedure text discovered by NEUGEBAUER discusses the calculation of Column Φ and says in line 13 and 16 (reverse):

17,46,40 is the increase or decrease in 18 years.

By the inaccurate expression '18 years' the Saros period is meant, which contains exactly 223 synodic months and approximately 239 anomalistic periods of the moon. The text therefore says that the quantity Φ increases or decreases by 17, 46, 40 in 223 months. Naturally it is possible that this number is to be multiplied by a power 60^n or 60^{-n}.

By applying his method of Diphantine Equations, NEUGEBAUER verified that the assertion of the procedure text is correct: the difference of two Φ-values 223 months apart is indeed

$$(21) \qquad \Phi_{224} - \Phi_1 = \pm\, 0; 0,17,46,40.$$

Next NEUGEBAUER compared two G-values 223 months apart, and he found that their difference $G_{224} - G_1$ is just $-\frac{2\,8}{3}$ times the difference just found:

$$(22) \qquad G_{224} - G_1 = -\tfrac{2\,8}{3}(\Phi_{224} - \Phi_1)$$
$$= \pm\, 0; 2,45,55,33,20.$$

But 0; 2,45,55,33,20 is just the monthly difference d of Φ:

[1]) O. NEUGEBAUER: 'Saros' and lunar velocity. Mat-fys. Meddelelser Kong. Danske Videnskab. Selskab *31*, No. 4 (1957).

(23) $$\Phi_1 - \Phi_0 = \pm d = \pm 0; 2,45,55,33,20^1)$$

and since the sign of $G_{224} - G_1$ is the same as that of $\Phi_1 - \Phi_0$, we have the important relation

(24) $$G_{224} - G_1 = \Phi_1 - \Phi_0.$$

This formula is valid on the linearly increasing and on the linearly decreasing branch of the function G i.e. when G lies between 2;53,20 and 4;46,42,57,46,40 (see the dotted lines in our Table for G). In the neighbourhood of the maximum and minimum of Φ, (24) holds only if the function Φ is 'truncated'. We shall return to this presently.

As NEUGEBAUER noted, the numbers 0; 0,17,46,40 and $\frac{28}{3}$ occurring in (21) and (22) play an important role in the calculation of G from Φ. In fact,

$$\varphi = 0; 0,17,46,40$$

is just the difference between successive Φ-values from Φ_0 to Φ_9 and from Φ_{25} to Φ_{34} in the table for G, and

$$\varepsilon = \frac{28}{3} = 9;20$$

is the slope of the function G on the linearly increasing and on the linearly decreasing branch.

A first conclusion to be drawn from (24) is, that G and Φ are expressed in the same units. Now G is a time, measured in ^{H} or $°$. Hence Φ is also a time, measured in ^{H} or in $°$. This excludes KUGLER's interpretation. So far NEUGEBAUER.

Instead of (24) we may also write

(25) $$(G_2 + G_3 + \ldots + G_{224}) - (G_1 + G_2 + \ldots + G_{223}) = \Phi_1 - \Phi_0.$$

This equation remains valid if 29 days are added to each G_n. It is still valid if, in the months in which the sun moves through less than 30°, the correction J is subtracted from each sum $29^d + G$, provided J is zero for months no. 1 and 224. Hence we may replace each G in (25) by $29^d + G - J$, which is the exact duration of the month in question. Equation (25) is therefore equivalent to

(26) $$S_1 - S_0 = \Phi_1 - \Phi_0,$$

S_0 and S_1 being the durations of two Saros cycles beginning with months no. 1 and 2 respectively.

[1] Here Φ_0 and Φ_1 are the Φ-values in two successive months, and *not* the Φ-values in the first two lines in the Table for G.

Equation (26) is satisfied if each S differs from the corresponding Φ by a constant only:

$$S_1 = \Phi_1 + c$$
$$S_0 = \Phi_0 + c.$$

The order of magnitude of any sum like S_0 or S_1 is $6\ 585^d + 2^H$, and the order of magnitude of Φ is 2^H. Hence, in my paper, I conjectured:

(27) $$S = 6\ 585^d + \Phi,$$

in other words: Φ *is just the excess of a Saros period of 223 months over $6\ 585^d$.*

If this conjecture is true, formula (26) must hold not only on the linearly increasing and decreasing branches of the function G, but everywhere without exception. To attain this, one has to replace Φ by a truncated function Φ^* or B^*, as shown in fig. 16a.

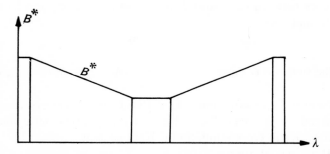

Fig. 16a. The function Φ^* or B^*, the excess of a Saros period over $6\ 585$ days.

Hence my conjecture: *In system A the excess of a Saros period over 6 585 days is a truncated function like the one pictured in fig. 16a, which agrees with Φ on the linearly decreasing and on the linearly increasing branch.*

In the German edition of the present book (1966) this conjecture was justified by a rather complicated chain of reasoning. Luckily, it is no longer necessary to reproduce this argument, for in 1968 AABOE[1]) published a text BM 36 311 + BM 36 593, which he called Text E, in which the function Φ actually appears truncated at the values 2;13,20 and 1;58,31,6,40. Thus, 'VAN DER WAERDEN's conjecture is happily confirmed', says AABOE.

---

[1]) A. AABOE- Some lunar auxiliary tables and related texts from the late Babylonian period. Kon. Danske Vidensk. Selskab Mat.-fys. Meddelelser *36*, 12 (1968).

In fig. 16a, B^* is called a 'function', but what is the independent variable? In other words: What is the meaning of the abscissae in fig. 16a? One possible answer to this question is as follows. In the Babylonian calculating mechanism, the quantities F (lunar velocity) and G (duration of a month) are both given as functions of the independent variable Φ, but G also depends on whether Φ is decreasing or increasing (see our Table for G). Therefore it seems natural to introduce a new independent variable x, defined as follows:

Let M be the maximum and m the minimum of the linear zigzag function Φ. Now put

$$x = 0, \text{ if } \Phi = M$$
$$x = M - \Phi, \text{ if } \Phi \text{ is decreasing}$$
$$x = M - m, \text{ if } \Phi = m$$
$$x = (M - m) + (\Phi - m), \text{ if } \Phi \text{ is increasing.}$$

Thus, x steadily increases, no matter whether Φ increases or decreases. In an anomalistic period, x goes from 0 to 2 $(M - m)$.

We may also replace x by another argument λ going from 0 to 360 and defined by

$$\lambda = \frac{360}{2(M - m)} x.$$

This variable was used in fig. 16 and called 'the longitude of the moon, reckoned from the point in the lunar orbit where the lunar velocity is maximal' (or in modern terminology: from the perigee of the lunar orbit).

The main result of this investigation is: Φ^*, *the truncated frunction* Φ, *is a piecewise linear function of* λ, *as shown in fig. 16a. Its meaning is: the excess of a Saros period over 6 585 days.*

The basic assumptions of System A

Study of the rules of System A for the calculation of solar and lunar longitudes, lunar latitudes, extents of eclipses and month length shows that all these rules follow logically from a small number of basic assumptions. These are:

1) The sun travels monthly 30° from 13° Virgo to 27° Pisces, and 28°7'30'' from 27° Pisces to 13° Virgo.

2) The Full Moon is in opposition to the sun, the New Moon has the same longitude as the sun. Hence in one month the moon travels 360° more than the sun.

3) The duration of daylight is a piecewise linear function of the sun's longitude. At 10° (1) the duration is 3^H. For every degree increase in solar longitude the daylight increases by 40' to 10° (2), by 24' to 10° (3) and by 8' to 10° (4), where the maximum of $3^H36°$ is reached. It then decreases in a similar manner to its minimum $2^H24°$, etc. (see fig. 13).

4) The nodes of the lunar orbit move retrograde each month by $k = 1°33'55''40'''$. The moon's latitude is a piecewise linear function of the distance from the nodes. The function's maximum is $6° = 7,12$ še, its minimum $-7,12$ še. Its variation in the nodal zone from $-2°$ to $+2°$ is 8 še per degree, outside this zone 4 še per degree (fig. 15).

5) If the absolute value of the moon's latitude at Full Moon is less than 17;24 fingers (1 finger $= 6$ še $= 5'$), an eclipse of the moon is possible. The extent of this eclipse in fingers is

$$F = 17;24 \pm E/6,$$

with the positive and negative signs for the ascending and descending nodes respectively.

6) The length of a 'saros period' of 223 synodic months increases as a function of lunar longitude linearly to a maximum, where it remains constant for a while; it then decreases linearly to a minimum, where it again remains constant for a while (see fig. 16a). The period of repetition of this function is the anomalistic period of the moon, given by the equation:

6 247 months = 6 695 anomalistic periods.

Further period relations follow from assumptions (1) to (6), e.g.

1 year = 12;22, 8 months.

An approximation procedure

From assumption 1) it follows that the sun moves through $30°$ or $28°7'30''$ in a mean synodic month. However, the true synodic month differs slightly from the mean. This situation is covered by the application of a characteristic approximation procedure. The moon can deviate up to $6°$ from its mean longitude; therefore the moment of conjunction or opposition with the sun can deviate by half a day from the mean. Hence the position of the sun at the moment of true New or Full Moon can deviate by half a degree from the positition given by calculation on the assumption of uniform month length.

This deviation must have been known to the originator of system A. He knew that the months are not uniform in length, nut nonetheless he calculated positions of the sun on the basis of months of equal length. He could do this because the deviations affected the end result by only half a degree at most, this being the maximum distance travelled by the sun in half a day.

In the next step of the approximation procedure, the time the moon needs to overtake the sun is calculated. An error of $\frac{1}{2}$ degree in the position of the sun causes an error of less than an hour in the time of the Full or New Moon.

A similar approximation procedure is also applied, as we shall see, in planetary calculations. Here too the times from one planetary phenomenon to its next occurence are assumed to be constant, and the planetary positions are calculated on this basis. These positions deviate but little from the true positions, especially in the cases of Jupiter and Saturn, because these planets move only slowly and hence a time error of several days had not more than a slight effect on the positions. In the next step of the approximation the exact time of the phenomenon in question is calculated.

The role of observation

To determine a linear zigzag function numerically, the values of four parameters are required, namely:
1) the monthly difference d,
2) the period p,
3) the mean value $\mu = \frac{1}{2}(M + m)$, and
4) an initial value.

For such functions as Φ or F, which pass through their maximum and minimum once in the course of a month, the period p is given by

$$p = \frac{2\Delta + d}{2\Delta} = 1 + \frac{d}{2\Delta},$$

where $\Delta = M - m$. Given p and d, we can calculate Δ. If further we know μ, we can find the maximum M and minimum m:

$$M = \mu + \tfrac{1}{2}\Delta, \; m = \mu - \tfrac{1}{2}\Delta.$$

The fundamental columns of system A, from which all the others are calculated, are Φ, B and E. Now it turns out that just these quantities Φ, B and E can be observed directly with the requisite degree of accuracy. This will now be shown.

Φ (or rather the modified function Φ^*, from which Φ can easily be determined) is the excess of a saros period over 6 585 days. Φ^* can be empirically determined by the observation of two lunar eclipses separated by three saros periods. The threefold saros or 'Exeligmos', which contains approximately a whole number of days, is mentioned in a cuneiform text from Uruk and in a Greek treatise by GEMINOS. The time-difference between two such eclipses permits a fairly accurate determination of the time Φ^*.

The quantity B is the lunar longitude at the time of Full Moon. The exact moment of a Full Moon is easily determined during a total eclipse: it lies in the middle between the beginning and end of the total stage. To determine the lunar longitude, the distance to a nearby ecliptic star needs to be known. The longitudes of the fixed stars could be taken by the Babylonians from their star catalogues, and so the lunar longitude could be calculated.

The length of the sidereal year can be determined as follows. Two eclipses separated by long time intervals are compared and so the path of the sun w in a large number n of synodic months is calculated. The sidereal year then contains $n(360/w)$ months.

In system A we have

$$1 \text{ year} = 12;22, 8 \text{ months.}$$

This year is still somewhat longer than the sidereal year of modern calculations and much longer than the tropical year. This indicates that the year length was determined not by observation of the equinoxes, but rather, as indicated, by observation of the positions of the eclipsed moon with respect to the fixed stars.

The non-uniformity of the sun's motion could easily be established by comparing positions of the moon at eclipses separated by 6-month intervals. Observation shows that in one part of the ecliptic, from Virgo to Pisces, the sun moves almost 180° in six months, in the other part significantly less. The simplest hypothesis to explain this is the assumption of two velocities in the two parts of the zodiac. For the larger velocity the value of 30° per month was adopted, and for the ratio of the velocities 16 : 15. To determine the arc L of the ecliptic for which the lower velocity should hold, we have the equation

$$\frac{360 - L}{30} + \frac{16}{15} \cdot \frac{L}{30} = 12;22, 8,$$

the solution of which is

$$L = 166°.$$

The position of one boundary point could be established by observing the distance covered by the sun from an eclipse in the slow sector to an eclipse in the fast sector of the ecliptic. The position of the other is them given by the addition or substraction of 166°.

There is yet another method for determining the non-uniformity of the solar motion. According to PTOLEMY (Almagest, III 4), HIPPARCHOS found a time of $94\frac{1}{2}$ days from vernal equinox to summer solstice, $92\frac{1}{2}$ days from summer solstice to autumnal equinox and $178\frac{1}{4}$ days from autumnal to vernal equinox. From these three times HIPPARCHOS and PTOLEMY determined the eccentricity of the sun. But the Babylonians had no such accurate observations of the equinoxes and solstices. It is therefore unlikely that they used a method like that of HIPPARCHOS.

Once the sun's movement on the ecliptic has been determined numerically, all that is needed is a single observation of an equinox to establish its position at 10° Aries or Libra. The positions of the other equinox and of the solstices are then found by adding 3 or 6 or 9 signs.

The highly accurate value of $3^H 36°$ for the longest duration of daylight was known already in the Assyrian period. If now the increase or decrease in day length for every

30° of solar longitude from vernal to autumnal equinox is assumed to be given by an arithmetical sequence of the form:

$$+5x, \ +3x, \ +x, \ -x, \ -3x, \ -5x,$$

the equation

$$5x + 3x + x = 36°$$

yields $x = 4°$. And therewith we have the whole scheme for calculating the duration of daylight.

The latitudinal motion of the moon

The motion of the nodes of the lunar path can be determined by two observations of widely separated eclipses, both at ascending or both at descending nodes, when the same part (north or south) of the moon's face is eclipsed each time. A count of the number of months, a determination of the lunar longitudes and a count of the number of passages through the nodes in the meantime are all that is required for an accurate calculation of the motion of the nodes. If then a further comparison is made of two eclipses of equal magnitude on different sides of the ascending or descending node, it may be concluded that the argument $u = \lambda - \Omega$ has opposite values both times; from which the exact position of the node can be derived. This is just the way PTOLEMY calculated the values, using Babylonian eclipse reports.

The maximum latitude of the moon can easily be determined by approximate observations: it is about 5°. If now a linear zigzag function is set up with maximum 5° and minimum −5°, it turns out that the slope of the function is too small in the neighbourhood of the nodes: too many eclipses and too great magnitudes are obtained. To remedy the situation, the slope was doubled in the nodal zone (see fig. 15). The limits of the nodal zone were taken as ± 2°. The maximum lunar latitude now becomes 6°, but this matters little, because the Babylonian mathematicians seem to have been concerned principally with producing a good representation of the eclipses.

We see that a very few observations suffice to establish the constants of System A. It is possible that mean values of repeated observations were taken. But the constants were apparently not checked later; otherwise, for example, the ever increasing error of the equinoxes would have been found. System A was used for centuries without any change in the constants.

The scientific character of System A

System A is probably the oldest example of a theory that is empirical on the one hand and mathematically exact on the other, like modern science. On the basis of observations covering many years the attempt was made to develop laws corresponding to the observations, involving the simplest possible assumptions about the motion of the heavenly bodies. The assumption of uniform solar motion did not achieve the desired result, so a division of the ecliptic into two parts with different constant velocities of travel was tried. In the case of the moon, a similar assumption would have given such bad results that it had to be abandoned and replaced by a regularly increasing and decreasing velocity.

It is instructive to observe that in system A some calculations were carried out accurately, whereas in other cases an approximation was accepted. Column Φ was calculated accurately to many sexagesimal places, and so was Column G, which was derived from Φ by a complicated calculation. Had G been calculated only approximately, say by rounding off to one degree of time, the errors would have accumulated in the course of the years with the result that after 60 years there could have been an error of half a day or more in the timing of eclipses. G was therefore calculated to 7 sexagesimal places. Three or four places would, in fact, have been sufficient.

Similarly the differences in lunar latitudes

$$E = E_n - E_{n-1}$$

were calculated to 4 sexagesimal places. Here too the summation of the individual errors would have resulted in a more substantial error in the magnitudes of eclipses.

On the other hand, the lunar velocities, which were not summed, were computed only approximately. Apparently the originator of system A though out carefully where he could allow himself a convenient approximation, and where he was obliged to calculate precisely.

Geometrical considerations and trigonometrical calculations are not needed for deriving the mathematical procedures of system A. The solution of linear equations with one unknown and the summing of arithmetical series — these are the only mathematical tools needed for system A.

The simplicity of the mathematical apparatus should not, however, be allowed to conceal the magnitude of the scientific achievement that the construction of system A represents. The whole system rests on a small number of hypotheses, whose consequences were followed to their strictly logical conclusions. The first problem was the selection of the hypotheses, the second the empirical determination of the constants, the third the numerical computation of the phenomena from the hypotheses. Complicated phenomena, such as the overtaking of the sun by the moon with due consideration for the non-uniformity of the motion of both bodies, had to be analysed into their simpler components to make the computation feasible.

The system produced such good agreement with experience that it could survive unaltered for centuries. KUGLER (Mondrechnung, p. 155) compared the calculated eclipse magnitudes for the years -173 to -161 as given in a system A text with modern calculations and found that the modern and the Babylonian values in general rise and fall to-

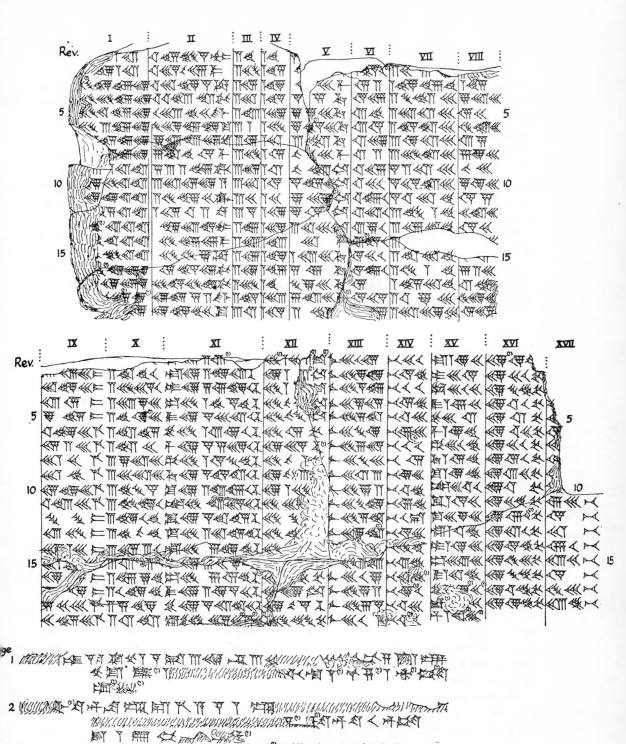

Fig. 17. The 'Crescent Table' ACT 122, copied by Pinches. From A. Sachs: Late Babylonian Astronomical Texts (Brown Univ. Press 1955), No. 66. On the lower edge the name of the astronomer Kidinnu is written

gether; the ratio of the Babylonian values to the modern ones was found to be nearly as
10 : 12. Yet by −162 system *A* had already been in use for some 300 years without any
change in the values of the constants. The system must therefore have been fitted most
meticulously to the observations in the beginning.

Once the theoretical system had been completed and checked by observation, a program
for the calculation of phenomena was still required, i.e. the rules of computation had to
be so formulated that any scribe could derive one column after another, following fixed
rules. This too was accomplished, as the instructional texts which have come down to us
show.

When we review the theory as a whole, we cannot deny our admiration for the author
of system *A*.

His name was probably NABU-RIMANNU. The subscript of the lunar table ACT 18,
'*Tersitu of Nabu-rimannu*', cannot be satisfactorily interpreted except as 'Equipment of
NABU-RIMANNU' (see NEUGEBAUER, ACT I, p. 12-13).

SYSTEM B

System *B* is simpler than system *A* in its logical structure. Procedures requiring such
refined and complicated derivations as columns *E* and *G* of system *A* are not encountered
in system *B*. Yet the numerical values and periods used in system *B* correspond still better
with reality. For this reason KUGLER concluded that system *B* was devised later than
system *A* — an opinion in which I concur. It would, in fact, have been ridiculous for the
highly intelligent author of system *A* to have replaced the simple procedures of system *B*
by more complicated ones, with periods and constants that gave inferior results!

The 'Crescent Table' ACT 122

This large text from Babylon, which EPPING and KUGLER took as their starting point
in their study of Babylonian lunar calculation, consists of 17 columns of 40 lines each
(20 on the front and 20 on the back). The text has been assembled from 9 fragments, the
largest fragment being SH 272 (81 − 7 − 6) = BM 34 580. On the lower edge is the
legend '*Tersitu* of *Ki-din-nu*', which probably means 'KIDINNU's Equipment'. The
astronomer KIDENAS (= KIDINNU) is also mentioned by Greek authors, as we shall see
in the next chapter.

The best copy is that of PINCHES, which we reproduce in fig. 17. A transcription of
columns *A* to *L* in modern numbers is to be found in KUGLER's 'Mondrechnung', p. 12-13.
An explanation of columns XII to XVII was given by SCHAUMBERGER in the third Er-
gänzungsband to KUGLER's 'Sternkunde'. NEUGEBAUER has given a transcription of the

whole text with commentary in ACT I (Commentary) and III (Text) under number 122.

The text is concerned with the New Moon and the first visibility of the Crescent for the years 208-210 of the Seleucid Era. The beginnings of the first ten lines of the reverse are given below. In the designation of the columns by letters T, A, B, C, D I shall follow NEUGEBAUER. The date column T and the beginning of column A have been restored; the date is completely certain.

	T	A	B		C	D
	VII	29;30, 1,22	11;45,59, 4	(8)	2,40	1,40
	VIII	29;48, 1,22	11;34, 0,26	(9)	2,29	1,45
	XI	29;57,56,38	11;31,57, 4	(10)	2,25	1,47
	X	29;39,56,38	11;11,53,42	(11)	2,31	1,44
	XI	29;21,56,38	10;33,50,20	(12)	2,43	1,38
	XII	29; 3,56,38	9;37,46,58	(1)	3, 1	1,29
210	I	28;45,56,38	8;23,43,36	(2)	3,18	1,21
	II	28;27,56,38	6;51,40,14	(3)	3,29	1,15
	III	28;11,22,42	5; 3, 2,56	(4)	3,35	1,12
	IV	28;29,22,42	3;32,25,38	(5)	3,31	1,14

The meaning of Columns A-D

Column A gives the motion of the sun in one month. One sees at once that A is a linear zigzag function with parameters:

Difference	d	$= 0;18$
Maximum	M	$= 30; 1,59$
Minimum	m	$= 28;10,39,40$
Amplitude	Δ	$= M - m = 1;51,19,20.$

The period of Column A is calculated as follows. In one month A increases or decreases by d. The number of months to complete a cycle from minimum through maximum and back to minimum is evidently given by:

$$p = \frac{2\Delta}{d} = \frac{3;42,38,40}{0;18} = 12,22, 8,53,20.$$

This value agrees approximately with the year length given by system A:

$$J = 12;22, 8.$$

We shall see later that column J, which likewise depends on the anomalistic motion of the sun, has a period of exactly 12;22, 8 months.

A different year length may be obtained from Column A as follows. The mean monthly motion of the sun is

$$\mu = \tfrac{1}{2}(M + m) = 29; \, 6,19,20.$$

In one year the sun travels exactly 360°. The year therefore has

$$\frac{360}{\mu} = 12;22, \, 7,52 \text{ months.}$$

This value is slightly more accurate than the value 12;22, 8 of system A.

Column B contains the longitude of the sun at New Moon at the end of the month. Each longitude B_n is obtained by the addition of the monthly motion A_n to the preceding longitude B_{n-1}, e.g.

$$(8) \; 11;45,59, \, 4 + 29;48, \, 1,22 = (9) \; 11;34, \, 0,26.$$

The duration of daylight is stated in column C. If the sun is at 8°(1), the duration of daylight is 3^H. From 8°(1) to 8°(2) the duration increases by 36′ (instead of 40′ as in system A) for every degree of solar longitude, from 8°(2) to 8°(3) by 24′ per degree (as in system A), from 8°(3) to 8°(4) by 12′ (instead of 8′ in system A). The longest day is thus

$$3^H + 18° + 12° + 6° = 3^H 36°,$$

just as in system A. After the maximum the duration of daylight decreases again, first by 12′, then by 24′, then by 36′, and so on. This scheme fits the reality still better than system A.

Column D gives the duration of half the night. If the daylight C is substracted from 6^H, the result halved and then rounded off to the nearest whole time degree, the answer is always just the figure in column D.

Column Ψ: Magnitudes of eclipses

The next column Ψ (KUGLER's notation E) was interpreted by KUGLER as the latitude of the moon. In NEUGEBAUER's 'Untersuchungen zur antiken Astronomie III' (Quellen u. Studien Gesch. Math. B 4, p. 308) KUGLER's interpretation was accepted; but later on (Isis, 36, p. 14) NEUGEBAUER showed that within the nodal zone, which alone is of significance for eclipses, the meaning of Ψ is the eclipse magnitude.

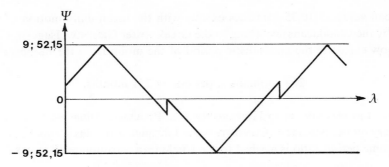

Fig. 18. Eclipse Magnitude Ψ according to System B.

In System A, as we have seen, eclipse magnitudes were deduced from the lunar latitude E by the formula

$$\Psi = 17;24 \pm E/6.$$

It is quite possible that the author of System B thought of a similar formula, but in the texts which have been preserved there is no column giving the moon's latitude itself. The eclipse magnitudes were simply extrapolated linearly, from one passage through a node backwards to the immediately preceding one. The graph of the function Ψ is shown in fig. 18.

The maximum of E is $9;52,15$, the minimum $-9;52,15$; the monthly difference is $3;52,30$. If after the passage through the node the absolute value of Ψ exceeds 3, one has to subtract 3, which explains the discontinuities in the figure.

This column takes no account of the anomalistic motion of the sun. Other texts contain, besides Ψ, two additional columns $\Delta\Psi'$ and Ψ'. The difference column $\Delta\Psi'$ depends on the anomalistic motion of the sun; its method of formation has not been completely elucidated. For further details the reader is referred to NEUGEBAUER, ACT I.

On calculating the period of column Ψ, we find

5 923 draconitic months = 5 458 synodic months.

This very good period ratio was known to HIPPARCHOS; see PTOLEMY, Almagest IV, 2.

Column F: Lunar velocity

In System B, the velocity of the moon (in degrees per day) is a linear zigzag function F with parameters:

Maximum	15;16, 5
Minimum	11; 5, 5
Difference	0;36.

The mean value 13;10,35 coincides exactly with the mean daily motion of the moon assumed by the Chaldaeans according to the Greek writer GEMINOS (Isagoge, Chapter 6).

If we now calculate the anomalistic period of the moon from the numbers given, we find

269 anomalistic periods = 251 months.

The ratio too was known to HIPPARCHOS (see PTOLEMY, Almagest IV 2). In a Greek commentary on the Almagest (CUMONT, Neue Jahrbücher für das klassische Altertum 27, p. 8) the same period ratio is acribed to the Chaldaean astronomer KIDENAS.

Column G: Uncorrected duration of the month

This column gives the excess of the month over 29^d in Long Hours — on the assumption of uniform solar motion. It corresponds to column G of System A, but its formation is simpler. It is just a linear zigzag function with parameters

Maximum	4;29,27, 5
Minimum	1;52,34,35
Difference	0;22,30.

The period of column G is the same as that of F, and hence also the same as the anomalistic month according to HIPPARCHOS. A further point of agreement with HIPPARCHOS was found by KUGLER, who calculated the mean synodic month from the mean value of column G. The result was

29;31,50, 8,20 days,

exactly as in HIPPARCHOS (PTOLEMY, Almagest IV 2).

These three coincidences prove, as KUGLER rightly remarks, that HIPPARCHOS was acquainted with the periods of System B.

Columns H and J: Correction to the duration of the month

The uncorrected duration of the month (Column G) was calculated on the assumption that the sun travels the same distance s each month. In fact the sun travels $s + h$, where h is a small correction term, so that the moon needs somewhat more (or less) time to overtake the sun. The time J, which has to be added to G, is proportional to h to a very good approximation.

In System B the sum $s + h$, and hence also h, is a linear zigzag function, that is, h increases linearly from its minimum to its maximum and then decreases again linearly.

It would therefore be logical to expect the correction J to increase and decrease linearly too.

This expectation is not fulfilled. The correction J does increase to a maximum and then decrease again, but the monthly increase or decrease is not constant: it is given by means of a difference column H, which is in its turn a linear zigzag function with maximum 21°, minimum 0 and difference $d = 6;47,30$. The period of this column H is almost half a year:

$$P = \frac{2\Delta}{d} = \frac{42}{6;47,30} = 6;11, 2,35.$$

Column H serves merely as an auxiliary for the calculation of the next column J. The maximum of J is 32;28, 6, or in abbreviated form 32;28 (time degrees), the minimum $-32;28$, 6 or $-32;28$. The difference of column J is given by column H. If the addition of H_n to the preceding J_{n-1} gives an answer exceeding the maximum M, the normal procedure for linear zigzag functions is used: the excess is subtracted from M. Similarly for the minimum.

The mean value of H is 10;30. The mean period if J is therefore

$$P_J = \frac{2(M - m)}{10;30} = \frac{2, 9;52}{10;30} = 12;22, 8.$$

This year length coincides exactly with that of System A.

The correction J is analogous to the correction J of System A. Both corrections derive from the non-uniformity of solar motion. In System A the sun had two constant velocities; from this followed as the logical consequence a constant negative correction for the months in which the sun had the lower velocity. Had the same considerations prevailed in System B as well, a normal linear zigzag function for J would have resulted. Instead a much more complicated function was applied, unrelated to the assumed model of solar motion. The strict logic which rules in System A is not to be found in System B.

Columns K, L and M

The addition of the correction J to the provisional monthlength G yields the final month-length:

$$K = G + J.$$

Column L gives the time of the New Moon, calculated by the rule

$$L_n = L_{n-1} + K,$$

or, if the sum $L_{n-1} + K$ exceeds 1 day

$$L_n = L_{n-1} + K - 6^H.$$

The times in column L are reckoned from midnight. The next column M gives the time of the New Moon before or after sunrise or sunset. Since D was the length of half the night, we have:

$$
\begin{aligned}
\text{before sunrise} \quad & M = D - L \\
\text{after sunrise} \quad & M = L - D \\
\text{before sunset} \quad & M = 6^H - (L + D) \\
\text{after sunset} \quad & M = L + D - 6^H.
\end{aligned}
$$

The remaining Columns

Following M in text 122 there are five more columns: N, O_1, P_1, P_3, O_3 (NEUGEBAUER's notation). Column $N =$ XIII gives the time from New Moon to sunset on the evening of the first visibility of the New Moon. Column $O_1 =$ XIV gives the elongation of the moon at this moment, column $P_1 =$ XV the time from sunset to moonset on this evening. Column $P_3 =$ XVI gives the time from moonrise to sunrise on the morning when the moon is visible for the last time, and column $O_3 =$ XVII the elongation of the moon on this morning.

The calculation of these columns has not yet been completely elucidated. See J. SCHAUMBERGER, third Ergänzungsheft to KUGLER's 'Sternkunde', and NEUGEBAUER, ACT I, p. 81 and 145.

NEUGEBAUER assumes in his commentary that columns N, O_1 and P_1 were calculated in advance for the evening on which the first visibility of the New Moon was expected, and P_3 and O_3 for the morning on which the last visibility was expected. He did not, however, succeed in discovering any criteria to form the basis of such expectations. In my opinion, it could be that the columns in question were calculated after the event for the morning or evening on which the crescent was actually observed. Perhaps it was not even the purpose of these calculations to make predictions about the moon's visibility.

Columns P_1 and P_3 are found in System A too, and we know from instructional texts how they were calculated (ACT I, p. 65, 208 and 230).

In the lunar tables according to System A it frequently happens that the quantities P_1 and P_3 were calculated for two different dates. In such cases we are sure that the calculations were made beforehand. The scribe did not yet know that actual morning or evening in which the moon would be visible for the last or first time. We do not know whether there were any definite criteria for deciding in favour of any particular morning or evening.

Obv.	I	II	III	IV	V	VI	VII	VIII	IX	X	XI	XII	Obv.
1.	[bar] 1	1,38,9 múl	gu₄ 1	30,13,30	sig 1	29,48	[šu]1	28,23,21	izi 1	27,57,51	kin 1	27,32,21	1.
	2	2,37,18	2	1,12,39 maš	2	30,47,9	2	29,22,30	2	28,57	2	28,31,30	
	3	3,36,27	3	2,11,48	3	1,46,18[ku]šú	3	30,21,39	3	29,56, 9	3	29,30,39	
	4	4,35,36	4	3,10,57	4	2,45,27	4	1,20,48	a 4	30,55,18	4	30,29,48	
5.	5	5,34,45	5	4,10, 6	5	3,44,3[6]	5	2,19,57	5	1,54,27 absin	5	1,28,57 rin	5.
	6	6,33,54	6	5, 9,15	6	4,43,[4]5	6	3,19, 6	6	2,53,36	6	2,28, 6	
	7	7,33, 3	7	6, 8,24	7	5,42,[5]4	7	4,18,15	7	3,52,45	7	3,24,15	
	8	8,32,12	8	7, 7,33	8	6,4[2,]3	8	5,17,24	8	4,51,54	8	4,23,24	
	[9]	9,31,21	9	8, 6,42	9	7,41,12	9	6,16,33	9	5,51, 3	9	5,22,33	
10.	[10]	[10]30,30	10	9, 5,51	10	8,40,21	10	7,15,42	10	6,50,12	10	6,21,42	10.
	[11]	[11,2]9,39	11	10, 5	11	9,39,30	11	8,14,51	11	7,49,21	11	7,20,51	
	[12]	12,28,4[8	12	11, 4, 9	12	10,38,39	12	9,14	12	8,48,30	12	8,20	
	[13]	13,27,57	13	12, 3,18	13	11,37,48	13	10,13, 9	13	9,47,39	13	9,19, 9	
	[14]	14,27, 6	14	13, 2,27	14	12,36,57	14	11,12 18	14	10,46,48	14	10,18,18	
15.	[15]	15,26,15	[15]	[14, 1,36	15	13,36, 6	15	12,11,27	15	11,45,57	15	11,17,27	15.
	[16]	16,25,24	[16]	[15, ,45	16	14,35,15	16	13,10,36	16	12,45, 6	16	12,16,36	
	[17]	17,24,33	[17]	15,59,54	[17]	15,]34,24	17	14, 9,45	17	13,4[4,]15	[17]	1]3,15,45	
	[18]	18,23,42	[18]	16,59, 3	[18]	16,33,33	18	15,8,[54]	18	14,[43,24]	[18]	14,14,[54]	
	[19]	19,22,51	[19]	17,58,12	[19]	17,32,42	[1]9	[1][6, 8, 3	19	15,42,[33]	[19]	15,1[4, 3	
20.	[20]	20,22]	[20]	18,57,21	[20]	18,31,51	20	17, 7,12	20	16,41,4[2]	[20]	16, 13,12	20.
	[21]	21,21, 9	[21]	19,56,30	[21]	[19,31]	21	18, 6,21	21	17,40,51	[21]	17, 12,21	
	[22]	22,20,18	[22]	20,55,39	[22]	20,30, 9	22	19, 5,30	22	18,40	[22]	18,1]1,30	
	[23]	23,19,27	[23]	21,54,48	[23]	21,29,18	[23]	20, 4,39	23	[19,39, 9]	[23]	19,10,]39	
	[24]	24,18,36	[24]	22,53,57	[24]	22,28,27	[24]	21, 3,48	2[4	20,38,18	[24]	20, 9]48	
25.	[25]	25,17,45	[25]	23,53, 6	[25]	23,27,36	[25]	22, 2,57	[25]	21,37,27	[25]	21, 8]57	25.
	[26]	26,16,54	26	2[4,[52,15]	[26]	24,26,45	26	23,[2,6]	[26]	22,36,36	[26]	22, 8,] 6	
	[27]	27,16, 3	27	25,51,[24]	[27]	25,25,5]4	27	24,[1,15]	[27]	23,35,45	[27]	23, 7,15	
	[28]	28,15,12	28	26,50,33	[28]	2[6,25, 3	28	25[,.]24	[28]	24,34,54	[28]	24, 6,24	
	[29]	29,14,2]1	29	27,49,42	[29]	27,]24,12	29	25,59]33	[29]	25,34, 3	[29]	25, 5,33	
30.			30	2[8,48,[51]			30	[26,58, 4]2	[30]	26,33,12	[30]	[26, 4,]42	30.

Fig. 19. Text 185. Daily motion of the Sun.

Auxiliary tables

As we have seen, column *A* is an auxiliary column for the calculation of the lunar longitude, column *B*. Similarly columns *G*, *H*, *J* and *K* are only auxiliary columns for calculating column *L*, which gives the time of New Moon. Our text 122, which comes from Babylon, contains all these auxiliary columns. On the other hand, they are all, or almost all, omitted in the Uruk texts. The Uruk tables are further abbreviated by the rounding off to a small number of sexagesimal places. The auxiliary columns and the precise values of the principal columns were calculated separately in so-called 'auxiliary tables' (ACT I, p. 164-177).

The auxiliary tables give us, as NEUGEBAUER says, a good insight into the way in which the calculations were made. In these tables we frequently find little wedges which indicate that the calculated values were checked after a certain number of steps. This control is obviously most useful. Modern astronomers too keep a continual check on their calculations, and they too generally use in their auxiliary calculations a larger number of decimal places than in their final results.

THE DAILY MOTION OF THE SUN AND THE MOON

The sun's motion

Text ACT 185 (fig. 19), from Uruk, gives the sun's position from day to day for year 124. The text is calculated on the assumption of uniform solar motion of 59′9″ per day. Fragments 186 and 187 are similarly calculated.

The purpose of these tables is not clear. I imagine that they were used as auxiliary tables for planetary calculations. For in planetary calculations, as we shall see, uniform solar motion is always assumed as the basis, whereas in lunar calculations the anomaly of the sun's motion is regularly taken into account.

The moon's motion

Four tables from Uruk (ACT I, p. 179) give the moon's position from day to day for the years 117, 118, 119 and 130 of the Seleucid Era. Similar tables have also been found in Babylon. The way in which these tables were calculated is very remarkable.

First, a linear zigzag function F^* was calculated with a period of 248 days. This gives the daily motion of the moon. The maximum and minimum of this function are

$$M = 15;14,35 \quad m = 11; 6,35.$$

The mean daily motion of the moon is therefore

(1) $$\tfrac{1}{2}(M + m) = 13;10,35.$$

The daily increase or decrease in F^* is

(2) $$d = 0;18.$$

Hence it follows that the function F^* passes through its maximum exactly 9 times in 248 days.

Both (1) and (2), as well as the exact rules of formation of the linear zigzag function F^*, are to be found also in the *Isagoge*, i.e. 'Introduction' of the Greek writer GEMINOS; they are there correctly ascribed to the Chaldaeans. The lunar period of 248 days is found, combined with a more accurate period of 3 031 days, in two Greek papyri of the Roman period[1]. Both periods are also found in the Pañchasdidhântikâ of VARÂHA MIHIRA (Ch. 2, Stanza 2-6) and in South Indian Tamil astronomy[2]

All this shows how far the influence of Babylonian astronomy spread. We shall return to this point in the last chapter.

THE DATE OF INVENTION OF BABYLONIAN LUNAR THEORIES

The date of System A

Until quite recently, all known lunar tables were from the Seleucid Period. In NEU-GEBAUER's publication ACT, the earliest lunar table was No. 70 (ACT I, p. 117), calculated for the years from −272 to −251.

The texts known to KUGLER were still more recent. Yet, KUGLER concluded from the position of the equinoxes in Systems A and B that both systems were much older. His reasoning was as follows. He compared the solar longitudes in Tablet ACT 122 with modern longitudes and found that the spring equinox, which was placed in this tablet at 8° Aries, had an error of 5 degrees. The tablet belongs to System B and was computed for the years −103 to −101. According to KUGLER's calculation, an error of this magnitude would accumulate in 287 years. Hence KUGLER concluded: 'Since our tablet dates

---

[1]) Papyrus Lund 35a: E. J. KNUDTZON and O. NEUGEBAUER: Bull. Soc. Royale des lettres de Lund, 1946—47 II, p. 77. Papyrus Ryl. 27: O. NEUGEBAUER, Danske Vid.-Selsk. hist. Meddelelser 32, No. 2 (1949) and VAN DER WAERDEN: Centaurus 5 (1958) p. 177.

[2]) See VAN DER WAERDEN: Tamil Astronomy. Centaurus 4 (1956), p. 221.

from the year 103 B.C., the determination of the spring equinox would fall on 390 B.C. ± several years'.

KUGLER also investigated Tablet ACT 60 (old signature SH 93), which belongs to System *A* and in which the spring equinox was assumed at 10° of Aries. His conclusion was: 'An analogous calculation for tablet No. 93 would bring us back to 500 B.C. ± several years'.

In 1928, FOTHERINGHAM made a new calculation, based upon the best known value of the apparent acceleration of the sun's motion, and concluded: 'The position NABURIANOS assigns to the equinox ties him down to the neighbourhood of 500 B.C.'[1])

In 1963, I made an attempt to estimate the accuracy of ancient Babylonian observations of the equinoxes and solstices[2]). I found that about 400 B.C. or even earlier the summer solstice was known to within 1 or 2 days. My conclusion, as stated in the German edition of this book, was: 'If the author of System *A* made an error of 1° at most in his determination of the equinoxes and solstices, his observations were made between −560 and −440. If the maximum error was 2°, the observations were made between −620 and −380. A larger error seems unlikely'.

A recently discovered text, published by AABOE and SACHS[3]), fully confirmed my conclusion. Two fragments of this text (Text C and Text D) and one duplicate (Text B) are preserved. The text belongs to System *A*. It was calculated, according to AABOE and SACHS, for the years −474 to −456 (XERXES, year 11 to ARTAXERXES I, year 8).

Under the Assyrian reign, astronomy was on a much lower level than during the Neo-Babylonian and Persian periods. The Assyrian reign ended in 612 B.C. Therefore, I feel we cannot well place the invention of System A before −610. Hence we may conclude: *System A was invented between −610 and −470*. The second half of this period, from −540 to −470, i.e. the beginning of the Achaemenid reign, seems more probable than the first half.

Similar calculations can be made for System B: they would lead to a date between −500 and −260. To narrow this range, we shall consider the evidence of Greek texts.

METON *and* EUKTEMON

These two astronomers observed the summer solstice in Athens in −431 (PTOLEMY, Almagest III 1). They constructed a 19-year intercalary cycle. METON placed the equinoxes and solstices at 8° Aries, 8° Cancer, etc. (COLUMELLA, De re rustica, Book 9, Chapter 14), exactly like the Babylonian System B-calculations. EUKTEMON published a

[1]) J. K. FOTHERINGHAM: The indebtedness of Greek to Chaldaen astronomy. The Observatory *51*, No. 653 (1928).
[2]) VAN DER WAERDEN: Das Alter der babylonischen Mondrechnung. Archiv für Orientforschung *ä0*, p. 97.
[3]) A. AABOE and A. SACHS: Two Lunar Texts of the Achaemenid Period from Babylon. Centaurus *14*, p. 1 (1969).

parapegma, i.e. a star calendar, in which the equinoxes and solstices, the annual risings and settings of the fixed stars and the relevant weather indications were noted. See F. BOLL: Griechische Kalender III, Sitzungsber. Heidelberger Akad. (1911).

In his 'Parapegmastudien' (Abh. Bayer. Akad. München, Phil.-Hist., Neue Serie *19*, 1941, p. 29) A. REHM pointed out that many details of METON's and EUKTEMON's para-pegmas can be traced back to Babylon with a high degree of probability. In particular, REHM mentions: the division of the ecliptic into twelve parts, the 19-year cycle, the anom-aly of the sun's motion, the observational apparatus used (the heliotropion). I could add that EUKTEMON's parapegma has many points of similarity to the calendar of fixed star risings in ^{mul}APIN. Both calendars are divided into a date list and a time interval list. The date list, in ^{mul}APIN as in EUKTEMON, is based on a division of the solar year into 12 artificial months defined by the course of the sun in the zodiac. In the date list the equinoxes and solstices are also entered. The time interval list, again in both cases, gives the time intervals between the star phases in days.

Hence it follows that METON and EUKTEMON were probably acquainted with Babylonian astronomy.

Two points indicate that they actually knew the Babylonian lunar theory. The first has already been mentioned above: METON takes the year points at 8°, like System B. The second is the anomaly of the sun's motion. EUKTEMON assumes that the sun takes 31 days each to pass through the signs Aquarius, Pisces, Aries, Taurus, Gemini and only 30 days each for the remainder. This looks very much like the devision of the ecliptic into a slow and a fast part which we found in System A.

Now it is, of course, possible that EUKTEMON discovered the anomaly of the sun's motion independently of the Babylonians, but for this he would have had to observe either a large number of eclipses or the equinoxes and solstices. No information about such observations has been handed down to us, apart from the one solstice observation with METON. Since EUKTEMON demonstrably took over many other elements from the Babylonians, it is much more likely that his division of the ecliptic into a slow and a fast sector was inspired by the Babylonian theory of the moon.

The date of System B

For System B we can find an upper and a lower limit, as follows.

1. METON observed the summer solstice in −431, and he fixed it at 8° Cancer according to COLUMELLA. If we assume that COLUMELLA was not making a mistake, and that METON took over the 8 degrees from System B, it would follow that System B was already in existence about −440.

2. The other limit can be found by the same method used for System A, namely by considering the time for which the placing of the year points at 8° is exactly correct. According to SCHNABEL and FOTHERINGHAM, this leads to a date arount −375. To reach

a date around −440 an observational error of about 1° must be assumed. This would certainly be possible, but not a date much further back. For if we were to go back as far as −500, 10° would be the correct position, and there would be no rational basis for the author of System B to correct the 10° of System A to 8°. The period between −480 and −440 fits best with all the available information.

A high point of Babylonian astronomy

The similarity between Systems A and B is so great that I am inclined not only to assume some dependence between them, but also to ascribe both to the same peak period of Babylonian astronomy. This would place this period of finest achievement between −600 and −440, with preference for the century from −540 to −440.

In observational astronomy too, this century saw a renaissance. The text STRASSMAIER KAMBYSES 400 of −521 has been discussed above. The unpublished text BM 36 823, which is No. 1393 in the Descriptive Catalogue of the collection of A. SACHS (Late Babyl. Texts, Providence, 1955), contains observations of Jupiter for the years −536 to −489, arranged in 12-year groups. From the 30 years preceding this text (−566 to −537) we have no planetary observations. Our texts are mostly collections assembling the observations of many years. For eclipses the collections run in an unbroken series from −747 to −159. Hence the fact that in all the many texts that have come down to us the first planetary observations are for −536 can probably be taken to show that the Babylonians themselves had no continuous series of planetary observations from earlier times. This impression is strengthened by the fact that we have two texts with planetary observations from the period −536 to −489, and three from the period −468 to −399, with observations of all the planets. It thus appears that a period of intensive observational activity set in shortly after −540. By that time there were so many older observations of the moon (stretching over 200 years), that accurate periods could be calculated, as required for the theory of the moon.

It is only natural that increased attention was paid to the calendar at the same time. We have already seen that from −528 to −502 an 8-year intercalary cycle was used, and from −498 a 19-year cycle, which was carried on into the early years of our era.

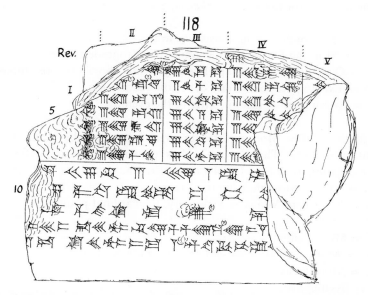

Plate 29. Text 603 with Procedure Text 821 (BM 34 571). Above Photograph British Museum, below copy of PINCHES, reproduced from A. SACHS, Late Babylonian Texts, No. 118. The upper part of the text is a table for Jupiter, calculated according to system A for the years 147—218 of the Seleucid Era (—164 to —93). The columns I to V give: Longitude of Morning Station, Date and Longitude of Opposition, Date and Longitude of Evening Station. The procedure text below the line explains the method of calculation.

CHAPTER VII

BABYLONIAN PLANETARY THEORY

General survey

We owe the decipherment of the first planetary tables to the same Jesuit father, FRANZ XAVER KUGLER, who explained the Babylonian lunar theory. The tables available to him were principally concerned with Jupiter. In his 'Sternkunde und Sterndienst in Babel' I (1907) he distinguishes 'Jupiter tables of the first, second and third types'. NEUGEBAUER labelled the types *A*, *A'* nad *B*, because the first two (*A* and *A'*) are related to the lunar system *A*, the third (*B*) to system *B*.

The principal purpose of the lunar tables was, to determine the positions of the Full and New Moon and the exact times of these phenomena. Similarly, the prime object of the planetary tables is the determination of the positions and dates of certain characteristic points in the orbits of the planets, which will here be called *cardinal points*.

The cardinal points for the *superior planets*, Saturn, Jupiter and Mars, are:

Γ = MF = Morningfirst = first visibility in the morning.
Φ = MSt = Morning Station = beginning of retrograde motion.
Θ = Op = Opposition (or perhaps Evening Rising shortly before Opposition)
Ψ = ESt = Evening Station = end of retrograde motion.
Ω = EL = Eveninglast = last visibility in the evening.

The designations Mf = Morningfirst, etc., were introduced by SCHOCH in LANGDON-FOTHERINGHAM-SCHOCH: The Venus Tablets of Ammizaduaga, Oxford, 1928. The Greek-letter notation is due to O. NEUGEBAUER. The notations MF, etc. seem to be more suggestive; that's why I shall use them there.

For the *inferior planets*, Venus and Mercury, the cardinal points are

Γ = MF = Morningfirst.
Φ = MSt = Morning Station = end of retrograde motion.
Σ = ML = Morninglast.
Ξ = EF = Eveningfirst.
Ψ = ESt = Evening Station = beginning of retrograde motion.
Ω = EL = Eveninglast.

KUGLER succeeded in explaining the calculation of the positions of Jupiter's cardinal points. PANNEKOEK and VAN DER WAERDEN found the rules used for the calculation of

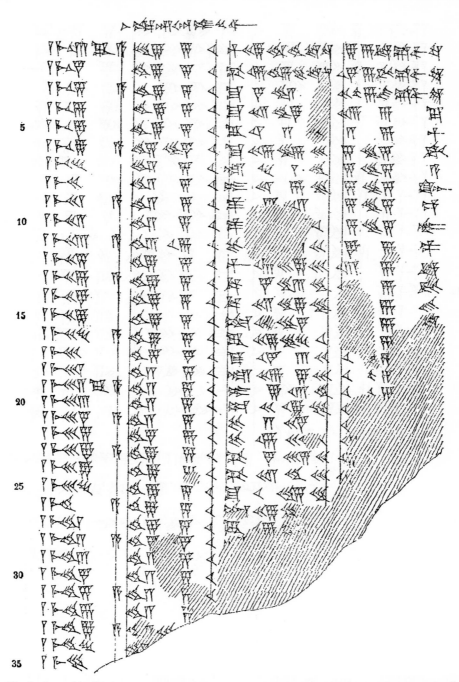

Fig. 20. Jupiter table 600 (Louvre Museum AO 6457). The year number 113 on the upper left is written as 100 + 13, with a special sign for 100 and the usual notation for 13. From A. THUREAU-DANGIN: Tablettes d'Uruk (Paris, Geuthner 1922) Plate 50.

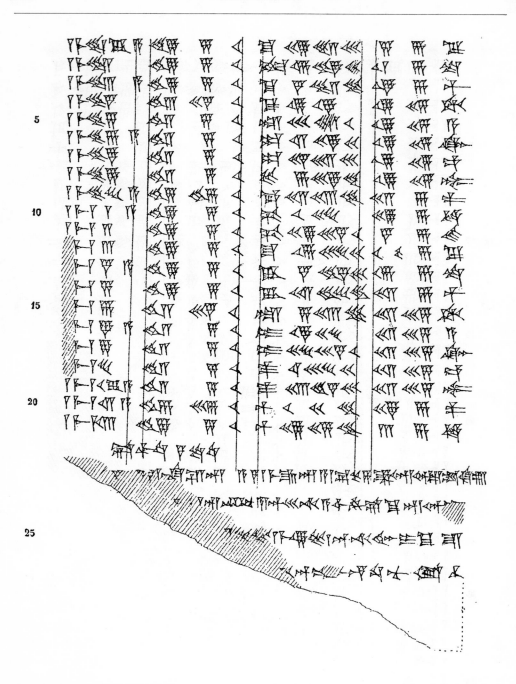

Fig. 21. Jupiter table 600, continued. Years 151—173. The years are written as 100 + 51 to 100 + 1,13.
Copied by A. THUREAU-DANGIN: Tablettes d'Uruk, Plate 51.

the corresponding dates. THUREAU-DANGIN, SCHNABEL and especially NEUGEBAUER published further texts through which it became possible to elucidate the methods of calculation for the other planets too.

The text numbers again refer to NEUGEBAUER's standard work ACT, where the texts are to be found in Vol. III and the commentary in Vol. II. Year numbers quoted without a minus sign are always years of the Seleucid era.

The tables in which the positions and times of the cardinal points are noted will be called *cardinal tables*. NEUGEBAUER used the name Ephemerids, but this word has already several other meanings.

JUPITER

System A

The law of formation of the Jupiter tables of system A is best illustrated by the cardinal table ACT 600. This table, which was found in Uruk, contains dates and positions for the Morning Station (MSt) of Jupiter for the years 113 to 173, i.e. from -198 to -138. The text bears the date 118 VII 12 and was written by *Anu-aba-uter* in the reign of ANTIOCHOS III. A copy of the main part of the table is reproduced in figs. 20 and 21. The numbers are easy to read. The texts begins as follows:

Year	Time interval	Date	Position
113 U	48; 5,10	I 28;41,40	8; 6 (10)
114	48; 5,10	II 16;46,50	14; 6 (11)
115 A	48; 5,10	IV 4;52	20; 6 (12)
116	48; 5,10	IV 22;57,10	26; 6 (1)
117	48; 5,10	VI 11; 2,20	2; 6 (3)
118 A	45;54,10	VII 26;56,30	5;55 (4)
119	42; 5,10	VIII 9; 1,40	5;55 (5)
120	42; 5,10	IX 21; 6,50	5;55 (6)
121 A	42; 5,10	XI 3;12	5;55 (7)

The numbers in brackets again denote signs of the zodiac. The letters U and A after the year numbers denote intercalary years with a second Ululu or Adaru. The time intervals are given, not in days, but in *Tithis*, with 1 tithi equal to a thirtieth of a synodic month. There are thus always 30 tithis in a month, which coincide approximately with the 29 or 30 days in the month. The word tithi is not actually found in the cuneiform texts: it comes from Sanskrit literature.

Tithis are a much more convenient unit for calculation than days. If the units were days, the scribe would have to know exactly for all the 61 years of the text which months had 29 days and which 30. The use of tithis does away with this. If the 48; 5,10 tithis in the second column are added to the date I 28;41,40 of the year 113, and then another 12 months, we arrive at the date II 16;46,50, since the year 113 has a second Ululu. In the civil calendar the date might be II 16 of II 17: it does not matter much, because exact dates of the stationary points cannot be accurately observed anyhow.

The positions in the last column are calculated by the following rule, as was recognized by KUGLER: *From 30°(8) to 25°(3) Jupiter covers 36° in a synodic period, but from 25°(3) to 30°(8) only 30°.* In the present case a synodic period is from one Morning MSt to the next MSt. The rule can easily be checked in the text. The addition of 36° to 8°6'(10) brings us to 14°6'(11), and so on.

For the transition cases, when the addition of 36° or 30° takes the planet across the boundary points 25°(3) or 30°(8), the procedure texts give the following rule:

'The excess over 25°(3) multiply by 0;50 and add to 25° (3). The excess over 30°(8) multiply by 1;12 and add to 30°(8)'. This we read in text 821, which is added as explanation to table 603.

The factors given, namely

$$0;50 = 5/6 = 30/36, \text{ and } 1;12 = 6/5 = 36/30,$$

lead to just the numbers that we find in our text. For instance, if we add 36° to the position 2;6 (3) of the year 117, we obtain 8;6 (4), which is 13;6 degrees beyond the boundary point 25° (3). Multiplication of 13;6 by 0;50 gives 10;55, the addition of which to 25° (3) gives the final position 5;55 (4), given in the table.

The sidereal period of Jupiter

If the rule just formulated governs the motion of Jupiter in a synodic period, what is the sidereal period of Jupiter?

One method to answer this question is, to substitute an imaginary 'mean Jupiter' for the actual. This mean Jupiter is characterized by the absence of any retrograde motion: it moves forward from one MSt to the next with a velocity of 30° per synodic period on the slow arc and 36° on the fast arc. If this 'mean Jupiter' coincides at any MSt with the 'true Jupiter', then it will clearly coincide again at the next MSt, and so on. Thus the sidereal period of the mean Jupiter will be equal to that of the true.

The fast arc from 30° (8) to 25° (3) contains 205°. To cover it, the mean Jupiter requires

$$\tfrac{205}{36} = 5;41,40 \text{ synodic periods.}$$

Just so one obtains for the slow arc

$$\frac{155}{30} = 5;10 \text{ synodic periods.}$$

In all, Jupiter will require

$$10;51,40 = \frac{391}{36} \text{ synodic periods}$$

to pass through the whole ecliptic. Hence we obtain the period relation

(1)   36 sidereal periods = 391 synodic periods.

The same period relation is basic to all three types of Jupiter tables. The mean synodic arc of Jupiter is therefore

$$\frac{360}{10;51,40} = 33°8'45'' \ldots,$$

a very accurate value: it differs by as little as 2'' from modern calculation.

It is possible that the notion of a 'mean Jupiter', which moves uniformly on the slow as well as on the fast arc, was foreign to the line of thought of the Babylonian astronomers. Another method of deriving the period relation (1) was indicated by AABOE[1]). To explain this derivation, let us divide the fast arc into 205 equal parts of 1°, and let us call these parts *steps*. On the 'slow arc', we define a *step* to be $\frac{5}{6}$ of 1°, or 50'. The ratio 5 to 6, which was used in this definition, is just the ratio 30 to 36 of the synodic arcs. Thus, the number of steps in a synodic arc of Jupiter is always 36, no matter whether the synodic arc lies wholly on the fast or slow arc or partly on the fast and partly on the slow arc. In other words:

In every synodic period Jupiter moves 36 steps forward.

The fast arc contains 205 steps, and the slow arc $155 \cdot \frac{6}{5} = 186$ steps. Hence the whole ecliptic contains

$$205 + 186 = 391$$

steps. In 391 synodic periods Jupiter takes 391 times 36 steps, i.e. the planet moves 36 times through the ecliptic. Hence we obtain, once more, the relation (1):

36 sidereal periods = 391 synodic periods.

We shall see that the notion of 'step' is an important notion in Babylonian planetary theory, especially in the theory of Mars. It is possible that AABOE's derivation of the period relation (1) is quite close to the original Babylonian line of thought.

[1]) ASGER AABOE: On Period Relations in Babylonian Astronomy. Centaurus *10* (1964) p. 213.

The calculation of the time intervals

From the transcription of text 600 we see that a synodic arc of 36° always has a time interval of 48; 5, 10, while an arc of 30° always has a time interval of 42; 5,10, to which in each case a further 12 months are to be added. The difference of the time intervals is 6 tithis and that of the arcs is 6°. In year 118 the time interval is 2;11 tithis shorter than in the preceding year, and the arc is correspondingly 2;11 degrees shorter. Hence there is a constant relation between the path S and the time T:

(1) $$T = S + c, \text{ where } c = 6,12; \ 5,10.$$

All time calculations in the cardinal tables depend on relations of the form (1). In the procedure texts these relations are deduced from the following principle:
It is assumed that the phenomena MF, MSt, Op, etc. always occur when the planet is a certain definite distance from the sun. This I call the *sun-distance principle*.
It follows from the sun-distance principle that in one synodic period of Jupiter, i.e. in our case from one MSt to the next MSt, the sun must cover the same distance as Jupiter and a complete orbit in addition. The same holds for Saturn and Mars; in the case of Venus and Mercury the complete orbit drops out. Now let the path covered by Jupiter in a synodic period be S. Then the path of the sun is $360 + S$. The time required by the sun to cover this distance is T. Hence T can be calculated.
In this calculation only the uniform motion of the sun is taken into account. To move through 360° the sun requires, according to the lunar theory

$$12;22, \ 8 \text{ months} = 12 \text{ months} + 0;22, \ 8 \text{ months}$$
$$= 360 \text{ tithis} + 11; \ 4 \text{ tithis}.$$

Therefore to cover 1 degree at mean velocity the sun requires

$$\frac{360 + 11; \ 4}{360} = 1 + \frac{\varepsilon}{360} \text{ tithis } (\varepsilon = 11; \ 4).$$

In one procedure text (No. 813) the somewhat too small value 11; 3,20 appears; otherwise, ε is always assumed equal to 11; 4.
The time for the sun to move $360 + S$ is therefore

(2) $$T = (360 + S)\left(1 + \frac{\varepsilon}{360}\right) = S + 360 + \varepsilon + \mu$$

where

(3) $$\mu = \frac{\varepsilon}{360} S.$$

Since $\varepsilon/360$ is a small factor, it makes little difference if the mean synodic arc is substituted for the synodic arc S in (3). Then μ becomes a constant, and equation (2) assumes the required form

$$T = S + c.$$

In our case it is found that

$$c = 360 + \varepsilon + \mu = 6{,}12; \ 5, \ 8, \ 8,$$

which can, for all practical purposes, be taken as 6,12; 5,10. Thus, equation (1) is justified.

From cardinal point to cardinal point

The procedure texts 813 (section 2) and 814 (section 2) show how the position of one cardinal point is derived from the preceding one. In the following table we give the arcs described by Jupiter according to these texts:

	Slow Arc 25°(3) to 30°(8)	Fast Arc 30°(8) to 25°(3)
MF to MSt	16;15	19;30
MSt to Op	−4	−4;48
Op to ESt	−6	−7;12
ESt to EL	17;45	21;18
EL to MF	6	7;12
Total	30°	36°

Proof that these rules were actually followed in the calculation of the cardinal tables can be found by a comparison of four cardinal tables from Uruk (ACT 600, 604, 601 and 606) for the phenomena MSt, Op, ESt and EL. One of these we have already discussed above. Tables 600 and 601 were written in the same year 118 by *Anu-aba-uter*. P. HUBER[1]) has proved that all four tables were calculated from the year 108 as origin. There can therefore be no doubt about the coherence of these four tables.

If now we compare the positions for the year 108 in these four tables, we find that the motions on the slow arc

---

[1]) P. HUBER, Zur täglichen Bewegung des Jupiter. Zeitschrift für Assyriol., New Series *18*, p. 265, especially §6.

EL to MSt: 22;15
MSt to ESt: −10
ESt to EL: 17;45

agree exactly with those calculated from the procedure text. Only the arc from MSt to
Op, which according to our procedure texts should equal 4, is 4;25 in the Uruk tables.
The times to cover these arcs in the year 108 were, according to the Uruk texts,

EL to MSt: 150 tithis
MSt to Op: 61 tithis
Op to ESt: 61 tithis
ESt to EL: 130; 5,10 tithis.

These times too are in good agreement with the values mentioned in the procedure
texts. For a detailed discussion the reader is referred to the article by P. HUBER just quoted.

System A'

System A' is still better known than A. It is described in a number of texts from Babylon
and Uruk. Three tables from Uruk for the years 116, 117 and 119 and nine tables from
Babylon which cover at least the period from 134 to 274 are calculated according to this
system.

In system A' the ecliptic is divided by 4 boundary points into 4 arcs. On the 'fast arc'
from 2° (10) to 17° (2) Jupiter covers 36° in a synodic period, on the 'slow arc' from
9° (4) to 9° (8) it covers 30°, and on the two remaining 'intermediate arcs' 33°45'. If the
sidereal period is calculated on this basis, exactly the same period relation (1) is found as
in system A. In deriving this period relation, one can use the notion 'mean Jupiter' or the
notion 'step': the result is always the same. The times too are calculated just as in A.

A *table of velocities* has been extracted from procedure texts by KUGLER and NEUGE-
BAUER. For the fast arc it is as follows:

After MF 30 days velocity   15'   per day
3 months to MSt   8'   per day
4 months retrograde   5'   per day
3 months from ESt on   7'40''   per day
30 days to EL   15'   per day
30 days to MF   15'   per day.

For the slow arc these velocities have to be multiplied by 5/6 and for the intermediate
arcs by 15/16, while the times remain unchanged.

NEUGEBAUER and I interpreted the 'days' mentioned here as tithis, but HUBER showed in the paper just quoted (Z.f.Assyriol., *18* p. 274), that it is real days that are used here. He further showed that three Uruk texts which describe the motion of Jupiter from day to day were calculated in exact accordance with this table of velocities.

If the month is taken to have 30 days, the table of velocities can be used to calculate the paths that Jupiter covers in the sectors of the ecliptic. For the fast arc from 2° (10) to 17° (2) we find

MF	to MSt	19°30′
MSt	to ESt	−10°
ESt	to EL	19°
EL	to MF	7°30′,

in total 36°, which is as it ought to be. By multiplying by 5/6 and 15/16 the distances on the slow and intermediate arcs are obtained.

In the great cardinal table 611 for the years 180-252 of the Seleucid era (KUGLER, Sternkunde I, p. 128) Jupiter covers 19°30′ from MF to MSt on the fast arc, which again agrees with the above calculation. Hence the procedure texts and cardinal tables from Babylon and the tables for the daily motion from Uruk are based on the same system.

The total of the times given in the table of velocities amounts to 390 days, that is 13 months and 6;12 tithis. However, in the cardinal tables and procedure texts much more accurate times are used. These are calculated from the 'sun-distance principle', as follows:

13 months 18; 5,10 tithis on the fast arc,
13 months 15;50,10 tithis on the intermediate arcs,
13 months 12; 5,10 tithis on the slow arc.

The times given in the table of velocities should therefore be taken as only an approximation. In fact, HUBER was able to prove that in one Uruk text the time intervals from MF to MSt and from MSt to ESt were extended by 4 and 6 days respectively.

System B

This system too is encountered in Uruk as well as in Babylon. From Uruk we have table 620, in which the time and position of the opposition are given for the years 127-194 of the Seleucid era. A few lines are broken off at the beginning. The signature shows that the table was written under ANTIOCHOS III, i.e. in 125 at the latest. The date used as the origin for the calculations in this table has been found (see my paper in Eudemus, Vol. 1, p. 45) as

113 IV 1 = −198, June 21.

In all system B texts both the paths S covered (that is the differences between two successive Jupiter longitudes) and the times T are linear zigzag functions. The difference d between successive values of S or T in the rising or falling part is always

$$d = 1;48.$$

The maxima and minima are:

Minimum of S:	28;15,30	of T:	40;20,45
Maximum of S:	38; 2	of T:	50; 7,15
Mean value of S:	33; 8,45	of T:	45;14

For both maxima and minima, and thus for the mean values as well, the following relation holds:

(4) $$T = S + 12; 5,15,$$

where 12 months have to be added in every case to the time (in tithis). The sun-distance principle leads us to expect a relation of the form $T = S + c$, but from our earlier calculations c should have been 12; 5, 8, 8 or 12; 5,10 if rounded. The difference amounts to only one day in 520 years and is thus insignificant.

The relation (4) does not hold exactly for individual values of S and T. The deviation in table 620 is only 0; 0,15, but it is 1; 1 for EL in table 622.

System B'

A variant of system B is described in sections 21 and 22 of the procedure text ACT 813. In this variant B' the mean value of S is 33; 8,45, as in system B, but the maximum M and the minimum m differ, and so does the difference d. As a result, the period of the linear zigzag function S differs from the period of T.

System B' also appears in Uruk in a cardinal table, ACT 640, written by *Anu-aba-uter* in the year 119. One year earlier the same scribe had calculated cardinal tables ACT 600 and 601 according to system A. System A' tables for daily motion were computed in Uruk for the years 116-119. The cardinal table ACT 620, belonging to system B, was computed only a few years later. Thus we see that about −190 all four systems A, A', B and B' were in use at Uruk.

An arithmetical series of the third order

The Jupiter positions calculated according to system A form an arithmetical series of the first order: the differences are constant in both the slow and the fast sectors of the ecliptic. The positions given by system B form a series of the second order: their differences form arithmetical series of the first order.

A masterpiece of Babylonian mathematical astronomy is afforded by texts 654 and 655, in which the daily motion of Jupiter is treated. For the final elucidation of the law of formation of this text we are indebted to P. HUBER (Zeitschr. f. Assyriol., New Series, Vol. 18, p. 279). HUBER first showed that both texts are fragments of one table. The table contained positions of Jupiter from day to day from MF of the year 147 to EL or MF of the year 148, together with their first and second differences. The (reconstructed) first lines read as follows:

	$\Delta^2 B$	ΔB	B	
147 IX 1	0	12,40, 0	29	(8)
2	-6	12,39,54	29;12,39,54	(8)
3	-12	12,39,42	29;25,19,36	(8)

For the reader's convenience I have multiplied ΔB and $\Delta^2 B$ by 60^3.

Thus the planet became visible for the first time in the morning of day IX 1 at 29° Scorpio. On the preceding day it covered 12'40''. The second differences form an arithmetical series with initial term 0 and difference -6. Therefore the next ΔB is derived from that of the first line by subtracting 6. The addition of this next ΔB to the Jupiter longitude B of the first line gives the next B. This process continues up to the morning stationary point:

		ΔB^2	ΔB	B
(5)	148 I 5	$-12,12$	9,42	16; 8,27,36

From here on the second differences ΔB^2 increase with constant differences $+10$. In the next line, therefore, we have $\Delta^2 B = -12,2$. Further, the sign of ΔB is tacitly (or erroneously) reversed, so that the next ΔB is calculated as follows:

$$-9,42 -12, 2 = -21,44.$$

In the table itself there are no signs. The scribe had to pay close attention to see whether a difference was to be added or subtracted; so an error of sign could easily occur.

Since ΔB has now become negative, the motion is retrograde, and indeed ever more so, since ΔB always decreases. But at the second stationary point ΔB must be either zero or almost zero. Hence ΔB cannot be allowed to decrease beyond the middle of the retrograde motion; thereafter it must increase again. In other words, $\Delta^2 B$ must remain negative up to the opposition (Op) and from there on become positive.

The retrograde motion of Jupiter lasts for four months according to the procedure texts. Therefore the sign of $\Delta^2 B$ must be reversed after two months. This is just what the writer of the table does. The date of the Morning Stationary Point was I 5. Two months later, towards the time of the opposition, we have

$$\text{III } 5 \qquad \Delta^2 B = -2,22 \qquad \Delta B = -7,14,30.$$

Now the sign is reversed and the constant third difference $\Delta^3 B = 10$ is added. So in the next line we have

$$\text{III } 6 \qquad \Delta^2 B = +2,32 \qquad \Delta B = -7,11,58.$$

This continues up to the Evening Stationary Point, when ΔB again becomes positive:

$$\text{V } 3 \qquad \Delta^2 B = +12, 2 \qquad \Delta B = -12, 4$$
$$\text{V } 4 \qquad \Delta^2 B = +12,12 \qquad \Delta B = +8.$$

After the Evening Stationary Point the reconstruction is very uncertain, because the text is badly damaged.

According to this text, the motion from MF to ESt varies in a smooth curve. This approximation is a great improvement on that produced by the assumption of piecewise constant velocities.

SATURN

Two systems, A and B, are known to us for Saturn. These are quite similar to systems A and B for Jupiter, but the numerous variants which make the Jupiter theory so interesting and informative are almost completely lacking. We shall not, therefore, devote much space to Saturn.

System A

This system is known only from two procedure texts, 801 and 802, both from Uruk. The name of the 'proprietor' of table 802, *Anu-aba-uter*, enables us to ascribe this table to the period around -190. Text 801 relates to Mercury and Saturn, whereas 802 is a duplicate of the Saturn section of 801. It begins thus:

Regarding Saturn.
From 10° (5) to 30° (11) slow
From 30° (11) to 10° (5) fast.

Next we have a table of velocities given for each part of the ecliptic, the slow and the fast. The velocities, in minutes of arc per day, are as follows:

		slow	fast
a)	Near the Sun	5	6
b)	After MF 30 days	5	6
c)	3 months to MSt	3;20	4
d)	MSt to Op retrograde 52½ days	14;...,40	15; 4,24
e)	Op to ESt retrograde 60 days	3;20	4
f)	3 months	3;35,30	4;18,40
g)	30 days to EL	5	6

The velocities in the sectors a), b), c), e) and g) are in the ratio 5 : 6. For sector f) the same ratio holds approximately. If we follow KUGLER in assuming the same ratio for d), we should have 14;13,40 as the velocity in the slow arc.

Lines 5 and 13 give the total retrograde motion:

slow 7;33, 7,30 degrees
fast 9; 3,45   degrees.

These numbers are in the correct ratio 5 : 6, but they are not in exact accordance with the table of velocities.

System B

System B for Saturn was used in Uruk and Babylon. In this system the synodic arc is a linear zigzag function with parameters:

Minimum m = 11;14, 2,30
Maximum M = 14; 4,42,30
Mean   = 12;39,22,30
Difference d = 0;12

Two periods can be deduced from these numbers: first, the anomalistic period, that is the time from one minimum to the next, and second the sidereal period, which is the time required by Saturn to pass through the whole ecliptic at mean velocity. The anomalistic period is

$$P_a = \frac{2(M - m)}{d} = 28;26,40 \text{ synodic periods;}$$

the sidereal is

$$P_s = \frac{360}{\mu} = 28;26,40 \text{ synodic periods.}$$

The two periods thus coincide exactly.

Multiplying the sidereal period by 9, we obtain the fundamental period relation

9 sidereal periods = 256 synodic periods.

MARS

It is very difficult to account for the motion of Mars, because this motion is extremely irregular. Let us now see how the Babylonians overcame this difficulty.

We shall confine ourselves here to system A, which is found in both Uruk and Babylon. The Uruk texts are cardinal tables for the years 89-131, 92-161 and 123-202 of the Seleucid era. The last of these three (ACT 501) was written in 124 by *Anu-uballit*.

Of special interest is a procedure text, 811a from Babylon. The following account of the theory of Mars depends primarily on this text.

Calculation of the Synodic Path

Our procedure text first gives a rule for calculating the longitudes of the phenomena EL, MF and MSt. The 'synodic path' is thus the path that Mars covers from one EL or MF or MSt to the next. For the calculation the ecliptic is divided into six sectors, each containing two zodiacal signs:

(2)+(3), (4)+(5), (6)+(7), (8)+(9), (10)+(11), (12)+(1).

The rules for calculating the synodic arc are as follows:

In (2) and (3) the path is 45°. The excess over (3) is multiplied by 2/3.

In (4) and (5) the path is 30°. The excess over (5) is multiplied by 4/3.

In (6) and (7) the path is 40°. The excess over (7) is multiplied by 3/2.

In (8) and (9) the path is 60°. The excess over (9) is multiplied by 3/2.

In (10) and (11) the path is 90°. The excess over (11) is multiplied by 3/4.

In (12) and (1) the path is 67½°. The excess over (1) is multiplied by 2/3. In each case 360° is to be added to the path given.

Example. Text 501 (from Uruk) gives the following positions for MSt:

Year 123	17;30	(2)
Year 125	1;40	(4)
Year 127	1;40	(5)
Year 129	2;13,20	(6).

The first position lies in the sector (2)+(3). Adding first 45°, we obtain 2;30 (4). The excess over (3) amounts to 2°30′. Subtracting from this one third, namely 50′, one gets 1°40′ (4). Adding 30° once, one obtains 1;40 (5), in accordance with the text. If one would add once more 30°, one would obtain 1;40 (6). To the excess over (5) one third, or 0;33,20 has to be added. This finally gives 2;13,20 (6).

Steps

We shall now calculate the sidereal orbit time for Mars according to system A. To simplify the calculation, we shall divide each synodic path into 18 parts. Once more, these parts will be called 'steps'. The lengths of the steps differ in the different sectors of the zodiac. The values are:

In (2) and (3)	45/18 = 2;30
In (4) and (5)	30/18 = 1;40
In (6) and (7)	40/18 = 2;13,20
In (8) and (9)	60/18 = 3;20
In (10) and (11)	90/18 = 5
In (12) and (1)	67;30/18 = 3;45 degrees.

When I introduced the concept of 'steps' in my paper 'Babylonische Planetenrechnung' (Vierteljahrsschr. Naturf. Ges. Zürich *102*, p. 39), I was not yet aware that sections of just these lengths appear in the Babylonian procedure text 811, Section 3 (ACT II, p. 381). In the procedure text we have 2;15 and 3;40 instead of 2;13,20 and 3;45, but the other figures coincide exactly. This means: the Babylonian theoretical astronomers realized the importance of the 'steps'.

The respective sectors of the zodiac thus contain

       24   36   27   18   12   16   steps,

so that the whole ecliptic has 133 steps. The rules given above for the calculation of the synodic path can now be very conveniently summarized:

Mars moves 133 + 18 = 141 steps in every synodic period.

The sidereal period

In 133 synodic periods Mars takes 133 times 151 steps, i.e. it moves 151 times through the ecliptic. Hence

(1)   151 sidereal periods = 133 synodic periods.

151 orbits have 15; 6, 0 degrees. Correspondingly, we read in text 811a, section 11:

2,13 phenomena 2,31 revolutions 15, 6, 0 degrees movement.

This means

133 repetitions of the same phenomenon = 151 full revolutions = 151 times 360° movement.

To obtain the mean synodic path, we must divide 15, 6, 0 by 2,13. Accordingly the text asks:
What must be multiplied by 2,13 to obtain 15, 6, 0?
and gives the answer:

6,48;43,18,30 times 2,13 is 15, 6, 0.

The mean synodic path is thus a complete orbit (360 degrees) plus 48;43,18,30°. Hence the text:

Write 48;43,18,30 as the mean path.

We see that this text gives not only the rules for calculation, but also the justification of the rules. The quotient 6,48;43,18,30 is correct to the last sexagesimal place.

The sun-distance principle

According to the sun-distance principle the phenomena EL, MF and MSt always occur when Mars is at a certain distance from the sun. Consequently, in any one synodic period (from EL to EL, or MF to MF, or MSt to MSt) the sun always covers the same distance as Mars and one complete orbit in addition.

In 133 synodic periods Mars completes 151 revolutions. According to the sun-distance principle, the sun in the same period completes

$$151 + 133 = 284 \text{ revolutions.}$$

Hence

(2) $\quad\quad$ 151 sid. periods = 133 syn. periods = 284 years.

This Mars period, as we saw above, was already known under the Persian reign.

In the procedure texts the sun-distance principle is used to derive a relation between the synodic path S and the corresponding time T. The calculation proceeds exactly as in the case of Jupiter. If Mars covers a path S, the sun must cover $360 + S$. The time needed for this is

(3) $\quad\quad T = (360 + S)\left(1 + \dfrac{\varepsilon}{360}\right)$, where $\varepsilon = 11;4.$

This can be re-written in the form

(4) $\quad\quad T = S + c,$

where

(5) $\quad\quad c = 360 + \varepsilon + \mu$

and

(6) $\quad\quad \mu = \dfrac{\varepsilon}{360} S.$

In the calculation of the small correction term μ the Babylonian mathematicians substituted for S its mean value

(7) $\quad\quad \bar{S} = 6,48;43,18,30.$

Multiplying (7) by

$$\frac{\varepsilon}{360} = \frac{11;4}{6,0} = 0;\ 1,50,40,$$

one obtains

(8) $\quad\quad \mu = 12;33,51,52,47,21.$

Exactly this value is to be found in the procedure text 811a, section 6. Shortly before, in section 5, the factor 0; 1,50,40 is also mentioned. Hence it is clear that the writer used in his calculations exactly the formula

(9)
$$\mu = \frac{\varepsilon}{360} \, \bar{S}.$$

For subsequent calculations μ was rounded to

$$\mu = 12;33,52.$$

Adding to this

$$360 + \varepsilon = 6,11; \, 4,$$

one obtains

(10) $c = 6,23;37,52.$

This value of c is the one to be used in evaluating $T = S + c$, as we see from section 3 of the procedure text:

'To the distance between one phenomenon and its next occurrence add 23;37,52 and you have the time.'

The 12 months or 6, 0 tithis contained in c according to our equation (40) were tacitly added.

The elongations

So far we have used two equivalent formulations of the solar distance principle, namely:

I. The phenomena EL, MF and MSt always occur at fixed distances from the sun.

II. In one synodic period the sun covers the same distance as Mars and a complete orbit in addition.

The author of the text 811a used the principle in form II. The question arises, whether he also knew formulation I, and, if so, what numerical values he assumed for the elongation of Mars at the time of the EL, MF and MSt.

Section 5 deals with the phenomenon EL. The text runs:

[. . .] 5 degrees, that Mars is separated from the sun, . . .

NEUGEBAUER tentatively restored the damaged figure at the beginning of the line as 15 and interpreted the 15° as the elongation of Mars at the time of EL.

The sun moves faster than Mars, so that the elongation of Mars decreases. We shall see later that it was assumed to decrease by 30° up to MF, so that it is −15° at MF. From MF to MSt it decreases by a further 105°. Therefore the morning stationary point occurs at $-120°$. In fact the number 2, 0 ($= 120$) is mentioned in the same section in connection with MSt. The procedure text is therefore based on the assumption that Mars disappears at an elongation of $+15°$, reappears at $-15°$ and turns retrograde at $-120°$.

On the basis of these numbers we can understand the calculations carried out in sections 6 to 9. The subject in these sections is the calculation of the times t_1, t_2, t_3 corresponding to the distances s_1, s_2, s_3 covered by Mars from EL to MF, from MF to MSt and from MSt to EL. Over these stretches the sun must cover the same distance as Mars and an additional $30°$, $105°$ or $225°$ respectively, which we shall denote by by r_1, r_2, r_3.

Then the time required for the sun to cover $s_1 + r_1$ is

$$(11) \qquad t_1 = (s_1 + r_1)\left(1 + \frac{\varepsilon}{360}\right) = s_1 + c_1,$$

where $c_1 = r_1\left(1 + \dfrac{\varepsilon}{360}\right) + \dfrac{\varepsilon}{360}\, s_1$.

Again substituting for s_1 its mean value $\bar{s}_1$, we obtain

$$(12) \qquad t_1 = s_1 + c_1$$

$$(13) \qquad c_1 = r_1\left(1 + \frac{\varepsilon}{360}\right) + \mu_1$$

$$(14) \qquad \mu_1 = \frac{\varepsilon}{360}\, \bar{s}_1.$$

In my article Babylonische Planetenrechnung (Vierteljahrsschr. Naturf. Ges. Zürich *102*) I showed that these formulae do in fact form the basis of the calculations carried out in the procedure text. Let us start with (14). The calculation of $\bar{s}_1$ is based on the following assumption: *the number of steps covered by Mars from EL to MF, from MF to MSt and from MSt to EL is 33, 60 and 58 respectively.* The sum of these numbers is 151 steps, as it should be. The mean length of a step is

$$\tfrac{360}{133} = 2;42,24,21,40.$$

Multiplying by 33, 60 and 58, one obtains:

$$\bar{s}_1 = 1,29;19,23,55$$
$$\bar{s}_1 = 2,42;24,21,40$$
$$\bar{s}_3 = 2,36;59,32,56,40.$$

Remembering that $\varepsilon/360 = 0;\ 1,50,40$, we now substitute these numerical values in (14). The value obtained for μ_1

$$\mu_1 = 2;44,45,\ 6,46,40$$

is exactly that given in the text (section 6). Hence it is clear that the text is based upon formula (14). Just so one obtains for μ_2:

$$\mu_2 = 4;59,32,55,57,46,40.$$

The text here differs in two places, having 22 for 32 and 47 for 57. The former difference is certainly due to a scribal error, because μ_2 is subsequently rounded off to 4;59,33. We may suppose that 47 is also a scribal error for 57.

The correct value of μ_3 according to (14) is

$$\mu_3 = 4;49,33,50,\ 5,51,\ 6,40,$$

in accordance with the text. In sections 7-9, the text uses the correct rounded values:

$$\mu_1 = 2;44,45$$
$$\mu_2 = 4;59,33$$
$$\mu_3 = 4;49,33,50.$$

In these sections equation (13) is worked out at length. In section 7, the step number $r_1 = 30$ is first multiplied by $\varepsilon/360 = 0;\ 1,50,40$; then $r_1 = 30$ is added, giving

$$r_1\left(1 + \frac{\varepsilon}{360}\right) = 30;55,20;$$

finally $\mu_1 = 2;44,45$ (the text erroneously says 1;44,45) is added, giving

$$c_1 = 33;40,\ 5\ \text{(text erroneously 33;40).}$$

Sections 8 and 9 run similarly. Thus we see that formula (13) is really fundamental to the procedure text. Further we see that the values we calculated for r_1, r_2, r_3 from the elongations $+15°$, $-15°$ and $-120°$ are indeed those that were taken by the author of the text as his basis. These elongations are to be taken from the mean sun: the sun's anomaly is neglected in all these calculations.

Summary

We have seen that system A is a logical system built up on the following hypotheses:
I. Mars moves with different velocities in six sections, each formed of 2 zodiacal signs:

$$(2)+(3), (4)+(5), (6)+(7), (8)+(9), (10)+(11), (12)+(1).$$

Each of these sectors is divided into

24	36	27	18	12	16

equal parts, which we have called 'steps'. The step lengths are thus

2°30′	1°40′	2°13′20″	3°20′	5°	3°45′.

II. The number of steps covered by Mars from EL to MF, from MF to MSt and from MSt to EL is 33, 60 and 58 respectively.

III. The solar year contains 12;22, 8 mean synodic months, or 360 + 11;4 tithis.

IV. The phenomena EL, MF and MSt occur at elongations of $+15°$, $-15°$ and $-120°$ from the mean sun.

The procedure text 811a for Mars contains not only (as do the majority of these texts) rules for calculation, but also gives their justification. These must go back to the author of system A. It must therefore be assumed that text 811a is based on some treatise by this author in which he expounded the basic concepts of his system. The procedure text itself is certainly a copy: the numbers in it contain typical copyist's errors which are recognizable from the fact that they do not influence the subsequent calculations.

Deviations between cardinal tables

According to the procedure text 811a, Mars covers 33 steps from EL to MF and 60 steps from MF to MSt.

In the cardinal tables the numbers of steps from EL to MF and from MF to MSt are likewise integers, but they deviate in certain cases from the figures given above. Thus in the Uruk text No. 502 the following positions are given for MF and EL:

Obverse:	MF		Reverse:	EL	
Line 12	1;40	(4)	Line 1	2;30	(3)
Line 13	1;40	(5)	Line 2	11;40	(4)
Line 14	2;13,20	(6)	Line 3	11;40	(5)

Obv.		I		Obv.	Rev.		I		Rev.
1.	[20]	gír-tab	igi	1.	0.	[11,15	ḫun	šú]	0.
	[30]	máš	igi			[2,30]	maš	[šú]	
	[1]5	ḫun	igi			[11,40]	kušú	[šú]	
	5	maš	igi			[11,40]	a	šú	
5.	[1]3,20	kušú	igi	5.		[15,3]3,20	absin	šú	
	[1]3,20	a	igi		5.	[25,3]3,20	rín	šú	5.
	17,46,40	absin	igi			[2]3,20	pa	šú	
	27,46,40	rín	igi			[1]5	zib	šú	
	26,40	pa	igi			[1]5	múl	šú	
10.	18,45	zib	igi	10.		[30]	maš	šú	
	17,30	múl	igi		10.	[30]	kušú	šú	10.
	1,40	kušú	igi			[30]	a	šú	
	1,40	a	igi			[10]	rín	šú	
	2,13,20	absin	igi			[30]	gír-tab	šú	
15.	[1]2,13,20	rín	igi	15.		[15]	gu	šú	
	[3,]20	pa	igi		15.	[26,]15	ḫun	šú	15.
	[20]	gu	igi			[12,3]0	maš	šú	
	[30]	ḫun	igi			[18,]20	kušú	šú	
	[15]	maš	igi			[18,]20	a	šú	
20.	[20]	kušú	igi	20.		[2]4,26,40	absin	šú	
	[20]	a	igi		20.	6,40	gír-tab	šú	20.
	[26,40]	absin	igi			10	máš	šú	
	[10]	gír-tab	igi			30	zib	šú	
	[15]	máš	igi			25	múl	šú	
25.	[3,45]	ḫun	igi	25.		6,40	kušú	šú	
	[27,30]	múl	igi		25.	6,40	a	šú	25.
	[8,20]	kušú	igi			8,53,20	absin	šú	
	[8,2]0	a	igi						
	[11,]6,40	absin	igi						
30.	[21,]6,40	rín	igi	30.					
	[16,]40	pa	igi						
	[7,]30	[zib	igi]						
	[10	múl	igi]						

Fig. 22. Text 502. Cardinal Table for Mars, from Uruk. Obverse ME, Reverse AL. from NEUGEBAUER, ACT III, Plate 175.

The distance from the first EL to the second MF (Line 13), and similarly from the second EL to the third MF (Line 14) is 30 steps. Since in passing from one line to the next Mars always covers exactly 18 steps, the distance from one EL to the subsequent MF remains 30 steps in all the following lines.

Similarly in the Babylon text No. 504 the difference between MF and MSt is always 63 steps.

The Uruk text 502 is not dated, but it can be related to text 500, which gives MSt and Op for the years 89-131. If it is assumed that 502 relates to the years 92-161, the two texts can be combined into a single table for EL, MF, MSt and Op. The number of steps from EL to MF is then 30, from MF to MSt 61 and from MSt to EL 60. Any other dating of the text 502 gives less satisfactory figures for the numbers of steps.

The retrograde motion

The theory discussed so far is valid only for the phenomena EL, MF and MSt. The retrograde motion from MSt through Op to ESt is handled in a completely different way. According to NEUGEBAUER (ACT II, p. 305), there are four different schemes, R, S, T and U, according to which, starting from MSt, the positions of Op and ESt can be calculated. All four make the arc from MSt to Op dependent on the position of MSt. According to scheme R the arc is always equal to 6° if MSt occurs in the zodiacal signs (2) or (3); for (4) or (5) the value is 6;24, for (6) or (7) 6;48, for (8) or (9) 7;12. After this the numbers decrease in the same fashion. Scheme T is analogous, except that the maximum is 7;30. In scheme U the arc increases linearly from the minimum 6 to the maximum 7;30, and then decreases linearly again. In scheme S signs in which the arc is constant alternate with signs in which it increases or decreases linearly. In this scheme the total retrograde motion from MSt to ESt is $2\frac{1}{2}$ times the arc from MSt to Op. We do not know how ESt was calculated in the other schemes.

System B

There is a Mars table from Uruk (ACT 510) that is based on system B. Actually only a small fragment is preserved, but P. HUBER[1]) succeeded in reconstructing from it the law of formation of the table.

In NEUGEBAUER's transcription the fragment runs as follows (I shall replace the names of the zodiacal signs by numbers for the reader's convenience):

[1]) See A. AABOE, Babylonian Planetary Theories, Centaurus 5 (1958) p. 246.

. . .	(7)
. . . 17	(9)
. . .,35	(12)
. . . 6,13,51	(2)
. . . 29,52, 8	(3)
. . . 5,30,25	(4)
. . . 30,25	(5)
. . .,30,25	(7)
. . . 30,25	(9)
. . .	(11)

HUBER reconstructed this text as follows:

[0]	I	
48,36,40	22,20,37	(7)
1, 5,36,40	27,57,17	(9)
1,17,38,17	15,35,34	(12)
1, 0,38,17	16,13,51	(2)
43,38,17	29,52, 8	(3)
26,38,17	26,30,25	(4)
25	21,30,25	(5)
42	3,30,25	(7)
59	2,30,25	(9)
1,16	18,30,25	(11)

Column I is derived by summation from the difference column [0]. The latter is a linear zigzag function with parameters

$$\text{Maximum } M = 1,20; \ 7,28,30$$
$$\text{Minimum } m = \quad 17;19, 8,30$$
$$\text{Difference } d = \quad 17.$$

If the period ratio is calculated from this, it is found to be exactly the same as in system A:

$$151 \text{ sidereal periods } = 133 \text{ synodic periods.}$$

The mean synodic motion also coincides with the System A value, being

$$\tfrac{1}{2}(M + m) = 48;43,18,30.$$

VENUS

For Venus there are three systems, A_0, A_2 and A_1.

System A_0

It so happens that this very simple system has survived only in Uruk. Text 400 gives the dates and longitudes for EF, i.e. for the first visibility of Venus as an evening star, for the 24 years from 111 to 135, as follows:

Year	Date	Longitude	
111	V 27;30	3	(7)
113	I 20;40	8;30	(2)
114	VIII 13;50	14	(9)
116	III 7	19;30	(4)
117	X 30;10	25	(11)
119	V 23;20	30;30	(6)

We see that the longitudes increase in one synodic period by 7 zodiacal signs and $5\frac{1}{2}$ degrees, the dates likewise by 19 months and 23;10 tithis. The path covered in one synodic period is thus

$$S = 19 \text{ signs} + 5\frac{1}{2}° = 9,34;30 \text{ degrees,}$$

and the time

$$T = 9,53;10 \text{ tithis.}$$

The relation between S and T is

$$T = S + 17;40.$$

The figure 17;40 is presumably rounded off. On the basis of the sun-distance principle, and taking the year to have 12;22,8 months, one would obtain

$$T = S + 17;41,28,40.$$

If S is multiplied by 5, we obtain 8 complete revolutions less $2\frac{1}{2}$ degrees, hence

$$5 \text{ synodic periods} = 8 \text{ sidereal periods} -2°30'.$$

If S is multiplied by 720, we obtain 1152 complete revolutions. Hence

720 synodic periods = 1152 sidereal periods = 1152 years.

System A_0 is simpler than the system A for Saturn, Jupiter and Mars, because in system A_0 the synodic arc S does not depend on the region of the ecliptic in which Venus happens to be. In fact this anomaly is much smaller for Venus than for the other planets, so that no great harm results from neglecting it.

Systems A_2 and A_1

Later mathematicians attempted to improve system A_0 by making the arc S dependent on the region of the ecliptic. Two systems, A_2 and A_1, emerged, of which the latter is somewhat better than the former: neither is very good.

System A_2 is best studied from text 420 (from Babylon); a photographic reproduction is shown in Plate 17. We see that the table consists of an upper part, a narrow belt and a lower part. The belt contains a so called Colophon, a heading, which reads thus:

Venus, relates to the years from 180 to 241. *Marduk-shum-iddina*, son of *Bēl-iddina*, descendant of *A-ku-ba-ti-la*, opposite . . . .-*iddina*, scribe of *Enūma Anu Enlil*, son of *Bēl-uballitsu* . . .

A second scribe was here named 'opposite' *Marduk-shum-iddina*; the exact significance of 'opposite' is not known. *Bēl-uballitsu*, the father of the second scribe, lived around 186, for in that year he calculated a cardinal table (No. 430) for Venus.

The upper part of our text is a cardinal table for all 6 cardinal points EF, ESt, EL, MF, MSt, ML. The lower part is an procedure text 821b, which tells us how the table was calculated.

The procedure text contains six sections for the six cardinal points. We here reproduce the second section relating to the Evening Stationary Point ESt. The zodiac is divided into 5 parts, each containing 2 or 3 signs. For each such part we are given first the path S from one ESt to the next and then the time T:

Zodiacal signs	Path S	Time T
(11) (12)	3,43;30	9,51
(1) (2) (3)	3,37;30	10, 1
(4) (5)	3,38;30	9,59
(6) (7) (8)	3,29;20	9,46
(9) (10)	3,28;30	9,49

Plate 30. Venus Table ACT 420 with Procedure Text 821b, from Babylon. The upper part is a Cardinal Table for Venus, computed for the years 180 to 241 (Seleucid Era) according to System A₂. The middle strip contains the name of the scribe Marduk-shum-iddina and of another scribe, called his 'opposite'. The lower part is a procedure text, which tells us how the table was calculated.

This rule of formation was in fact used in computing cardinal table 420. The table begins thus:

Year	Date	Position
180	XI 16	12;20 (12)
182	VI 7	25;50 (7)

The difference between the dates is 9,51 tithis and the path covered is 7 signs and 13;30 degrees, which is as it should be according to the procedure text.

Summing the five times T, we obtain 99 months less 4 tithis: the familiar 8-year Venus period. Summing the five paths S (and adding a complete revolution to each S), we obtain a total of 8 orbits minus 2;40 degrees in the sections on ESt, EL and MSt, but 8 orbits less 2;30 degrees in the sections on MF and ML. NEUGEBAUER's explanation for this is that the former three sections and table 420 were calculated from System A_2, the latter two (MF and ML) from system A_1.

This mixing of the two systems leads to great confusion. For the short time from EL to MF Venus should move retrograde, but table 420 sometimes makes the motion direct. For instance, in the year 241 Venus would move forward, according to 420, through $1\frac{1}{2}$ degrees in one day!

Comparison with modern calculations shows that system A_2 is very poor. A motion of 8 revolutions less 2;40 degrees in 5 synodic periods is much too slow. Consequently the longitudes calculated from system A_2 are too small throughout, the errors becoming ever greater with the passage of time.

System A_1 is somewhat better than A_2, but still not very good. The anomaly of Venus' motion is made much too large in either case. Further, both systems have the inconvenient property of not being indefinitely extensible either forwards or backwards. The longitudes decrease by 2°30′ or 2°40′ every 8 years. Consequently, after a time one of the longitudes comes out of the ecliptic sector (11) (12) or (1) (2) (3) etc. The relevant path S then alters by a large amount, and the sum of the five paths becomes much too big or too small.

It is therefore only for a limited period that it is possible to maintain a system like A_2 without change. In my paper 'Babylonische Planetenrechnung' (Vierteljahrsschrift Naturf. Ges. Zürich *102*) I made use of this fact to date system A_2. The result was that A_2 must have been invented between −186 and −125.

The resultant chronology of the three Venus systems is thus:

> A_0 was known in Uruk about −200;
> A_2 was invented between −186 and −125, probably in Babylon;
> A_1 was invented about −125 in Babylon in *Bēl-uballitsu*'s circle.

MERCURY

System A₂

The oldest planetary tables that have come down to us are Mercury tables from Babylon, ACT 300a and 300b. The former relates to the years 4 to 22, the latter to 10 to 18 of the Seleucid era. Several lines have been broken off at the beginning of both tables; it is therefore possible that they began some years earlier still. We shall not go far wrong if we assume that both texts were calculated about the year 11 of the Seleucid era, i.e. about −300.

Both texts belong to the same system, A_2. In this system the last visibility in the morning (ML) and in the evening (EL) are first calculated. The addition of a variable invisible sector gives the next reappearance at evening (EF) and morning (MF) respectively.

For the calculation of ML the ecliptic is divided into 4 parts, in which different synodic paths *w* are taken, namely:

from   (4) 0 to   (6) 30 $w_1 = 1,47;46,40$
from   (7) 0 to (10)   6 $w_2 = 2, 9;20$
from (10) 6 to   (1)   5 $w_3 = 1,37$
from   (1) 5 to   (3) 30 $w_4 = 2, 9;20.$

The number of synodic periods needed for Mercury to pass through the whole ecliptic is therefore:

$$\frac{1,30}{1,47;46,40} + \frac{1,36}{2, 9;20} + \frac{1,29}{1,37} + \frac{1,25}{2, 9;20} = \frac{1223}{388}$$

Thus 1223 synodic periods make 388 years. This ratio is quite close to that mentioned in text 800:

145 synodic periods = 46 years.

For the calculation of EL the ecliptic is likewise divided into four parts:

from   (4) 0 to   (9) 30 $w_1 = 1,48;30$
from (10) 0 to (11) 30 $w_2 = 2, 0;33,20$
from (12) 0 to   (1) 30 $w_3 = 1,48;30$
from   (2) 0 to   (3) 30 $w_6 = 2,15;37,30$

Starting with an ML, in order to calculate the next EF, a certain distance was added to the position of the ML, this distance being a piecewise linear function of that position. The procedures for EL and MF are analogous. For further details the reader is referred to NEUGEBAUER, ACT II, p. 296.

System A_1

In one Uruk text, ACT 300, and in six Babylonian texts we find another system A_1, in which the calculation is done in exactly the opposite way, the position of the preceding last visibility being derived from the position of the first visibility (MF or EF). For the calculation of MF or EF the ecliptic was divided into 3 parts in which different synodic arcs, w, were assumed, namely for MF

from (5) 1 to (10) 16	$w_1 = 1,46$
from (10) 16 to (2) 30	$w_2 = 2,21;20$
from (3) 0 to (5) 1	$w_6 = 1,34;13,20$

and for EF

from (4) 6 to (7) 26	$w_1 = 2,40$
from (7) 6 to (12) 10	$w_2 = 1,46;40$
from (12) 10 to (4) 6	$w_3 = 1,36.$

Daily motion

In the Uruk text 310 (ACT III, Plate 168) the positions of Mercury are given from day to day for 7 months. By way of example, let us take the first half of the second month:

Day	Difference	Position	
1	1;45	5;37	(6)
2	1;45	7;22	(6)
3	1;45	9; 7	(6)
4	1;45	10;52	(6)
5	1;45	12;37	(6)
6	1;37,30	14;14,30	(6)
7	1;33,18	15;47,48	(6)
8	1;29, 6	17;16,54	(6)
9	1;24,54	18;41,48	(6)
10	1;20,42	20; 2,30	(6)
11	1;16,30	21;19	(6)
12	1;12,18	22;31,18	(6)
13	1; 8, 6	23;39,24	(6)
14	1; 3,54	24;43,18	(6)
15	59,42	25;43	(6)

We see that the differences are at first constant and then decrease arithmetically. The positions thus form arithmetical sequences of the first and second order.

THE TIME OF INVENTION OF BABYLONIAN PLANETARY THEORIES

Observations of lunar and solar eclipses were available in the Babylonian archives since −748. They formed the necessary observational basis for the two lunar theories A and B. As we have seen, the lunar System A was probably invented between −540 and −470, and System B between −480 and −440.

The same archives also contain numerous observations of the planets, but these observations do not start before −536. Now for a planetary theory one needs observations during a period of several years, say during 8 years at least for Venus, 12 years for Jupiter and even more for the slow-moving Saturn. Therefore we may safely assume that planetary systems A and B were not invented before −530. In studying these systems, one gets the strong impression that they were modelled after the lunar systems A and B, hence −530 seems to be the earliest possible date indeed.

On the other hand, by −300 there were already Mercury tables belonging to System A. Hence the planetary theory of System A was invented between −530 and −300.

These limits are pretty certain. By using probability arguments, we may obtain more narrow limits. The arguments will be denoted by a), b), c).

a) System A for the Moon, for Jupiter and for Mars are admirable logical systems, and very similar in their logical structures. Therefore we may conjecture that they were invented by the same man, or at least elaborated by the same group of astronomers. Now, System A for the moon existed already by −470, as we have seen in Chapter 6. Hence it seems probable that System A for Jupiter and Mars was invented between −530 and −430.

b) As we have seen in Chapter 6, there are texts from the years −445 and −418, in which positions of planets with respect to zodiacal signs are recorded. Thus, the text 1387 of Pinches-Sachs[1]) (= BM 45 674) says that the Eveninglast of Venus in the year −445 took place 'at the end of the fishes'. Just so, the diary VAT 4924 says that Jupiter and Venus were in Nisannu −418 'at the beginning of Gemini', and that in Addaru II of the same year Jupiter was 'at the beginning of Cancer'. In a horoscope for the year −409, positions of planets with respect to zodiacal signs are recorded. In later texts, we often find indications of the following kind: 'On a certain date a certain planet entered a certain zodiacal sign'.

How could the Babylonians obtain such dates? There are two possibilities: by observation or by calculation. Let us examine the two possibilities.

If one tries to determine entrances of planets into zodiacal signs by observation, one meets two difficulties. First, the limits of the signs are not marked at the sky. One can only observe distances to fixed stars, and then by means of a catalogue of longitudes of stars calculate the longitudes of the planets. Secondly, planets are often invisible,

---

[1]) A. Sachs: Late Babylonian Astronomical Texts, Providence 1955.

because they are too near to the sun or because the sky is clouded. In these cases one has to interpolate between earlier and later observations.

Thus we see that observations alone are not sufficient: they must in any case be combined with calculations.

Moreover — and this is the third difficulty — horoscopes are often required for a date in the past, for which no observations are available.

All these difficulties disappear if the entrances are calculated from planetary tables. I shall explain the method by means of an example.

In Text ACT 600, belonging to System A for Jupiter, we find in the second line a date for EL:

Year 115.   Date XII 18;30,10. Position 29;24 (12).

Now if this position is taken for granted, at what date will Jupiter enter the next sign (1) Aries?

According to a procedure text belonging to System A', the velocity of Jupiter between EL and MF is 15' per day on the fast arc, i.e. between 2° (10) and 17° (2). Now, System A usually agrees with A' on the fast and slow arc. Hence let us assume that in System A too the velocity was 15' per day. It follows that after 2 days Jupiter's position would be 29;54 (12). After that, it would take Jupiter less than half a day to reach the end of the sign (12). Hence the date of entry of Jupiter into Aries would be $2\frac{1}{2}$ days after XII 18;30, or XII 21. In System A with its piecewise constant velocities, calculations of this kind are easy.

The conclusion is that calculations of positions at a given date, or of entrances of planets into signs, are an easy matter as soon as one has planetary tables, but are difficult and often impossible if one has to rely upon observations. Up to the present day, astrologers always use tables, and practically never make observations.

For these reasons it is not unreasonable to assume that the planetary positions in our texts for the years -445, -418 and -409 were calculated from tables belonging to System A or A'. If this is assumed, it follows that System A must have existed by -420 or even earlier.

c) In my paper The Date of Invention of Babylonian Planetary Theory, Archive for History of Exact Sciences 5, p. 70, I have studied a set of planetary tables without dates for Saturn, Jupiter and Mars. I have found that the most probable dates for the first line of the Mars table are

$$-498 \text{ or } -419$$

For line 2 of the Saturn table, the most probable dates were found to be

$$-510 \text{ or } -451 \text{ or } -392.$$

Since the tables for Mars and Saturn are quite similar, and very much different from the usual kind of dated tables, we may suppose (with a certain degree of probability) that they were computed by the same man or the same group of astronomers, and that their initial dates do not differ by more than 20 years. Under these assumptions, the only possible pair of dates is

$$-498 \text{ for the Mars table,}$$
$$-510 \text{ for the Saturn table.}$$

If the span of 20 years is extended to 30 years, another solution would be

$$-419 \text{ for the Mars table,}$$
$$-392 \text{ for the Saturn table.}$$

If this pair of dates is accepted, the positions of Saturn do not fit as well as in the first case, and the span between the two dates is now 27 years, as compared with 12 in the first case. Therefore, the first pair of dates

$$-498 \text{ and } -510$$

seems more probable.

This pair of dates falls within the reign of DARIUS (-521 to -485). Hence, combining the arguments a), b), c) we may conclude that the most probable time of invention of System A for the planets is the reign of DARIUS.

If System A for the planets was invented by the same man as System A for the moon, then his name was probably NABU-RIMANNU.

It is quite possible that the activity of this great astronomer started already during the reign of KAMBYSES (-529 to -521), and that the text 'Strassmaier Kambyses 400', which contains observations of the Moon, Jupiter, Venus, Saturn and Mars, is a sign of his activity. We have already mentioned the fact that some entries in this text were calculated, not observed. It seems possible that the calculations were made by means of the lunar theory of System A.

The next planet which NABU-RIMANNU studied seems to have been Jupiter. We have one text containing observations of Jupiter for the years -525 to -489, ordered in groups of 12 years (PINCHES-SACHS, Nr. 1393; see Chapter 4). Such a collection of observations would be extremely useful for any astronomer who wants to make a theory of Jupiter. The observations were made during the reigns of KAMBYSES and DARIUS.

A man named 'NABU-RIMANNI, son of BALATU, descendant of the priest of the moon-god' witnessed two legal documents in the years -490 and -489, during the reign of DARIUS. It is possible that this man was the astronomer NABU-RIMANNU. See A. T. OLMSTEAD: History of the Persian Empire, p. 202. The texts of the documents (VAT 18 and 73) were published in Vorderasisatische Schriftdenkmäler 5 (1908), Nr.104 and 105.

CHAPTER VIII

THE SPREAD OF BABYLONIAN ASTRONOMY

As we have seen, the cradle of horoscopic astronomy was in Babylonia. As early as −410, horoscopes were cast in Babylon. Two-and-a-half centuries later, horoscopes were cast all over the ancient world.

Now, in order to cast horoscopes, one must know how to calculate longitudes of planets. Also one has to calculate the 'ascendent' or 'horoscope', i.e. the point of the ecliptic just rising over the horizon at a given hour. Therefore, whenever people want to cast horoscopes, they must learn how to use astronomical tables.

For computing such tables, two kinds of method were available in late antiquity. We may call them 'Babylonian' and 'Greek' methods; a more accurate description would be *linear methods* and *trigonometric methods*. Linear methods are based upon rising and falling arithmetical sequences such as we find them in cuneiform texts from Babylon and Uruk. Later Greek authors such as HIPPARCHOS and PTOLEMY preferred the more accurate trigonometric methods, but trigonometry was not available before 200 B.C. Besides, linear methods are much easier to apply than trigonometric calculations. Therefore, even after −200, linear methods remained very popular with astrologers. Even as late as 550 A.D., linear methods of the Babylonian type were explained in a Sanskrit astronomical treatise[1]) alongside with trigonometric methods.

HIPPARCHOS and PTOLEMY did not use linear methods, but they did make use of Babylonian observations and lunar and planetary periods. The marvellous edifice of their geometrical astronomy was erected on the solid foundation laid by the Babylonians through their diligent observations and calculations. Without the work of the Babylonian scribes, Greek precision astronomy would not have been possible.

In this chapter we shall follow the spread of Babylonian astronomy as shown by Greek, Latin, Sanskrit and Egyptian sources. In order to get a complete picture, a certain amount of repetition will be unavoidable.

EARLY GREEK EVIDENCE

The eclipse of THALES

In Chapter 4 we have seen that THALES, in his prediction of an eclipse, probably used Babylonian methods.

[1]) VARÂHA MIHIRA: Pañcasiddhântikâ, translation and commentary by O. NEUGEBAUER and D. PINGREE, Kon. Danske Vidensk. Selskab Hist.-Fil. Skrifter *6*, 1, Part I and II.

Gnomon and division of the hours

HERODOTOS reports (Hist. II 109): 'Polos and gnomon and the twelve parts of the day did the Greeks learn from the Babylonians'.

The Greek divided the day and the night into 12 equal parts each, which they called *horai* (hours of the day or night). The length of the hours therefore depended on the season. Babylonian knowledge of the twelvefold division of the day and night is confirmed by the British Museum Ivory prism, in which the durations of the twelfths of day and night are given for every month of the year.

The same division of the day and night was also used by the Egyptians. See K. SETHE, Die Zeitrechnung der Aegypter, Nachr. Ges.Wiss. Göttingen (Phil.-Hist.) 1919 and 1920.

The *Polos* of which HERODOTOS speaks is possibly the shadow caster of a hemispherical solar clock. See the article *Horologium* in Pauly-Wyssowa's Realenzyklopädie des klass. Altertums (Neue Bearbeitung).

A *Gnomon* is a vertical rod that casts its shadow on a horizontal plate. Its main purpose is to find the time of day by observing the gnomon shadow. The Babylonians achieved this with the aid of tables such as we find in ^{mul}APIN. This text contains three tables: one for the winter solstice, one for the equinox and one for the summer solstice. In each case the time of day for a given shadow-length is given. Between these points the time seems to have been ascertained by linear interpolation.

The Greeks had much more accurate methods. They inscribed hour lines on the gnomon plate, constructed so that at the end of the first hour of the day the point of the shadow fell on the first hour line, and so on. ANAXIMANDROS erected a gnomon in Sparta, which also showed the solstices and equinoxes (DIOGENES LAERTIOS II 1).

The gnomon tables of ^{mul}APIN leave the user in the lurch around noon; for the shadow length alters but little at this time. The only means of finding the exact noontime by means of the gnomon is to observe the direction of the shadow when it points due North. Therefore I suppose that the Babylonians drew the North-South line on their gnomon plates, just as the Greeks did.

Numbers and heaven according to the Pythagoreans

According to ARISTOTLE (Metaphysics A5) the Pythagoreans occupied themselves with the mathematical sciences, and because they saw that numbers are so very important in these sciences, they arrived at the following views:

'Heaven is harmony and number',
'Number is the essence of the Whole',
'Things exist by imitation of number'.

Further, ARISTOTLE says 'They constructed the heaven from numbers' (De Caelo III and Metaphysics M6).

How did the Pythagoreans reach these conclusions? In what sense did they 'construct the heaven from numbers'?

The astronomy of ANAXIMANDROS and later Greek astronomers is primarily geometrical. The Greeks thought of the paths of the Sun, Moon and planets as circles in space, or they imagined rotating spheres carrying the planets with them in their motion. The hour lines on the gnomon depend on geometrical constructions and not on calculation. Much later the constructions were replaced by trigonometrical calculations, but the Pythagoreans had not yet reached this stage.

In contrast the Babylonians had from the very beginning an arithmetical astronomy in which numbers played the leading part. If we assume that PYTHAGORAS and his school were acquainted with this arithmetical astronomy, their accentuation of the importance of numbers becomes intelligible.

Of the numbers which enter into astronomical calculations those which define the ratios of the orbital periods are of special importance. The Pythagoreans were certainly interested in these periods, for they speculated about the 'Great Year', which is a common multiple of all orbital periods. The determination of planetary periods, however, necessitates serial observations over long periods, much longer than those available to the Greeks at the time of PYTHAGORAS. Even at much later dates KALLIPPOS, HIPPARCHOS and PTOLEMY had to use Babylonian observations in order to find accurate period relations. This suggests that the Pythagoreans likewise obtained their knowledge of planetary periods from Babylonian sources, perhaps indirectly by way of Egypt.

This conclusion is confirmed by the fact that the 59-year Saturn period known to us from the cuneiform texts appears in CENSORINUS (De die natali 18) as 'Great Year of the Pythagorean PHILOLAOS' and in AETIOS II 32 as 'Great Year of OINOPIDES and PYTHAGORAS'.

It is not likely that the Pythagoreans of the fifth century who lived in Southern Italy came into direct contact with Babylonian astronomy. The distance from Italy to Babylon is large, and the Persian wars did not promote cultural exchanges. I therefore suppose that it was PYTHAGORAS himself, who came from Samos and lived before the Persian wars, who handed on to his adepts astronomical knowledge from Mesopotamia or Egypt.

This conclusion is in full agreement with Greek tradition, which calls PYTHAGORAS a pupil of the Magi or Chaldaens or of the 'Chaldaean ZARATAS'. Even if the reports about his travels in Egypt and Babylon are not reliable in detail, they still indicate that the Greeks recognised a dependence between Egyptian and Babylonian doctrines on the one hand and Pythagorean doctrines on the other.

The zodiac

The most impressive proof of the great influence of the Babylonians on the general development of astronomy and astrology is provided by the history of the zodiac. For a full account of this history see my 'History of the Zodiac', Archiv für Orientforschung 16 (1953), p. 216. Here I shall restrict myself to the most important points.

We have seen that the obliquity of the solar path was known to the scribe of the text ^{mul}APIN (about -700). In this text the path was divided into 4 parts and the year into 12 schematic months, such that the sun spent 3 months in each of the four parts. From here it is only a short step to the twelvefold division of the sun's path. The 4 parts of the ecliptic need only be divided into three parts, in each of which the sun remains one month. Since the months were usually reckoned to have 30 days, it was only natural to divide each sign of the zodiac into 30 'degrees'. The resulting division of the zodiac into 12 signs of 30 degrees each was fundamental not only in astronomy, but also in astrology: the practice of horoscope astrology is based upon it.

In Greece the zodiac with its twelve signs was not, as in Babylon, the product of a long development. We find the Greek zodiac fully developed at the end of the sixth century. PLINIUS tells us (Nat. Hist. II 31):

> The obliquity (of the zodiac) is supposed to have been made known first by ANAXIMANDROS of Miletus in the 58th Olympiad (548-545 B.C.). Subsequently KLEOSTRATOS made known the signs in it, starting with Aries (the Ram) and Arcitenens (the Archer).

The statement that ANAXIMANDROS made known the obliquity of the zodiac is certainly correct, for we know from other sources that in his system the paths of the sun and moon were inclined circles. It thus appears that PLINIUS' information stems from a good source. What PLINIUS says about the Ram and the Archer is somewhat puzzling[1]; but the statement that KLEOSTRATOS of Tenedos made the zodiacal signs known in Greece is quite clear and definite. KLEOSTRATOS probably lived before -500. He is said to have carried out astronomical observations from the base of Mount Ida[2].

The names of the signs

The Greek names from which the modern descriptions of the zodiacal signs are derived are mostly translations of much older Babylonian star names. Let us go through the series.

[1] See the discussion between FOTHERINGHAM and WEBB in the Journal of Hellenic Studies, Vol. 39, 41, 45 and 48.
[2] A. REHM, Parapegmastudien, Abh. Bayer. Akad. München (Neue Folge) 19 (1941), p. 135.

(1) Instead of the Babylonian 'hired labourer' (ḪUN·GA) the Greeks had a Ram.

(2) GU·AN·NA means 'bull of heaven', hence our Bull.

(3) MAS·TAB·BA·GAL·GAL means 'the great twins', hence the Greek designation Didymoi, which means twins.

(4) The origin of our Crab has not been explained.

(5) UR·A probably means Lion or Lioness.

(6) Spica, the principal star of Virgo, is called in the cuneiform texts AB·SIN, i.e. furrow. But in ^{mul}APIN we read 'The star AB·SIN is the corn-ear of the goddess Shala'. The idea of a goddess or virgin carrying an ear of corn appears in a line drawing of the Seleucid period (Plate 11c). The Greek star name Spica means 'ear of corn'.

(7) *Zibānītu* means Scales.

(8) GIR·TAB = *zuqāqīpu* means Scorpion.

(9) Our Archer was portrayed in Roman Egypt (e.g. at Dendera, Plate 14b) as a winged centaur shooting with a bow. A very similar fabulous being is found on a Babylonian boundary stone of the Cassite period (Plate 14a). The animal has two tails and two heads: a dog-head looking backwards and a man's head with a high cap looking forwards. All these attributes are again found at Dendera. The Babylonian origin of the Graeco-Egyptian Archer is thus indubitable.

(10) The constellation SUḪUR-MÁŠ appears in ^{mul}APIN among the 'stars in the path of the moon'. SUḪUR means Goat and MÁŠ Fish. A fabulous beast with a goat's head and fish's body is to be found on a boundary stone from the Cassite period (Plate 14c). Just this combination of goat and fish is also portrayed at Dendera in the place of our Capricorn (Plate 14d). The attitude of the forelegs is the same as on the boundary stone. The Greek name Aigokeros means goat-horned (Latin: Capricornus).

(11) The meaning of GU·LA is not known to us, but the idea of a god pouring water from two jars, which we find portrayed at Dendera (Plate 14f), stems from the Old-Babylonian period (Plate 14e).

(12) The Greek conception of the constellation Pisces was two fishes whose tails were tied together by a band in the region of α Piscium. The expression 'Band of the Fishes' *(rikis nūni)* is also to be found in cuneiform texts. The constellation Pisces is generally called 'the tails' *(zibbāti*^{mes}*)*. In earlier cuneiform texts we find two constellations ŠIM·MAḪ and *anunitum*, which were considerably more extensive than the two small fishes in the Greek zodiac.

Sidereal and tropical divisions of the zodiac

The Babylonian division of the zodiac is *sidereal*, i.e. the limiting points of the signs have a fixed position with respect to the fixed stars. For instance, Spica always lies quite near the end of the sign Virgo.

In this system, the longitudes of the fixed stars are constant: they were given in a 'star catalogue', which was used in ancient and in more recent times. Longitudes of the moon and the planets were determined by observing their distances to fixed stars. Longitudes of the sun were probably determined by observing eclipses.

In this system the location of the equinoxes may vary. Three determinations are known:

^{mul}APIN (−700): equinox at 15° Aries (13° would be correct)
System A (−500): equinox at 10° (correct)
System B (−440): equinox at 8° (9° would be correct).

On the other hand, most Greek authors define the zodiacal signs by means of the equinoxes and solstices. The initial points of Aries, Cancer, Libra and Capricorn are, by definition, the points at which the sun's center stands at the equinoxes and solstices. This is the *tropical division* of the zodiac.

A consequence of these definitions is a quite different order of the observations and a different structure of the theory. HIPPARCHOS started with accurate determinations of equinoxes and solstices. Next he determined the eccentric motion of the sun. PTOLEMY followed the same road: a table of the motion of the sun is basic for his theory. From the longitude of the sun, the longitude of the moon can be found, e.g. by observing eclipses. Longitudes of planets and fixed stars are determined by observing their distances from the moon.

The first astronomer who introduced the tropical division of the zodiac seems to have been EUKTEMON, who lived at Athens. In the year −431 METON and EUKTEMON observed the summer solstice (PTOLEMY, Syntaxis III 1). Starting with this observation, EUKTEMON constructed a *parapegma*, i.e. a calendar, in which the annual risings and settings of several fixed stars were noted[1]. He divided the solar year into 12 'months' (not lunar, but solar months) defined by the 12 signs of the zodiac. In the month 'Cancer' the sun dwelt in the sign Cancer, and so on. The first day of the month 'Cancer' was the day of the summer solstice, the first day of 'Libra' was the autumnal equinox, and so on. EUKTEMON's tropical division of the zodiac differed from the Babylonian division by 8 or 9 degrees at the time of EUKTEMON.

The Athenian METON, who also composed a parapegma, did not use EUKTEMON's new division of the zodiac, but used the original Babylonian norm. As COLUMELLA (De re rustica XI, 14) informs us, METON located the vernal equinox at 8°. This agrees with the Babylonian System B.

EUKTEMON's solar year began with the summer solstice. The first five 'months' had 31 days each, the last seven 30 days. Hence EUKTEMON assumed that the sun passes through one part of the zodiac with a constant velocity of 30° per 31 days, and through the remaining part with a velocity of 30° per 30 days. This model of the motion of the sun is quite similar to the Babylonian System A.

[1] A. REHM: Griechische Kalender III, Sitzungsberichte Heidelberger Akad. (hist.) 3rd Abhandlung, 1913.

In EUKTEMON's calculation of lunar months he used an intercalation cycle of 19 years. METON too used this cycle. This cycle was also known to the Babylonians.

EUKTEMON's star calendar consisted of a date list and a date-difference list. Just so, the text ^{mul}APIN contains a list of dates of annual risings and a list of date differences, as we have seen in Chapter 3.

EUDOXOS (−370) also composed a parapegma. According to COLUMELLA, he located the equinoxes and solstices at 8°, just as METON did. EUDOXOS also wrote a treatise called 'Phainomena', which served as a model for the poem 'Phainomena' of ARATOS. In this treatise of EUDOXOS as well as in the poem of ARATOS, the equinoxes were located at 15° of the signs Aries and Capricorn[1]), just as in the Babylonian text ^{mul}APIN.

Observations and periods

When ALEXANDER conquered the Persian empire, the ties between Babylonian and Greek civilization became closer than ever before. KALLISTHENES, a historian, who accompanied ALEXANDER on his expedition, sent his uncle ARISTOTLE observations from Babylon at the latter's express wish[2]). Since ALEXANDER took Babylon in −330 and KALLISTHENES was executed in −326, the observations must have been sent between these two dates. At this time ARISTOTLE was at Athens. His astronomical adviser was the Athenian KALLIPPOS, who observed the summer solstice in −329. From a fragment of HIPPARCHOS, which by chance has been preserved[3]) we know that KALLIPPOS compared his observations with earlier Babylonian ones and thus found that the year has $365\frac{1}{4}$ days. Perhaps the observations he used were just those which ARISTOTELES had received from KALLISTHENES[4]).

In PORPHYRIOS' report it is stated that these observations covered a period of 31 000 years down to the time of ALEXANDER. These 31 000 years are of the same order of magnitude as the 36 000 years which in BEROSSOS' chronology separated the deluge from CYRUS. BEROSSOS enumerates the Babylonian kings since the flood and their reigns. It is quite possible that the Babylonians cast horoscopes for some of these kings and calculated planetary positions in retrospect. Such calculated positions may have been included among the observation reports which KALLISTHENES passed on to ARISTOTLE. Even to-day we find the greatest difficulty in distinguishing calculated results from observations in the cuneiform texts. The notion of real observations over a period of 31 000 years is incredible.

[1]) R. BÖKER: Die Entstehung der Sternsphäre Arats, Berichte sächs. Akad. Leipzig 99 (1952).
[2]) PORPHYRIOS quoted by SIMPLIKIOS, Commentary on De Caelo p. 506.
[3]) THEON of Alexandria: Commentary on the Almagest III 1, ed. ROME =Studi e Testi Bibl. Vat. 106, p. 836.
[4]) See J. K. FOTHERINGHAM: The Indebtedness of Greek to Chaldaen Astronomy. Quellen u. Studien Gesch. Math. B2, p. 28.

PTOLEMY (about +140) used the observations of his Greek predecessors and made observations himself, but he also made extensive use of Babylonian eclipse and planetary observations. The eclipse observations he used were made between −720 and −380.

In Babylonian goal-year texts, the following approximate planetary periods were used:

Saturn	59 years
Jupiter	71 and 83 years
Mars	47 and 79 years
Venus	8 years
Mercury	46 years.

HIPPARCHOS used the same periods, as we are told by PTOLEMAIOS (Syntaxis IX 3). HIPPARCHOS also used the lunar periods of the Babylonian System B, as we have seen in Chapter 6.

More accurate planetary periods are mentioned by the astrologer RHETORIOS in an excerpt from ANTIOCHOS (Catalogus codicum astrologorum graecorum I, p. 163), namely

Saturn	265 years (9 sidereal orbits)
Jupiter	427 years (36 sidereal orbits)
Mars	284 years (151 sidereal orbits)
Venus	1151 years (720 synodic periods)
Mercury	480 years (1513 synodic periods).

The same periods were also used in the Babylonian planetary theories.

We shall now see that the Greeks and Romans took over from the Babylonians not only observations and periods, but methods of calculation as well.

The rising and setting of the moon

As we have seen in Chapter 2, the earlier Babylonian texts calculate the rising and setting of the moon on the basis of the assumption that the daily retardation of the moon' setting in the first half of the month (up to the full moon) and the daily retardation of the moon's setting in the second half are both equal to 1/15 of the whole night.

Elementary rules for calculating the rising and setting of the moon are also found in the 'Anthology' of the astrologer VETTIUS VALENS, in the 'Natural History' of PLINIUS and in the 'Geoponica' of CASSIANUS BASSUS. In my article Babylonian Astronomy III (J. of Near Eastern Studies, 10, p. 27) I showed that all these rules rest on the same basic assumption about the daily retardation of the rising and setting of the moon in the night.

Only the author of the Geoponica gives his source, namely 'ZOROASTER'. Two other fragments ascribed to ZOROASTER, likewise from the Geoponica of CASSIANUS BASSUS, have already been discussed in Chapter 5 in the section 'Sirius and the Harvest'. We have seen that these fragments belong to a primitive stage of zodiacal astrology which probably arose in Babylon in the time of the Chaldaean kings (-625 to -538). Presumably the Magi passed on this primitive zodiacal astrology and ascribed it to their prophet ZARATHUSTRA.

Rising times of zodiacal signs

Important for astrology are the times in which the twelve zodiacal signs rise above the horizon in their daily rotation. Rules for calculating these rising times are to be found in the works of MANILIUS, VETTIUS and FIRMICUS MATERNUS. MANILIUS gives the rising times only for the climate (i.e. for the geographical latitude) of Babylon, but FIRMICUS takes six, and VETTIUS seven climates into account. For each climate the rising times of the first six signs form an ascending, the last six a descending arithmetical progression (see O. NEUGEBAUER, Trans. Amer. Philos. Soc., 32, p. 257).

In a surviving work called Anaphorikos the Greek astronomer HYPSIKLES explains the method of calculation of these arithmetical progressions. He discusses only the climate of Alexandria, but his method can be applied to any climate, as soon as the length of the longest day for that climate is known.

HYPSIKLES assumes that the beginning of sign (1) is the vernal point. Let the rising times of the signs (1), (2), . . . be t_1, t_2, . . . The times t_1, . . ., t_6 are supposed to form a rising, t_7, . . ., t_{12} a descending arithmetical progression, the terms in the second progression being the same as those in the first but in the reverse order:

$$t_7 = t_6, t_8 = t_5, \ldots, t_{12} = t_1.$$

Let the length of the longest day for the climate in question be given. The problem is to determine the rising times t_1, . . ., t_{12}.

The solution is based on the following basic idea. If the sun just enters a sign, say the sign (2), the initial point of this sign rises at sunrise. In the course of the day the signs (2) (3) (4) (5) (6) (7) rise in succession. At the end of the day the sun sets, so then the opposite point of the ecliptic rises. This opposite point is just the end point of the sign (7). Thus the duration of the day, if the sun be at the beginning of sign (2), is

$$C_2 = t_2 + t_3 + t_4 + t_5 + t_6 + t_7.$$

Similar equations can be formed for the initial points of all signs. In particular, we have

$$C_1 = t_1 + t_2 + t_3 + t_4 + t_5 + t_6$$

and

$$C_4 = t_4 + t_5 + t_6 + t_7 + t_8 + t_9.$$

Now $t_1 + t_2 + t_3 = 3t_2$, because t_1, t_2, t_3 form an arithmetical series. Similarly for $t_4 + t_5 + t_6$, etc. Hence the equations can be simplified to

(1)
$$C_1 = 3t_2 + 3t_5$$

(2)
$$C_4 = 3t_5 + 3t_8 = 6t_5$$

C_1 is the length of an equinoctial day, C_4 that of the longest day. These two values are known, so t_5 can be calculated from (2), and t_2 from (1). The difference d of the arithmetical series is

(3)
$$d = \tfrac{1}{3}(t_5 - t_2).$$

Now the whole series is known.

For the climate of Babylon all our authors take the ratio of longest day to shortest night as 3 : 2, as do the cuneiform texts. If the day-lengths $C_1, C_2, \ldots, C_{12}$ are calculated for this climate, exactly the same values are found as in the lunar system A.

The whole mathematical scheme is typically 'linear'; it requires no trigonometry. The Babylonian horoscope casters naturally needed the rising times $t_1, \ldots, t_{12}$ just as much as their Greek and Roman colleagues. They already had systems A and B, but they were ignorant of trigonometry. On these grounds I follow NEUGEBAUER in assuming that the Babylonian astronomers knew and used the arithmetical progressions $t_1, \ldots, t_6$ and $t_7, \ldots, t_{12}$, at least for the climate of Babylon.

If HYPSIKLES' hypothesis is modified by making the difference between the middle terms of the progression $(t_4 - t_3)$ twice as large as the other differences, equation (3) becomes

(4)
$$d = \tfrac{1}{4}(t_5 - t_2).$$

If now $t_1, \ldots, t_6$ are calculated afresh, a new series of rising times is obtained, which is in fact found for various climates in Michigan Papyrus III 149 and for the climate of the Hellespont in KLEOMEDES and MARTIANUS CAPELLA. Also GERBERT, who later became Pope SYLVESTER II, knew this sequence (see the paper of NEUGEBAUER quoted before).

The second climate belongs, according to the Michigan Papyrus, to Syria. If the durations of daylight $C_1, C_2, \ldots, C_{12}$ is calculated anew for this climate, the values obtained are exactly those of the lunar system B. The papyrus states that the vernal point is at 8°; this too fits system B. Once again we have confirmation that the whole linear theory of rising times is of Babylonian origin.

It is questionable whether the Babylonians themselves calculated rising times for more than one climate. Until more evidence becomes available, we must assume that this extension of the theory is Greek.

THE EVIDENCE FROM GEMINOS

The calculation of the moon's velocity

GEMINOS, who lived at Rhodos about 70 B.C., tells us in his 'Isagoge' (ed. MANITIUS, Chapter 18) how the 'Chaldaeans' calculated the daily motion of the moon. The passage is important for our understanding of Babylonian astronomy, because GEMINOS gives not only the method, but also the train of thought leading to it.

According to GEMINOS, the constants determining the motion of the moon are:

Smallest daily motion	11° 6′35″
Mean daily motion	13°10′35″
Greatest daily motion	15°14′35″
Daily increase or decrease	18′.

The cuneiform texts 190-196 (NEUGEBAUER, ACT I, p. 179-183) from Uruk and Babylon are all based on the method reproduced by GEMINOS. In these texts the position of the moon from day to day is calculated by addition of the daily motions, as we have seen in Chapter 6.

The Chaldaeans' train of thought was as follows, according to GEMINOS. The period taken as the starting point was the 'Exeligmos', i.e. an approximate 54-year lunar period of 669 synodic months or 19 756 days[1]). In this time the moon passes 723 times through the zodiac and moves 32 degrees more. Thus, the total motion is 260 312 degrees in 19 756 days. By dividing these numbers the Chaldaeans found, says GEMINOS, that the mean daily motion of the moon is 13°10′35″. His report is credible, for we find in the cuneiform texts both the 54-year lunar period and also the mean daily motion of 13°10′35″.

The Exeligmos contains, according to GEMINOS, 717 anomalistic periods and 19 756 days. If the number of days be divided by 717, then an anomalistic period is found to be 27;33,20 days, says GEMINOS[2]). Dividing this by 4, we obtain 6;53,20. This is the number of days the moon requires from its smallest velocity to the mean, or from the mean to the largest velocity.

Observation gives the smallest daily motion of the moon as being between 11 and 12 degrees and the largest between 15 and 16 degrees, says GEMINOS.

Now let us assume that the daily motion increases or decreases every day by the same

---

[1]) The same period is also mentioned by PTOLEMY, Syntaxis IV 2. According to him, the 54-year period was obtained by tripling the 18-year lunar period in order to obtain an integer number of days. In a cuneiform text from Uruk (THUREAU-DANGIN, Tablettes d'Uruk No. 14) both the 18-year and the 54-year periods are mentioned.

[2]) In fact the result of the division is 27; 33, 13. O. NEUGEBAUER drew attention to this error of GEMINOS.

amount d, so that we are dealing with arithmetical sequences. The difference d is to be such that $6;53,20$ times d, added to the mean motion $13;10,35$, gives a maximum between 15 and 16, and subtracted from $13;10,35$ a minimum between 11 and 12. These requirements are met by $d = 0;18$. For if this be multiplied by $6;53,20$, the result is $2; 4$. The largest daily motion then becomes

$$13°10'35'' + 2°4' = 15°14'35''$$

and the smallest daily motion

$$13°10'35'' - 2°4' = 11°6'35''.$$

THE CHALDAEANS AND THEIR ASTROLOGY

GEMINOS quotes the 'Chaldaeans'. Who were they?

From the agreement between the record of GEMINOS and the cuneiform texts we may conclude that the Chaldaeans were Babylonian astronomers and that GEMINOS, who lived on the island of Rhodos about 70 B.C., was well-informed about their theory of the moon.

In Chapter 2 of the same Isagoge, GEMINOS gives an account of the astrological doctrine of the 'aspects'. Two planets may have a trigonal or tetragonal aspect (angle of 120° or 90°) or they may be in opposition (180°). GEMINOS ascribes this doctrine and its application to nativities to the 'Chaldaeans'. Hence the Chaldaeans of GEMINOS were not only astronomers, but they also cast horoscopes.

When ALEXANDER the Great was on his way to Babylon, he came across 'Chaldaean diviners', who urged him not to enter the city because 'they knew from the stars that the king's death would occur at Babylon'. The story is told by DIODOROS (XVII 112), by ARRIANOS (Anabasis VII 16) and by PLUTARCHOS (Life of Alexander 73). Most probably, their source was a record of an eye-witness (PTOLEMAIOS LAGU or ARISTOBULOS). According to the authors just quoted, the Chaldaeans were priests of Bel-Marduk, and they also made predictions to ALEXANDER's successors ANTIOGONOS and SELEUKOS.

A still more ancient source is HERODOTOS (−450), who mentions a group of priests of the god Bel whom he calls 'Chaldaeans' (Histories I 181-183).

The way of life of these 'Chaldaeans' is described by STRABON in his Geography, Book 16, Chapter 1, as follows:

> In Babylon a settlement is set apart for the local philosophers, the Chaldaeans, as they are called, who are concerned mostly with astronomy; but some of them, who are not approved of by the others, profess to be genethlialogists.

There is also a tribe of the Chaldaeans, and a territory inhabited by them, in the neighbourhood of the Arabians and of the Persian Sea . . . There are also several tribes of the Chaldaean astronomers. For example, some are called Orchenoi, others Borsippenoi, and several others by different names, as though divided into different sects which hold to various dogmas about the same subjects. And the mathematicians make mention of some of these men; as, for example, Kidenas and Naburanos and Sudines. Seleukos of Seleukeia is also a Chaldaean . . .

As we have seen, the names KIDENAS = KIDINNU and NABURIANOS = NABU-RIMANNU occur in cuneiform texts. NABU-RIMANNU probably invented System A and lived about −500 under DARIUS, whereas KIDENAS lived about −440 and probably invented System B. SUDINES lived about −200 and was astrologer at the court of ATTALOS I of Pergamon. SELEUKOS of Seleukeia was one of the few followers of ARISTARCHOS of Samos, who lived about −280 and proposed the heliocentric theory. So the 'so-called Chaldaeans' of STRABON all lived during the Persian and Hellenistic age.

STRABON makes a distinction between the 'so-called Chaldaeans', who were philosophers and astronomers (and some of them also astrologers), and the tribe of the Chaldaeans, who lived in the South of Babylonia near the Persian gulf. This distinction is correct. In the time of NEBUCHADNEZZAR the Chaldaeans were just the people living in that southern region, and the kings of Babylon belonged to them. Later on the name 'Chaldaeans' came to denote a class of priests living in Babylon, who occupied themselves with astronomy and astrology.

The Chaldaeans were active as astrologers already under the Persian kings (539-331 B.C.). This we know from three sources:

A) GELLIUS reports in Noctes atticae XV 20: A Chaldaean predicted from the stars the brilliant future of EURIPIDES to his father.

B) CICERO reproduces in De divinatione II 42 a saying of EUDOXOS: 'One should not believe the Chaldaeans in their predictions of the fate of a man from the day of his birth'.

C) PROKLOS reports in his Commentary on the Timaios (p. 151 Diehl): 'THEOPHRASTOS tells us that his Chaldaean contemporaries possessed an admirable theory. It predicted every event, the life and the daeth of every human being, not only general effects as e.g. good or bad weather'.

EURIPIDES had his first success as a tragedy-writer in −441. EUDOXOS lived about −370, and THEOPHRASTOS about −330. So our three testimonies describe activities of 'Chaldaeans' living under the Persian kings. Even if the testimony of GELLIUS is rejected as unreliable, the other two testimonies from excellent sources remain.

Most important is CICERO's quotation from EUDOXOS. CICERO says that EUDOXOS has stated 'in writing' his opinion on the predictions of the Chaldaeans. So CICERO has seen a written statement of EUDOXOS. He does not expressly say that the predictions were made from the stars, but since we know that horoscopes were cast at Babylon as early as −410, forty years before EUDOXOS, it seems reasonable to assume that the predictions EUDOXOS alludes to were based upon birth horoscopes. CICERO too interpreted the statement of EUDOXOS as bearing on horoscopes, for he uses it as an argument in his refutation of horoscope astronomy.

The whole second book of CICERO's De divinatione deals with the Chaldaeans and their horoscopes. CICERO's main source is the stoic philosopher PANAITIOS, who lived at Rhodos about −140 and who was the only stoic to reject astrology.

Evidence referring to the Chaldaeans

We have already mentioned three most instructive testimonies about the astronomical and astrological doctrines of the 'Chaldaeans', namely:

1) GEMINOS' exposition of the calculation of the daily motion of the moon, which is in accordance with the cuneiform texts,

2) GEMINOS' account of the theory of 'aspects',

3) CICERO's exposition of the astrological ideas of the Chaldaeans according to PANAITIOS.

To these, several more quotations and testimonies may be added:

4) An exposition of the main features of the doctrine of 'the Chaldaeans from Babylon' in DIODOROS II 30-31, consisting of seven parts:

a) On the order and regularity of the Cosmos, on Divine Providence, and on astrological predictions,

b) On the planets and their power,

c) On the fixed stars and the zodiac,

d) On the influence of the planets on the birth and life of man,

e) On 24 important fixed stars outside the zodiac[1]),

f) On the Moon, on eclipses, and on the form of the earth,

g) On observations extending over 473 000 years until ALEXANDER's expedition.

DIODOROS indicates that his source contained much more information. In part d) he informs us that the Chaldaeans made predictions for several kings, including ALEXANDER, ANTIOGONOS and SELEUKOS the Victor. This SELEUKOS reigned from 312 to 280 B.C., hence the treatise DIODOROS used was written after 312 B.C., probably by a Greek author who lived not much later than SELEUKOS.

5) In book 7 of his 'Naturales quaestiones', SENECA discusses several theories concerning the nature of the comets. SENECA mentions two authors: APOLLONIOS of Myndos (about 220 B.C.) and EPIGENES of Byzantium (about 200 B.C.), who both assert that they have studied with the Chaldaeans, but who held different opinions on the comets.

---

[1]) For a commentary to parts c) and e) see VAN DER WAERDEN: The thirty-six stars, J. of Near Eastern Studies 8 (1949) p. 6.

APOLLONIOS maintained, in agreement with the Chaldaeans, that the comets are stars. They come from the highest parts of the Cosmos, and they appear only when they reach the lowest part of their orbits. Their brightness increases as they come nearer, just as in the case of the other planets. A very good theory!

A. REHM calls SENECA's exposition 'remarkably clear'[1]). The same character of clearness can also be observed in several other expositions of Chaldaean doctrines, e.g. in GEMINOS' account of the theory of the motion of the moon according to the Chaldaeans, and also in his account of the doctrine of aspects.

6) PLUTARCHOS reports in 'Isis and Osiris' 48:

> The Chaldaeans declare that of the planets, which they call 'tutelary gods', two are beneficient, two maleficent, and the other three are median and partake of both qualities.

7) In Chapter 5 we have discussed the 'Dodecaeterids of Zeus', in which predictions are given from the zodiacal sign in which Jupiter dwells. One of these Dodecaeterids was ascribed to 'ZOROASTER', one to 'ORPHEUS', others to 'the Chaldaeans'[2]). From this we may conclude that dodecaeterids were contained in books ascribed to ZOROASTER, to ORPHEUS, and to the Chaldaeans. The last of these three conclusions is confirmed by CENSORINUS, who declares:

> The dodecaeterids are Chaldaean (De die natali 18,7).

8) PLINIUS informs us (Nat. Hist. XVIII) that a 'Parapegma of the Chaldaeans' existed. A parapegma is a star calendar: a list of dates of annual risings and settings of fixed stars, with weather predictions. PLINIUS reproduces 10 entries from the Parapegma of the Chaldaeans.

There are reasons to assume that all quotations referring to 'the Chaldaeans' come from one treatise or from a group of treatises, written in Greek, in which the astronomical and astrological doctrines of the Chaldaeans were exposed in a systematic and clear fashion. This treatise was written at the beginning of the Hellenistic era (say between -320 and -170). It seems that many later astrological writings were influenced by this textbook[3]).

---

[1]) A. REHM: Das siebente Buch der Nat. Quaest. des Seneca, Sitzungsber. Bayer. Akad. München (hist.) 1921.
[2]) See BIDEZ et CUMONT: Les mages hellénisés, or Catalogus codicum astrologorum graec. II, p. 139; V (1), p. 171; VIII 3, p. 189; V (4), p. 171; IX 2, p. 170.
[3]) See my paper 'Die Aegypter und die Chaldäer' in Sitzungsberichte der Heidelberger Akademie 1972, 5. Abhandlung.

For our knowledge of the early history of Indian astronomy we are indebted principally to two works of the sixth century A.D., namely the *Âryabhatiya* of ÂRYABHATA and the *Pañchasiddhântikâ* of VARÂHA MIHIRA.

The astronomy we find in the *Âryabhatiya* is of the same kind as Greek astronomy: it is based on an epicyclic model and uses trigonometrical tables. There is an almost complete absense of historical data. In this respect the work of VARÂHA MIHIRA is much more instructive.

The Pañchasiddhântikâ

The text of this work has been published first by THIBAUT and DVIVEDI with commentary and English translation (Lahore, 1930), and next by NEUGEBAUER and PINGREE with a better translation and a new commentary[1]). The attribution to the sixth century is confirmed in two ways:
1. Mention is made in the work itself of the epoch 505 A.D.
2. The Indian tradition gives the date of VARÂHA MIHIRA's death as 587 A.D.

Pañcha means five, and Siddhânta Handbook of astronomy. The Pañchasiddhântikâ contains extensive excerpts from five Siddhântas, which are now lost but were extant in the time of VARÂHA MIHIRA. Three, namely

> Sûrya-Siddhânta
> Romaka-Siddhânta
> Pauliśa-Siddhânta

use trigonometrical methods. The other two:

> Paitâmaha-Siddhânta
> Vâsistha-Siddhânta

are much more primitive. The methods used in these two Siddhântas are *linear methods* of the same kind as those used in Babylonia. In fact, we shall see that there are many points of contact between the latter two Siddhântas and Babylonian astronomy.

VARÂHA MIHIRA tells us that the three first-named Siddhântas are more accurate than

---

[1]) O. NEUGEBAUER and D. PINGREE: The Pañcasiddhāntikā of Varāhamihira, 2 Vols, K. Dankse Videnskab. Selskab Hist. Skrifter *6* (1970).

the last two. In fact, the trigonometric methods used by HIPPARCHOS, PTOLEMY and
ÂRYABHATA are more accurate than the linear methods used by the Babylonians, by
HYPSIKLES and in the Paitâmaha- and Vâsistha-Siddhânta.

On the other hand, the linear methods are much easier to learn and to apply. One
needs only additions, multiplications and divisions, no trigonometric tables. Therefore
it is not astonishing that VARÂHA MIHIRA thought it worth while to make excerpts not
only from the three more accurate Siddhântas, but also from the two more primitive
treatises.

We shall now discuss these two treatises in some detail.

1. Paitâmaha-Siddhânta

Paitâmaha or Pitâmaha (= Great Father) is one of the commonest names of Brahma.
Paitâmaha-Siddhânta thus means 'astronomical doctrine of Brahma'. There were several
works with the title Brahma- or Paitâmaha-Siddhânta, one of which as in fact survived.
Here we are concerned only with the Paitâmaha-Siddhânta of VARÂHA MIHIRA (Chapter
12 of the Pañchasiddhântikâ).

The epoch of the Paitâmaha-Siddhânta is 11 January A.D. 80. The Siddhânta was
probably composed not long after this epoch.

As THIBAUT remarks in the introduction to the Pañchasiddhântikâ, the Paitâmaha-
Siddhânta belongs to an early stage of Indian astronomy. Babylonian influence shows
most clearly in the last verse of Chapter 12, in which instructions for calculating the
length of the day are given. The rule says: When the sun moves to the North (i.e. in the
period from the winter to the summer solstice), take the number of days elapsed since
the winter solstice. After the summer solstice take the number of days to the next winter
solstice. To this number (hereafter denoted by x) add 732, multiply by 2, divide by 61
and subtract 12. The result is the length of the day in muhûrtas, 1 muhûrta being 1/30 of
a complete day. This rule is equivalent to the formula

$$t = \tfrac{2}{61}(732 + x) - 12 = \tfrac{2}{61}x + 12,$$

where x runs from 0 to 183 and back again. The length of the day is thus a linear zigzag
function with minimum 12 and maximum 18. The ratio of longest to shortest day is 3 : 2,
as in the Babylonian texts.

For more information about the Paitâmaha-Siddhânta see NEUGEBAUER-PINGREE II,
p. 80-83.

2. *Vasistha-Siddhânta*

A. *General Information*

From NEUGEBAUER-PINGREE I, p. 10 I quote:

> There existed a Vasisthasiddhānta already in A.D. 269/70, as Sphujidhvaja writes in his Yavanajātaka (LXXIX, 3):
> 'By following the opinion of the sage Vasistha some of those concerned with (astronomical) rules (believed that this great lunisolar yuga) is best; for those led by the Yavanas[1] . . . (the lunisolar yuga) is 165 years'.
> Varāhamihira states in II, 13 that the shadow-problem in II, 12-13 is from the Vasisthasamāsiddhānta (presumably an abridgement of a longer original Vasisthasiddhānta). We are inclined to believe that the rest of II is also from the Vasistha.

Following THIBAUT and NEUGEBAUER-PINGREE, I shall assume that Chapter 2 of the Pañchasiddhântikâ is from the Vasistha-Siddhânta.

Chapter 2 contains only 13 stanzas. The first six teach us how to calculate the positions of the sun and moon. Stanza 8 concerns the duration of the day and the night. Stanzas 9-13 teach the calculation of the shadow-length of the gnomon.

In the whole chapter no use is made of trigonometry, only of addition, subtraction, multiplication and division with remainder. The length of the day (Stanza 8) is a linear zigzag function with minimum 12 and maximum 18 muhûrtas, as in the Paitâmaha Siddhânta and Babylonian lunar theory. In stanza 2 we find a lunar period of 248 days used, as in the cuneiform texts in the calculation of the daily motion of the moon. In stanza 5 use is made of zodiacal signs, degrees and minutes.

B. *Motion of the moon*

The method for computing the motion of the moon according to stanzas 2-6 was first investigated by T. S. KUPPANA SASTRI in Journal of Oriental Research 25 (1957), p. 19, and in greater detail by NEUGEBAUER and PINGREE in the commentary to their edition of the Pañcasiddhântikâ (Part II, p. 15-22). SASTRI has shown that the longitudes of the moon from day to day were calculated from an initial longitude by adding the daily motions, which were computed by means of a linear zigzag function, just as in the Babylonian theory. The period of the linear zigzag function, viz. 248/9 days, is exactly

---

[1] The Yavanas (Ionians) are the Greeks (VAN DER WAERDEN).

the same as in the cuneiform texts. A larger period of 3031 days, known from Greek papyri, is also used in the stanzas 2-6. For the mean daily motion NEUGEBAUER and PINGREE calculated three slightly different values, viz.

$$\mu_1 = 13;10,34,52$$
$$\mu_2 = 13;10,34,43$$
$$\mu_3 = 13;10,34,17.$$

All three values are quite near to the Babylonian value

$$\mu = 13;10,35.$$

C. Motion of the planets

The first 60 verses of the last chapter of the Pañchasiddhântikâ form a unit, clearly distinct from the preceeding chapters. Here I shall restrict myself to verses 1-56, in which the planets are treated in the following order:

1- 5 Venus
6-13 Jupiter
14-20 Saturn
21-35 Mars
36-56 Mercury.

At the end of the Venus section, there is a note saying: 'Venus in the Vâsisthasiddhânta'. Since the other planets are treated in just the same way as Venus, we may suppose that verses 1-56 are all from the Vâsisthasiddhânta.

Each of the five sections begins with a rule for calculating the First Visibility. For Jupiter, Saturn, Mars, and Mercury these rules are based upon the period relations

Jupiter: 36 sidereal revolutions = 391 synodic periods
Saturn: 9 sidereal revolutions = 256 synodic periods
Mars: 151 sidereal revolutions = 133 synodic periods
Mercury: 217 sidereal revolutions = 684 synodic periods.

The same relations are found in Babylonian planetary texts (see O. NEUGEBAUER, ACT p. 283).

For Venus, the text states that the progress in longitude in every synodic period is 7 zodiacal signs and 5° degrees plus a fraction of a degree. THIBAUT and DVIVEDI proposed to read this fraction as $\frac{1}{3}$ degree. OLAF SCHMIDT corrected this into $\frac{1}{2}$ degree[1]), thus obtaining a complete agreement with the Babylonian value, which is $5\frac{1}{2}$ degrees. NEUGEBAUER and PINGREE translated $5\frac{1}{2} + \frac{1}{3}$ degree. This is a possible reading of the text, but the reading $5\frac{1}{2}$ seems equally possible. The Sanskrit text has something like 'Her progress on the threefold path is $5\frac{1}{2}$ degrees of Scorpio' (i.e. 7 signs and $5\frac{1}{2}$ degrees). I am indebted to PETER WIRTH for this observation. If the text is interpreted in this way, it is in accordance with the Babylonian theory for all the planets.

Next, the text describes for each planet its motion during a synodic period. The simplest description is for Venus. The starting point is the Eveningfirst (Text: 'Venus rises in the West'). The text proceeds thus:

XVII, 3. In three (periods) of sixty (days) Venus travels 70° increased by 4, 3, and 2 (i.e. 74°, 73°, and 72° respectively). In $27\frac{1}{2}$ (days) 20°, and in 3 (days) $1\frac{1}{4}$ degree.

The addition of these motions

$$74° + 73° + 72° + 20° + 1\tfrac{1}{4}°$$

would give a direct motion of $240\frac{1}{4}$ degrees from EF to ESt, which is too small in any reasonable theory. NEUGEBAUER and PINGREE conclude: 'At any event the description of the motion of Venus as given in our text seems incomplete'.

However, the text can be interpreted in another way, suggested by PETER WIRTH in a forthcoming paper[2]). WIRTH starts with the remark that the numbers 74, 73 and 72 are given in the text as $70 + 4$, $+ 3$ and $+ 2$ respectively. Just so, the 3 days and $1\frac{1}{4}$ degree may be interpreted as $27\frac{1}{2} + 3$ days and $20 + 1\frac{1}{4}$ degrees. Thus one would obtain the velocity scheme:

$$74° \quad \text{in 60 days}$$
$$73° \quad \text{in 60 days}$$
$$72° \quad \text{in 60 days}$$
$$20° \quad \text{in } 27\tfrac{1}{2} \text{ days}$$
$$21\tfrac{1}{4}° \quad \text{in } 30\tfrac{1}{2} \text{ days.}$$

The addition would give

$$260;15° \text{ in 238 days,}$$

which is perfectly reasonable.

In Verse 4, the text describes the retrograde motion:

Then it retrogrades 2 (degrees) in 15 (days); then it sets in the west in 5 (days) and rises in the east in 10 (days). Venus goes 4 (degrees) in 20 (days).

[1]) See O. NEUGEBAUER: Babylonian Planetary Theory. Proc. Amer. Philos. Soc. 98 (1954) p. 79, footnote 49.

[2]) P. WIRTH: Die Venustheorie des Vasistha ..., to appear in Centaurus 1973.

PETER WIRTH proposed the following interpretation:

$$\text{After ESt} \quad - \quad 2° \text{ in 15 days}$$
$$- \quad 5° \text{ in } 5 \text{ days}$$
$$\text{After EL} \quad -10° \text{ in 10 days}$$
$$\text{After MF} \quad - \quad 4° \text{ in 20 days}$$

The addition would give

$$-21° \text{ in 50 days}$$

which is very reasonable.

In verse 5, the direct motion from MSt through ML to EF is described:

> Proceeding in direct motion, (Venus) travels in the opposite direction to setting in the east. Proceeding 75° in 60 (days) Venus is (again) visible in the west. Venus in the Vāsisthasiddhānta.

The interpretation of PETER WIRTH is based upon the plausible assumption that the velocities from MSt to ML are the same as from EL to ESt, but in opposite order:

$$21\tfrac{1}{4}° \text{ in } 30\tfrac{1}{2} \text{ days}$$
$$20° \quad \text{in } 27\tfrac{1}{2} \text{ days}$$
$$72° \quad \text{in } 60 \quad \text{days}$$
$$73° \quad \text{in } 60 \quad \text{days}$$
$$74° \quad \text{in } 60 \quad \text{days.}$$

The motion from ML to EF is, according to the text,

$$75° \text{ in 60 days.}$$

The total motion in a synodic period would be

$$574\tfrac{1}{2}° \text{ in 586 days.}$$

These figures are not far from the values given in verse 1:

$$575\tfrac{1}{2}° \text{ in 584 days.}$$

Hence, the interpretation of verses 3-5 given by WIRTH seems very plausible.

Very remarkable indeed is the description of the motion of Mars in stanzas 29-35. The ecliptic is divided into six parts, each consisting of two zodiacal signs, namely

$$(2)+(3), \ (4)+(5), \ (6)+(7), \ (8)+(9), \ (10)+(11), \ (12)+(1),$$

exactly as in system A of the cuneiform texts for Mars. But the similarity goes still further.

The cuneiform texts calculate the retrograde motion of Mars by four methods according to system A. Method R is based on the assumption that in six sectors of the zodiac the retrograde arcs from the Morning Station to the Opposition have the values:

$$6;48 \quad 7;12 \quad 6;48 \quad 6;24 \quad 6 \quad 6;24.$$

Method S takes the same values as R in the signs

$$(2) \quad (4) \quad (6) \quad (8) \quad (10) \quad (12).$$

For this method we also know the total retrograde stretches from Morning Station to Evening Station. They can be obtained by multiplying the previously given values by $2\frac{1}{2}$. The results are:

$$17° \quad 18° \quad 17° \quad 16° \quad 15° \quad 16°.$$

Exactly the same values for the total retrograde stretches in the six sectors of the zodiac are given in the text of Varâha Mihira too, as was remarked by NEUGEBAUER. Thus the Mars calculation of the Vâsistha-Siddhânta may certainly be taken to derive from Babylonian astronomy.

D. On the origin of the Vâsishtha-Siddhânta

Right at the beginning of our section on the Vâsistha-Siddhânta we have quoted a passage from the astrological poem Yavanajâtaka of SPHUJIDHVAJA. The word Yavana in the title of the poem means Ionian, or Greek in general. According to PINGREE[1]) the poem goes back to a Greek astrological composition written in Alexandria in the first half of the second century A.D., which was translated into Sanskrit by YAVANESVARA about 150. Another Greek astrological text was also translated in the second century. It seems that later Indian horoscopy is mainly based on these two Sanskrit translations.

The last part of SPHUJIDHVAJA's poem contains a planetary theory which, according to PINGREE, coincides exactly in system and numerical constants with the cuneiform tablets of the Seleucid period. The transmission thus followed the following path:

Babylon (Seleucid era)
Alexandria (around 100 A.D.)
India (YAVANESVARA around 150, SPHUJIDHVAJA around 270).

[1]) D. PINGREE: Astronomy and Astrology in India and Iran, Isis 54, p. 235.

There is another case in which NEUGEBAUER has succeeded in establishing the path of
the transmission with fair certainty[1]). There is a schematic calculation of the rising times
of the zodiacal signs which belongs to system A of the Babylonian lunar calculation.
The Anthologia of VETTIUS VALENS (152-188) contains, as we have already seen, just such
a calculation. The same sequence of numbers as in VETTIUS is found, figure for figure,
in VARÂHA MIHIRA's astrological tract Brhat Jataka. In this instance too, the Babylonian
methods were first taken over by Hellenistic astrologers and next transmitted to India.

In this transmission Persia possibly played an intermediate role. At any rate VETTIUS
VALENS' Anthologia was translated into Middle Persian, as AL-BIRUNI informs us[2]).

Great periods

The system of great periods or yugas, which we find fully developed in Sanskrit astron-
omical treatises, is relatively old. It is explained in detail in the twelfth book of the
Mahâbhârata and somewhat more shortly in the first book of the Laws of MANU.
According to G. BUHLER[3]), both explanations derive from a common source. Now the
Laws of MANU in the form known to us existed as early as the second century A.D., so
that the common source must be ascribed to a date earlier than this.

MANU and *Mahâbhârata* make a 'year of the gods' equal to 360 ordinary years.
12,000 'years of the gods', that is 4 320 000 ordinary years, make up a *yuga* of the gods.
Later astronomers called this period *Mahâyuga*, i.e. great yuga or great year.

This great yuga was divided already in the earlier sources into four smaller yugas,
whose lengths were in the ratio 4 : 3 : 2 : 1. The last partial period, the *Kaliyuga*, in
which we are now living, thus contains 432 000 years. In the four periods things get steadily worse, as in the golden, silver, bronze and iron ages of HESIODOS.

A thousand yugas of the gods were said to form a 'day of Brahman', or *Kalpa*. Thus,
a day of Brahman contains 4 320 millions of years. The night of Brahman is the same
length. At the beginning of his day he each time creates the world anew. All creatures
behave in each new creation exactly as in each earlier creation.

We thus encounter in India at the beginning of the Christian era the same views on the
'great year' and the perpetual recurrence of all events as we found earlier in the Orphic,
Pythagorean and Stoic teachings. To be sure, the numbers given for the Indian yuga do
not agree with the numbers mentioned in the Greek sources.

At the same time, it is just these numbers that betray the ultimate origin of the yuga
system. For they are all divisible by 60^3. The Mahâyuga contains 20 times 60^3 years, and
the four smaller yugas

$$8.60^3, \ 6.60^3, \ 4.60^3, \ 2.60^3$$

[1]) O. NEUGEBAUER, Archives Internat. d'Histoire des Sciences 38 (1955), p. 166.
[2]) O. NALLINO, Raccolta di Scritti VI, p. 291—296.
[3]) The Laws of MANU, Sacred Books of the East XXV (1886) p. lxxxii-xc.

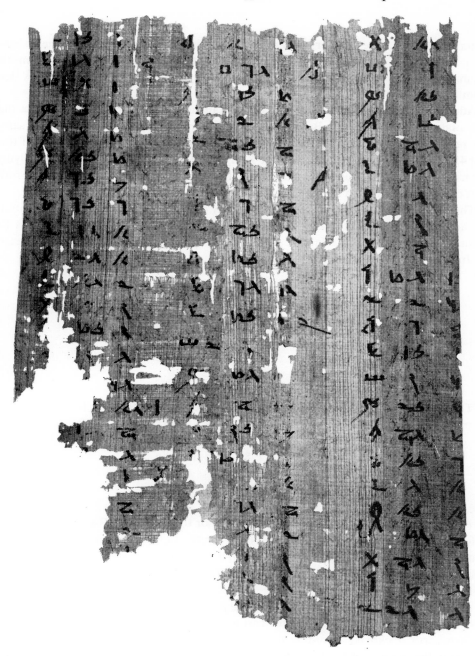

III   II   I

Plate 31. The first three columns of Papyrus P. 8279, from Fayum in Egypt, now in the Berlin Museum.
Published by W. SPIEGELBERG, Orient Literaturzeitung 5 (1902). Latest edition: O. NEUGEBAUER and
R. A. PARKER: Egyptian Astronomical Texts III (1969). The three columns I, II, III are to be read from
right to left and from top to bottom.

years respectively. The numbers thus become very simple when expressed in the Babylonian sexagesimal system. The Indian number system was purely decimal from the
beginning. Hence we may conclude that the Mahâyuga and the four smaller Yugas stem
from Babylon.

Additional confirmation is to be found in a statement by BEROSSOS[2]) to the effect that
the total of the reigns of the Babylonian kings before the Flood amounts to 120 saroi,
where a saros (Babylonian SAR) contains $60^2 = 3600$ years. BEROSSOS' 120 saroi thus
last 432 000 years, exactly the same as the Kaliyuga of the Indian tradition. The Kaliyuga
forms part of the Mahâyuga, and likewise the 120 saroi of the kings before the flood form
part of BEROSSOS' 'Great Year'.

The great creation period, called *Kalpa* or 'Day of Brahman' in these texts, is mentioned, according to PINGREE (Isis 54, p. 238), in an eschatological context as early as the
stone edicts of King ASHOKA (about −250). Thus the yuga system appears to have reached India in the early Hellenistic period.

EGYPTIAN PLANETARY TABLES

The tables

Three Egyptian planetary tables, which we shall designate P, S and T, have been totally
or partially preserved, namely:

> P: Papyrus P 8279 from Berlin
> S: 'Stobart Tables'
> T: Teptunis Papyrus II 274.

A section of text P is reproduced in Plate 31. For the full text of P and S the reader is
referred to the basic publication by O. NEUGEBAUER, Egyptian Planetary Texts, Trans.
Amer. Philos. Soc. 32 (1942), p. 209, or to the new edition of the same tables in NEU-
GEBAUER and PARKER, Egyptian Astronomical Texts III (Brown Univ. Press, Providence
1969).

All these texts contain *dates of entry of the planets into the signs of the zodiac*, that is,
just the dates an astrologer needs for casting horoscopes. P covers the years 14 to 41
of AUGUSTUS, reckoned according to the Egyptian calendar. The year *x* of AUGUSTUS
begins in the summer of the Julian year −30 + *x*; so the text begins in −16 and ends in
+12.

---

[1]) P. SCHNABEL, Berossos (1923), Fragments 29—30a.

S consists of three parts:

Part A for the 7 years 4-10 of VESPASIANUS (A.D. 71-78),
Part C for the 14 years from TRAIANUS 9 to HADRIANUS 3 (A.D. 105-119),
Part E for the 7 years 11-17 of TRAIANUS (A.D. 126-133).

The Greek text T contains only a few entry dates for the years 10-18 of TRAIANUS. We shall not consider this text further here, but concentrate on P and S, which are both written in demotic script.

NEUGEBAUER proved that text S uses not the Egyptian, but the Alexandrine calendar. In the former every year has 365 days, in the latter every fourth year is an intercalary year of 366 days.

The division of the ecliptic

On comparing the planetary positions in P and S with modern calculations, NEUGE-BAUER found that in the second decade of the reign of AUGUSTUS the longitudes of the texts are an average of 4° greater than modern values, and that this sytematic difference decreases with time. If the modern longitudes are reduced to a sidereal division of the ecliptic, which begins with the vernal point of the year −100, the systematic difference becomes a constant equal to 4 to 5 degrees, as in the Babylonian texts. This means that the Egyptian mathematicians worked on the basis of a sidereal division of the ecliptic which almost concided with the Babylonian division.

How were the tables calculated?

It was noticed by NEUGEBAUER that the tables note the entry of the planets into the zodiacal signs even in cases where the planets are invisible. The dates must therefore have been at least partially computed. The question is, how.

Two kinds of theories of planetary motion existed at the time when the tables were computed, namely:

Type A (so called after the Babylonian system A): Theories in which the velocity is constant for some time and then changes suddenly,

Type C (C means Continuous Change of Velocity): The velocity does not jump, but changes steadily.

Of type A are all Babylonian system A theories. Of type C are:

all Greek theories based upon epicycles or eccenters,
all Babylonian System B theories, and
the Babylonian theory of Jupiter, in which the longitude of the planet is represented by a third order arithmetical sequence.

My theses are:

Thesis 1. Text S is based upon a theory of Type A.

If this is true, there must be a velocity scheme, from which the velocities and the jumping points can be calculated for every particular planet.

Thesis 2. For Venus the velocity scheme of Text S coincides exactly with that of Varâha Mihira *in the domain of fast motion.*

This velocity scheme is as follows:

> Venus covers 72° in 60 days,
>   next 73° in 60 days,
>   next 74° in 60 days until Morninglast,
>   next 75° in 60 days until Eveningfirst,
>   next 74° in 60 days,
>   next 73° in 60 days,
>   next 72° in 60 days.

After these 420 days, a much slower motion begins: Venus covers 20° in $27\frac{1}{2}$ days, and next $21\frac{1}{2}$ degrees in $30\frac{1}{2}$ days. After this comes the retrograde motion, next comes a slow direct motion, and then the velocity jumps once more to 72° in 60 days.

For text P, this scheme does not hold. In this text, the change from quick to slow motion and conversely occurs less suddenly. The motion of Venus in text P is quite similar to the motion of the same planet in cuneiform texts, like Rm 678 and SH 103, but the details of the velocity scheme underlying text P are not yet known: much remains to be done in this field.

The arguments in favour of Theses 1 and 2 will be given presently. We now turn to Mars.

Thesis 3. The motion of Mars in Text S was computed by means of a division of the zodiac into 6 parts

$$(2)+(3), (4)+(5), (6)+(7), (8)+(9), (10)+(11), (12)+(1)$$

just as in the Babylonian System A.

As we have seen, Varâha Mihira uses the same division. The common source of Varâha Mihira and text S is, without any doubt, the Babylonian System A for Mars.

Thesis 4. For Mars, the velocity scheme of Text S is the same as in the Babylonian System A.

Strictly speaking, Thesis 4 holds only for the direct motion from Eveninglast (EL) through Morningfirst (MF) to the Morning Stationary Point (MSt). For the retrograde motion from MSt to ESt and for the direct motion from ESt to EL the situation is more complicated, as we shall see presently.

Thesis 5. For Jupiter, the velocity schemes of Text S and of Text P are based on the Babylonian System A'.

The details of the velocity schemes for Jupiter are not yet known. The reason for this is, that Jupiter moves so slowly. During a synodical period, the total motion of Jupiter lies between 30° and 36°, so that we usually have only one entry into a new zodiacal sign in any synodical period, which is not sufficient for a determination of the velocities.

The arguments in favour of my five theses were fully exposed in my paper 'Aegyptische Planetenrechnung' in Centaurus 16 (1972). In this book I shall restrict myself to the most instructive points. I shall consider first Venus, next Mars, and finally Jupiter.

The motion of Venus in text S

For the year 9 of TRAIANUS, the dates of entry of Venus into the signs according to text S are

(6) Virgo	I 16	24 days
(7) Libra	II 10	24 days
(8) Scorpio	III 4	25 days
(9) Arcitenens	III 29	23 days
(10) Capricorn	IV 22	24 days
(11) Aquarius	V 16	24 days
(12) Pisces	VI 10	24 days
(1) Aries	VII 4	25 days
(2) Taurus	VII 29	25 days
(3) Gemini	VIII 24	24 days
(4) Cancer	IX 18	25 days
(5) Leo	X 13	25 days
(6) Virgo	XI 8	38 days
(7) Libra	XII 16	

The first two columns contain the numbers and names of the zodiacal signs, the next two the month and day on which Venus enters the sign in question. The months all have 30 days; the months XII is followed by 5 epagomenal days (or 6, if the year has 366 days). The last column gives the number of days Venus stays in each zodiacal sign.

From the last column one sees that Venus dwells 24 or 25 days (or in one case 23 days) in each of the signs from Virgo to Leo: the velocity is nearly constant. At the end of the year the motion suddenly becomes slower: Venus needs 38 days to pass through Virgo. This sudden change in velocity is an argument in favour of Thesis 1, but not yet a full proof.

In a theory of type A, with piecewise constant velocities, it is easy to calculate the dates of entry. In a theory of type C, with steadily changing velocities, the calculation is much more difficult. Since the author of the text S has calculated hundreds of entries, it seems much more probable that he used a theory of type A. Once more, this is only a probability argument, not a valid proof.

In my paper in Centaurus quoted before, the proof was given as follows.

Let us consider two hypotheses:

Hypothesis A: The velocity of Venus was assumed to be piecewise constant. In this case the longitude λ would be a piecewise linear function of the time t, as pictured in Fig. 23.

Hypothesis C: The velocity of Venus was assumed to change steadily. In this case the diagram for λ as a function of t would be a smooth curve (Fig. 24).

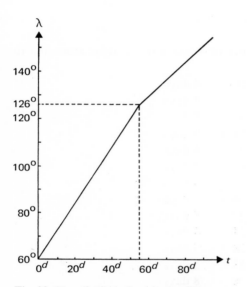

Fig. 23. Hypothesis A. Longitude of Venus as a function of time.

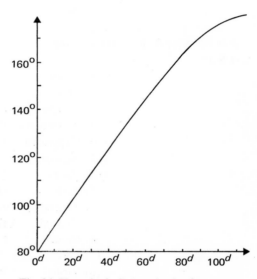

Fig. 24. Hypothesis C. Longitude of Venus as a function of time.

In both cases one may take on the λ-axis a segment of 30 degrees, say from $x - 30$ to x, and calculate (or construct from the drawing) the time Δt Venus needs to cover this segment. This time Δt is a function of λ, which can be plotted in a diagram. Under Hypothesis A one obtains a function which remains constant up to the point $x = a$ at which the velocity jumps to a lower value. From a to $a + 30$ the function Δt increases linearly (Fig. 25), and next it becomes again constant, unless another jumping point makes it increase once more. On the other hand, under Hypothesis B the function Δt would be represented by a smooth curve (Fig. 26). Figures 24 and 26 were taken from a modern table, but the epicycle hypothesis would yield curves of just the same type.

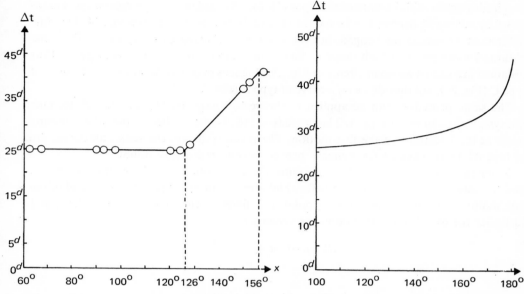

Fig. 25. Hypothesis A. The time Δt Venus needs to go from longitude x - 30 to longitude x.

Fig. 26. Hypothesis C. The time Venus needs to go from longitude x - 30 to longitude x.

The last three entries in the last column of our table for TRAIANUS 9 would give three points of our Δt-curve with ordinates

$$25, \quad 25, \quad 38.$$

Three points are not sufficient to decide between our Hypotheses A and C. To obtain more points, one can consider other years differing from our year

$$\text{AD } 105 = \text{TRAIANUS } 9$$

by a multiple of 8 years. Such years are

$$\text{AD } 113 = \text{TRAIANUS } 17$$
$$\text{AD } 129 = \text{HADRIANUS } 14.$$

Now 8 years are nearly 5 synodic periods of Venus. After these 5 periods Venus has the same longitude as before minus $2\frac{1}{2}$ degrees, and all motions are nearly as in the year TRAIANUS 9. This one can check from the text itself: the deviations never exceed 1 day. Hence the longitudes given in text S for TRAIANUS 17 and HADRIANUS 14, namely the

longitudes of the initial points of the signs (3), (4), (5), and (6), can be reduced to TRAIA-
NUS 9 by adding $2\frac{1}{2}$ degrees for TRAIANUS 17, and $7\frac{1}{2}$ degrees for HADRIANUS 14. The time
differences Δt remain unchanged, but the x-values are increased by $2\frac{1}{2}$ or $7\frac{1}{2}$. Thus one
obtains 8 more points, which ought to lie on the same curve. The $3+8=11$ points thus
obtained are shown as small circles in Fig. 25. One sees that they do not lie on a curve of
type C (Fig. 26), but they do lie on a curve of type A (Fig. 25).

The same procedure can be applied to the years TRAIANUS 11, 13, 14, and 16. One
always obtains curves of type A. The procedure can also be applied to the other jumping
point at the beginning of the fast motion. The result is always the same: all curves are
of type A. Thus, Thesis 1 for Venus is proved beyond reasonable doubt.

From the curves one can also determine the exact situation of the jumping points
and the values of the velocities just before and after the jumping points. At the end of the
fast motion, just before the jumping point, one finds a velocity of 30° in 25 days, and
just after the end of the fast motion the velocity is

$$30° \text{ in } 41 \text{ or } 42 \text{ days.}$$

Comparison with VARÂHA MIHIRA

In the year 9 of TRAIANUS the jumping point found from our diagram lies at 5° in
Virgo. Let us make the check:

Venus enters Virgo on XI 8. To reach the jumping point at 5° with a velocity of 30° in
25 days Venus needs $4\frac{1}{6}$ days. From the jumping point to the end of Virgo Venus has to
cover 25 degrees. To cover the first 20 degrees Venus needs, according to VARÂHA
MIHIRA, just $27\frac{1}{2}$ days. For the next 5 degrees we have to assume, according to PETER
WIRTH's reading of the text of VARÂHA, a velocity of $21\frac{1}{4}$ degrees in $30\frac{1}{2}$ days.

Hence the time Venus needs to cover 5 degrees is

$$\frac{5}{21\frac{1}{4}} \cdot 30\frac{1}{2} = 7\frac{3}{17} \text{ days.}$$

The total time needed for 30 degrees is

$$4\frac{1}{6} + 27\frac{1}{2} + 7\frac{3}{17} \text{ days}$$

or nearly 38 days. The Egyptian text has just 38 days: the agreement with VARÂHA
MIHIRA is perfect.

Let us now extend the comparison to the other years of VESPASIANUS, TRAIANUS and
HADRIANUS.

According to WIRTH's interpretation of the text of VARÂHA MIHIRA, Chapter 17,
Verses 3 and 5, the velocity scheme for the direct motion of Venus is as follows:

Slow motion: $21\frac{1}{4}$ degrees in $30\frac{1}{2}$ days
              20   degrees in $27\frac{1}{2}$ days
Rapid motion: 72   degrees in 60 days
              73   degrees in 60 days
              74   degrees in 60 days until ML
              75   degrees in 60 days until EF
              75   degrees in 60 days
              73   degrees in 60 days
              72   degrees in 60 days
Slow motion: 20   degrees in $27\frac{1}{2}$ days
              $21\frac{1}{4}$ degrees in $30\frac{1}{2}$ days.

Let us first consider the rapid motion, totalling 513°, i.e. slightly more than 17 zodiacal signs. At the beginning and end of this course the velocity is

$$72° \text{ in } 60^d, \text{ or } 30° \text{ in } 25^d,$$

and in the middle part from ML to EF it is

$$75° \text{ in } 60^d, \text{ or } 30° \text{ in } 24^d.$$

In the intermediate intervals, in which Venus covers 73° or 74° in 30 days, the velocity would be

$$30° \text{ in } 24.7 \text{ or } 24.3 \text{ days}$$

respectively. Hence, if text S is calculated according to this scheme, we must expect:

first, that we always have at least 16 whole zodiacal signs belonging to the region of quick motion,

secondly, that the time needed to cross one of these signs, rounded to whole days, is always 24 or 25 days,

thirdly, that at the beginning and end of the stretch of the quick motion Venus crosses the first two and the last two signs in exactly 25 days,

fourthly, that the middle two of the 16 signs are crossed, as a rule, in 24 days each. Exceptions from this rule are to be expected only if Morninglast or Eveningfirst, at which the calculation starts anew, takes place just in the sign in question.

In the *fifth* place, we may also expect that after the stretch of quick motion the velocity becomes

$$20° \text{ in } 27\frac{1}{2} \text{ days}$$

and next

$$21\frac{1}{4} \text{ degrees in } 30\frac{1}{2} \text{ days.}$$

This means that in the region of slow motion Venus covers 30° in 41 to 42 days.

If one now examines the text S, one sees that these five rules always hold, with exceptions for rules 2 and 4 only if a ML or EF occurs just in the zodiacal sign in question. The rules 1, 3 and 5 hold without any exception.

This conclusion is valid only for text S. In text P and in Babylonian almanacs like Rm 678, SH 103 or SH 492, these rules are not valid.

Thus, Thesis 2 is justified.

The motion of Mars in text S

Thesis 3 asserts that the motion of Mars in text S was calculated by means of a division of the zodiac into 6 parts, each consisting of an even sign $(2n)$ and an immediately following odd sign $(2n+1)$, just as in the Babylonian system A for Mars.

To see this, let us consider the direct motion of Mars in any synodical period. The first complete period is contained in the years VESPASIANUS 5-7. The times Mars needs to cross the signs in direct motion are

(7)	(8)	(9)	(10) (11)	(12) (1)	(2)	(3)	(4)	(5)	(6)	(7)
48	41	41	38	38 40	38	44	41	54	54 48	68

The last figure 68 is much larger than all the others. Obviously, the last sign (7) does not belong to the stretch of fast motion. Leaving out this sign, we are left with 5 pairs of signs $(2n)$ and $(2n+1)$. In three cases the times within these pairs are equal:

$$41=41, \ 38=38, \ 54=54.$$

In the middle part of the synodic period, in the region of Eveninglast and Morningfirst, this rule does not hold any more. In this region, the times are usually smaller, i.e. the motion between EL and MF is quicker. In what follows, we shall affix the letter i to these 'irregular' numbers. We shall see later that they are not really irregular: they only obey another law than the 'regular' numbers.

The period VESPASIANUS 8-9 shows the following figures:

(9)	(10) (11)	(12) (1)	(2)	(3)	(4)	(5)	(6)	(7)	(2)	(9)
43	38	38 41	41	46	43i	48i	53	48	48 43	61

The larger number 61 at the end does not belong to the region of fast motion. Once more, one finds 3 pairs of equal numbers:

$$38=38, \ 41=41, \ 48=48$$

and in the middle part two 'irregular', i.e. smaller numbers.

The next complete synodic period, TRAIANUS 11-12, is quite similar: The pairs 38=38, 41=41 and 48=48 are just the same as in the preceeding period.

The next synodic period is TRAIANUS 13-14. Here too the 'irregular' numbers are smaller than their neihgbours:

(12)	(1)	(2)	(3)	(4)	(5)	(6)	(7)	(8)	(9)	(10)	(11)
43	43	48	48	53	49i	45i	48	42	42	38	39

Once more, we have three equal pairs:

$$43=43, \quad 48=48, \quad 42=42,$$

whereas at the end the number 39 is slightly larger than the preceeding 38.

In all these cases we may notice one characteristic feature: every time one passes from one pair like (12)+(1) to the next pair (2)+(3) the velocity suddenly jumps to another constant value. The constant values occurring most frequently are:

$$
\begin{aligned}
&\text{in } (2) + (3)\text{: } 30° \text{ in } 46 \text{ days,} \\
&\text{in } (4) + (5)\text{: } 30° \text{ in } 54 \text{ days,} \\
&\text{in } (6) + (7)\text{: } 30° \text{ in } 48 \text{ days,} \\
&\text{in } (8) + (9)\text{: } 30° \text{ in } 42 \text{ days,} \\
&\text{in } (10) + (11)\text{: } 30° \text{ in } 38 \text{ days,} \\
&\text{in } (12) + (1)\text{: } 30° \text{ in } 41 \text{ days.}
\end{aligned}
$$

I shall call these numbers of days *normal numbers.*

In the second half of any synodic period, after the Morningfirst, the 'normal numbers' occur almost without exceptions, whereas in the first half, before Eveninglast, there are several exceptions. Consider e.g. the years TRAIANUS 13-14. Here we find before EL

$$
\begin{aligned}
&\text{in } (12) + (1) : 43 = 43 \text{ instead of the normal 41,} \\
&\text{in } (2) + (3) : 48 = 48 \text{ instead of the normal 46,}
\end{aligned}
$$

whereas after ML we find the normal numbers:

$$
\begin{aligned}
&\text{in } (7) : 48 \\
&\text{in } (8) + (9) : 42 = 42 \\
&\text{in } (10) : 37.
\end{aligned}
$$

In an earlier paper[1]) I have explained why the motion in the text S is irregular before

[1]) VAN DER WAERDEN: Babylonische Methoden in ägyptischen Planetentafeln. Vierteljahrsschrift Naturforschende Gesellschaft Zürich *105* (1960) p. 97.

EL, but perfectly regular after MF. The explanation is: In each synodic period the calculation starts anew with EL. The motion from EL to MF and from MF to the Morning Stationary Point (MSt) is perfectly regular, and in accordance with system A. However, for the retrograde motion after MSt another set of rules was adopted. The Babylonians had four velocity schemes R, S, T and U, as we have seen in Chapter 7. The Egyptians probably used one of these. The retrograde motion ends with the Evening Stationary Point (ESt). Now, if one would apply to the following direct motion (from ESt to EL) the normal velocity scheme, the date and place of EL would come out wrong, i.e. not in accordance with the Babylonian system A. Therefore, the man who computed text S had to use larger numbers of days in the year TRAIANUS 13 in the signs (12)+(1) and (2) + (3), in order to arrive at the right date for EL.

Now let us have a closer look at the 'normal' times of passage t_{norm}. They are, as we have seen

	(2)+(3)	(4)+(5)	(6)+(7)	(8)+(9)	(10)+(11)	(12)+(1)
t_{norm} =	46	54	48	42	38	41

In the Babylonian system A, each pair of zodiacal signs is divided into a certain number of 'steps'. Within each pair of signs, all steps have the same lenght, namely

$$\sigma = \quad 2°30' \quad 1°40' \quad 2°13'20'' \quad 3°20' \quad 5° \quad 3°45'$$

Now if we compare t_{norm} with σ, we see that to a larger σ always corresponds a smaller value of t_{norm}. The connection between t_{norm} and σ can be expressed by the formula

(1)
$$t_{norm} = 30 + \frac{40}{\sigma}.$$

The values of t_n resulting from this formula are

$$46 \quad 54 \quad 48 \quad 42 \quad 38 \quad 40\tfrac{2}{3}$$

If the last number is rounded up to 41, we obtain exactly the normal times t_{norm}. Note that the σ were drawn exclusively from cuneiform texts, whereas the t_{norm} were calculated from the Egyptian text S. Yet, the two sets of numbers coincide exactly.

We have seen that in each part of the zodiac Mars was assumed to have a constant normal velocity. The reciprocal velocity is t/s (time divided by length of the path). In our case s is 30° for each zodiacal sign. Dividing (1) by $s = 30$ and writing t instead of t_{norm}, one obtains

$$\frac{t}{s} = 1 + \frac{4}{3\sigma}.$$

This relation is valid not only for a whole zodiacal sign or pair of signs $(2n, 2n+1)$, but also for any segment within such a pair of signs, because the velocity s/t is constant within such a pair of signs. Multiplying by s, one obtains the *equation of motion*

(2)
$$t = s + \frac{4}{3} \frac{s}{\sigma}.$$

Here, s/σ is the number of steps contained in the line segment s. If this number is called y, the equation (2) can be written as

(3)
$$t = s + \tfrac{4}{3} y.$$

If a line segment s on the ecliptic does not lie within one pair of signs $(2n, 2n+1)$, one can divide it into parts lying within such pairs. The total number of steps y is the sum of the numbers $y = s/\sigma$ calculated for the parts. Since (3) holds for any such part, it follows that (3) holds for the whole segment s, as long as the segment belongs to the region of normal fast motion.

Now let us see whether an equation of the same kind as (3) also holds for the fastest motion between EL and MF. Since the motion is faster, the time t_{min} Mars needs to cover a certain distance s must be smaller than the time $t = t_{norm}$ given by (3). Let us try the simplest possible formula

(4)
$$t_{min} = s + y.$$

If the segment s lies within a pair of zodiacal signs $(2n, 2n+1)$, we may replace y by s/σ, as before. Thus we would have

(5)
$$t_{min} = s + \frac{s}{\sigma}.$$

If the segment s is a whole zodiacal sign, we have $s = 30$ and hence

(6)
$$t_{min} = 30 + \frac{30}{\sigma}.$$

This assumption would give us the following minimal time intervals

	(2)+(3)	(4)+(5)	(6)+(7)	(8)+(9)	(10)+(11)	(12)+(1)
$t_{min} =$	42	48	$43\tfrac{1}{2}$	39	36	38

In fact, these figures occur rather frequently in the middle part of the motion. Thus we find:

Sign (1), years VESPASIANUS 4 and 6: $t = 38$
    (3), VESPASIANUS 9 and TRAIANUS 9: $t = 42$
    (4), TRAIANUS 11: $t = 48$
    (4), HADRIANUS 11: $t = 48$
    (6) and (7), TRAIANUS 16: $t = 43$ and $t = 44$
    (8), TRAIANUS 18: $t = 39$
    (9), HADRIANUS 1 and 16: $t = 39$
    (10), HADRIANUS 1: $t = 36$.

In several other cases, the values of t are slightly larger than the minimal values t_{min}. This was to be expected, because it often happens that a zodiacal sign belongs partly to the region of fastest motion (between EL and MF) and partly to the region of normal fast motion (before EL and after MF). In such cases the time t ought to be larger than t_{min}, but less than t_{norm}.

On the other hand it very seldom happens that t is less than t_{min}. It never happens in the region of MF, but it does happen in the region of EL, where the motion is often irregular, for the reason explained before.

We may summarize our results as follows. Between EL and MF, the equation of motion is

$$(7) \qquad\qquad t = s + y$$

and after MF, as long as the fast motion of Mars lasts, the equation is

$$(8) \qquad\qquad t = s + \tfrac{4}{3}y.$$

Just before EL, formula (8) holds in some cases, but in other cases the t-values were changed in order to ensure the continuity of the motion at the point EL.

Now let us see whether equation (7) is in accordance with system A. Let us apply formula (7) to the whole segment s from EL to MF. According to the Babylonian theory, the number of steps from EL to MF is a constant c_1, hence (7) reduces to

$$(9) \qquad\qquad t = s + c_1.$$

Now this is exactly the formula by which the time interval t between EL and MF is calculated in the Babylonian system A. According to the Procedure Text 811 a, formula (9) holds with $c_1 = 33;40$. This value of c_1 is nearly equal to the value obtained from text S.

For further details see my papers in Vierteljahrsschrift Naturf. Ges. *105* and Centaurus *16* quoted before.

For Thesis 5, I cannot claim the same degree of certainty as for the Theses 1 to 4. Let me therefore reformulate Thesis 5 with some caution:

The velocity schemes for Jupiter in Texts P and S are probably based on System A'.

From cuneiform texts three theories for Jupiter are known: Systems A, A', and B. Only A and A' are based upon the assumption of a piecewise constant velocity. In A the synodic arc is

$$30° \text{ from (3) } 25° \text{ to (8) } 30°,$$
$$36° \text{ from (8) } 30° \text{ to (3) } 25°.$$

In A' the synodic arcs are

$$30° \quad \text{from (4) } 9° \text{ to (8) } 9°,$$
$$33°45' \text{ from (8) } 9° \text{ to (10) } 2°,$$
$$36° \quad \text{from (10) } 2° \text{ to (2) } 17°,$$
$$33°45' \text{ from (2) } 17° \text{ to (4) } 9°.$$

In B the synodic arc decreases linearly from a maximum in (12) to a minimum in (6) and then increases again. A similar statement holds for all theories of type C.

Now let us see which theory fits the texts best. In system A, the times Jupiter needs to cover one zodiacal sign or 30° ought to be equal for the 5 successive signs (4), (5), (6), (7), (8). In system A', the times ought to be qual in (5), (6), (7) but less in (4) and (8). In system B, they should increase with nearly constant differences in (4), (5), (6), and decrease just so in (6), (7), (8).

The actual numbers of days Jupiter dwells in the signs (4) to (8) according to the texts P and S are given by the following tables:

Table 1. Times in Text P

Signs	(4)	(5)	(6)	(7)	(8)
Augustus, years 17-20			395	397	396
years 26-32	393	400	400	400	403
years 38-41	393	400			

Table 2. Times in Text S

Signs	(4)	(5)	(6)	(7)	(8)
Vespasianus, years 4-6				387	380
Traianus, years 9-13			395	394	392
Traianus 19 - Hadrianus 2	393	398			
Hadrianus 12-17	393	398	398	396	147

The number 395 for the sign (6) in the first line of Table 1 is wrong according to all theories: it must be excluded. Just so, the number 403 at the end of the second line has to be discarded. The remaining numbers in Table 1

$$397 \quad 396$$
$$393 \quad 400 \quad 400 \quad 400$$
$$393 \quad 400$$

are in good accordance with system A', but not with A or B.

Before passing to text S, let us first answer the question: How long should Jupiter dwell in each of the signs (5), (6), (7) according to the theory of system A'?

The answer is not quite unambiguous. In any case, the signs (5), (6), (7) belong to the region of slow motion, in which Jupiter advances 30° in every synodic period. Hence the time Jupiter needs to cross each one of these signs is just one synodic period. In a first approximation the Babylonians assumed all synodic periods to be of equal duration. Since 391 synodic periods were assumed to be equal to 427 years, the duration of a mean synodic period would be

$$\tfrac{427}{391} \cdot 365\tfrac{1}{4} \text{ days}$$

or nearly 399 days. In Table 1, the actual figures in the signs (5), (6), (7) are

$$397, \quad 400, \quad 400, \quad 400 \text{ and } 400 \text{ days.}$$

The agreement with the theoretical value 399 is not bad.

In a second approximation, the Babylonians used the sun-distance principle and found in the region of slow motion a synodic period of 12 months and 42;5,10 tithis, or $395\tfrac{2}{3}$ days, as we have seen in Chapter 7. Hence, if the time Jupiter needs to cover a sign (5), (6) or (7) were 395 or 396 days, this too would be in accordance with system A'.

Now let us pass to text S. In Table 2, the numbers of days for signs (4) and (8) are, without exception, considerably smaller than for signs (5), (6) and (7). This excludes system A. Now let us see whether the numbers in columns (5), (6) and (7) of Table 2, viz.

$$387$$
$$395 \quad 394$$
$$398$$
$$398 \quad 398 \quad 396$$

are in accordance with system A'.

The number 387 in the first line has to be discarded in every theory. The three numbers 398 in the third and fourth line are equal: this is a strong argument in favour of system A'. The remaining numbers 395, 394 and 396 are of the right order of magnitude, but they are not exactly equal, as they should be in system A'. Anyhow, system A' fits better than any other theory.

Thus, Thesis 5 seems justified.

Comparison of text P with Babylonian texts

We now return to Venus. We have seen that in text S the motion of Venus was computed by means of the velocity scheme of VARÂHA MIHIRA. On the other hand, text P was certainly not calculated by the same scheme. The motion of Venus in text P is not at all similar to the motion in text S, but it is similar to the motion assumed in Babylonian almanacs, as we shall see presently.

In the Babylonian text Rm 678, published by EPPING and STRASSMAIER (Zeitschr. f. Assyriol., 5, p. 354), we find the entry dates of Venus into the signs of the zodiac for the year −83. On taking the differences, we obtain the times required to pass through the signs (4) to (11), namely:

$$24 \quad 25 \quad 25 \quad 25+25 \quad 26 \quad 28+35.$$

Here the plus sign indicates that the total time taken to pass through the two signs is the sum of the two figures. The actual entry date into the sign (11) is lost, but the divisions are a plausible restoration. We see that in the fast part of the motion the numbers are slowly increasing from 24 through 25 and 26 to someting like 28, which never happens in text S.

Very similar series of numbers are found in two texts for the year −75, SH 103 and SH 492, published by KUGLER (Sternkunde und Sterndienst II, p. 471). But the series in text P is similar too. For years 16 and 17 of Augustus the times given by P for the passage through the zodiacal signs in the direct part of the motion are as follows:

(10)	(11)	(12)	(1)	(2)	(3)	(4)	(5)	(6)	(7)	(8)	(9)
25	25	25	25	25	24	22	22	23	24	24	25
25	25	26	27	29	35						

Here too the number 25 occurs very frequently, as in the Babylonian texts. Apparently a constant velocity of 30° per 25 days was assumed for Venus over long stretches. Towards the end of the direct motion the velocity gradually decreases: the time for a sign becomes 26, then 27, then 29 and finally 35 days.

We conclude that P and S are not based on the same scheme. The similarity between P and the Babylonian texts allows us to conclude with some degree of probability that P was calculated according to a Babylonian velocity scheme. The reconstruction of this scheme could well be a most rewarding task for future investigation.

An Egyptian Mercury Table

A papyrus has recently been published by R. A. PARKER[1]) which proves much more directly that in the times of the Roman Emperors the Egyptians used Babylonian methods for calculating planetary positions. The papyrus in question is Carlsberg 32. O. NEUGE-BAUER's evidently correct interpretation, which PARKER gives in a note at the end of his article, is that the subject is the motion of Mercury, calculated from day to day, from the Morning Stationary Point to the Morninglast. The table contains, like the cuneiform texts, *sexagesimal numbers*. It begins:

0; 5,27,17	0; 5,27,17
0;10,54,34	0;16,21,51
0;16,21,51	0;32,43,42
0;21,49, 8	0;54,32,50
. . . . .	. . . . .

We see that the numbers in the first column form an arithmetical series with constant difference 0; 5,27,17. Those in the second column result from the summation of the first column; they thus form an arithmetical series of the second order. The first column gives the daily motion of Mercury, the second the total path covered.

Similar methods were used by the Babylonians in text 310 (O. NEUGEBAUER, ACT II, p. 326 and III, Plate 169, col. I) to calculate the motion of Mercury.

According to PARKER, the text was probably written during the Roman period.

SUMMARY

In chapters 6 and 7 we became ecquainted with the 'linear methods' of the Babylonian astronomers. In chapter 8 we have seen that these were used in late antiquity everywhere from Rome and Egypt to India. While they were less accurate than the trigonometrical, they were much easier to handle. It should not, therefore, occasion any surprise that the astrologers particularly preferred the linear methods and remained faithful to them even after APOLLONIOS, i.e. after −200, when the more accurate trigonometrical methods became available. In Egypt linear methods were still in use even in the time of HADRIANUS (117-138), in India as late as the sixth century. Subsequently, they were superseded by trigonometrical methods.

In our treatment of the rising times of the zodiacal signs we saw that the linear methods

---

[1]) R. A. PARKER, Two demotic astronomical papyri, Acta Orientalia 25 (1960), p. 143.

were further developed and refined by the Greeks. The calculation of the entry dates of the planets into the zodiacal signs would appear to present a similar case. In the Egyptian planetary tables of the age of AUGUSTUS the gradual reduction in the velocity of Venus before the Evening Stationary Point is quite similar to that in cuneiform texts from the years -83 and -75. In the later text S from the time of HADRIANUS, however, we find a completely different velocity law, according to which the velocity suddenly decreases with a large jump. This law, as we have seen, reappears in VARÂHA MIHIRA in the sixth century A.D. The Venus theory underlying text S is more exact and better than systems A_0, A_1 and A_2 of the cuneiform texts.

How the improved linear theory was transmitted to India is not known. Apparently, 'the wise VASISTHA', who lived before $+270$, already knew it.

INDEX

1. ABBREVIATIONS

A = Asiatic collection Oriental Institute Chicago

ACT = O. NEUGEBAUER: Astronomical Cuneiform Texts. Lund Humphreys, London 1955

AO = Antiquités orientales, collection du Louvre, Paris

BIDEZ-CUMONT = J. BIDEZ et F. CUMONT: Les mages hellénisées. Paris 1938 (2 Vol.)

BM = British Museum

CBS = Catalogue Babylonian Section, University of Pennsylvania Museum

EF = Eveningfirst

EL = Eveninglast

ESt = Evening Station

FESTUGIERE = A. -J. FESTUGIERE: La révélation d'Hermès Trismégiste. Paris, Gabalda et Cie. 1949–1954 (4 Vol.)

HARPER = R. P. HARPER: Assyrian and Babylonian Letters. Chicago 1892–1914

HS = Hilprecht-Sammlung Jena

MF = Morningfirst

ML = Morninglast

MM = Metropolitan Museum, New York

MSt = Morning Station

NYBERG Religionen = H. S. NYBERG: Die Religionen des alten Iran, Leipzig 1938

Op = Opposition

PINCHES-SACHS = Late Babylonian astronomical and related texts, copied by T. G. PINCHES and J. N. STRASSMAIER, published by A. J. SACHS. Brown University Press, Providence 1955

Reports = R. C. THOMPSON: The reports of the magicians and astrologers. London 1900

Rm = RASSAM collection (Brit. Mus.)

SH = SHEMTOB collection (Brit. Mus.)

Sp = SPARTOLI collection (Brit. Mus.)

U = URUK collection Istambul Museum

VAT = Vorderasiatische Tontafelsammlung Staatliche Museen Berlin

2. CUNEIFORM TEXTS AND PAPYRI

3. PROPER NAMES AND SUBJECTS

4. LIST OF PLATES